# 100 MOST POPULAR SCIENTISTS FOR YOUNG ADULTS

# 100 MOST POPULAR SCIENTISTS FOR YOUNG ADULTS
## Biographical Sketches and Professional Paths

Kendall Haven
and
Donna Clark

1999
Libraries Unlimited, Inc.
Englewood, Colorado

Libraries Unlimited, Inc.
P.O. Box 6633
Englewood, CO  80155-6633
1-800-237-6124
www.lu.com

**Library of Congress Cataloging-in-Publication Data**

Haven, Kendall F.
  100 most popular scientists for young adults : biographical sketches and professional paths / by Kendall Haven and Donna Clark.
     xv, 525  p.      19 x 26  cm. -- (Profiles and pathways series)
  Includes bibliographical references and index.
  ISBN 1-56308-674-3
  1. Scientists--Biography.   2. Science--History--20th century.
I. Clark, Donna Lynn.   II. Title.   III. Title: One hundred most popular scientists for young adults.   IV. Series.
Q141.K424   1999
509′.22--dc21                                                    99-13755
                                                                        CIP

This book is dedicated to two awe-inspiring groups:
to the thousands of dedicated scientists
who pour their hearts, minds, and passions
into the progress of science, and
to the dedicated teachers
who bring the world of science into thrilling,
vivid life for their students.

# Table of Contents

# Introduction

When we hear about renowned scientists at the pinnacles of their careers who have made earth-shaking discoveries, we are filled with admiration, awe, and wonder. We wonder how they got there. Is that what they always wanted to do? Did they always know they were going to be in that field of science? Did they know they would be good at it? What do they really *do* in that field of science? How did they get into that field?

When they were children, did they want to be scientists? Were they good in high school? Were their parents smart? What did they do in college? Did they ever change careers? Fields? Why did they pick *that* field of science?

These are questions that are never asked by those eager to find out about the latest discovery, the most recent awe-inspiring accomplishment. But they are exactly the questions that are most important for someone standing at the very beginning of a career in science. And that is why we wrote this book.

This book contains biographical sketches of 100 of the most prominent and interesting American scientists of the twentieth century. We chose this group to profile because their struggles, early decisions, concerns, dilemmas, course selections, post-graduate options, and advice will be more relevant to modern teens than would be life histories of scientists from more distant places and times.

Our focus in compiling these profiles was not simply to highlight their major achievements, but rather to document the trail they carved out in getting to a position of prominence. We wanted to uncover their early intentions and plans and the early life events that shaped their career choices. We wanted to create road maps for others to use as guides in beginning and shaping successful science careers. Each of these career paths has proven successful. Each of these paths has produced a world-class scientist. From them perhaps teens will uncover keys to launching their own greatness.

The scientists in this book have come from all possible backgrounds and groups of people. Some were raised in cities, others on farms. While some were rich, others were poor. Some of these scientists had educated parents, but others had parents who never got past the third grade. Most were good students who stayed in school to obtain doctorates, but several flunked out of high school and two never earned a high school diploma. Some always felt strongly drawn toward the sciences, while others never considered the sciences until they found themselves doing something "scientific." A few wandered along convoluted paths through many careers before finding their rightful niche. Most marched in a very linear and direct way straight into their chosen field.

Many of these scientists did their work in laboratories; others worked in the field. Many spent most of their time pondering and working with paper and pencil or chalkboard. A number of them spent most of their time teaching and working with students. Many of the scientists described in this book have achieved world fame, including several who have won science's highest prize, the Nobel Prize. A few have been largely unrecognized, and others are still on the climb to the top of their careers. Some stumbled accidentally into discoveries of the greatest magnitude. Most worked with great persistence over many years to make their discoveries. Some have worked doggedly and diligently through a long and productive career without a single major breakthrough.

Yet these widely differing and fascinating scientists do have six charac-teristics or traits in common. First and foremost among these is *curiosity*. If you are not curious and do not feel a need to answer the questions your curiosity creates, you will likely struggle in a science career. Closely coupled with curiosity is *wonder*—a deep, almost reverent wonder about life, nature, the world, and the universe.

Next, certainly, is *passion*. Each of these scientists expressed a deeply felt passion for his or her field and work. Passion is a driving engine of success. All of these successful scientists seemed to overflow with *persist-ence* and with boundless *energy*. They never seemed to give up or to lack the energy to pursue a new idea or new question. Finally, they all searched for ideas *beyond the accepted convention*. They didn't accept prevailing wisdom at face value but rather let their curious minds search for flaws and for alternate explanations. One conclusion of this research and writing effort has been that these six traits seem to substantially increase a person's chances for scientific success and, it is likely, for success in general.

Selection of the 100 scientists to be included in this book consumed three months of review and evaluation. Over 500 names were nominated by the authors, by students, and by science teachers who agreed to serve on a review committee. Nominations were limited to scientists whose primary work was performed during the twentieth century, because their career paths and struggles will be more relevant to today's students than would those of earlier times. Future editions of this book will continue to emphasize new, upcom-ing, and recent scientists and scientific developments.

The hardest single task of this project was reducing our initial list of over 500 noble and worthy scientists down to 100. In truth there are thousands of dedicated men and women who deserve to be in this book. We had to leave out almost all of them, including Kendall's personal heroes from his days in the graduate school of oceanography. Don't think those not included in these pages are any less worthy of study or emulation.

In editing the list from 500 to the final 100, we sought a balanced mix of the many fields of science, of the type of work performed, and of gender and ethnicity of the scientists, a balance between well-known scientists whose work (and often whose life) has been completed and current researchers who have made significant contributions, but whose greatest work may still lie ahead. We sought to include both well-known scientists whose names have become part of our common vocabulary and researchers whose names are not known outside their own field, but whose work has already become important. Finally, we wanted to provide a wide variety of early life histories and early career paths.

Reference and biographical information on the final 100 was collected from both published and unpublished sources (provided by the various institutions where the scientists had worked). All living scientists on the final list were also interviewed to ensure the accuracy of the entries in this book. Nothing has been fictionalized for these entries. Quotes are only included where they were reported by one of the participants or observers. The same is true for scenic detail and character feelings, reactions, and motives. We have only included here what the actual participants reported or what is preserved in photographic and other evidence.

The 100 scientists included here represent the physical, earth, and life sciences and include representatives of most of the major fields of science. Almost one-third are women. The list includes representatives of virtually every major ethnic group in America. They are split among basic researchers, applied researchers, and field researchers; between teachers and non-teachers; between theorists and experimentalists. They were each deeply engaged in the process of "doing" science and can each serve as inspiring models for us all.

We owe a great debt of thanks to many individuals who helped us compile the vast amount of information and references used in developing this text. We want to extend a special thanks to the staff at the Sonoma State University library for their ongoing support and assistance, to Janis Goldblum at the National Academy of Sciences, to Debra Brandt at the National Academy of Engineers, to Rex Ellis and Susan Strange at the Smithsonian Institute, to Dr. Judy Goodstein at the California Institute of Technology Library, and to Barbara Ittner for her enthusiastic encouragement and suggestions. We also want to thank the many busy scientists described in this book who took the time to be subjected to our interviews and to the many other working scientists who assisted in theory and data collection.

Finally, we want to extend thanks to you, the reader, for having the curiosity to explore these pages. If you are thinking of a career in one of the sciences, let the histories of these eminently successful men and women serve as your guides. Let their experiences and advice help you set your course. It was a thrill for us to learn about these wonderful people whom we had only known before as names on theorems, principles, and discoveries. We hope you are equally fascinated and inspired by reading their stories.

# How to Use This Book

This book is designed to present the experiences of notable modern scientists to help readers prepare for, plan, and more accurately envision their own careers in one of the fields of science. Each entry is divided into six sections:

**Career Highlights**: A quick listing of some of the major awards and achievements of each scientist.

**Important Contributions**: A summary of the scientist's major contributions and their significance.

**Career Path**: A narrative description of significant early events in the scientist's life and the path each followed to lead to a successful science career.

**Key Dates**: A chronological listing of the scientist's major life events.

**Advice**: Advice and recommendations in the scientist's own words for how to start a successful career in that field of science.

**References**: A short list of additional references to extend the reader's information about both this scientist and the field. See your school or public librarian for additional titles.

Internet references for the major scientific disciplines are included in an appendix. There is also an appendix listing the scientists by subject area.

The individual entries in this book are short (1,400–1,500 words each) and therefore are certainly not comprehensive reviews of each scientist's life, accomplishments, and career. Selected references are included to help readers extend and complete their understanding of each scientist and his or her field. The Internet references are good starting points for exploring avenues and options related to individual scientific fields.

# Luis Alvarez

*"The Wild Idea Man"*                              Physics

## Career Highlights

- Discovered over 70 new elementary particles
- Awarded Nobel Prize for Physics, 1968
- Awarded the National Medal of Science by the National Science Foundation, 1964
- Awarded the Collier Trophy, the highest aviation award in the United States, 1946

## Important Contributions

Luis Alvarez is most famous for his Nobel Prize-winning effort to discover and study over 70 new elementary particles, many of which exist for less than 1/1,000,000 of a second. As part of this effort, Alvarez created the world's first linear proton accelerator with detection bubble chamber and revolutionary stereophotography system.

But Luis Alvarez can also claim credit for a wide-ranging list of discoveries and inventions, from ground-control radar approach systems for landing planes (now standard at all commercial airports), to the first nuclear chain reaction not using uranium, to methods for producing very slow neutron beams, to the creation of important radioactive isotopes of helium and mercury. In fact, there is hardly an area of physics-related discovery and invention on which Luis Alvarez did not leave his mark.

## Career Path

During his junior year of college in 1930, Luis Alvarez was given $50 as a Christmas present, a substantial sum during the Great Depression, a period of severe economic hardship that started with the failure of the stock market in 1929. Rather than use the money for food, school books, or the new slide rule he needed, or to pay back loans from friends, Luis used his

$50 to buy flying lessons. He had always been fascinated by flying and wanted to know what it felt like to soar, free as a hawk, through the sky and clouds.

The flight instructor said that $50 would only buy three and one-quarter hours of lessons, not nearly enough to qualify for a solo flight, and that Luis should come back when he had $150. Feeling that $150 was an impossible sum to acquire, he answered that that was all the money he had and he'd take what he could afford. In two and three-quarters hours Luis qualified for solo flights and used the last 25 minutes of his flying time to soar with the birds. It was the fastest flight qualification to that date in the state of Illinois. Luis Alvarez applied that same relentless enthusiasm and energy to all his efforts, usually with equally successful results.

Luis began his studies at the University of Chicago in 1928, planning to major in chemistry because his father, a physician and biochemistry professor, had given him a solid foundation in the practice and theory of chemistry. During his sophomore year two teachers influenced him to switch to physics. Luis made a smooth and successful transition, graduated with highest honors in 1932, and stayed on campus for graduate work, receiving his Ph.D. in 1936.

Alvarez moved to California after graduation to accept a research position at the University of California, Berkeley. The UC Berkeley physics department was an exciting place during the late 1930s. Ernest Lawrence had invented the cyclotron there. Using this wondrous "atom-smasher," discoveries seemed to pile up faster than they could be written up. Vague ideas for new experiments turned into major revelations before new theory could be developed to explain what had been observed. The whole department vibrated with the thrilling sense that they had become the world leaders in physics research.

Everyone in the department fought for time on the cyclotron. Alvarez used his turns to explore what happened when heavy metals were bombarded with a slow neutron stream. While engaged on this work, he created a new isotope of mercury ($Hg^{198}$), which later became important as the standard for length measurements for the U.S. Bureau of Standards.

Alvarez discovered new radioactive isotopes of hydrogen and helium that later became important in low-temperature research. He also developed a new method for producing beams of ultra-slow neutrons. The Alvarez method opened whole new fields of study for the cyclotron.

World War II temporarily scattered the Berkeley physics brain trust. After spending two years designing a series of important radar and microwave systems for the U.S. Air Force (including the first ground-control approach radar for airplane instrument landings, which soon became standard equipment at every commercial airfield in the country), Alvarez joined the Manhattan Project, the United States government's secret effort to build an atomic bomb, and was present at the first atomic detonation in 1945.

Because of the importance of his contributions to the effort to create an atomic bomb (and because of his flying experience), Luis Alvarez was selected as the one scientific observer to fly in the B-29 observer plane that flew with the *Enola Gay,* which dropped the atomic bomb on Hiroshima, Japan. He was thus the only person to watch both of the first two nuclear explosions on earth.

The power unleashed by the atomic bomb frightened—even terrified— many, but it inspired Alvarez. Back at Berkeley after World War II, he searched for better ways to explore the still-mysterious atom. All of the particle accelerators built up to that time accelerated either an electron or a neutron. Alvarez began to wonder what would happen if he accelerated a proton to near light speed and smashed it into an atom. It took a decade to complete the basic research on how to isolate, control, direct, and accelerate a stream of protons.

By 1958 Alvarez had designed and built the first 40-foot-long linear proton accelerator. Concrete walls surrounded the polished metal chamber. Thirty-ton magnet collars were spaced along its length. When it was running at full power, researchers could literally smell the ionized energy pulsing through the beast.

Alvarez hoped to study new subatomic particles created by proton collisions. However, the high-energy particles he produced had such short lives—tiny fractions of a second—they could not be tracked with existing technology.

By 1959 Alvarez's team had developed a new bubble chamber of superheated liquid. When high-energy particles slammed through it—even those that lived for less than a micro-second—they left trails of gas bubbles, which could be photographed and studied. To do the photographic work, the team designed a revolutionary stereophotographic system, nicknamed "Frankenstein," which took simultaneous, high-speed photographs through three different cameras.

The system went operational in 1960. Over the next several years, because of Alvarez's efforts, the number of known elementary subatomic particles rose from 30 to over 100. To analyze the millions of photographs taken each year, Alvarez used banks of the (then) highest-speed computers. His extensive particle discoveries earned him the 1968 Nobel Prize for Physics.

By his own admission Alvarez always loved to play with gadgets and, when he wasn't inventing them, he was tinkering with them. In the 1950s he invented an indoor electronic golf training system, which was used by President Eisenhower. He invented a novel kind of color television system that never caught on. His tinkering with core sampling equipment led Luis and his son, Walter, to first propose the theory that a giant meteor crash killed the dinosaurs.

Because his ideas and contributions spanned such an incredibly wide range of physics specialties and included such a large number of important, innovative concepts, Luis Alvarez has often been called the "wild idea man" of physics. But Alvarez saw his life differently. At every turn in the road he saw a new idea as exciting to him as a shiny new penny is to a young boy. He saw himself as forever being "in the position of a boy who finds a penny and thinks he is on his way to becoming a millionaire." Millionaires or not, because of Luis Alvarez's work, we are all much richer.

## Key Dates

| | |
|---|---|
| 1911 | Born in San Francisco on June 13 |
| 1932 | Received B.S. from University of Chicago |
| 1936 | Received Ph.D. from University of Chicago; appointed research assistant in nuclear physics at University of California, Berkeley |
| 1938 | Appointed instructor at UC Berkeley |
| 1940 | Worked on military weapons development programs |
| 1943 | Moved to Los Alamos, New Mexico, to work on the Manhattan Project |
| 1945 | Returned to UC Berkeley as full professor |
| 1968 | Awarded Nobel Prize for Physics |
| 1985 | Retired |

## Advice

*Luis Alvarez was a worker, an experimenter, and a tinkerer, and would advise students considering a career in physics to do the same. It is not enough to study theory. You must do the lab work to see for yourself how it works. A blindly accepted theory is a limiting wall rather than a springboard to new development. Become intimately familiar with the measurement and research tools of your field and learn how to use and modify them. Prove every theorem and concept to yourself in the lab. Then you'll be ready to extend theories into new areas and make significant advances in your field.*

## References

Alvarez, Luis. *Alvarez: Adventures of a Scientist.* Berkeley: University of California Press, 1987.

Boose, Henry, and Lloyd Motz. *The Atomic Scientists: A Biographical History.* New York: John Wiley, 1991. (Good biographical and field review.)

Daintith, John, et al., eds. *Biographical Encyclopedia of Scientists.* 2d ed. Vol. 1. Philadelphia, Pa.: Institute of Physics Publishing, 1994. (Summary entry on Alvarez's work.)

Tanor, Joseph, ed. *McGraw-Hill Modern Men of Science.* New York: McGraw-Hill, 1986. (Strong summary of Alvarez's work.)

Wasson, Tyler, ed. *Nobel Prize Winners.* New York: H. W. Wilson, 1987. (Excellent summary of Alvarez's work.)

# Isaac Asimov

*"From Science Fact to
Science Fiction"*

Biochemistry
and Writing

Boston University Photo Services

## Career Highlights

- Authored almost 500 books on a variety of subjects, from science fiction to Shakespeare and biochemistry
- Received the Hugo Award in 1963, 1966, 1973, 1977, and 1983
- Won the Nebula Award, Science Fiction Writers of America, 1973 and 1977
- Received the Glenn Seaborg Award from the International Platform Association, 1977

## Important Contributions

Isaac Asimov is considered one of the world's best and most prolific science fiction authors. He had a talent for explaining complicated scientific theories—from nuclear fusion to the theory of numbers—clearly, simply, and lucidly. He could explain science intelligibly to the general public in an accurate and often amusing style, so he was much loved both as a writer and as a lecturer. His scientific career spanned 40 years of biochemistry and teaching, but it is for his hundreds of books that he will be most remembered.

## Career Path

Isaac Asimov was born in Russia in 1920; his family moved to the United States when he was three years old. His parents bought a candy store in Brooklyn, New York, and young Isaac begged his father to let him read the magazines with the glossy covers. His father steadfastly refused, claiming fiction magazines were "junk—not fit to read."

In 1929, a new magazine, *Science Wonder Stories*, appeared. Isaac convinced his father to let him read this magazine because it had the word "science" in the title. His father reluctantly agreed and Isaac devoured every issue. Then he secretly read magazines without the word "science" in the title, figuring he could later argue that permission to read one such magazine implied permission to read them all. The young boy became a devoted fan of pulp fiction. He read all the magazines in the store, as well as almost everything he could find at libraries within a 10-mile radius of his home.

When he was 11 years old, Isaac attempted to write his first pulp fiction story. He called it "The Greenville Chums at College," fashioned after the Hardy Boys book, *The Darewell Chums at College.* After struggling through eight chapters, Isaac abandoned the story. He was a junior-high-school boy in a shabby Brooklyn neighborhood trying to write about small-town life at college. Sadly he had to admit that he didn't know what he was talking about.

That first bitter failure didn't sour Isaac's love for writing, however. At age 17, after publishing several small pieces in his high school's literary semiannual, he decided to try again. This time he would write about what he *did* know. Life in his Brooklyn neighborhood, however, bored him, so he returned to the only other topic he knew well, science and science fiction from his years of pulp fiction reading. Isaac began a story called "Cosmic Corkscrew," in which he first used what would become his typical science fiction plot formula: He took a scientific gimmick and built a story around it.

It took the young writer a year to finish that one short story. Weeks disappeared in researching a single idea or in reworking one passage. By the time he finished, John W. Campbell (one of the best-known science fiction writers of the time) had become editor of *Astounding Science Fiction* (the most prestigious publication of its genre).

Asimov's father suggested he submit his story to Campbell for publication. Although Isaac was intimidated by the idea, he agreed to give the best science fiction magazine in the country a shot. Since it cost 12 cents to mail it and only 10 cents to take the subway round trip, he decided to deliver his precious story to the editor's secretary personally.

What happened next was a would-be writer's dream. Instead of handing his story to the secretary and leaving, Asimov was shown into Campbell's office, and they talked together for over an hour. Campbell agreed to read the story himself.

Two days later Asimov received the story back in the mail. Campbell had rejected it. He did, however, offer extensive suggestions for improvement. This was the beginning of a years-long relationship between Asimov and Campbell, during which Campbell guided the young author to become a better and better science fiction writer.

Meanwhile, Asimov rapidly progressed through the public schools, earning an undergraduate degree in chemistry from Columbia University when only 19 years old. He received his M.A. in chemistry two years later, in 1941. While he loved writing, Isaac also loved the mysteries of science, and what he learned in his science classrooms became fuel for his pen.

Both Asimov's academic career and his writing were disrupted for four years by his service during World War II. After his discharge, he returned to Columbia University to earn his Ph.D. in chemistry in 1948. He then joined the faculty of the Boston University Medical School, gradually working up through ranks from instructor, to assistant professor, to associate professor, and finally to professor of biochemistry.

Although he maintained a full academic workload, Asimov never abandoned his first love, writing. His first two science fiction books were published in 1950, less than a year after he was hired as a chemistry instructor. A steady stream of books followed throughout his life.

Isaac Asimov is perhaps best known for the two dozen short stories and three novels he wrote on robots (he coined the term "robotics"). Before he came along, robots had always been portrayed as mechanical monsters beyond the control of humans. Isaac "humanized" robots, creating his famous Three Laws of Robotics, which became so popular that many people felt that when robots became a reality they would indeed be programmed with Asimov's three laws.

Asimov's "Foundation" series (1951–1953) was also enormously popular. He wrote it as a future history—a story being told in the distant future that tells about that future society's history. In 1966, a special Hugo Award was bestowed on the "Foundation" series for being the "best all-time science fiction series."

But Asimov also wrote nonfiction, with his first factual book, a medical text called *Biochemistry and Human Metabolism,* published in 1964. He said that writing that book, "introduced me to the delights of nonfiction. I went on to discover the even greater ecstasies of writing science for the general public." His natural talent for explaining difficult concepts in a lively and clear manner made him a good teacher as well as nonfiction writer. He published over 20 nonfiction science books, including *Building Blocks of the Universe, The Intelligent Man's Guide to Science,* and *The History of Physics.*

Asimov called himself a working scientist. "I don't want to write poetically; I want to write clearly." He wanted his stories to stimulate curiosity and the "desire to know." He continued to write distinguished science fiction and non-fiction science up until his death in 1992, upon which science lost one of its most prolific and capable spokespersons.

## Key Dates

| | |
|---|---|
| 1920 | Born in Petrovichi, Russia, on January 2 |
| 1923 | Moved to the United States with his parents |
| 1939 | Received B.S. from Columbia University |
| 1941 | Received M.A. from Columbia University |
| 1942–1945 | Worked as civilian chemist at U.S. Navy Air Experimental Station, Philadelphia |
| 1945–1946 | Served in the U.S. Army |
| 1948 | Received Ph.D. from Columbia University |
| 1949–1951 | Worked as instructor at Boston University |
| 1950 | Published first books, *Pebble in the Sky* and *I, Robot* |
| 1951–1953 | Published "Foundation" series |

| 1951– | Worked as assistant and then as associate professor at |
| 1979 |     Boston University |
| 1979– | Became professor of biochemistry |
| 1992 | |
| 1992 | Died April 6 |

## Advice

*Asimov once wrote, "There must be such a thing as a born writer. At least I can't remember when I wasn't on fire to write." To be a science or a science fiction writer, you must know science and burn with a passion to write. "If the feel of telling a story is in your blood, take classes to learn the craft of writing." Campbell said of young Asimov, "he was lean and hungry, and very enthusiastic. He couldn't write, but he could tell a story. You can teach a guy how to write, but not how to tell a story."*

*In undergraduate work, concentrate on gaining a breadth of knowledge in the physical sciences (especially physics, chemistry, and space sciences) and in general biology. Wait for graduate studies to specialize in the particular field that most interests you.*

## References

Asimov, Isaac. *Asimov on Science Fiction.* New York: Doubleday, 1979.

———. *The Foundation Trilogy.* New York: Ballantine Books, 1984. (Asimov's most famous science fiction.)

———. *In Memory Yet Green: The Autobiography of Isaac Asimov, 1920–1954.* New York: Doubleday, 1979.

Erlanger, Ellen. *Isaac Asimov: Scientist and Storyteller.* New York: Lerner, 1986. (A biography, good for younger readers.)

Gunn, James. *Isaac Asimov: The Foundations of Science Fiction.* Oxford: Oxford University Press, 1982.

Horton, H. Robert. *Principles of Biochemistry.* New York: Prentice Hall Press, 1996.

Williamson, J.N. *How to Write Tales of Horror, Fantasy, and Science Fiction.* Cincinnati, Ohio: Writer's Digest Books, 1987. (A collection of essays on writing by master writers in the fields of horror, fantasy, and science fiction.)

# Robert Bakker

*"Hot Blooded Dinosaurs"*                    Paleontology

Courtesy of Casper College, by Donna Davis

## Career Highlights

- Discovered that dinosaurs were warm-blooded, agile runners, and good parents
- Discovered that birds are descended from dinosaurs
- Received AAPG Award for writing about geology, 1988
- Received Gem and Mineral Society research award, 1990

## Important Contributions

Dinosaurs were plodding, cold-blooded monsters. They were sluggish, dull-gray, and so dumb they weren't capable of decent parenting. That was the classical view of dinosaurs through the first half of the twentieth century. That was how dinosaurs were depicted in illustrations. That was what expert paleontologists believed. Robert Bakker shattered those beliefs.

Robert Bakker was the first to claim that dinosaurs were warm blooded, colorful, quick, and agile. He was also the one who first proposed that birds were descended from dinosaurs.

Bakker first expressed these ideas as a graduate student, and was ridiculed and scoffed at by established paleontologists. Twenty-five years later, the body of evidence collected to support his views is overwhelming. A reluctant scientific community has grudgingly admitted that Robert Bakker was right all along.

Bakker also discovered and named six new species of dinosaurs and eleven species of early mammals. Robert Bakker is the man who completely rewrote the book on dinosaurs.

## Career Path

Robert Bakker can remember the exact day he decided to study dinosaurs. It was in the fall of 1953 when, as a nine-year-old fourth grader, he visited his grandfather in rural New Jersey. He saw a magazine lying on a porch table: the September 7, 1953, issue of *Life*. A snarling dinosaur glared back from the cover. Inside Robert found not just glorious dinosaur pictures, but an article entitled "The Pageant of Life." In his own words, "It was the story of how evolution worked. It was wonderful. What got me was not just that dinosaurs were neat and grotesque, but that they were part of a much bigger story, a great historical pageant."

That first exposure to the wondrous tale of evolution instantly inspired and fascinated the young boy. He had already developed a love of nature and birds thanks to a fourth grade teacher who led her class on bird walks around town, and now he became a certified dinosaur junkie.

From suburban New Jersey it was a short car trip to the American Museum of Natural History in New York City. Robert begged for someone to drive him there every weekend. He'd take his drawing tablet and make sketches of the skeletons and of what the dinosaurs must have looked like who wore those bones. His mother would patiently sit and read.

Robert pushed for family trips to the zoo so he could watch animals move and study their legs. Was a panther's leg different from an impala's? Did a chicken's leg bend differently than a zebra's? How did those differences relate to the different activity of each animal? How did form dictate function for each animal and how did function dictate form?

At home Robert carefully tore apart chickens destined for the family dinner table to see how muscles moved bones and how muscles and joints related to motion. What he learned from chickens he applied to dinosaurs. What did the shape of a dinosaur's joints and the size of its bones say about how it must have moved and functioned? He tried to account for this motion and the implied probable muscle masses to control and move each bone in his drawings.

Robert graduated from high school in 1964 on the class honor roll and entered Yale University to study paleontology. A great revelation swept over him one night during his sophomore year. As he walked through the darkened museum, faint bits of light caught the dinosaur skeletons and made them appear to move through the shadowed stillness. It occurred to Robert as he studied the familiar bones that these creatures had ruled the earth for 165 million years. They couldn't have been stupid, cold-blooded, and sluggish. Intelligent mammals were around and would have taken over unless the dinosaurs kept winning because they were fundamentally better.

Robert Bakker set out—all alone—to prove that the prevailing view of dinosaurs was completely wrong. He turned to four disparate sources of information to develop his case: comparative anatomy (comparing the size and shape of similar parts of different species), latitudinal zonation (where the animals live), the cumulative fossil record (all previously collected dinosaur bones and skeletons), and ecology (relationship of a species to its environment).

For three years Bakker exhaustively studied the bones of mammals and found that they were, as were dinosaur bones, rich in blood vessels and lacked growth rings—just the opposite of cold-blooded reptiles. He found that Cretaceous dinosaurs thrived in northern Canada where cold-blooded reptiles could not have survived. Finally he studied African and north American ecosystems and found that warm-blooded predators eat six to eight times as much per pound of body weight as do reptile predators. By studying the fossil record, Bakker found that the ratio of predators to herbivores in dinosaur ecosystems matched what would be expected of a warm-blooded ecosystem.

Dinosaurs had to have been warm-blooded. Their bones, relative numbers, and locations proved it.

Bakker compared leg bone size, shape, and density for hundreds of modern animals with those of dinosaurs. He found that dinosaur leg bones closely matched the bone structure for running mammals—not those who sprint for 10 seconds when alarmed, but those who regularly run for 20 minutes.

Dinosaurs were runners. Their structure proved it. That also meant that they were agile. No sluggish, clumsy oaf would be a natural runner.

Again turning to the fossil record, Bakker found that very few baby and juvenile dinosaur skeletons had been discovered. This meant that few had died, which, in turn, meant that parent dinosaurs had to have been very successful at protecting, sheltering, and feeding their young.

Dinosaurs were good parents.

The old myths were shattered. Bakker published his findings while still a graduate student at Harvard. He was met with glacial antagonism from the paleontology establishment. Prestigious professors sneered that it was ridiculous for a mere student to oppose theories accepted by every top paleontologist in the world. Bakker mused that his Harvard professors would rather have stoned him than listen to a young punk who was trying to destroy all their cherished beliefs. Bakker was shunned. He feared that his career was destroyed. He struggled to find relevant post-graduate work.

It took 20 years of intense data collection and analysis for the tide of belief to turn in Bakker's direction. Even after it did, he was still viewed with suspicion as an untrustworthy radical.

Now Robert Bakker splits his time between long weeks at digs in the Badlands of Wyoming and long weeks at home piecing together the bone fragments he has found, trying to interpret their meaning and significance. Often on digs, the wind blows hot and dense. Always the work is tedious and slow. As he says, "The bones are full of cracks. You can't just yank the bones out. You have to carefully chisel out a block of rock that contains the skeleton. Then you cover the whole block with plaster of Paris so the whole mass of rock and bones don't shift and crack. Back home you scrape the rock off with needles and very small knife blades."

Bakker is deeply committed to improving education to support and sustain children's natural fascination with and love of nature and dinosaurs. He is also eagerly looking forward to the next find and the next discovery. "Who knows?" he says. "We may have found evidence of feathered dinosaurs."

## Key Dates

| | |
|---|---|
| 1945 | Born in Ridgewood, New Jersey, on March 24 |
| 1968 | Received B.S. from Yale |
| 1976 | Received Ph.D. from Harvard |
| 1976–1984 | Worked as instructor of paleontology at Johns Hopkins University |
| 1984–present | Moved to Boulder, Colorado; appointed adjunct professor of paleontology at University of Colorado and curator of paleontology at the university museum |
| 1986 | Published *The Dinosaur Heresies* |

## Advice

*If you are considering a career in paleontology, Robert Bakker would advise you to spend a lot of time at zoos. Watch animals move. See the architecture and choreography of bones moving. Study how muscles, joints, and skeleton interact and what those motions imply for the shape and function of the animal.*

*Bakker would also advise you to get hold of a dead chicken—one with the feet and head still attached. Take the chicken apart. Pull on the meat to see how muscles move bones. Clean and boil the skeleton. Then take it to a museum and compare it to the skeleton of a velociraptor or a Tyrannosaurus Rex. You will find that they are very similar.*

*For coursework, Bakker would advise you to study the basic sciences, of course, but also study history. Learn science within the context of evolution, that is, in the context of changing time.*

## References

Bakker, Robert. *The Dinosaur Heresies.* New York: Morrow Books, 1968. (Review of dinosaur anatomy and function and of the process of paleontology.)

Daintith, John, et al., eds. *Biographical Encyclopedia of Scientists.* 2d ed. Vol 1. Philadelphia, Pa.: Institute of Physics Publishing, 1994. (Summary entry on Bakker's work.)

Krishtalka, Leonard. *Dinosaur Plots.* New York: William Morrow, 1989. (Good review of major palentology methods and issues.)

Officer, Charles. *The Great Dinosaur Extinction Controversy.* Reading, Mass.: Addison-Wesley, 1996. (Excellent recap of issues and methods.)

Stille, Darlene. "Dinosaur Scientist," in *Science Year, 1992.* New York: World Book, 1993. (Excellent interview with Bakker about his work and life.)

# Robert Ballard

*"Titanic Discoveries"*  Marine Geology

Institute for Exploration

## Career Highlights

- Discovered the *Titanic* in 13,000 feet of water on the floor of the Atlantic Ocean, 1985
- Named Scientist of the Year by *Discover* magazine, 1987
- Awarded the American Geological Institute Award, 1990
- Awarded the Newcomb Cleveland Prize by the American Association for the Advancement of Science, 1981

## Important Contributions

Robert Ballard will be forever famous for finding the greatest ship ever lost. In the pitch-black, icy-cold depths 13,000 feet under the choppy surface of the Atlantic Ocean, Ballard found the *Titanic*. He also discovered the wreck of the mighty German battleship, the *Bismarck*, and the American World War II aircraft carrier, *Yorktown*, sunk during the Battle of Midway.

Far more important than these headline-grabbing discoveries has been Ballard's work to explore and map the ocean floor. He has designed the two most flexible, versatile, and powerful deep-sea submersibles on earth. With them he has discovered new living communities and life forms and has mapped vast tracts of the ocean depths. Robert Ballard, part geologist, part ocean engineer, part explorer, has opened up a new world of deep-sea exploration and changed the nature of oceanographic exploration.

# Career Path

The dozen men in the electronics control room of the French research vessel *Argonne* stood as reverently transfixed and hushed as if visiting a holy shrine. The three black-and-white monitors they stared at showed a fuzzy landscape of silt, mud, and small stones, all partially obscured by a thick layer of algae that shone in the camera floodlights like a fine snow, giving an other-worldly look to the bleak ocean bottom scene. A huge metal cylinder loomed into the picture, looking as out of place as a swing set on the moon.

"A boiler," muttered the man at the controls. The camera-mounted deep-sea submersible *Argo-Jason* veered around the five-story-high monolith. Less than 100 yards away the towering bow and slime- and growth-covered railings of a giant ship rose like a silent wraith from the mud of the ocean floor, like a towering mountain above the tiny remote. *Titanic* had been found.

Yet the discovery of this illusive treasure was inevitable. Robert Ballard, the man who designed and built *Argo-Jason*, who designed the search, and who spent over a year researching the *Titanic's* sinking in libraries, on computers, and in wave tanks, made it so.

When Robert Ballard was two years old, his family moved to southern California, where his father, Chester Ballard, worked as a flight test engineer at the government's testing ground in the Mojave Desert. The sight and sound of jet aircraft screaming into the sky are among Robert's earliest memories.

In the mid-1950s, Robert's father was appointed to be the U.S. Navy's representative at the Scripps Institute of Oceanography in La Jolla, California. There the young boy fell in love with the ocean. His main pastimes were bodysurfing at the beach and reading about famous ocean explorers. His favorites were Osa and Martin Johnson, the photographic explorers of the South Pacific who worked in the 1940s.

Robert took a wide smattering of ocean-related science and engineering courses in college, winding up with a B.S. in geology and chemistry in 1965, although no specific academic field captured his interest. He applied to Scripps for graduate school but was turned down because he hadn't studied physics. Still wanting to pursue some oceanic field, he enrolled in the Institute for Geophysics at the University of Hawaii and found a job training dolphins to cover his school expenses.

In the late 1960s, Ballard entered the Navy to fulfill his military service and was assigned as a liaison officer to Woods Hole Oceanographic Institute in Massachusetts. The assignment was a gift from heaven. He would work at Woods Hole for the rest of his career.

In January 1972, Ballard attended an international conference on the Mid-Atlantic Ridge. He proposed using manned submersibles to probe and document the ridge. Other scientists scoffed at the use of manned submersibles, claiming that the work could only be accomplished from the surface.

Ballard convinced both Woods Hole administrators and the National Science Foundation that a Mid-Atlantic Ridge survey would be the perfect opportunity to demonstrate the new three-man submersible, *Alvin*, which Woods Hole was developing with Navy funding.

Through early 1974, research ships towed unmanned vehicles (including an underwater acoustical radar sled that Ballard designed) above the ridge so that scientists could pinpoint the most productive spots for dives by *Alvin*. That summer *Alvin* made 17 dives totaling over 100 hours of bottom time, produced over 1,000 pictures of volcanic features along the ridge line and rift valley, and collected hundreds of rock samples. Ballard was onboard *Alvin* for most of its dives. His work documented areas of incessant "microearthquakes," violent lava flows, lightless deep-sea communities, and new species never before seen, and produced a vast wealth of unique information.

*Alvin* was so successful that the National Science Foundation decided to use it for a survey of the Cayman Trough, a 24,000-foot-deep gash in the floor of the Caribbean just south of Cuba, and then for the Galapagos Hydrothermal Expedition. In both explorations *Alvin* provided critical data that could not have been obtained otherwise.

But manned submersibles had serious limitations. *Alvin* could only make 100 dives a year, could not remain on the bottom very long, and couldn't go below 12,000 feet. Ballard dreamed of creating versatile, robotic, unmanned submersibles that could pull harder, deeper duty. The Office of Naval Research supported his five-year development of the *Argo-Jason* system, featuring side-scanning radar, computer-enhanced underwater cameras, powerful strobe lights, and mechanical arms for sample collection.

Ballard came up with an ingenious plan to test the *Argo-Jason*. He had always been fascinated by the wreck of the *Titanic*. Countless explorers and salvage crews had hunted for the illusive wreck, but none could find her. He convinced the Navy that finding *Titanic* would be a suitable test for the *Argo-Jason* system and a historically significant event. To help ensure that the test would be successful, he spent a year researching the sinking in the library and modeling the fall of the ship from surface to the bottom in simulation tanks and on computers.

By the summer of 1985 Ballard had narrowed *Titanic's* possible resting site to a 225-square-mile grid on a 13,000-foot-deep plain. A French research vessel swept the entire search area with towed sonar equipment in the same back and forth pattern you would use to mow the lawn. Every promising sonar echo was plotted and logged, but none proved to be *Titanic*.

Argo was deployed during the next phase of the expedition; in less than a week *Argo's* floodlights and cameras swept across a massive ship's boiler.

Ballard turned the remote vehicle, and less than 100 yards away *Titanic* lay patiently waiting.

Through dozens of television specials, 14 books, and over 100 technical articles, Ballard has worked to popularize deep-sea exploration. He has discovered the wrecks of two other famous giant ships, the German battleship *Bismarck*, and the American aircraft carrier, *Yorktown*.

But Robert Ballard's most important and most lasting legacy will be the very concept of manned and unmanned deep-sea submersibles as a practical and proven tool for underseas exploration. He has stirred our hearts and imaginations with his photographs and discoveries. He has immeasurably enriched our knowledge of the hidden deep-sea portions of the earth. Still in his late fifties, he certainly isn't through making his mark on the ocean sciences and our world.

## Key Dates

| | |
|---|---|
| 1942 | Born in Wichita, Kansas, on June 30 |
| 1965 | Received B.S. in geology and chemistry form UC Santa Barbara |
| 1966–1967 | Worked for North American Aviation, Ocean Systems Division in deep submersible engineering |
| 1967 | Attended University of Hawaii |
| 1967–1969 | Served as Navy liaison officer to Woods Hole Oceanographic Institute |
| 1970–1974 | Worked as research associate in ocean engineering at Woods Hole Oceanographic Institute |
| 1974 | Received Ph.D. in marine geology form University of Rhode Island |
| 1974–1976 | Worked as research assistant in geology at Woods Hole Oceanographic Institute |
| 1976–1979 | Worked as associate scientist in ocean engineering at Woods Hole Oceanographic Institute |
| 1979–1980 | Worked as visiting scholar in geology at Stanford University |
| 1980–1983 | Worked as associate scientist in ocean engineering at Woods Hole Oceanographic Institute |

1983–    Works as senior scientist in ocean engineering at Woods
present      Hole Oceanographic Institute

1992–    Serves as president, Institute for Exploration, Mystic,
present      Connecticut

## Advice

*Robert Ballard would advise any-one considering a career in marine geology to study all facets of oceanography and marine engineering rather than focusing exclusively on geology. The fields of oceanography are inter-connected. Without a working knowledge of all of the fields it will be difficult to advance in any of them. Spend as much time as possible on the ocean and in the ocean. Find out early if you are comfortable at sea. It will be difficult to study an environment if you do not have direct, personal, physical knowledge of it. Finally, learn about marine equipment as early as possible. The more time you spend working in the field, the faster your career will advance.*

## References

Archbold, Rick. *Deep Sea Explorer: The Story of Robert Ballard.* New York: Scholastic, 1994. (Good review of Ballard's work and methods.)

Ballard, Robert. *The Discovery of the Bismarck.* New York: Warner Books, 1990. (Good review of the process of undersea exploration.)

———. *The Discovery of the Titanic.* New York: Warner Books, 1989. (Good review of the process of undersea exploration.)

———. *Explorations.* New York: Hyperion, 1995. (Good autobiographical review of all Ballard's explorations.)

———. *Finding the Titanic.* New York: Scholastic, 1993. (Good review of the process of undersea exploration.)

———. *Photographic Atlas of the Mid-Atlantic Ridge Rift Valley.* Boston: Springer-Verlag, 1977. (Good introduction to the process of systematic underwater mapping and grid work.)

*Current Biography Yearbook, 1986.* New York: H. W. Wilson, 1987. (Good review of Ballard's early work.)

# John Bardeen

*"Taming the Transistor"*

Physics and
Electrical
Engineering

## Career Highlights

- Received Nobel Prize for Physics, 1956 (shared with Walter H. Brattain and William Shockley) for inventing the transistor
- Received Nobel Prize for Physics, 1972 (shared with Leon N. Cooper and J. Robert Schrieffer) for the theory of superconductivity
- Awarded the Presidential Medal of Freedom, 1977
- Won the National Medal of Science, 1966

## Important Contributions

John Bardeen was the first person ever to be awarded two Nobel Prizes in physics. He won his first Nobel Prize for inventing the transistor. The transistor has been the backbone of every computing, calculating, communicating, and logic electronics circuit built in the last 50 years.

Bardeen won his second Nobel Prize for elucidating the theory of superconductivity, which has been called "one of the most important achievements in theoretical physics since the development of quantum theory." Superconductivity at higher temperatures has led to such feats as frictionless, ultrafast trains lifted magnetically above their rails, traveling on superconductive tracks.

## Career Path

John Bardeen taught physics at the University of Minnesota from 1938 to 1941. There, as a 30-year-old assistant professor, he found the first research question that stirred both his intellectual curiosity and his passion.

He discovered the mystery of superconductivity. Superconductivity is the state where, at temperatures a few degrees above absolute zero, many metals lose all resistance to the flow of electricity. Electricity will flow through them unimpeded forever.

At the turn of the century, Kammerlingh Onnes discovered that mercury lost all electrical resistance when chilled to 4.2° K. He and other scientists struggled to understand this phenomenon, but an explanation had never been found. For the first time in his life, John Bardeen was fascinated.

John had been a true child prodigy, attending an experimental elementary school in Madison, Wisconsin, where he skipped the fourth, fifth, and sixth grades. He received his bachelor's degree at age 20 and his master's degree at age 21, both from the University of Wisconsin. He breezed through school with minimal difficulty and no real challenges.

Following graduation, he worked as a geophysicist for Gulf Research, where he helped develop new techniques for locating petroleum deposits. With a year of grueling field work under his belt, Bardeen decided to re-enter academic life. In 1933, he enrolled in Princeton University to study theoretical physics. He completed his Ph.D. in 1936 while studying as a research fellow at Harvard.

Then, as an assistant professor at the University of Minnesota, Bardeen found superconductivity and became engrossed in the search for a theory to explain the phenomenon. He developed the idea that a gap in the energy levels available to electrons would trap them in superconducting states. But this theory was proved incorrect by later experiments. Before he could revise his theory, World War II claimed his time and attention, designing electrical proximity fuses for naval mines.

After the war, Bardeen was hired by Bell Laboratories, a high-tech communications and electronics research plant. In the fall of 1947 he joined forces with William Shockley and Walter Brattain, who were already studying the possible use of semiconductor materials in electronics. Shockley shared the "industrial dream" of freeing electronics from the bulkiness, fragility, heat production, and high power consumption of the vacuum tube. To allow semiconductors to replace tubes, Shockley had to make semiconductor material both amplify and rectify electric signals. All of his attempts up to that point had failed.

Bardeen first studied and confirmed that Shockley's mathematics were correct and that his approach was consistent with accepted theory. Shockley's experiments should work. But the results they found using germanium, a common semiconductor, didn't match the theory.

John Bardeen theorized that unspecified surface interference on the germanium must be blocking the electric current. The three men set about testing the responses of semiconductor surfaces to light, heat, cold, liquids, and the deposit of metallic films. On wide lab benches they tried to force electric current into the germanium through liquid metals and then through soldered wire contact points. Most of November 1947 and much of December were consumed with these tests.

The three scientists found that the contact points worked—sort of. A strong current could be forced through the germanium to a metal base on the other side. But rather than amplifying a signal, it actually consumed energy.

Then Bardeen noticed something odd and unexpected. He accidentally misconnected his electrical leads, sending a micro-current to the germanium contact point. When a very weak current was trickled through from wire solder point to base, it created a "hole" in the germanium's resistance to current flow. A weak current converted the semiconductor into a superconductor. He had to repeatedly demonstrate the phenomenon to convince both himself and his teammates that his amazing results weren't fluke occurrences. Time after time the results were the same with any semiconductor material they tried: high current, high resistance; low current, virtually no resistance.

Bardeen named the phenomenon, "transfer resistors," or transistors. It provided engineers with a way to both rectify a weak signal and boost it to many times its original strength. Transistors required only one-fiftieth the space of a vacuum tube and one-millionth the power and could out-perform a vacuum tube. For this discovery, the three men shared the 1956 Nobel Prize for Physics.

But rather than seeing transistors as an end point, Bardeen hoped that semiconductors would hold his long-sought key to superconductivity. As important as they were, transistors proved a disappointment to him in that they were another dead end in his search for a superconductivity theory.

In 1951, Bardeen left Bell Laboratories to become a professor of physics and electrical engineering at the University of Illinois, where he again took up his investigation of superconductivity. This time, he worked with graduate students J. R. Schrieffer and Leon Cooper.

After five years of fruitless study, Bardeen, Cooper, and Schrieffer made a breakthrough in 1957. They were able to demonstrate that, at super cold temperatures, the electrons in a lattice of atoms bonded in pairs of opposite spin and momentum. Once an electric flow was induced, the electrons in a pair traveled coupled together; these pairs were later called Cooper pairs. If one electron was refracted, its pair-mate refracted in the opposite way so that the net momentum of the flow was unchanged. The current would continue forever until some outside force acted to stop it.

For this successful model of superconductivity, Bardeen, Cooper, and Schrieffer were awarded the Nobel Prize for Physics in 1972. Their success generated a powerful resurgence of interest in superconductors and their potential applications. These scientists paved the way for a brand new industry to emerge based on the possibilities of exploiting superconducting materials.

## Key Dates

| | |
|---|---|
| 1908 | Born in Madison, Wisconsin, on May 23 |
| 1928 | Received B.S. from University of Wisconsin |
| 1929 | Received M.S. from University of Wisconsin |
| 1930–1933 | Worked as geophysicist with Gulf Research and Development Corporation |
| 1936 | Received Ph.D. in physics and mathematics from Princeton University |
| 1935-1938 | Served as Junior Fellow, Harvard University |
| 1938–1941 | Worked as assistant professor of physics, University of Minnesota |
| 1941–1945 | Worked as physicist at U.S. Naval Ordnance Laboratory |
| 1945–1951 | Worked as research physicist at Bell Telephone Laboratory |
| 1951–1975 | Worked as professor of electrical engineering and physics, University of Illinois |
| 1956 | Received Nobel Prize for Physics |
| 1959–1962 | Served as member of President's Science Advisory Committee |
| 1972 | Received Nobel Prize for Physics |
| 1975 | Retired |
| 1991 | Died on January 30 |

# Advice

*John Bardeen believed that understanding and discovery come only as the result of care and persistence. "Never give up" was the advice Bardeen most commonly offered his students. Don't ever give up on a problem, a dream, or a career. When Bardeen left for Stockholm to receive his first Nobel Prize, his partners were ready to abandon their study of superconductivity, but at his insistence they continued. It took Bardeen almost 20 years to devise an accurate theory of superconductivity.*

*Electrical engineering is one of the most rapidly changing fields in all science. It will be a full-time job just to stay current with the field once you gain a solid understanding. Major advances are made by merging electrical theory with a knowledge of materials and physics or chemistry. As an undergraduate, branch out from electrical engineering as widely as possible.*

# References

Aaseng, Nathan. *American Profiles: Twentieth-Century Inventors.* New York: Facts on File, 1991. (Good entry on Bardeen's work and life.)

———. *The Inventors: Nobel Prizes in Chemistry.* Minneapolis, Minn.: Lerner, 1988. (Good entry on Bardeen's work and life.)

Bardeen, John. "Semiconductor Research Leading to the Point Contact Transistor," in *Nobel Lectures: Physics, 1942–62.* Amsterdam: GRD Publications, 1964.

Burns, Gerald. *High-Temperature Superconductivity: An Introduction.* Boston: Academic Press, 1992.

Vidali, Gianfranco. *Superconductivity: The Next Revolution?* Cambridge, England: Cambridge University Press, 1993.

# George Beadle

## *"Bread Mold to Nobel Prize"*       Genetics

## Career Highlights

- Awarded the Nobel Prize for Physiology and Medicine, 1958
- Discovered how genes and DNA physically exert control over cell development
- Awarded the Kimber Genetics Award of the National Academy of Sciences, 1960
- Awarded the Lasker Award by the American Public Health Association, 1950

## Important Contributions

Genes are strung along chromosomes and contain directions for the operation and growth of individual cells. But how can a molecule of nucleic acid (a gene) direct an entire complex cell to perform in a certain way? George Beadle answered this critical question and vastly improved our understanding of evolutionary genetics.

Beadle discovered that each gene directs the formation of a particular enzyme. Enzymes then swing the cell into action. His discovery filled a huge gap in our understanding of how DNA blueprints are translated into physical cell-building action. Beadle's ground-breaking work shifted the focus of the entire field of genetics research from the qualitative study of outward characteristics (what physical deformities are created by mutated genes) to the quantitative chemical study of genes and their mode of producing enzymes.

## Career Path

George Beadle was supposed to be a farmer. He was born on a farm outside Wahoo, Nebraska, in 1903. His mother died when George was four years old and his older brother died in a farm accident when George was eight. His father assumed that George, the only surviving heir, would take over the family's 40-acre farm.

Then a high school physics teacher kindled George's interest in science and persuaded him to go to college. The only way his father would agree to four years of college was if the schooling would help George run the farm. So the young man enrolled in the College of Agriculture at the University of Nebraska. Through the agronomy department George assisted in a study of the genetics of hybrid wheat. That study was his first exposure to the field of genetics; it turned his world upside down.

All thoughts of running the family farm had vanished by the time George Beadle graduated with a B.S. in 1926. He was hooked on the wonder of genetics. He couldn't imagine spending his life on anything else. In 1926 genetics was still a new field, buzzing with the electric excitement of important discoveries to be made. The general concepts of genetics were known, but no one understood the physical mechanisms that made the concepts occur. That is, they had a good sense of *what* happened, but barely a hint of *how* it happened.

George shifted to Cornell University, one of the national centers of genetics research, to continue his studies. His assigned work was to collect and review all published literature on the genetics of maize (field corn). He wrote his dissertation on common mutations in the chromosomes and genes of corn.

Chromosomes are strands of genetic material in the nucleus of plant and animal cells. Genes are long chain molecules of DNA attached to chromosomes. Genes carry the actual blueprint instructions for the construction and operation of every living cell. Genetics research in the late 1920s was shifting from the outward effect of chromosomes to the study of the effects of individual genes. Studies were conducted on organisms with simplistic gene structures such as field corn or fruit flies so that changes in outward appearance could be traced back to mutations in individual genes.

Beadle received his Ph.D. in 1931 and accepted a fellowship at Caltech so he could continue his studies under famed geneticist Thomas Morgan, who had spent 20 years studying mutations in fruit fly genes. After studying under Morgan for two years, he accepted a number of short-term teaching appointments until, at the age of 34, he landed an appointment with the genetics faculty at Stanford University in 1937.

Stanford wanted to develop their study of biochemical genetics. The study of genetics was 80 years old. But biochemical genetics, or the molecular study of how genetic signals are created and sent to cells, was still in its infancy. Beadle teamed with microbiologist Edward Tatum to try to determine how genes exercise their controlling influence.

In concept their work was simple. In practice it was painstakingly tedious and demanding. They searched for the simplest life form they could find, choosing the bread mold *Neurospora* because its simple gene structure had been well documented. They grew trays upon trays of colonies of *Neurospora* in a common growth medium. Then Beadle and Tatum bombarded every colony with X-rays, which were known to accelerate genetic mutations. Within 12 hours some colonies were continuing to grow normally (they were unmutated), some had died (X-rays had destroyed them), and some still lived but failed to thrive (gene mutations now made them unable to grow).

This third group was most interesting because it had undergone some genetic mutation that made it impossible for the mold to grow on its own. If Beadle and Tatum could discover exactly what this mutated mold now needed to grow, they would learn what its mutated gene had done on its own before it had been damaged.

Beadle and Tatum placed individual spores from one of these colonies into a thousand different test tubes, each containing the same standard growth medium. To each tube they added one possible substance the original mold had been able to synthesize for itself, but which the mutated mold might not be producing. Then they waited to see which, if any, would begin to thrive.

Only one tube began to grow normally: tube 299, the one to which they had added vitamin $B_6$. The mutation to the mold's gene must have left the mold unable to synthesize vitamin $B_6$ and thus unable to grow. That meant that the original gene had produced something that made the cells able to synthesize the vitamin on their own. The second step of Beadle and Tatum's experiment was to search for that something.

Beadle found that when he removed, or blocked, certain enzymes, the mold stopped growing. He was able to trace these enzymes back to genes and to show that the mutated gene from tube 299 no longer produced any enzyme. Through this experiment he discovered how genes do their job. He proved that genes produce enzymes and that enzymes chemically direct cells to act. It was a discovery worthy of a Nobel Prize.

For the rest of his career George Beadle drifted among teaching, research, and university administration. But his first love was always hands-on genetic research. He remained active until the end of his life in this exciting field of research, which he had done so much to shape and develop.

# Key Dates

| | |
|---|---|
| 1903 | Born in Wahoo, Nebraska, on October 22 |
| 1926 | Received B.S. in agriculture from University of Nebraska |
| 1931 | Received Ph.D. in genetics from Cornell University |
| 1931–1933 | Worked as post-doctoral lab assistant at the California Institute of Technology |
| 1933–1937 | Held teaching positions at various U.S. and European institutions |
| 1937–1946 | Worked as professor of genetics at Stanford University |
| 1946 | Accepted chair of the genetics department at the California Institute of Technology |
| 1958 | Awarded Nobel Prize for Physiology and Medicine |
| 1962 | Appointed president of the University of Chicago |
| 1968 | Retired to return to private genetics research |
| 1970 | Returned to Caltech as a trustee |
| 1989 | Died on June 9 |

## Advice

George Beadle believed that studying at the best graduate school under a leading researcher was the key to launching a successful genetics career. But first you must work hard enough as an undergraduate to have your pick of graduate schools and then post-doctoral positions. Always choose situations that will enable you to study under the leading experts in your field.

During your career, expect lots of hands-on lab work. There is no substitute for consistent and precise lab work. Learn lab technique as well as a solid foundation in theory. As an undergraduate, study a wide range of subjects: chemistry, physics, biology, biochemistry, and biophysics, and, especially, math. No significant study rests within the confines of one narrow field. Look for ways to bridge information and concepts from different fields to provide a new perspective on challenging problems.

## References

Beadle, George. *Language of Life: An Introduction to the Science of Genetics.* New York: Doubleday, 1966. (Excellent primer on the field of genetics through the mid-1960s.)

Davern, Cedric. *Genetics: Readings from Scientific American.* San Francisco: W. H. Freeman, 1981. (Excellent series of readings on genetics.)

Edey, Maitland. *Blueprints: Solving the Mystery of Evolution.* New York: Penguin Books, 1986. (Good review of the field of genetics.)

Moritz, Charles, ed. *Current Biography Yearbook, 1990.* New York: H. W. Wilson, 1991. (Good review of Beadle's work.)

Tanor, Joseph, ed. *McGraw-Hill Modern Men of Science.* New York: McGraw-Hill, 1986. (Strong summary of Beadle's work.)

Wasson, Tyler, ed. *Nobel Prize Winners.* New York: H. W. Wilson, 1987. (Good summary of Beadle's work.)

# Jacob Bjerknes

*"The King of Atmospheric Sciences"*          Meteorology

## Career Highlights

- Awarded the U.S. National Medal of Science, 1967
- Awarded the Losey Medal by the Institute of Aerospace Sciences, 1963
- Developed the first quantitative system for weather prediction
- Awarded the Meritorious Civilian Service Medal of the U.S. Air Force, 1946

## Important Contributions

Working jointly with his father, Jacob Bjerknes developed the theory of weather prediction by air mass analysis. It was Jacob Bjerknes who coined the term "front" to describe the boundary between two air masses and who developed the polar front theory of cyclones. Jacob Bjerknes was also the first to study the climate controlling interactions between the ocean surface and the lower atmosphere, to explain the El Niño phenomenon, and to determine the effect of equatorial ocean temperature on mid-latitude rainfall.

In the early 1900s, Jacob and his father, Vilhelm, were jointly called "the fathers of modern meteorology" because of their successful efforts to develop predictive models for atmospheric movement and change. In the 1950s and early 1960s, meteorology underwent another revolution. Rocket and satellite data and photographs of air masses and cloud systems became available for the first time. It was Jacob Bjerknes who pioneered the use of this new data source to improve atmospheric calculations. For the second time in a century, Jacob Bjerknes ushered in a new approach to meteorology and was again called "the father of modern meteorology."

# Career Path

Jacob Bjerknes was born in 1897 into two worlds. One was a world of science. His father, Vilhelm, was a meteorologist and a professor of mathematical physics. His grandfather was a professor of mathematics. His mother was a zoologist and embryologist and became Norway's first woman professor. Jacob was raised in a house of science talk, science books, and science visitors.

But Jacob Bjerknes was also born into a world of prejudice and discrimination. The Bjerknes family was Norwegian, but lived in Sweden. Even in kindergarten Swedish classmates taunted and teased Jacob. The harassment grew much worse after Norway withdrew from its union with Sweden in 1905. Shy and reserved by nature, the young boy withdrew and lived his early years as a loner, spending solitary afternoons watching the Swedish clouds and sky. While still a schoolboy, Jacob began to assist his father with his atmospheric research because he needed something to do and because he had already developed a deep affection for the sky.

The family moved home to Norway when Jacob was 12 years old. His father was offered a position at the University of Christiania, where he would focus on "developing the world's first quantitative physics to describe and predict atmospheric phenomena and change." Young Jacob continued to assist his father in this effort.

Long before completing his high school studies, Jacob was committed to studying the atmosphere as a career. There was never any doubt in his mind about his career choice. He entered the University of Christiania to study under his father while he continued to assist him with his atmospheric research.

In 1916 Jacob followed his father in a move to the University of Leipzig and took a position as one of his father's two paid assistants while he began his graduate studies. Less than a year later, senior and junior Bjerkneses were both offered positions at the new Bergen Museum Geophysical Institute. While his father headed the physics teaching department, Jacob served as teaching assistant and chief weather forecaster.

Jacob pledged to complete the research tasks his father had been unable to finish and find a quantitative system for describing the movement of atmospheric air. However, no one had figured out how to record measurements in the *upper* atmosphere. All available data reflected conditions at or near ground level. Jacob Bjerknes believed studies of the little-understood upper atmosphere were the key to successful weather modeling and prediction.

Bjerknes spent a full year adapting and testing temperature, altitude, and wind velocity measuring equipment so that they would work on a balloon mount. This equipment recorded continuously while the balloon ascended. At a preset altitude, the balloon would partially deflate and sink to the ground, where the data could be recovered and analyzed.

It was an ingenious plan. But too many balloons were never recovered. Too often equipment malfunctioned. Project costs skyrocketed. Precious little information was collected.

Bjerknes added a radio transmitter to the balloon platform both to serve as a locator beacon and to transmit data to the ground as it was collected. His crew spent almost a decade launching balloons, repairing damaged sensors, and correlating surface weather conditions with the upper atmospheric data they collected.

From this study Bjerknes made several ground-breaking observations. Air moved in great masses. These air masses moved along generally predictable seasonal tracks. He also noticed that significant weather events happened along the borders between substantially different air masses. He named these borders "fronts."

Bjerknes was able to produce enough data to define the movement of upper atmosphere air masses and the ways in which waves of upper-atmosphere energy transferred into the lower atmosphere. He developed methods of identifying an air mass, of predicting its probable track and interactions with other air masses, and of evaluating the effect of fronts that would probably occur along the boundary of this mass with other air masses.

He was then able to measure the violent interactions of both upper- and lower-atmosphere air masses along their fronts as they crashed into, or rubbed their way past, other air masses to substantiate his quantitative model. The accuracy of near- and long-term weather forecasting took an instant tenfold leap forward.

While pursuing this research, Bjerknes noticed that air masses surrounding low pressure centers characteristically spun in a counter-clockwise, or cyclonic, direction. He named these air masses cyclones and noted that most major weather conditions were associated with these air masses.

Bjerknes was on a lecture tour in the United States, presenting his findings, in April 1940, when the German Army invaded Norway. He was unable to return home. He was offered a professorship at the University of California at Los Angeles, which he accepted. There, on the edge of the Pacific Ocean, Bjerknes turned his research attention to the interaction between tropical ocean and atmosphere.

Using balloon- and ship-mounted measuring equipment, Bjerknes discovered flows of water, heat, and energy between the tropical ocean surface and lower atmosphere just as he had between upper- and lower-atmosphere air masses. Wind energy transferred to the ocean to create waves. Ocean thermal energy and moisture transferred into the lower atmosphere to exert a dominant influence over mid-latitude air flows and weather patterns.

This body of research by Bjerknes finally explained the El Niño phenomenon first observed almost a century earlier. For the first time a single, comprehensive theory tracked air mass and energy flows between the upper atmosphere, lower atmosphere, and major oceanic surfaces. The art of weather forecasting became for the first time a science.

But even now, when he had completely rebuilt the standard approach to meteorology, Bjerknes wasn't satisfied. Rockets were routinely reaching the upper atmosphere. The first satellites had been launched. He was the first to recognize the potential of this new technology. He reinvented meteorology all over again by incorporating satellite and rocket data and photographs into his models and into his system of predictions.

Twice the same man earned the title "father of modern meteorology" by radically improving the existing technology and methodology used for atmospheric studies. Throughout 55 years of productive research, Jacob Bjerknes produced 57 technical papers and earned the undisputed reputation as the king of atmospheric sciences.

## Key Dates

| | |
|---|---|
| 1897 | Born in Stockholm, Sweden, on November 2 |
| 1909 | Family moved to Norway |
| 1916 | Received B.A. from University of Christiania |
| 1916 | Entered University of Leipzig to study with his father |
| 1917 | Hired to work at the Geophysical Institute at Bergen under his father |
| 1918– 1931 | Worked as chief forecaster for Bergen weather forecasting service |
| 1924 | Received Ph.D. in meteorology from the University of Oslo |
| 1931 | Appointed professor of meteorology at Bergen Museum |
| 1940 | Immigrated to America; appointed professor of meteorology at the University of California at Los Angeles |
| 1952 | Was first meteorologist to use orbital and rocket data for weather analysis |
| 1975 | Died on July 7 |

# Advice

Jacob Bjerknes believed that exploring nature and reading are the two great adventures of childhood. A career in meteorology should start very early with relevant reading and with careful observation of wind, weather, clouds, and sky. In high school and college begin any serious study of the sciences with a thorough understanding of mathematics. All science requires the application of numerical models and other mathematics. Study math, physics, and inorganic chemistry in addition to atmospheric sciences. Finally, every field of science requires dedicated, persistent, diligent study over a long period of time.

# References

Caskey, James, ed. *A Century of Weather Progress: A Collection of Addresses Presented at a Joint Symposium.* Boston: American Meteorological Society, 1980. (Good historical entries on the development of quantitative meteorology.)

Eggenberger, David. *The McGraw-Hill Encyclopedia of World Biography.* New York: McGraw-Hill, 1983. (Good summary biographical entry.)

Gillispie, Charles, ed. *Dictionary of Scientific Biography.* New York: Charles Scribner's Sons, 1978. (Good biographical and work summary.)

Lockhart, Gary. *The Weather Companion: An Album of Meteorological History and Science.* New York: John Wiley, 1988. (Good historical review of the field.)

Nese, Jon M., Lee M. Grenci, David J. Mornhinweg, and Timothy W. Owen. *A World of Weather: Fundamentals of Meteorology.* Dubuque, Iowa: Kendall/Hunt Publishing Company, 1996. (Textbook and laboratory manual containing real-life examples and nontraditional problems.)

# Niels Bohr

*"Cracking the Code"*                                      Physics

## Career Highlights

- Awarded Nobel Prize for Physics, 1922
- Awarded Ford Foundation Atoms for Peace Award, 1957
- Awarded Gold Medal from Royal Danish Academy of Sciences, 1907

## Important Contributions

Marie Curie opened the century by proving that there *was* a subatomic world. Einstein, Dirac, Heisenberg, Born, Rutherford, and others provided the theoretical descriptions of this subatomic world. But *proving* what lurked within an atom's shell, and what governed its behavior, lingered as the great physics challenges of the early twentieth century.

It was Niels Bohr who developed the first concrete model of the placement, motion, radiation patterns, and energy transfer of the electrons that circled an atom's nucleus. Bohr's theory solved a number of inconsistencies and flaws that existed in previous attempts to guess at the structure and activity of electrons. Niels Bohr successfully combined direct experiment with advanced theory to derive an understanding of electrons. It was an essential step in science's march into the nuclear age. For this reason he is often called the "father of atomic physics."

## Career Path

There is theory, and then there is experimental data. Theories need data to prove their correctness. Data can only be explained through theories. Unfortunately, few scientists work with both, so theoreticians' concepts and lab researchers' results are often at odds. In early 1912 Niels Bohr realized that just such a morass of confusion surrounded the structure of an atom.

Niels Bohr was only 26 in 1912, very young to be stepping into the middle of a heated worldwide physics controversy, but his upbringing and training made him eminently qualified. Niels had been born into a well-to-do Danish family in 1885. His father was a professor of physiology, and the elite of Copenhagen regularly gathered at the Bohr house for lively discussion and intellectual debate.

The tall, hospitable young man grew up in a carefree world of privilege. He was an excellent athlete, but was also sensitive and needed a steady flow of reassurance and sympathy. Niels was considered a "fair-haired" golden boy who seemed to glide comfortably through life.

His senior project at the University of Copenhagen on the surface tension of water earned a Gold Medal from the Royal Danish Academy of Sciences in 1907. Niels stayed at the university for his master's degree and his doctorate before deciding to broaden his studies.

Bohr spent three months at Cambridge University studying under J. J. Thompson (who first hypothesized the existence of the electron in 1897) and a year at the University of Manchester, where he joined Ernest Rutherford's group studying atomic structure and radioactive elements. Rutherford's work, in particular, was an important step in the path leading Bohr toward his own discoveries. It was at Manchester that he formed an early concept of his later model of atomic structure.

In the spring of 1912, Bohr realized that atomic theory no longer matched the growing body of experimental atomic data. When he was offered a professorship at the University of Copenhagen that fall, Bohr assumed a position in which he could correct this glaring discrepancy.

The infant field of atomic physics boiled with new ideas and new discoveries, each seemingly more exciting than the last. What made the work hard was that there was no way to actually see an atom, no way to peer inside and directly observe what was going on. Theoretical physicists often felt like police investigators, sifting through mountains of indirect observations and data for the few, key bits of evidence, and then having to build a theory to explain the entire atomic structure from these few scattered clues.

Bohr had helped Rutherford conduct experiments to measure the angle at which alpha particles were deflected when they struck an atom. The large angle of deflection they measured suggested that the alpha particle had to have hit a dense, solid mass.

Other experimenters had established that protons were thousands of times more massive than electrons. Neutrons had been discovered and were considered to be about the same size as protons. Still, protons and neutrons combined accounted for only a tiny fraction of the total volume of an atom. Rutherford hypothesized that the protons and neutrons must be massed in a dense nucleus at the atom's center to account for the dense mass his experiments suggested. He theorized that electrons must be circling this nucleus as planets circle the sun in the vast empty space of the outer atom.

It sounded promising. But by 1912 Bohr had shown that classical electrodynamics predicted that an orbiting electron would continuously lose energy and slowly spiral into the nucleus. The atom would collapse and implode. But that didn't happen. Atoms were amazingly stable. Something was wrong with the theory.

As Bohr began to organize his observations and theories into a formal model of the atom in 1913, two new ideas entered his thinking and changed the direction of his model. Enrico Fermi and others had been experimenting with radioactivity and atomic radiation. They found that energy tended to be emitted from an atom in discrete quanta of energy. These findings supported the theories of Max Plank, Albert Einstein, and Max Born.

The second new idea came from chemists who were busy cataloging the physical and electrical properties of the atoms of each element. One of the experiments being conducted measured the atomic radiation emitted by atoms of different elements. The chemists found that if they passed this radiation through a prism, the radiation was not continuous over the whole frequency spectrum, but came in sharp spikes at certain discrete frequencies. Different elements showed different, characteristic patterns in these energy spikes. But no one could make sense out of the patterns, or even out of the existence of the spikes themselves.

Bohr studied and compared these different, and apparently unrelated, bits of data. They didn't fit any existing theories. Still, he realized that they had to relate somehow. They all dealt with characteristics and emissions from the same source: atoms. Sifting and re-sifting the data and the theories over an eight-month period, he arrived at a revolutionary idea: Electrons must not be as free as previously thought.

Bohr theorized that the electrons circling an atom's nucleus could only exist in certain, discrete, fixed orbits. To jump to a closer orbit, an electron would have to give off a fixed amount of energy (the observed spikes of radiated energy). If an electron were to jump into a higher orbit, it would have to absorb a fixed quanta of energy. Electrons couldn't go wherever they wanted or carry any amount of energy. Electrons had to be in one or another of a few specific orbits. They must gain and lose energy in specific quanta. The atomic model Bohr created was revolutionary and a complete departure from previous ideas, and it earned him the Nobel Prize for Physics. Although revolutionary, the model fit well with experimental observations and explained all of the inconsistencies of previous theories. His findings received instant acclaim and acceptance. A score of researchers set about proving Bohr's model. The effort to prove his theory conclusively consumed much of the next 20 years of his life.

Throughout the last 40 years of his long and productive life, Niels Bohr worked to refine and improve quantum mechanics. He contributed to the Manhattan Project (the American efforts to create an atomic bomb during World War II) and spent much of his later time spearheading the International Atoms for Peace effort. But Bohr will always be remembered as the one who finally cracked the code, solved the mystery, and created an accurate model of the workings and mechanics of the electrons of an atom.

## Key Dates

| | |
|---|---|
| 1885 | Born in Copenhagen, Denmark, on October 7 |
| 1907 | Received B.S. in chemistry from University of Copenhagen |
| 1911 | Received Ph.D. from University of Copenhagen |
| 1912 | Appointed assistant professor at University of Copenhagen |
| 1913 | Published his revolutionary theory of atomic structure |
| 1914 | Held professorship at University of Manchester |
| 1916 | Held full professorship at University of Copenhagen |
| 1922 | Won Nobel Prize for Physics |
| 1955 | Retired from University of Copenhagen at mandatory retirement age of 70 |
| 1962 | Died on November 18 |

## Advice

*If you are considering a career in subatomic physics, Niels Bohr would advise you to start by gaining a solid understanding of math and classical physics methods. Then seek out the researchers at the forefront of the specialties that interest you most. Apply to those schools and find ways to study under the current leaders of your field, the ones breaking new and revolutionary ground. Volunteer if you must, but work with the leaders. Sign up for their classes. Attend all their lectures. Work with them until your own ideas and questions are begging to be investigated.*

## References

Aserud, Finn. *Redirecting Science: Niels Bohr and the Rise of Nuclear Physics.* London: Cambridge University Press, 1990. (Good look at relationship of science to funding and outside support.)

Blaedel, Niels. *Harmony and Unity: The Life of Niels Bohr.* Chicago: Science Technology Publications, 1988. (Powerful anecdotes about Bohr.)

Clive, Barbara. *The Questioners: Physicists and the Quantum Theory.* New York: Thomas Crowell, 1975. (Good review of the field.)

Moor, Ruth. *Niels Bohr: The Man, His Science, and the World They Changed.* Cambridge, Mass.: MIT Press, 1985. (Excellent biography.)

Murdoch, D. R. *Niels Bohr's Philosophy of Physics.* London: Cambridge University Press, 1989. (Excellent review of Bohr's physics.)

Rosenthal, S. *Niels Bohr: His Life and Work.* New York: John Wiley, 1977. (Good biography.)

# Max Born

## Career Highlights

- Awarded Nobel Prize for Physics, 1954
- Awarded Stokes Medal (Cambridge), 1936
- Awarded Macdougall-Brisbane Prize, 1945
- Awarded the Max Planck Medal, 1948
- Awarded the Hughes Medal of the Royal Society, 1950

## Important Contributions

In the first 20 years of the twentieth century, physics buzzed with the incredible discovery of the subatomic world. Long before microscopes were powerful enough to enable researchers to see an atom, scientists probed into the subatomic world of electrons, protons, and alpha and beta particles.

Einstein, Heisenberg, Dirac, and other famed researchers posed theories to explain this bizarre new territory. But it was quiet, unassuming Max Born who created a unified quantum theory that systematically, mathematically described the subatomic world.

Max Born's gift to the world was a brand-new field of study we now call "quantum mechanics," which is the basis of all modern atomic and nuclear physics and solid state mechanics. These fields trace their origins to the theories devised by other visionary scientists. But they owe their practical, unifying mathematical descriptions to Max Born. It is because of him—not Einstein, Bohr, or Heisenberg—that we are now able to quantitatively describe the world of subatomic particles.

## Career Path

Adrift again.

Standing droop-shouldered in the light German rain at the funeral of his mentor in the fall of 1909, 27-year-old Max Born was stabbed by a double-barrel sadness. He keenly felt the abrupt personal loss of his friend and mentor, Herman Minkowski, and also the bitter repercussions of the professor's death in his own professional life. Just two weeks earlier Born had been hired as an assistant professor at Göttingen University by Minkowski. It was to be his first paid position since he had earned his Ph.D. two years earlier. With Minkowski's death, his position evaporated and he was left adrift for the third time in his life.

Max Born was born in Poland in late 1882. His father was a professor of anatomy. His mother died when Max was four, and he was raised by part-time nannies, growing up in an adult world of university intellectuals and artists. It was a lonely world for a child without a mother, a world in which Max felt that he was left adrift, alone with his toys and number games. When the young boy entered school he was more comfortable with numbers than with people.

Max was an excellent student: diligent, quick, thorough, and quiet. He wanted to pursue either a math or an engineering career, but his father encouraged him to take a broad spectrum of courses and not specialize until he had sampled all the fields that the world of science offered. He entered the University of Breslau in 1901, based on his father's recommendation. In 1904 he transferred to Göttingen University, where he could better specialize in math and physics and pursue his love of numbers.

Famed mathematics professor Herman Minkowski was impressed with Max's abilities and made him his assistant. Minkowski had been grappling with the concepts of relativity for several years before Einstein published his general theory of relativity in 1905. For the last year of his university study, Max lived in a world abuzz with the wonder, implications, and potential of Einstein's bold and revolutionary theory.

Filled with enthusiasm and verve, Max graduated in 1907 with plans to continue his studies. But the post-graduate position and the funding he sought collapsed and the quiet, slight man of 24 was left adrift for the second time in his life.

Max returned home to live in his childhood room. Working alone for two years at the desk he had used for homework as a boy, he tried to apply Minkowski's mathematical approach to the problems of subatomic relativity as described in Einstein's theory. Through this work, Max Born discovered a simplified and more accurate method of calculating the minuscule mass of an electron.

Still unsure of his abilities, Born hesitated to publish his findings, sending his paper instead to Professor Minkowski for review. Minkowski was so impressed he offered him a full-time position at Göttingen University. Overjoyed at this confirmation of his scientific worth, Born left home for Göttingen, feeling that he had finally found his place in the world.

Two weeks after Born's arrival, Professor Minkowski died. The job evaporated and he was left adrift again. He went back home for another full year of independent study and wrote a second paper, a review of the mathematical implications of Einstein's relativity. Finally he was offered a lecturing position at Göttingen University.

Born arrived eager to grapple with the mysteries of the atom. However, the only available research funding was designated for the study of the vibrational energy in crystals. He was deeply disappointed, feeling excluded from the grand hunt for the structure of the atom. Still, he energetically immersed himself in the study of crystals, telling friends that it was another new world to learn about. For five years he and two assistants collected, grew, sliced into paper-thin wedges, studied, measured, and analyzed crystals.

By 1915 Born had discovered that the physical characteristics of a crystal depended on the arrangement of the atoms in each molecule of the crystal. He found that certain atoms vibrate at certain, specific frequencies and that the energy they absorb and radiate relates to those frequencies. From these discoveries, he was able to mathematically derive a wide range of the physical, electrical, and optical properties of crystals.

Born then shifted to the University of Berlin to work with physics giant Max Planck. He also met and began to correspond with Albert Einstein. Born and Einstein would become both good friends and a popular duet at university parties, Einstein playing sonatas on his violin, Born accompanying on the piano.

Planck and Einstein were at the hub of the race to unravel and understand the subatomic world. Born brought his mathematical superiority and his understanding of crystals to their efforts. It was a classic case of finally being in the right place at the right time with the right background.

Theories abounded about the peculiar behavior of subatomic particles. But theories, like guesses and hunches, were easy to propose. No one was able to write down the mathematics that proved and described those theories. The problem had mystified the greatest minds in the scientific world for almost 20 years. This seemed a problem ideally suited for Max Born.

It occurred to Born that the quantum phenomena physicists found so troubling in electrons looked remarkably similar to the behavior of the crystals he had studied for many years. Further, his focus on rigorous mathematical development allowed him to recognize the mathematical short-comings in the major theories. In 1916 he set to work on the immense and complex numerical problem. The work stretched the available mathematical tools to the limit of their potential. The effort, itself, stretched over nine years of tedious work on blackboards, on note pads, and with slide rules.

In 1925 Born, with the help of two assistants, completed work on a paper they entitled, "Zur Quantenmechanik," or "On Quantum Mechanics." The phrase had never been used before. The paper exploded across the scientific world. It clearly, mathematically laid out the fundamentals that Einstein, Planck, Dirac, Bohr, Minkowski, Heisenberg, and others had talked around. It concretely explained and described the amazing world of subatomic particles.

"Quantum mechanics" became the name of the new field of study that focused on a quantitative description of subatomic phenomena. Max Born became its founder. He was adrift no more.

When Max Born was awarded the Nobel Prize for Physics in 1954 for his development of quantum physics, two of his assistants had already received the award for work they performed under his supervision. But the world was forever changed in a very profound and fundamental manner by the mathematical principles of quantum mechanics he created. On his tombstone is written the central equation of his quantum theory:

$$pq - qp = h/2^l i$$

It is an equation that has unlocked countless wonders of the solid-state and subatomic world to better our lives, even though only a handful of scientists understand and can work with its implications.

✳ ✳ ✳

## Key Dates

| | |
|---|---|
| 1882 | Born in Breslau (now Wroclaw), Poland, on December 11 |
| 1907 | Received Ph.D. from Göttingen University in Germany |
| 1909 | Wrote first scientific paper describing a new method for calculating the mass of an electron |
| 1910 | Held assistant professorship at Göttingen University |
| 1913–1923 | Developed and published theories and principles of quantum mechanics |
| 1918 | Became full professor at Göttingen |
| 1936 | Fled to England to escape rising Nazi control |

1954    Awarded Nobel Prize for Physics

1970    Died on January 5

## Advice

*Max Born believed that mathematics is the true language of science. Every successful science career must begin with a full mastery of math. That foundation will allow you to understand and decipher the implications and relationships of all other fields. Born said during several speeches late in his life, "I always considered my knowledge of mathematics to be one of my greatest assets."*

*Max Born also advised students to resist the urge to specialize during their undergraduate studies. Instead, generalize. Study all the fields you can. Questions and studies will often lead you across field boundaries.*

## References

Born, Max. *Physics in My Generation.* London: Cambridge University Press, 1956. (Autobiography.)

House, J. E. *Fundamentals of Quantum Mechanics.* San Diego: Academic Press, 1998. (Good book for beginning students.)

Keller, Alex. *The Infancy of Atomic Physics.* Oxford: Clarendon Press, 1993. (Good review of the field.)

Tanor, Joseph, ed. *McGraw-Hill Modern Men of Science.* New York: McGraw-Hill, 1986. (Strong summary of Born's work.)

Wasson, Tyler, ed. *Nobel Prize Winners.* New York: H. W. Wilson, 1987. (Excellent summary of Born's work.)

# Jane Brody

*"From Test Tube to Sauce Pan"*

Science Writing and Nutrition

## Career Highlights

*The New York Times*

- Received Lifeline Award, American Health Foundation, 1978
- Received Howard Blakeslee Award, American Heart Association, 1971
- Received J. C. Penney-University of Missouri Journalism Award, 1978
- Received Science Writers' Award, American Dental Association, 1971, 1978

## Important Contributions

Much of the credit for nudging Americans into an understanding of the influence of diet and lifestyle on health belongs to journalist Jane Brody. As a columnist for *The New York Times* and *Family Circle* magazine, and as an author of five books on health, she has translated technical medical and biochemical information into language and concepts the average lay reader can understand and absorb. Consistently and reliably, over the course of almost 30 years, she has put the latest scientific information at the fingertips of all Americans and has helped them become more active participants in their own health maintenance.

While her writings have covered a wide range of lifestyle-related issues such as stress management, teeth grinding, and coping with anger, nutrition has been Jane Brody's greatest single focus. Nutrition and a balanced diet are new concepts in this country. In the early twentieth century, awareness of proteins, carbohydrates, and fats did not exist. People ate whatever was readily available, preferably smothered in a sweet sauce. As biochemical researchers unraveled the process of food absorption in the body, Jane Brody made the public aware of this information and helped people to understand its importance for their lives.

## Career Path

Two tragic events during high school shaped the early career decision of Jane Brody. One month before graduation, Jane's mother died of ovarian cancer, a disease she had been fighting almost a year. Two years before, her maternal grandmother also had died of cancer. Rather than wallow in fear, or succumb to the inevitability of death, Jane chose to fight back. She determined to learn everything she could to preserve her own health. To the young woman that meant that she would have to become a research chemical scientist.

Jane Brody was born in 1941 in Brooklyn, New York, the daughter of a lawyer and an elementary school teacher. She was raised near Brooklyn's Prospect Park, the neighborhood where she still makes her home. Jane recalled her childhood years as typical, but also truly liberated.

Nutrition and health were never uppermost on the family's mind. Jane was routinely exposed to rich Eastern European foods with a heavy emphasis on butter, lard, and chicken fat. But she remembers that good nutrition was also important in her family. Her father instilled in her his passion for certain healthy things: fresh fruit in every season; rich, dark bread and oatmeal for breakfast in the winter; shredded wheat for breakfast in the summer.

As a child Jane wanted to be a veterinarian. Later she decided to be a biologist. Her career goal shifted as she grew, but always lay somewhere in the sciences. After the death of her mother and grandmother, she was determined to be a research chemical scientist.

Jane Brody entered Cornell University in 1958 and majored in biochemistry to prepare her for a life of anti-cancer chemical research. Two experiences there changed her mind again. The first grew out of a general feeling of being lost on campus, and of "not being able to integrate into the Cornell community." A psychologist suggested that she volunteer to join the staff of the school magazine, the *Cornell Countryman*, since she had enjoyed working on the school newspaper during high school. Almost immediately, her uneasiness dissolved and she began to consider journalism as a valuable and viable activity.

The second experience that affected Jane's career choice involved a summer research position she obtained during her junior summer. She was hired onto a National Science Foundation project at the New York State Agricultural Experiment Station in Geneva, New York. For eight hours a day, five days a week, for ten weeks she conducted in-lab biochemical research. She quickly realized that "what was fun for ten weeks, when projected to ten years, was not so enticing. I could see myself shortly talking to test tubes." Full-time laboratory work would not be a part of her future. Chemical research was out.

As the editor of the *Cornell Countryman* during her senior year, Jane finally made a lasting career decision. "One day I realized that *this* is what I really love, finding out what other researchers are doing." It was then too late to shift majors. She graduated with a B.S. in biochemistry in 1962.

After one year of graduate school to earn an M.S. in journalism, specializing in science writing, Jane Brody landed a job as a reporter for the *Minneapolis Tribune*. Rather than being assigned to the science desk, she was given the beat of a city reporter—murders, school board elections, and programs in the park. The work was not what she wanted, but was still interesting. More important, she developed a flare for clear, concise, and understandable writing.

In 1965, a position as science writer opened at *The New York Times*. Brody was ideally suited for the job. She had a degree in science. She had science writing experience both during graduate school and for the undergraduate magazine. And she had the hands-on experience of a working reporter. The young reporter took the position in late 1965 and is still there, more than 30 years later.

In 1976, after 11 years of reporting, Brody was asked to start a "Personal Health" column in the Sunday weekly "Living" section. She exhibited a gift for sifting through the baffling blizzard of confusing and often contradictory raw medical information and incomprehensible medical and research language to glean reliable concepts and practical guidelines for her readers. Doctors often copied her articles for their patients. In 1986 she added a PBS program to her outlets for health information.

While Brody reads several newspapers every day and over 30 medical and technical journals every week, she writes only three or four days each week. In addition, she has to test each recipe she recommends and includes in books or articles.

Working on her cookbooks becomes a family affair. Brody does the cooking to test each recipe. Her twin boys wash the piles of dishes. Her husband organizes the tasting parties. During these periods she often cooks a dozen dishes a day, far more than her family could handle. Friends and neighbors are invited in to help test. Each guest receives a clipboard, pencil, and score sheet along with plate and fork.

Including a hundred recipes in a book may mean preparing 500 to 600 dishes. For every recipe approved, several will be rejected. Often either the flavor or the consistency of a dish won't be quite right and Brody will have to revise the recipe and retest it. She laughs that careful research is a lot of work whether you are working with test tubes in a lab, picks and shovels on an archaeological dig, or scrubbing pots and sauce pans in a test kitchen.

Throughout her 30 years of writing and thousands of columns and articles, Jane Brody has acted as a dependable, reliable, and critically important intermediary between the medical research world and the public. New information is of little value until it is used to better peoples' lives. She has been singularly successful at translating medical and technical jargon into compelling and practical public information.

## Key Dates

| | |
|---|---|
| 1941 | Born in Brooklyn, New York, on May 19 |
| 1962 | Received B.S. from Cornell University |
| 1963 | Received M.S. from University of Wisconsin |
| 1963–1965 | Worked as reporter for the *Minneapolis Tribune* |
| 1965–present | Works as science writer for *The New York Times* |
| 1986 | Began PBS television series on health and nutrition |
| 1987 | Received Ph.D. from Princeton University |

## Advice

*Brody once commented, "I get a kick out of having a job where I am paid to learn. I love learning about science and I get to, every day." A love of technical learning is the first prerequisite for a career as science writer. The second is a passion for writing. Writing clearly and concisely requires discipline and hard work.*

*Don't think too narrowly about how you will eventually work within the general fields of science and writing as an undergraduate. Learn the jargon and principles of all the major science fields. Finally, gain experience as a writer. Volunteer for the school paper, the local paper, the church paper. Freelance pieces. But force yourself into situations where you have to write for demanding editorial review.*

## References

Brody, Jane. *Jane Brody's Good Food CookBook.* New York: Norton, 1985.

———. *Jane Brody's Nutrition Book.* New York: Norton, 1981.

———. *Jane Brody's The New York Times Guide to Personal Health.* New York: Times Books, 1982.

Moritz, Charles, ed. *Current Biography Yearbook, 1996.* New York: H. W. Wilson, 1997. (Good entry on Brody's work.)

Serifini, Anthony. *Legends in Their Own Time.* New York: Prentice Hall Press, 1994. (Good entry on Brody's work.)

Straub, Deborah, ed. *Contemporary Authors.* Vol. 23. Detroit: Gale Research, 1996. (Good entry on Brody's writing.)

# David Brower

*"Our Number 1 Conservationist"*

Environmental Science

## Career Highlights

Earth Island Institute

- Twice nominated for a Nobel Peace Prize
- Rated as the foremost militant environmental activist of the last half of the twentieth century
- Awarded the John Muir Award of the Sierra Club, 1977
- Awarded the Paul Bartsch Award from the Audubon Naturalist Society, 1967
- Awarded the National Parks Association Gold Award, 1956

## Important Contributions

David Brower has inspired generations of environmentalists and conservationists. He single-handedly shaped the major American environmental movement and turned the Sierra Club into a potent environmental defense force. He led the fights that stopped development at over 100 sites on natural park lands, including dams in the Grand Canyon, Dinosaur National Monument, and Kentucky's Red River Gorge. He fought for the preservation of California's old-growth redwoods, of Florida's Everglades, and of Maine's Allagash Wilderness.

Brower founded Friends of the Earth, the John Muir Institute, and the National Outdoor Recreation Resources Review and is generally considered to be America's Number 1 conservationist. Secretary of the Interior Udall called him, "The most effective single person on the cutting edge of conservation in this country."

## Career Path

When David Brower was just over a year old, he lost most of his front teeth in a fall from a baby carriage. It was 11 years before the second set of teeth, somewhat misshapen, emerged from his damaged gums. As a boy, David was mercilessly teased and called the "toothless boob." He grew up painfully shy and afraid to smile.

A toothless mouth was not the only tragedy the young boy had to survive. Just as he started school, his father lost his job and the family had to survive off the meager rents they received from several houses they owned. Worse, David's mother lost her eyesight the next year, when he was eight. But even in that tragedy there was a slim silver lining. David later recalled, "I became her eyes during our walks through the wild Berkeley hills. I think that did a lot for my ability to observe. Seeing the world for someone else sharpened my appreciation of the beauty in natural things."

David became fascinated with butterflies and his naturalist's eye grew so sharp that by the time he was 15 he could identify the species of butterflies in flight. He would have chosen a career in entomology if his high school classmates at Berkeley High hadn't scorned insect-chasing as unmanly.

A quick learner, David willingly studied long, hard hours. He graduated early from high school and entered the University of California Berkeley (UCB) when he was only 16 years old. Surrounded by older classmates and under financial and emotional strain, he again felt like an outsider, and he dropped out of college in his sophomore year.

David Brower took a job as a clerk in a candy factory. His life seemed to be going nowhere. Winding hikes through nature were his only pleasure. Brower used all of his vacation time to hike and climb in the Sierra Mountains, often returning to favorite places where his family had camped when he was a child. In 1933 he joined the Sierra Club to take advantage of their excursions into the Yosemite wilderness area.

In 1935 Brower was fired from his candy clerk job for too often coming back days late from Yosemite camping trips. Almost penniless, he traveled back to the place he loved, Yosemite, and found a job with the Curry Company, which operated the valley facilities for the National Park Service. After a year in the accounting department, he was made park publicity manager.

In addition to gaining a reputation as the best mountaineer on the park staff and making over 70 first ascents of rugged Sierra peaks, Brower also came to be known for having a flare for dramatic and powerful publicity. He worked with famed photographer Ansel Adams on photo books, brochures, and silent films depicting the breath-taking grandeur of the valley.

From these book-publishing experiences, Brower was offered a position as editor at the University of California Press in Berkeley in 1941, where he shared an office with co-editor Anne Hus. They were married in 1943.

Brower proved to be a superb editor. Anne Hus later recalled, "He liberates what is good in an author's work. . . . He knows very little about English literature, yet he has a remarkable sense of the language."

Excluding a three-year absence while he fought during World War II, Brower worked for the UC Press for eight years. During that time he remained an active member in the Sierra Club. In 1952 he was offered the position of executive director of the club.

There, at age 40, Brower finally found his true niche. The club's founder, John Muir, had been an outspoken crusader for environmental protection. Since his death in 1914, the club had been far more social than political. Brower realized that through this organization he could unleash his zeal and passion. He quickly repositioned the club into a confrontational advocate for the environment. Club membership skyrocketed from 2,000 to 77,000.

Deciding that the club needed to test its new muscle in a big battle, Brower took on the U.S. Bureau of Reclamation's plan for dams on the Colorado River in Dinosaur National Monument in Utah and in the Grand Canyon in Arizona. The dams would flood national treasures, destroy riparian habitat and ecosystems, irrevocably alter the river flow and temperature regimes, and disrupt the life cycles of important fish species. Through a hard-fought and bitter battle, the Sierra Club won and plans for both dams were scrubbed.

David Brower's next act was to wield the lobbying power of the club to promote the passage of the Wilderness Act and to create the Point Reyes National Seashore near San Francisco. Sierra Club membership continued to climb. He enhanced the club's political clout with a carefully designed series of books and films documenting the beauty of many of the country's wilderness areas.

To diversify the kinds of actions environmentalists could take, Brower created two new organizations, Friends of the Earth and the John Muir Institute, both of which have joined the Sierra Club as powerful environmental defense forces.

David Brower didn't set out to be America's leading conservationist. He started with a deep appreciation of, and a love for, the natural environment. The rest "just fell into place over time."

Brower has edited over 50 books. He has won over 100 battles with state and federal governments for environmental protection, and has single-handedly shaped the organizations dedicated to American environmental conservation. David Brower's efforts have left both a deep imprint on our society and vast tracks of pristine wilderness for future generations to marvel at and enjoy.

## Key Dates

| | |
|---|---|
| 1912 | Born in Berkeley, California, on July 1 |
| 1928 | Enrolled at the University of California, Berkeley |
| 1930 | Dropped out in his sophomore year |
| 1930–1935 | Worked as a clerk in a candy factory |
| 1933 | Joined the Sierra Club |
| 1935–1941 | Hired by National Park Service to work at Yosemite, including five years as publicity manager |
| 1941–1952 | Appointed editor of the University of California Press |
| 1943–1945 | Served with US Army Tenth Mountaineering Division |
| 1952 | Appointed executive director of the Sierra Club |
| 1969 | Received B.S. from Claremont College |
| 1969 | Formed Friends of the Earth and the John Muir Institute |
| 1973 | Received Ph.D. in ecology from San Francisco State University |
| 1989–present | Is semi-retired; still active in publishing and writing for the Sierra Club and for Friends of the Earth |

# Advice

*David Brower believes that the key to a career in ecology or environmental protection is the ability to keenly observe and appreciate the natural world. You don't need to travel to exotic scenic wonders. Begin in your own neighborhood and backyard. Learn to recognize, respect, and cherish the spectacular grandeur all around us. Study the patterns and flows of the natural world. Then learn the interdependencies and interconnectedness of all living and non-living things.*

*You must love nature enough to dedicate long hours of work and effort to save and preserve it. This is your base. In school, study resource economics as well as the physical and biological sciences to gain an understanding of the interaction of the human economy with the natural environment.*

# References

Baskin, Yvonne. *The Work of Nature.* Washington, D.C.: Island Press, 1997. (Good review of conservation movement and its principles.)

Brower, David. *For Earth's Sake: The Life and Times of David Brower.* New York: Peregrine Smith Books, 1990. (Autobiography and good review of the environmental movement.)

Cozic, Charles, ed. *Global Resources: Opposing Viewpoints.* San Diego, Calif.: Greenhaven Press, 1998. (Good review of conservation issues.)

McPhee, John. *Encounters with the Archdruid.* New York: Farrar, Straus & Giroux, 1971. (Complete biography of Brower.)

Mooney, Louise, ed. *Newsmakers: The People Behind Today's Headlines.* Detroit: Gale Research, 1990. (Good review of Brower's work.)

Moritz, Charles, ed. *Current Biography Yearbook, 1990.* New York: H. W. Wilson, 1991. (Good review of Brower's work.)

# Luther Burbank

*"The Plant Wizard"*                    Horticulture

## Career Highlights

Luther Burbank Home & Gardens

- Introduced more than 800 new plant and vegetable varieties, including the Shasta daisy and the Burbank potato
- Laid the foundation for applied botanical genetics
- Awarded the gold medal of the National Institute of Social Sciences, 1915
- Received a gold medal from the St. Louis International Exhibition, 1904
- Has had more than 100 schools nationwide named for him; has a park in Santa Rosa, California, and the town of Burbank, California, named for him

## Important Contributions

Call it the American dream or the Cinderella syndrome. Call it what you will, Luther Burbank lived it. He was a poor boy with little money and less education who, through his own talent, determination, and hard work, went from obscurity to fame, who left the world a better place by doing what he loved best.

Luther Burbank introduced more than 800 new plants to the world. His creation of the spineless cactus turned a worthless desert growth into a valuable forage plant. He created scores of new fruits, including many plums and prunes. His nearly magical flair for recognizing the one better plant specimen out of a thousand nearly identical seedlings left the world with a richer and more abundant food supply—and left our flower gardens with more daisies and sweeter roses.

## Career Path

To average citizens in the California town of Santa Rosa it looked like a normal plum tree, exactly like the hundreds of others in Luther Burbank's orchard in 1890. But to a trained eye, this plum tree looked very odd, indeed. The leaves were deeper green on one branch, the leaf edges a bit smoother on another, the fruit earlier on some branches and later on others. It was as if every branch were a different variety of plum.

In fact, Luther Burbank had grafted over 600 promising seedlings onto the branches of that one sturdy tree. The tree had become a museum of the possible styles and variations in plums. By grafting this way, he would only have to wait a year instead of a decade to see if a seedling would produce an improved plum variety. This accelerated grafting technique was one of two strokes of genius he gave to horticulture. His was a genius weaned from years of labor, careful experimentation, and experience.

Luther Burbank was born in 1849 in Massachusetts, the son of a farmer, carpenter, and brick and pottery maker. Luther worked in the fields all through grade school. He never received formal education beyond those early years. At age 21, he scraped together the money to buy his own farm and began raising vegetables for a living.

A turning point in Luther's life occurred when he read Darwin's *Variations of Animals and Plants under Domestication.* The book thrilled him. Those were the most inspiring words he would ever read. He began reading all he could of Darwin and applied himself in earnest to cultivating new and better varieties of fruits, flowers, and vegetables.

On his Lunenburg, Massachusetts, farm, at the age of 24, Burbank produced his first new variety, the Burbank potato, which became the dominant potato in the commercial market because of its size, flavor, and disease resistance. It was even introduced in Ireland to help combat the blight epidemics. Burbank sold the rights to this potato for $150, and he used the money to move to Santa Rosa, California, in 1875.

On his arrival in Santa Rosa, Burbank said, "I firmly believe, from what I have seen, that this is the chosen spot of all this earth as far as Nature is concerned." He worked as a farmhand, slept in a greenhouse, saved some money, and soon bought a small tract of land, which he began to farm. Since his farm needed to support him financially, he divided his time between practical farming and experimentation. His first year in business he only spent $15.20 on supplies; three years later he earned more than $1,000 and published his first catalog. By 1881, he was filling orders as large as 20,000 plum trees. In 1888, he sold his interest in the nursery business to his partner but retained his operating name of "Santa Rosa Nurseries" so that he could devote all of his time and energies to experimentation.

Burbank applied Darwinian principles to breeding plants. He would cross two parental forms, then recross the resultant offspring to select plants with the greatest vigor and yield. He was a master at seeing, feeling, and smelling minute variations between seedlings. To other men each seedling looked like a half-dozen small leaves and a spindly stalk. To Burbank, each held a unique set of properties. More important, he learned to correlate those physical characteristics of leaf and stem to qualities of the fruit, flower, or vegetable the plant would eventually produce.

From 1,000 seedlings, Burbank could quickly discern the 10 or 20 that were most likely to produce the best fruit. The ability to recognize almost imperceptible differences between seedlings and to accurately correlate those differences to the quality of the fruit was the first of his strokes of genius.

Burbank's second stroke of genius was the grafting system he developed. Each promising seedling was immediately grafted onto a branch of a full-grown parent so as to quickly reveal the quality of the new variety. His goal was not to prove any scientific theory or to make scientific discovery; his sole aim was the production of better varieties of cultivated plants—plants that the public would buy.

Luther Burbank never grew rich from his efforts; for him, that was not the object. It was a labor of love. He made more than 100,000 separate experiments over the course of his career, growing some 1,000,000 plants annually for testing purposes. At the time of his death, he had some 3,000 extensive experiments in progress.

For over 50 years, Luther Burbank experimented with cultivating new varieties and species of plants, introducing hundreds of new plants to the world. While some were ornamental, useful only for their beauty (such as the Burbank rose, the Shasta daisy, and gladiola), he also introduced breeds of spineless cacti that were very important to the cattle industry; other grains and grasses that also improved cattle production; and new varieties of fruits and vegetables important to national agriculture, including varieties of corn, plums, peaches, quinces, tomatoes, and berries. Perhaps more important than the plants themselves, he introduced new techniques, new methods of experimentation, for cultivating and crossing plants.

While he was sometimes called "The Plant Wizard," Burbank himself did not like the term. He felt there was no magic in helping nature to evolve: "I merely aid nature to do in a few years what she alone would require centuries to accomplish. There is not a factor in my work which every plant grower does not have at his disposal."

\*  \*  \*

## Key Dates

1849    Born in Lancaster, Massachusetts, on March 7

1867–
1868    Attended Lancaster Academy, Massachusetts

1870–
1875    Worked his own truck farm in Lunenburg, Massachusetts

1875    Moved to Santa Rosa, California

1876    Bought his own farm in Santa Rosa

1885    Gave up commercial farming and devoted himself entirely
        to experimentation

1893–
1901    Published the annual *New Creations* catalog

1904    Burbank rose won a gold medal from the St. Louis
        International Exhibition

1905–
1911    Taught a course in plant breeding at Stanford University

1926    Died April 11 in Santa Rosa, California

# Advice

*Luther Burbank attributed his success to his ability to perceive minute differences between plants. If you are considering a career in horticulture, Luther Burbank would advise you to develop a keen sense of perception. Become a master of seeing, a master of feeling. Heightening your perception of slight variables will go a long way toward your success in this field. Read extensively on plant evolution, heredity, and adaptation. Study plant biology and physiology, and learn the processes of experimentation at as early an age as possible.*

# References

Burbank, Luther, and Wilbur Hall. *The Harvest of the Years.* San Francisco: Linwood Books, 1927. (Autobiography published posthumously.)

Callow, J. A. *Advances in Botanical Research.* Vol. 26. New York: Academic Press, 1997.

Camenson, Blythe. *Careers for Plant Lovers & Other Green Thumb Types.* Lincolnwood, Ill.: Vgm Career Horizons, 1995.

Garraty, John A., and Mark C. Carnes. "Luther Burbank," in *Dictionary of American Biography.* Vol. 2. New York: Charles Scribner's Sons, 1988.

Rudall, Paula. *Anatomy of Flowering Plants: An Introduction to Structure & Development.* New York: Cambridge University Press, 1993.

# Jocelyn Bell Burnell

*"A Little Bit of Scruff"*                    Astronomy

The Open University, courtesy AIP Emilio Segrè Visual Archives

## Career Highlights

- Discovered pulsars, for which her advisor (Anthony Hewish) won the Nobel Prize for Astronomy
- Awarded the Albert Michelson Medal of the Franklin Institute of Philadelphia, 1973
- Received the J. Robert Oppenheimer Memorial Prize, 1978
- Awarded the Herschel Medal by the Royal Astronomical Society, 1989

## Important Contributions

As a 24-year-old graduate student, Jocelyn Bell discovered pulsars, a new class of unimaginably dense, burned-out stars. Her discovery led to a greater understanding of the life and death of stars and opened up new fields of study in astronomy, superdense matter, gravitation, and superstrong magnetic fields. But as has happened to other women scientists, she did not win the Nobel Prize for her discovery. Instead, her graduate advisor did.

## Career Path

It looked like a forest after a bad fire, with all the leaves and branches burned from the bare tree trunks. Or maybe it resembled rows upon rows of pilings to support some monstrous, elevated platform. In truth, it was a four-and-one-half-acre radio antenna field strung across the English countryside. Twelve hundred telephone poles supported a criss-crossing network of 120 miles of wire. Once connected to a radio receiver, this gargantuan maze of wire was supposed to be the most sensitive radio frequency receiver on Earth, capable of detecting even the faintest of signals from the distant depths of space.

Who could have guessed in early 1967 that this gridlock mesh of wire and poles would reveal one of deep space's greatest secrets? Certainly 24-year-old astronomy graduate student Jocelyn Bell, who had felt like a slave laborer instead of a prized intellectual for the months of field construction, did not, although she would be the one to make the discovery. There could hardly be a less likely candidate for a Nobel Prize-winning discovery.

When Jocelyn Bell was an 11-year-old girl living in rural Northern Ireland, she took and failed her "eleven-plus" exam, the now-defunct British school examination, which meant she would not be allowed to go on to college. She attributed her failure to three things: (1) she was quite young when she took the exam, (2) she was a slow developer, and (3) her country school hadn't offered her an adequate education. Luckily, her parents believed in her potential and sent her off (at age 13) to a Quaker boarding school in England, where she got a second chance at higher education.

One of Jocelyn's father's jobs as an architect involved designing an addition to Northern Ireland's Armagh Observatory. While a student at the boarding school, she visited the observatory with her father and became interested in astronomy, reading all of her father's books on the subject. The staff at the observatory encouraged her to become a professional astronomer.

The idea appealed to the young woman, but her school's weak science department left her unsure of her abilities.

In 1961, she enrolled in the University of Glasgow in Scotland because it was one of the few places in Britain that offered a degree in astronomy. But the field of astronomy was highly competitive, with few positions available. Afraid that she didn't have the background or academic talent to compete successfully, Jocelyn changed her major to physics, which, if she survived her undergraduate years, still allowed the possibility of getting an advanced astronomy degree. She received—with honors—her bachelor of physics degree in 1965.

Jocelyn Bell then turned to Cambridge to work on her Ph.D. in astronomy. At that time, radioastronomer Anthony Hewish was designing a large radio telescope to detect radio waves (electro-magnetic radiation in the frequency band used for radio transmissions) emitted from objects in deep space. Extremely long radio antennas can be focused, like a telescope, to search for signals in a very narrow portion of space. Hewish planned to use 120 miles of wire strung out over 1,200 nine-foot-tall polls over a four-and-one-half-acre site to create the biggest and most tightly focused radio antenna array on Earth.

Bell spent her first two years at Cambridge helping Hewish build his radio telescope, spending more time digging postholes than studying astronomy. In July 1967, they switched it on. Bell's job switched then, too—from doing construction work to analyzing the volumes of data that the telescope spewed forth daily. As the radio telescope translated radio waves into lines made by pens moving across rolls of paper—nearly 100 feet of chart paper daily—it became her job to analyze these charts. But she couldn't keep up. Within six months her "in-basket" of charts needing to be reviewed stretched for over three and one-half miles—and was growing daily!

Two months after the telescope started up, Bell noticed the first "bit of scruff," as she called it. She had found an unusual pattern of lines, which kept time with sidereal time, or star-time. (Earth rotates every 24 hours with respect to the sun, but only 23 hours and 56 minutes in relation to the stars.) Since the bit of scruff kept time with the stars rather than the Earth, she interpreted this to mean that the signal was coming from deep space. She also noticed that the pulses were equally spaced: one and one-third seconds apart, indicating a regularly occurring, controlled emission. Bell immediately notified Hewish, who did not believe her. He felt that the signal must be manmade since it was so fast and so regular. Yet that too seemed impossible because the signal kept time with star-time, not Earth time.

Hewish and Bell seriously discussed the possibility that the signal was being sent by extraterrestrials (which they fondly dubbed LGM, Little Green Men). After all, radioastronomers believed that they would be the first ones to detect a signal from other lifeforms in space. But before they approached the public with that theory, Bell noticed another bit of scruff in a different part of the sky, this time 1.2 seconds apart. Since it seemed unlikely that there would be two separate groups of Little Green Men simultaneously trying to contact Earth on the same frequency, they ruled out the possibility that extraterrestrials were sending the signal.

Every theoretician at Cambridge was brought in to explain the scruff. After months of study and calculation it was concluded that those little bits of "scruff" were what we now call pulsars. When a huge star runs out of nuclear fuel, all the matter in the star collapses inward. This creates a gigantic explosion, called a supernova, and what remains becomes a hundred million million ($10^{14}$) times denser than ordinary matter. As it shrinks, it begins to spin faster and faster, like a skater who brings her arms closer to her body. As it spins faster, it creates magnetic and electric fields, which broadcast beams of powerful radio waves. These radio waves operate like lighthouse beacons, detectable from Earth with every rotation of the star—once or twice a second. From Earth, this type of neutron star appears to pulsate, thus the name "pulsars."

During the midst of the development of this astounding explanation for her discovery, Bell quietly turned her back on her work and left the field of astronomy. She married, changed her name to Jocelyn Bell Burnell, and proceeded to follow her husband around the globe as his government job moved him from place to place.

In 1974, the Nobel committee awarded the Nobel Prize for Astronomy to Anthony Hewish for his "decisive role in the discovery of pulsars." Many noted scientists disagreed with the Nobel committee and rebuked Hewish for his failure to give Bell Burnell proper credit. Since Hewish neither discovered nor explained pulsars, astronomer Jeremiah P. Ostriker notes, and since the Nobel Prize is given for a discovery as Alfred Nobel intended, then the prize should have included Jocelyn Bell Burnell. Yet she herself defended the Nobel committee's decision, arguing that "Nobel Prizes are based on long-standing research, not on a flash-in-the-pan observation of a research student."

Bell Burnell stayed out of the world of science for 20 years before her love of astronomy called her back to teaching and astronomical research. In 1991, she took a full-time job as a professor of physics at Britain's Open University. Since she herself benefited from a "second-chance" Quaker boarding school after flunking her eleven-plus exam, it seems fitting that she is now teaching at a second-chance institution, which offers instruction to adults who missed out on higher education in their youth.

✳ ✳ ✳

# Key Dates

| | |
|---|---|
| 1943 | Born in Belfast, Northern Ireland, on July 15 |
| 1954 | Failed her "eleven-plus," a now-defunct British school examination |
| 1956 | Entered Mount School, a Quaker girls' boarding school in York, England |
| 1965 | Received B.S. in physics from the University of Glasgow |
| 1965 | Entered astronomy department, Cambridge University |
| 1967 | Discovered pulsars |
| 1968 | Earned her Ph.D., married, and left field of radioastronomy |
| 1974 | Anthony Hewish received the Nobel Prize for Bell's discovery of pulsars |
| 1991–present | Works as full-time professor of physics in Britain's Open University |

# Advice

*Jocelyn Bell Burnell entered astronomy because she developed a love of the field as a child. She stayed in it because she could master the math and physics inherent in astrophysical research. She would advise young students to spend as much time as possible at planetariums and observatories. If you are fascinated by what you see, astronomy might be the field for you. Next gain a solid grounding in math and physics. Finally, as you begin serious astronomical study, also consider classes in electrical engineering, because astronomy is dependent on electronics.*

*Finally, Jocelyn would advise students that, if they get a poor start or get sidetracked during school, don't be devastated or downhearted. Look for the second chances to get where you want to go—because they are out there.*

# References

McGrayne, Sharon Bertsch. *Nobel Prize Women in Science: Their Lives, Struggles, and Momentous Discoveries.* New York: Carol Publishing, A Birch Lane Press Book, 1993.

Raymo, Chet. *365 Starry Nights: An Introduction to Astronomy for Every Night of the Year.* New York: Simon & Schuster, 1992.

Schaaf, Fred. *The Amateur Astronomer: Explorations and Investigations.* New York: Franklin Watts, 1994. (Written for young adults.)

Stille, Darlene R. *Extraordinary Women Scientists.* Chicago: Children's Press, 1995.

# Nolan Bushnell

*"King Pong"*

Electronics and
Video Technology

## Career Highlights

- Invented the world's first coin-operated video arcade games
- Invented the liquid crystal screen
- Founded Atari and Chuck E. Cheeses and numerous other companies

## Important Contributions

Today we take it for granted that we can walk into a video arcade, pop a quarter into any one of the hulking machines that line the walls, and play a fast-action, blood-pumping, adrenaline-rushing video arcade game. But there was a time—not too long ago—when there were no such things as video arcade games. For that invention, we have Nolan Bushnell to thank. Bushnell created Pong, the world's first successful coin-operated video game, the "great-granddaddy" of video games, the game that started the entire video game industry.

## Career Path

A large white dot jerkily bounced across a black screen. White bars slid up and down along either edge to intercept and reflect the "ball." A vertical white bar in the middle simulated a net. That was all Pong did—bounce a ball back and forth. But that was enough. At the time (1972) Pong was a revolutionary craze in America and its creator, Nolan Bushnell, was considered a genius. Pong machines drew crowds to watch and long lines of players waiting their turn at the simple controls.

Nolan Bushnell was born a tinkerer. His favorite childhood toys were erector sets, ham radios, and oscilloscopes (devices that displayed changes in electric current and voltage on television-like screens). He made electromagnets and batteries to show to his class and turned the family garage into a laboratory. Nolan nearly blew up the house when he built a liquid-fuel rocket engine and strapped it to a roller skate. By age 12, the young boy was repairing radios, television sets, and washing machines for spending money.

In 1961, Nolan enrolled in Utah State College. Two years later, he transferred to the University of Utah as an engineering major, where he played games on a school computer during his free time. Access to the university's giant mainframe computer was a perk for upper division engineering students. Nolan became an avid player of a computer game called Spacewar, playing it whenever he could. "I was hooked. I loved it way more than class!" He also realized that if he had had to pay to play, someone would have made a small fortune.

Bushnell toyed with the idea of creating a computerized video game that could be played at amusement parks; however, computers in those days were huge, expensive to build and to run, produced massive amounts of heat from countless vacuum tubes, and required a staff of people to maintain them. The computer that he played games on at school cost $8 million. At 25 cents a game, it would take hundreds of years to make any money. But he never gave up on the idea.

During summer vacations, Bushnell worked as the games manager at an amusement park arcade, where he studied people's spending habits and preferences. He realized that people liked games that were fairly simple, not too complicated, ones that tested their manual dexterity, ones that allowed the parents to go off for a while and leave the kids entertained.

After graduation, the young engineer landed a job at Ampex Corporation in Santa Clara, in the heart of the emerging Silicon Valley. There science caught up with his dream. With the invention of transistors, integrated circuits, and, in 1970, microprocessors, everything changed. Computer circuits were suddenly cheap, small, and reliable. Nolan's dream finally became plausible.

Each night Nolan Bushnell rushed home from work, tossed down a fast dinner, and shut himself into the workshop he had built in one of his two daughter's bedrooms. Long into the night he tore apart old pinball machines for parts and poured over technical diagrams. His elaborately wired circuits and processors resembled platters of spaghetti. Bundles of colored wires snaked across the floor and furniture. The bed looked like a jumbled electronics parts store. Boxes of spare parts spilled into the hallway and garage. He used a 19-inch black-and-white television for a video screen and wired together 185 integrated circuits to control and run this monster project.

By early 1971, it was done. Bushnell had created the world's first coin-operated video game: Computer Space. He worked out a manufacturing agreement with a local company and sat back to watch the money roll in. It didn't.

Computer Space was a dismal flop. It violated the rules Bushnell had learned at the amusement park. It was too sophisticated and not enough fun. His total proceeds from Computer Space were just under $500.

With that $500, Bushnell created a company, Atari, which is Japanese for "prepare to be attacked!" He hired a friend as programming engineer and set out to make a simpler, more visual and kinetic game. They decided to "start simple" and make a two-person game of ping pong.

In eight months Pong, with only 80 integrated circuits, was ready for the marketplace. By today's standards, Pong was laughably simple. Pong consisted of a black screen with a thick, dotted white line down the middle representing a net. Small white rectangles on either edge represented the players' paddles, which would bat a "ball" (a white circle) across the "net." The score was recorded with large numbers near the top.

The name of the company, Atari, turned out to be apt. Pong fairly "attacked" the country, selling more than 100,000 units in the first 18 months. Bushnell was able to move his lab into a real office and his daughter got her bedroom back.

Cash flow problems haunted the young company. Bushnell decided to diversify by creating video games for home use. They were an immediate hit. He also created the world's first liquid crystal screen, which became the industry standard for a dozen years. But none of these technical developments solved Atari's financial problems, and in 1976 Bushnell sold Atari to Warner Communications for $28 million ($15 million of which went directly to him). He walked away from Atari convinced that products focused on fun are profitable.

While at Atari, Bushnell had conceived of a new venture: Pizza Time Theaters, where patrons of the restaurant would have their choice of entertainment while they waited for their food: watching movies, playing video games, or watching a stage show performed by robots, including a large mouse named Chuck E. Cheese. Warner, the funding company, was not enthusiastic about the idea and only allowed one Pizza Time Theater to be set up. In 1978, Bushnell bought back all assets and rights from Warner for $500,000 and set out to do it on his own.

Sales at Pizza Time Theaters showed steady and impressive increases, moving to $99.2 million in 1982. But by 1983, the appeal had faded. In March 1984, Pizza Time Theaters filed for bankruptcy. Bushnell considered this his first "failure" and while it was disappointing, he noted that he was resilient, not someone who "sits around wringing his hands."

Ever resilient, the inventor went on to set up Catalyst Technologies, a kind of holding company that provided services to groups of inventors. He planned to once again prove to Wall Street that profit happens when people focus on fun. However, by 1986, most of Catalyst's firms no longer existed. Bushnell joined forces with Apple computer developer Steve Wozniak to build their own toy: NEMO, robots that could be steered by remote control or from audio signals encoded in television programs or from video cassettes. In his own words, these are "video games that spill off the screen and run around your feet." But this project, too, was abandoned.

From a background in science and engineering, Nolan Bushnell went on to become one of the most remarkably successful entrepreneurs of the century. He is always looking to the future, looking to see what's missing and how to fill that need. When asked what his favorite project is, he routinely answers, "The next one."

## Key Dates

| | |
|---|---|
| 1943 | Born in Clearfield, Utah, on February 5 |
| 1961 | Entered Utah State College |
| 1968 | Received B.S. in electrical engineering from University of Utah |
| 1968–1970 | Worked as games manager at Lagoon Corp. in Salt Lake City, Utah |
| 1970–1972 | Worked as engineer for Ampex Corp in Redwood City, California |
| 1971 | Built the videogame Computer Space |
| 1972 | Founded Atari, Inc.; created Pong |
| 1976 | Sold Atari to Warner Communications |
| 1977 | Opened Pizza Time Theaters, Inc., in Sunnyvale, California |
| 1981 | Founded Catalyst Technologies in Sunnyvale, California |
| 1984 | Pizza Time filed bankruptcy |
| 1985–1989 | Teamed up with Steve Wozniak |
| 1989–present | Retired; working on private projects |

## Advice

*If you are considering a career in video or electronics technology, Nolan Bushnell would advise two things. First, take a broad range of engineering courses, not just electrical engineering. Materials, structural, and corrosion engineering are important to the success of any development venture even though it might be an electronics product. Second, do something about it. Bushnell once commented to a journalist, "The critical ingredient is . . . doing something. A lot of people have ideas, but there are few who decide to do something about them now. Not tomorrow. Not next week. But today."*

## References

Cohen, Scott. *ZAP!: The Rise and Fall of Atari.* New York: McGraw-Hill, 1984.

Evory, Ann, and Peter Gareffa, eds. *Contemporary Newsmakers.* Detroit: Gale Research, 1985.

Herz, J. C. *Joystick Nation: How Videogames Ate Our Quarters, Won Our Hearts, and Rewired Our Minds.* Boston: Little, Brown, 1997.

Sullivan, George. *Screen Play: The Story of Video Games.* New York: Warne, 1983.

# Wallace Carothers

*"Mr. Nylon"*                                    Organic Chemistry

Archives of the National Academy of Sciences

## Career Highlights

- Elected to National Academy of Sciences, 1936
- Invented neoprene synthetic rubber, 1931
- Invented nylon, 1936
- Editor of *Organic Synthesis*, 1933

## Important Contributions

If you have worn nylon, dacron, neoprene, polyester, or any other synthetic polymerized fabric, you have benefited from the work of Wallace Carothers. More than anyone else, he actualized the long-sought goal of creating durable, affordable synthetic fibers. He invented neoprene and nylon and made possible the creation of a dozen other now-common synthetic fibers.

In nine years of working at the Du Pont experimental research laboratory, Wallace Carothers made seven major contributions to fundamental organic chemistry theory and laid the foundation for the creation of a whole group of industries producing the synthetic materials he developed. He changed the way we dress, work, and play, and had a far greater impact on America than his short 41-year-life span might suggest.

## Career Path

In fiction, tragedy is often made to ride tandem with triumph. In the real world of science, that coupling has happened many times. However, tragedy never rushed more senselessly in to snuff out sweet triumph than in the life of Wallace Carothers.

Because Wallace Carothers' father was a college professor, it was always assumed that Wallace, the eldest son, would follow in his father's teaching footsteps. The boy spent much of his time in high school assessing the available academic fields to pick his teaching specialty. Shy, withdrawn, uncomfortable with people, he never paused to question whether teaching was an appropriate profession for him. His father taught economics courses, while he preferred chemistry, finding it more comfortable.

Wallace completed high school in 1915 and entered Tarkio College in Missouri. With the shortage of teachers after the outbreak of World War I, he was asked to teach chemistry during his senior year. He developed mild nervous ticks and insomnia during his semester of teaching and graduated with good, but not extraordinary, grades in 1920.

Carothers transferred to the University of Illinois for a one-year master's program and then was hired to teach at the University of South Dakota. His two years of teaching were stressful and unproductive. The nervous disorders he had noticed at Tarkio grew worse. He returned to Illinois to pursue a doctoral degree, which he completed in 1924.

While at South Dakota, Carothers began to probe into the research area that would later bring him fame. The explosion of research into the structure and nature of the atom by worldwide physicists and chemists had produced mountains of information. Of greatest interest to him was the emerging concept of valence.

By 1921 it had been theorized that an atom's ability to bond with other atoms depended on the arrangement of its electrons. The number of electrons in an atom's outer shell was called its valence and seemed to determine both physical characteristics and bonding characteristics of the element.

So far, valence theory had only been applied to inorganic chemistry studies (for example, how metals bonded with non-metals). Carothers wanted to see if valence theory applied to organic chemistry and to the long, carbon-chain molecules that dominated organic life.

In 1926, the eager scientist was offered a position at Harvard University teaching organic chemistry. He eagerly accepted, feeling that this would be his long-term academic home. However, he stayed at Harvard less than two years. His inability to relate to and motivate students spun him into fits of deep depression. He began to question his basic abilities; his health deteriorated.

In 1928 E. I. Du Pont de Nemours and Company (it would become simply the Du Pont Company by 1936) created an experimental field research station at Wilmington, Delaware, as a new center for fundamental chemical research. They selected Carothers to lead the team in organic chemistry. He was offered lab space, a small team of trained research assistants, a generous budget of equipment and supplies, and an open assignment to work on problems of his own choosing.

Shy, withdrawn Carothers was reluctant to leave the structured safety of academic institutions. But this offer to prove his worth in a laboratory instead of in a classroom seemed too good to be true. Open-ended basic research was an unheard-of opportunity in the early twentieth century. It was, however, the best deal Du Pont ever made.

An intense and compulsive worker, Carothers drove his team as if the nation depended on their success. He set two areas of research as goals to investigate. The first was the general area of synthetic rubber. In particular, he decided to focus on the newly discovered low polymers of acetylene, vinylacetylene, and divinylacetylene.

This research produced hundreds of derivative products that had to be individually assessed and investigated. Among this vast array of compounds was one created by adding hydrochloric acid to vinylacetylene. This compound offered elastic properties similar to, but in many cases superior to, rubber. In 1931 the Du Pont Company patented and started to produce this synthetic rubber under the name neoprene.

The second area Carothers decided to investigate was the search for new synthetic fibers through the synthesis of polymers of high molecular weight through well-known reactions such as esterification and amide formation.

While this process can be described in one simple sentence, the work and subsequent investigation and cataloging of the properties of each new substance was grueling. The team explored literally thousands of new organic compounds.

Virtually all proved worthless. Many were too weak. Many had low melting points. Many were too brittle to form into fibers. Even those molecules that proved suitable for fiber formation failed to produce workable results. Either the fibers didn't adhere well to each other, they weren't tough enough to stand up as a woven fabric, or they weren't flexible enough to work as a fabric.

Out of this exhaustive and seemingly fruitless experimentation came a great advance in the understanding of the chemistry and properties of both natural and synthetic polymers. By 1935, Du Pont had begun a massive research effort into one of the new fiber-forming polymers Carothers had discovered. This fiber became nylon, first marketed in 1939, four years after he created it.

Carothers had always been subject to long, deep fits of depression and nervous illness. The stress of long years of seemingly unproductive effort took their toll. Prolonged melancholy set in, and his health began to fail in early 1937. In November of that year, he took his own life. He did not live to see the triumph of his creation: Nylon became the most successful, popular, and profitable synthetic fiber ever to reach the marketplace.

Wallace Carothers crowded a lifetime's worth of science into less than one decade of research at Du Pont. He made numerous major contributions to fundamental organic chemistry theory and laid the foundation for the creation of a whole group of industries producing the synthetic materials he developed. He published 62 papers and claimed 69 patents. During that period of intensive laboratory experimentation, Carothers made discoveries that have affected and benefited us all.

## Key Dates

| | |
|---|---|
| 1896 | Born in Burlington, Iowa, on April 27 |
| 1920 | Received B.S. in chemistry from Tarkio College, Missouri |
| 1921 | Received M.S. in chemistry from University of Illinois |
| 1921–1922 | Worked as instructor in chemistry, University of South Dakota |
| 1924 | Received Ph.D. in organic chemistry from University of Illinois |
| 1924–1926 | Worked as instructor at University of Illinois |
| 1926–1928 | Worked as instructor at Harvard University |
| 1928 | Appointed director of the Du Pont experimental station lab |

1937    Completed basic work on world's most successful synthetic fiber, nylon

1937    Died in Philadelphia, Pennsylvania, on April 29 at age 41

# Advice

*Wallace Carothers would advise you to research the range of possible jobs in a field as well as the field itself before choosing a career. Make sure you will enjoy the day-to-day work as well as the subject. In school take as wide a range of chemistry-related classes as possible. But don't rely on classwork alone. Read all relevant journals and periodicals to stay current. Developments happen too quickly to be incorporated into classroom courses.*

# References

Adams, Roger. *Biographical Memoirs.* Vol. 20: *Wallace Carothers.* Washington, D.C.: National Academy of Sciences, 1940.

Daintith, John, et al., eds. *Biographical Encyclopedia of Scientists.* 2d ed. Vol. 1. Philadelphia, Pa.: Institute of Physics Publishing, 1994. (Summary entry on Carothers's work.)

Eggenberger, David, ed. *The McGraw-Hill Encyclopedia of World Biography.* New York: McGraw-Hill, 1983. (Short entry on Carothers's work.)

Garraty, John, ed. *Encyclopedia of American Biography.* New York: Harper & Row, 1984. (Detailed summary of Carothers's work.)

Gillispie, Charles, ed. *Dictionary of Scientific Biography.* Vol. XV. New York: Charles Scribner's Sons, 1978. (Good summary of Carothers's work.)

# Rachel Carson

*"The World Took a New Direction"*                    Ecology

## Career Highlights

- Wrote several best-selling books on the environment, including *Silent Spring,* which prompted national and international awareness of the environment
- Won the 1951 National Book Award for nonfiction for her book *The Sea Around Us*
- Awarded the 1963 Conservationist of the Year Award from the National Wildlife Federation
- Awarded the Audubon Medal (first woman)

## Important Contributions

Rachel Carson was largely responsible for the birth of the modern environmental movement. She refused to believe that the destruction of the earth's natural resources and widespread pollution were necessary costs of economic progress. Through her research, her studies, and especially her influential and controversial book *Silent Spring,* she was the first to bring to the American people's attention the dangers of indiscriminate use of insecticides and pesticides. Because of her patient and well-documented research, many dangerous chemicals were banned or limited, making our world a safer place.

## Career Path

June 1958. A crop-dusting bi-plane dipped low over the western Massachusetts woods and fields surrounding a small township. Thick sprays of white billowed from each wing pod like tube-shaped clouds hanging ominously over the land. Before the mist settled like fog into the trees, eight song birds lay contorted and dead in the backyard of one nearby house. Several small squirrels violently twitched for long minutes before lying still and cold.

Within a day, lawns and woods were littered with the dead: birds, bees, rodents, small mammals, and butterflies as well as the mosquitoes the DDT had been designed to control. Desperate for help, the neighbors turned not to local and state governments, which promoted and approved the deadly spraying, not to the chemical corporations making millions by selling pesticide and insecticide sprays, but to one lone woman. They turned to Rachel Carson because they believed she would win.

Rachel Carson grew up on a 65-acre farm. She learned to love nature from her mother, a former schoolteacher. With her mother's encouragement, Rachel became an amateur naturalist and writer, publishing her first story in *St. Nicholas* magazine at age 10.

Rachel entered Pennsylvania College for Women with the intention of becoming a writer, but she switched her major to biology in her junior year after a biology class renewed her interest in natural sciences. Graduating magna cum laude in 1929 with a degree in zoology, she won a graduate scholarship to Johns Hopkins University, which awarded her a master's degree in marine zoology in 1932. She accepted a teaching position at the University of Maryland from 1932 to 1936, but spent much of her time studying the ocean and its life forms at the Woods Hole Oceanographic Institute in Massachusetts.

Rachel's father died in 1935, leaving her mother without financial support. Her sister died a year later, leaving two young daughters that Rachel and her mother decided to raise. As the sole support of this new family, Carson needed a better-paying job, and so accepted an aquatic biology position with the U.S. Bureau of Fisheries, becoming one of the first women to occupy a non-clerical position there. In 1940, the Fisheries Bureau became the Fish and Wildlife Service, and she moved into the information section. By 1949, she had advanced to editor-in-chief, overseeing conservation efforts and the new wildlife refuge network.

To supplement her income, she wrote articles on the sea and on marine ecology. One of these, "Undersea," was published in the *Atlantic Monthly,* and a publisher invited her to expand it into a full-length book. That book, *Under the Sea Wind,* was widely praised but did not sell well.

Carson took a leave of absence from work (thanks to the Eugene F. Saxton Memorial Fellowship) to write her next book, *The Sea Around Us.* Chapters of it appeared in the *New Yorker* magazine as part of prepublication publicity, so when the book appeared in 1951, it was an immediate hit. It was on the best seller list for 86 weeks, translated into 30 languages, and won the

National Book Award. In 1952, Carson won a Guggenheim Fellowship, which enabled her to resign from her position with the Fish and Wildlife Service to devote herself full time to her writing. Her third book, *The Edge of the Sea,* came out in 1955 and also became a best seller.

Then, in 1958, a friend wrote to her for help. As part of the Massachusetts mosquito-control program, a plane had sprayed the countryside with DDT, a powerful pesticide. This friend wrote of the horrible deaths of 14 robins after the spraying and asked for Carson's help. She decided to write an article about the dangers of DDT and other toxic chemicals used indiscriminately on the environment. But no one would publish it; it was too controversial. The pesticide business was a multimillion-dollar business, and no one wanted to battle it.

Carson decided to write a book, *Silent Spring*, the story of a rural valley and the horrors it endured after pesticide spraying. It took her years to research the effects of pesticide pollution, culling information from scientific reports and from interviews she conducted with scientists across the world. She found that more than a billion dollars worth of chemical sprays were being sold and used in America each year; those highly toxic materials were not only contaminating the environment and persisting for years in waters and soils, but were also accumulating in the human body. She proposed strict limitations on spraying programs and increased research efforts to develop safer, more natural controls for insects.

When *Silent Spring* was released in 1962, it immediately aroused the nation. Sales soared—it stayed for 31 weeks on the best seller list, selling 500,000 hardback copies and millions in paperback. The popularity of the book was due in part to the outrage of the public upon reading about the well-documented, massive damage to the ecosystem caused by unwise use of pesticides. It was also due in part to the chemical companies, which launched an attack against Carson to try to discredit her and her views. For the next two years she fought to maintain her personal reputation and to educate the public—and the government—about the dangers of pesticide use.

President John F. Kennedy set up a commission to study the pesticide problem in 1963. The commission's report vindicated Carson, upholding the basic premise of *Silent Spring*. She testified before a Senate committee examining the pesticide issue, and after her death in 1964, several regulations were passed requiring stricter labeling of ingredients and other pesticide controls.

In all of her books (and especially *Silent Spring*), Rachel Carson brought the fledgling science of ecology to the public's attention. Her books alerted the public to the dangerous environmental effects of man-made pesticides— as well as the collusion of big business and government regulatory agencies in the depletion and pollution of natural resources. These writings jolted the nation into action and led to the banning of DDT in 1972, and to a host of laws and regulations to protect the environment from future damage. As one writer put it, "A few thousand words from her, and the world took a new direction."

## Key Dates

| | |
|---|---|
| 1907 | Born in Springdale, Pennsylvania, on May 27 |
| 1929 | Graduated from Pennsylvania College for Women |
| 1932 | Received M.A. from Johns Hopkins University |
| 1931–1936 | Taught zoology at University of Maryland |
| 1936 | Worked as aquatic biologist with the U.S. Bureau of Fisheries |
| 1941 | Published *Under the Sea Wind* |
| 1947–1952 | Worked as editor-in-chief of the Fish and Wildlife Service's publications |
| 1951 | Published *The Sea Around Us*; won the 1951 National Book Award for nonfiction |
| 1951–1952 | Won a Guggenheim Fellowship for study in marine biology |
| 1955 | Published *The Edge of the Sea* |
| 1962 | Published *Silent Spring* |
| 1964 | Died April 14 in Silver Spring, Maryland, of cancer |
| 1965 | Published posthumously *The Sense of Wonder* |

## Advice

*The science of ecology is a mix of chemistry and biology, with heavy dashes of physics, engineering, and resource economics mixed in. But more important than completing this daunting course load, Rachel Carson would advise you to become active in your local environmental protection, conservation, and recycling groups. Spend time in nature and learn to observe keenly the details you see. Study the ecological relationships in your local ecosystems. Note how physical and chemical changes affect different flora and fauna. This practical experience you gain through self-study will be invaluable to your career success.*

## References

Carson, Rachel. *Silent Spring.* Boston: Houghton Mifflin, 1962.

Gartner, Carol B. *Rachel Carson.* New York: Frederick Ungar, 1983.

Henricksson, John. *Rachel Carson: The Environmental Movement.* Brookfield, Conn.: Millbrook Press, 1991.

Karleskint, George. *An Introduction to Marine Biology.* San Diego, Calif.: Harcourt Brace Jovanovich College & School Division, 1997.

Kudlinski, Kathleen V. *Rachel Carson: Pioneer of Ecology.* New York: Viking Penguin, 1988.

Lear, Linda. *Rachel Carson: Witness for Nature.* New York: Henry Holt, 1997.

# George Washington Carver

*"The Plant Doctor"*                Agricultural
                                    Chemistry

National Park Service, George Washington Carver National Monument

## Career Highlights

- Developed more than 400 synthetic materials from common farm crops and waste materials
- Awarded the Spingarn Medal for distinguished service to science by the NAACP, 1923
- Elected to the Royal Society, Britain's most prestigious scientific organization, 1916
- Awarded the Franklin Roosevelt Medal for "Distinguished Research in Agricultural Chemistry," 1937
- Has a national holiday named for him: January 5 has been designated George Washington Carver Day by the U.S. Congress

## Important Contributions

Despite the fact that George Washington Carver was born a slave and raised in poverty, he earned a master's degree in agriculture and succeeded in becoming a professor and head of the Department of Agriculture at Tuskegee University. There, in a laboratory where he made most of his own equipment and tools, came discoveries and products that first enriched the lives of the southern farmers he was trying to help—and then the lives of us all.

## Career Path

George Washington Carver, born a slave during the Civil War, never knew either of his parents. His father was killed in an accident when he was an infant, and his mother was kidnapped from the plantation when George was less than a year old. The plantation owners, the Carvers, raised him and his older brother and gave them their name.

The boy grew up sickly and lonely. There were no nearby schools for black children. Instead, he roamed the woods and fields and learned by studying nature. When he found sick or dying plants, he brought them home and nursed them back to health in his secret garden. Part of the barn became his "greenhouse" during the winter. Neighbors began to refer to him as the "plant doctor."

When he was 10 years old, George realized he would never be more than a slave boy until he got an education, so he bravely marched out alone in search of one. He wandered through Missouri and Kansas, attending school when he could, and working as a farm hand, cook, and laundry helper to pay his way. He stayed long enough in Minneapolis, Kansas, to graduate from high school. During this time, he developed an interest in drawing and painting. He sketched mostly plants and flowers, revealing his keen powers of observation in the lifelike details he sketched.

The first time he applied to college, Carver was rejected because he was black. The second time, at age 25, he was granted admission to Simpson College in Iowa. His art teacher felt that, despite his talents, a black man could never make a living as an artist, so she encouraged his interest in botany. She even wrote a letter of recommendation for him to her father, a professor of horticulture, at Iowa State College. After two years at Simpson, Carver was granted admission to the agricultural department at Iowa State.

Carver worked in the college greenhouse to earn money for living expenses and tuition. In 1894, he graduated with high honors and, while remaining in school to work on a master's degree in botany and agriculture, was made an assistant instructor and appointed director of the greenhouse. He began a study of mushrooms and fungal diseases and collected mushroom samples from across the south and south-central United States.

Carver received his master's degree in 1896, and in that same year, the president of Tuskegee Institute in Alabama (Booker T. Washington) asked him to become the head of the school's new Department of Agriculture. Part of this job would include teaching poor southern farmers how to use the soil more effectively by growing and harvesting a variety of crops—essentially, how to better support themselves and their families through farming. Deeply committed to helping black farmers, he accepted and moved to Tuskegee.

There was no laboratory space or scientific equipment at the new school. Carver had to improvise his own. He asked for a room for his laboratory and was given a dilapidated barn. An old lantern became his heater. He fashioned a mortar from a heavy cup. A flat piece of iron became the pestle that he used to grind up substances in the mortar. He found old bottles at the dump and cut the tops off to create beakers. He turned an ink bottle into an alcohol lamp. And he made his own wicks from plant fibers.

In 1897 Carver discovered a new species of fungus (*Taphrina carveri*—named after its discoverer). Through his work on cross-fertilization, mycology (fungi), and plant diseases, he established a name for himself in the field of botany.

The young teacher and experimenter was soon promoted to director of the Tuskegee Agricultural Experiment Station, where his mission was to demonstrate how science could benefit farmers through improved fertilization and planting practices. His greatest challenge was to persuade southern farmers to accept the new ideas of science and to grow more than just cotton. The south had long been a one-crop economy: cotton. However, since cotton uses up large amounts of minerals from the soil—and after years of planting cotton and nothing but cotton—the farmers had ruined the soil. It was difficult to grow a decent cotton crop in such depleted soils.

Carver tried to convince farmers to plant peanuts, plants that grow well in poor soils and add vital nutrients to the soil. The surface roots of peanut plants take in nitrogen particles from the air. When these roots are plowed into the soil after harvesting, they enrich the soil with nitrogen. But southern farmers would not listen to a black man who promoted revolutionary changes in traditional agricultural practices, nor would they give any credence to the logic of science, which they viewed as senseless foreign propaganda. It took the Mexican boll weevil, a beetle that feeds on the cotton plant and lays its eggs in the cotton beds, to change their minds. When the boll weevil eggs hatch, the larvae feed on the fibers of the cotton. Boll weevil infestations destroyed thousands of acres of cotton and persuaded cotton farmers to try another crop: peanuts.

When the peanut harvest came in, however, there were more peanuts than could be sold. Acres of them rotted in the fields. Carver needed to come up with a solution—and fast. He needed to create a market for peanuts. So he took the peanut apart—chemically. In his lab, he shelled peanuts, removed the papery skins, and ground the nuts into a fine powder. He heated the powder, pressed it, and extracted an oil. He then heated the oil at various temperatures to see what would happen. This process of grinding, pressing, and heating left him with the simple substances of the peanut: water, fats, oils, gums, resins, sugars, starches, pectoses, lysin, and amino acids. He then recombined these materials at different temperatures and with other substances to make new products.

Carver made paper from the peanut skins, as well as a soil conditioner and an insulating board from the shells. From the peanut itself he made soap, cooking oil, rubbing oil, a dairy-free milk, cheese, and other products. He eventually created more than 300 products from the peanut. From the sweet potato, he made over 100 products, including postage stamp and envelope paste. He created over 500 dyes from 28 kinds of plants and clays.

Although he worked alone with little monetary backing and although most of his equipment was discarded junk that he fashioned himself, George Washington Carver nevertheless managed to help shape the future of agriculture in the South. Through his inventions and by teaching sustainable farming practices, he taught southern farmers about crop rotation, waste utilization, and the benefits of new crops such as peanuts. In doing so, he relieved the South of its one-crop dependency, improved diet and nutrition, and raised poor farmers' hopes and achievements.

## Key Dates

| | |
|---|---|
| 1864 | Born near Diamond Grove, Missouri |
| 1894 | Received B.S. in agriculture from Iowa State College of Agriculture and Mechanical Arts |
| 1896 | Received M.S. from Iowa State College |
| 1896 | Appointed head of agricultural department and director of agricultural research at Tuskegee Institute in Alabama |
| 1897 | Discovered a new kind of fungus, *Taphrina carveri* |

1935    Appointed collaborator in the Department of Agriculture's Bureau of Plant Industry, Division of Mycology and Disease Study

1940    Established the George Washington Carver Foundation

1943    Died January 5 in Tuskegee, Alabama

1953    Plantation on which he was born was declared a national monument

## Advice

*George Washington Carver believed in learning through trial-and-error experimentation. Even more, he believed in designing his research to meet the practical needs of the local community. He would advise you not to worry about the titles of university departments or the labels of a degree. Focus on problems you want to address. Let real-world problems be your guides to classes and courses of study. Carver would also advise you to be active in your community, in agricultural clubs and bureaus. Volunteer if necessary to gain firsthand knowledge of the issues and problems that confront your community.*

## References

Altman, Susan. *Extraordinary Black Americans—From Colonial to Contemporary Times.* Chicago: Children's Press, 1989.

Elliott, Lawrence. *George Washington Carver: The Man Who Overcame.* Englewood Cliffs, N.J.: Prentice-Hall, 1966. (Popular biography.)

Hay, R. *Chemistry for Agriculture & Ecology.* Malden, Mass.: Blackwell Science, 1981.

Hayden, Robert C. *7 African American Scientists.* Frederick, Md.: Twenty-First Century Books, Henry Holt, 1992.

McMurry, Linda O. *George Washington Carver: Scientist and Symbol.* New York: Oxford University Press, 1981. (The only full-scale, documented biography.)

# Karen Chin

*"Messing Around with Dinosaur Poop"*

## Paleontology and "Paleoscatology"

Courtesy of Karen Chin

## Career Highlights

- Is the world's leading "paleoscatologist"
- Received Geological Society of America Research Grant & Outstanding Student Research Award, 1992, 1993
- Received American Association for the Advancement of Science First Place Award for Excellence, 1992
- Received Smithsonian Minority Museum Professionals Award, 1989

## Important Contributions

Karen Chin is a pioneer in a branch of science that is so unusual, so peculiar, and so new that it doesn't even have a formal name yet. She studies dinosaur dung. She is probably the world's leading "paleoscatologist"—one who studies fossilized scat. Chin's careful research has made significant strides in our understanding of coprolites (or fossilized feces) and the eating habits of the animals who produced them.

# Career Path

Karen Chin had been an excellent student in high school, and she fully expected college would be the same. She was wrong. The University of California at San Diego (UCSD) was primarily a pre-med college, so the students she competed with were top-notch students. She realized in dismay that she had never learned how to study and sank from being top in her class and winning science fairs in high school to receiving straight "D's" in college. It was a humbling experience for someone who had always loved to learn and had been one of the best and brightest.

As a young child, Karen Chin had an insatiable curiosity, especially about nature. She wandered through her Los Angeles neighborhood with a paper bag, collecting interesting tidbits to study—everything from cigarette butts and rocks to dead beetles and broken leaves.

Karen's parents fostered her interest in nature, giving her kitchen counter space on which to analyze her treasures and garage space for storage. They took her to Yosemite when she was a child, and she fell in love with the wonder, beauty, and majesty of the valley. By age nine, she had memorized all 17 types of coniferous trees in Yosemite and a good deal of other information about the park. Once, on a guided nature walk, the young girl correctly answered every question the park ranger asked of the crowd. The ranger was less than amused. But the crowd enjoyed watching a nine-year-old best a trained ranger and Karen was hooked. She decided to be a park ranger when she grew up.

In high school, Karen developed an interest in botany, a natural outgrowth of her love of nature. As a senior, she won first place in botany at the San Diego High Schools Science Fair for her exhibit "Floral Induction of *Xanthium strumarium in vitro*" in which she tried to make a cocklebur bloom in tissue culture. She took little pieces of stem, prepared a sterilized growing medium (made of a gel-like substance called agar), added vitamins and other necessities, and adjusted the photoperiod (day length) to try to induce a bloom. This project also won honorable mention in the California State Science Fair.

Karen entered UCSD in 1970 and eagerly looked forward to taking university science classes. So it was galling for her to watch her grades hover just above failing for the very classes she had gone there to master. She loved learning about nature, about how things grow and how they live, but she hated struggling to survive the coursework. She muddled through, barely managing to maintain an average grade level and, the summer after her junior year, got her childhood dream job as a seasonal park ranger.

After graduation, Chin hunted for a job that would combine her love of natural history with her interest in public education and research and decided to try a museum. She boldly approached the Museum of the Rockies, but was told she needed a graduate degree to work as a curator there. Undaunted, she enrolled in Montana State University to work on a master's degree. While in graduate school, she met a scientist who would forever change her career.

Professor Jack Horner introduced Chin to the mystery of paleontology, which soon became her passion. Horner also introduced her to coprolites (a scientific term for fossilized dung). As a youth, Horner had once worked shoveling elephant dung when the circus came to town. Later, as a paleontologist, he saw big ugly chunks of rock that looked surprisingly like the elephant dung. It didn't take long for him to realize he was looking at fossilized dinosaur feces.

Chin was also schooled in recognizing animal dung. As a park ranger, she more often encountered traces of the animals rather than the animals themselves and had soon learned to recognize and identify animal dung. It was a natural step for her to take up an in-depth study of dinosaur coprolites.

But this was not an easy task. Coprolites aren't often recognizable. The ugly chunks of stone can range in size from microscopic to over a foot long. They can be shaped as nuggets, crescents, pebbles, or just big blobs. Their color can range from orange, beige, or brown, to even aquamarine. And because of the "detached nature" of the droppings (you generally won't find one neatly piled beside the skeletal remains of the animal who dropped it) it can be virtually impossible to figure out who dropped what.

Chin had the advantage of studying coprolites with more technological muscle than had paleontologists who preceded her. With circular saws, diamond-edged blades, and grinding wheels, she tackled her subjects, cutting, grinding, and slicing them into samples thousandths of an inch thick. She examined them with light and electron microscopy and used biogeochemical analyses to investigate their biochemical profiles. She even used X-ray diffraction and electron microprobes to discover their mineral and elemental composition.

One group of specimens Chin studied was from Montana (near Choteau in the Two Medicine Formation). These specimens were large and formless, like huge cow pies that had been broken up. They were filled with dark fibrous material: remnants of shredded wood. They were probably the by-products of a very large vegetarian, but the young paleontologist had to figure out a way to prove that they were dinosaur dung.

First, Chin studied how the droppings were arranged in the excavation site. They were scattered about, as one might expect to find cow pie droppings. Second, since these specimens were found in a nesting ground of *Maiasaura* (a duck-billed vegetarian dinosaur), it was reasonable to make a connection between the two. Third, the short, angular fragments suggested that the wood had been chewed, not just stepped on. And fourth—the clincher.

Chin noticed different-sized tunnels running through some of the specimens. On a hunch, she took the specimens to Bruce Gill, a noted dung beetle specialist. To him it looked like the "perfect soil trace of a modern-day dung beetle." When they discovered "backfilled" burrows (tunnels that had been filled with dung or soil and then fossilized), they knew they were indeed looking at coprolites. Only dung beetles fill up tunnels with dung and dirt—and dung beetles only operate in dung! She had found the oldest evidence of dung beetle activity as well as the first evidence of dinosaur-insect interactions. Her biogeochemical analysis also provided the first evidence that *Maiasaura* ate flowering plants.

Karen Chin hopes her research will help answer a number of unanswered questions about dinosaurs, other ancient lifeforms, and their feeding habits and behavior. Such paleontological clues help scientists reconstruct ancient ecological webs, allowing glimpses into ecosystems that are long gone.

## Key Dates

| | |
|---|---|
| 1952 | Born in Montreal, Canada, on May 14 |
| 1975 | Received B.A. in biology at the University of California at San Diego |
| 1976–1978 | Worked as park interpretive specialist for California Department of Parks and Recreation |
| 1974–1988 | Worked as seasonal park interpreter for U.S. National Park Service |
| 1982–1985 | Worked as teaching assistant at Montana State University |
| 1984–1990 | Worked as research assistant at Museum of the Rockies |
| 1988 | Received M.S. in biology from Montana State University |
| 1988–1990 | Worked as Paleontology Field School instructor at Museum of the Rockies |
| 1990–present | Works as Dinosaur Workshop instructor for The Nature Conservancy |
| 1991–1992 | Worked as teaching assistant at University of California at Santa Barbara |

1994–
1996      Was a visiting scholar at Stanford University

1996      Received Ph.D. in geological sciences from the University
          of California at Santa Barbara

1996–
present   Is a visiting scientist for the U.S. Geological Survey

1997–     Works as sdjunct curator of paleobotany at the Museum of
present       the Rockies

1998–     Works as instructor for San Francisco State University
present

## Advice

*If you are considering a career in paleontology, Karen Chin would advise you to start by studying modern animals and ecosystems. Spend time in nature and observe the patterns of animal movement and how animals cluster in different combinations with other animals and plant groups. Volunteer to work at county and state nature parks. Spend time with park interpretive specialists and others working in the field. Search for summer jobs in park and interpretive centers. Bring this practical experience and knowledge to the classroom when you begin your formal studies. In college, take chemistry and history as well as biology-related courses.*

## References

Currie, P.J., and K. Padian [ed]. *Encyclopedia of Dinosaurs.* San Diego, Calif.: Academic Press, 1997. (Chin contributed pages 147–150 on coprolites.)

Farlow, J.O., and M. K. Brett-Surman [eds]. *The Complete Dinosaur.* Bloomington: Indiana University Press, 1997. (Chin contributed pages 371–382 describing what dinosaurs ate.)

Rudwick, Martin J. S. *The Meaning of Fossils: Episodes in the History of Paleontology.* Chicago: University of Chicago Press, 1985.

Sternberg, Charles H. *The Life of a Fossil Hunter.* Bloomington: Indiana University Press, 1990.

Wright, Karen. "What the Dinosaurs Left Us," *Discover* (June 1996): 59.

# Bernard Chouet

*"The Earth, My Laboratory"*     Volcanology

Courtesy of Bernard Chouet

## Career Highlights

- Is world's leading authority in volcanic prediction studies
- Was scientific expert for the French government during the volcanic crisis of La Soufriere Volcano in Guadeloupe, French West Indies
- Is scientific advisor to the Alaska Volcano Observatory, the Montserrat Volcano Observatory, and the government of Colombia for ongoing geophysical monitoring

## Important Contributions

As a youth, Bernard Chouet dreamed of creating a scientific, quantified system for volcanic predictions to replace the empirical approach that had been used in the past. As an adult, he manifested that dream. Chouet founded a new field of study—quantitative volcano seismology—and created the world's first quantitative predictive model for volcanoes.

## Career Path

Clutching his stomach, a 10-year-old boy rose from his seat in the gym, his chair scraping across the polished wood floor. A sheen of sweat covered the upper lip and forehead of his pasty-white face. His steps were halting and wobbly as he made his way toward the back of the cavernous room while rows of other 10-year-olds paused in their fevered work to watch. Retching, Bernard Chouet scurried out of the gym for the nearest bathroom. He had left his national placement examination for science.

In Switzerland, most children at around age 10 take entrance examinations that funnel them into specific careers. Because Bernard got sick and left in the middle of his test, he failed the exam—and shattered his dreams of a career in science. He was instantly slated for trade school. Fortunately, a teacher later recognized his science potential and made arrangements for him to retake the test, which he easily passed.

When he was 16 years old, Bernard saw a movie about a volcano in Africa. The volcano fascinated him, but there are no volcanoes in Switzerland, so it was not possible to study them in school. He picked a more practical field, engineering, but his heart had already picked volcanoes.

Bernard attended the Federal Polytechnic Institute in Lausanne, Switzerland, and graduated in 1968 with a B.S. in electrical engineering. He went to work for a bio-cybernetics (robotics) lab and soon realized that if he wanted to pursue this field, he would have to go to the United States, where all the advances in robotics were being made. So he sent applications to American universities. When his employer found out, his boss grew very upset and told him, "You're being too ambitious. There isn't a chance you'd make it in the United States. If you're so vain, you can go elsewhere for a job." Just like that, he was fired.

But Chouet prevailed. A letter of acceptance arrived from one of the most prestigious technical schools in the world: the Massachusetts Institute of Technology (MIT). He had six months before school began and so accepted a position with Club Med in Sicily. There he gave sailing lessons and then, by chance, began leading tours to Mt. Etna, a live volcano. Once again he fell in love with volcanoes, and once again he had no way to study them. He was, after all, going to be studying electrical engineering at MIT, and they didn't even have a program in volcanoes.

At MIT, the young scientist brought his knowledge of robotics to the study of aeronautics and astronautics in the man-vehicle lab, part of the Apollo program, which was going full swing. It was an exciting time; there were lots of new inventions and plenty of funding for research, so Chouet decided to become an astronaut.

Then the bottom fell out. NASA's budget got slashed. It was time to look for a new field.

In January 1971, Chouet ran into someone from MIT's Department of Earth Science who was working on volcanoes. They had worked together for a month when, in April, Mt. Etna erupted. Because he was familiar with Mt. Etna, he was asked to help prepare the logistics for an experiment that summer. He agreed. As soon as he graduated with an M.S. in aeronautics and astronautics in 1972, Chouet began to work on another master's degree, this time in earth and planetary sciences. He decided to "make the earth my laboratory."

Chouet wanted to try to combine the fields of seismology and volcanology into a single predictive science. His new graduate advisor scoffed that it was a wild pipe dream and too far fetched for serious consideration. Following that advisor's recommendation, he studied seismology and earthquakes and, in 1976, received his Ph.D. in geophysics.

But Chouet's heart still burned to study volcanoes. He took his new advisor to the Oregon Cascades to see volcanoes, and his new advisor fell in love with volcanoes too. Together they decided to build Chouet's dream, which was essentially to create a whole new field of study, which they called quantitative volcano seismology. They took the tools of seismology (a 50-year-old study) and applied them (with some modification and by inventing new tools as well) to volcanology.

The advisor and the budding volcanologist struggled to make sense of the chaos of information on the 600 live volcanoes on this planet. Each volcano looks different, has different seismic signals, different signatures, different events. It was a mountain of confusing data, an incredible catalog of events with no apparent pattern.

Chouet adapted seismic theory and applied it to that confusion, and the pieces started to fall into place. He called it "removing the mountain so you can see the plumbing." His theory helped scientists figure out what was happening underneath the ground. It was a quantum leap forward in the study of volcanoes and volcanic prediction.

But theories must be substantiated with data. Data collection means spending extensive time on the slopes of volcanoes. There are two primary field duties. The first is placing seismic and other test equipment using global satellite positioning. The second is keeping the equipment running, an often difficult task. Volcanic gases can be so corrosive that they can quickly eat through the connectors and insulation on the electric cables. Volcanic dust can filter into and ruin sensitive equipment. Even rats can be a problem, eating through and destroying cables.

Chouet has worked in ice storms, dealing with frozen equipment in the middle of a blizzard. He's been blasted with hot sand in sandstorms. And, of course, there's always danger from the volcano itself: "You never know what the volcano is going to do until you put down that equipment."

When not in the field, the volcanologist does a lot of computer work, "number crunching," interpreting the data collected from the field work. He also spends much of his time writing (scientific papers, proposals, articles, lectures), attending conferences, and speaking to groups all over the world.

Bernard Chouet hopes to create a curriculum for the next generation. He wants to write a textbook for this new field, quantitative volcano seismology, so that young people can build from where he leaves off. He wants to teach people how volcanoes work, to leave a legacy of ways to assess the hazards of volcanoes, and leave the world a safer place.

## Key Dates

| | |
|---|---|
| 1945 | Born in Nyon, Switzerland, on October 14 |
| 1963 | Received B.S. from Gymnasium Cantonal |
| 1968 | Received Electrical Engineering Diploma from Federal Institute of Technology |
| 1970–1972 | Worked as research assistant at Man-Vehicle Laboratory at Center for Space Research, MIT |
| 1972 | Received M.Sc. in aeronautics and astronautics from MIT |
| 1973 | Received M.Sc. in earth and planetary sciences from MIT |
| 1976 | Received Ph.D. in geophysics from MIT |
| 1976–1983 | Worked as research associate, Department of Earth and Planetary Sciences, MIT |
| 1983–1995 | Worked as geophysicist, Office of Earthquakes, Volcanoes, and Engineering, U.S. Geological Survey, California |
| 1995–present | Works as geophysicist, Volcano Hazards Team for the U.S. Geological Survey, California |

## Advice

*Volcanologists study the flow of the physical matter in the Earth and of the forces that control it. Thus, volcanology includes virtually all of the earth and physical sciences. Bernard Chouet would advise you to "Accumulate as much knowledge as you can from every field. In the past we taught sciences as separate fields. Now we're finding they're all interrelated. Now we know we should study science as a whole, looking at it holistically. So go ahead and study elasticity and wave propagation, but also study fluid dynamics, chemistry, thermodynamics, all branches of physics. It all fits together."*

*His parting advice is "Don't ever let anyone tell you 'you can't do it.' It doesn't matter where you start from. Don't say, 'Well it's too late now; I majored in Biology, that won't help me study volcanoes.' It's never too late." To Chouet it's the journey more than the destination that counts. Chouet doesn't see his job as one that has an end. If conditions change, he'll change also and find something new: "Who knows, twenty years from now, I might be studying whales."*

## References

Decker, Bob, and Barbara Decker. *Volcanoes*. 2d ed. New York: W. H. Freeman, 1995.

Lay, J., and R. Wallace. *Modern Global Seismology*. Orlando, Fla.: Academic Press, 1995.

MacDonald, Gordan A. *Volcanoes*. Englewood Cliffs, N.J.: Prentice-Hall, 1972.

Newhall, Christopher G., and Raymundo S. Punongbayan. *Fire and Mud: Eruptions and Lahars of Mount Pinatubo, Philippines*. Seattle: University of Washington Press, 1997.

Scarpa, T., and F. Tilling. *Monitoring and Mitigation of Volcano Hazards*. Minneapolis, Minn.: Springer-Verlag, 1996.

# Eugenie Clark

*"Shark Lady"*                    Marine Ichthyology

Photo by Andreas Rechnitzer

## Career Highlights

- Discovered shark intelligence; expert on shark behavior
- Received Society of Women Geographers Gold Award, 1975
- Received Lowell Thomas Award of the Explorers Club, 1986
- Received Cousteau Award, 1973
- Was director, Cape Haze Marine Lab, 1955–1966

## Important Contributions

Respected researchers warned Eugenie Clark that her attempt to measure shark intelligence would surely fail. They warned that she would look like a fool wasting valuable lab time searching for something that didn't exist. Everyone knew that sharks worked on primitive, even pre-historic instinct, and lacked a measurable amount of higher intelligence.

In only four weeks Clark trained four lemon sharks to nose an underwater target board and ring a bell before expecting to be fed. Within six weeks, she had trained them to nose the board, ring the bell, and swim completely across the pen.

Rather than looking foolish, Eugenie Clark's results were called remarkable and ground-breaking. Her detailed data from this experiment revolutionized shark research worldwide and led marine biologists to rethink their basic approach to behavior and intelligence research for many other marine species. Eugenie Clark became one of the foremost marine biologists of the last half of the twentieth century.

## Career Path

"You'll be fine," Eugenie remembered Dr. Hubbs of Scripps Institute of Oceanography saying as he latched her helmet face plate and helped her over the side for her first open ocean dive.

With a new Ph.D. in hand, Eugenie Clark had finally qualified for research assistant (RA) positions. Her first RA assignment was as part of a team cataloging Pacific coastal fish for the Scripps Institute. This was before SCUBA gear. Divers wore bulky suits and metal helmets with long air hoses trailing to surface support ships.

Dr. Hubbs, the lab and project director, dictated when RAs like her would dive and what they would look for once they reached the bottom.

She dropped into a blue-green wonder-world. Fish she had only seen in captive aquariums swam past. She felt she could see for miles through the rippling patterns of light and water. Her first glimpse of the ocean bottom was the most magical thing Eugenie would ever see.

As Clark hit bottom at 100 feet she began to feel groggy. One of her gloved hands groped across the back of her helmet to adjust the air flow knob. It didn't help. Her breath came in ragged gasps. She clawed at the air-control valve.

Nothing.

There was no air. Her head swam. Her eyes burned. Her vision blurred. She stumbled to her knees, gasping to find some air, struggling to open the valve even farther.

Then she accidentally released one of the helmet latches. Ice-cold sea water leaked in, stinging her face like a cold, hard slap. In a last, desperate act, she flipped all her helmet latches, tossed the helmet, and bolted for the surface.

As the neohpite diver recovered, gasping for air on the boat, Dr. Hubbs matter-of-factly reported, "Your air hose ruptured."

"I almost died down there!"

"It's fixed now. You're ready to head back down."

Clark gasped, "Dive again?!"

He shrugged. "Of course. You're a new Research Assistant."

Having obtained a Ph.D., Clark had arrived at what she thought was the top, only to find that, as an RA, she was really at the bottom all over again.

Eugenie Clark grew up in New York City. On Saturdays she accompanied her mother to the cigar and newspaper stand she ran in the Manhattan Athletic Club. To keep her daughter from being bored and under foot, Mrs. Clark allowed Eugenie to spend those Saturdays in the New York Aquarium in the building next door. Enthralled by every tank and spectacle, the young girl soaked in every fact and detail of each species and developed a deep fascination for marine fishes. She longed to push through the glass and swim with the fish. She *knew* she would be an oceanographer.

After graduation from Hunter College, Clark found that a B.A. degree in zoology had no value in the New York job market. She had to snatch the only job she could find, as a chemist for a plastics company, while she took graduate school classes for two years to earn her master's. But a master's degree opened only small, inconsequential oceanographic jobs to her. She went through six of these jobs over an eight-year period while she pursued her Ph.D., building a varied and extensive foundation of work experience.

As a new doctoral graduate, Clark found she was worth little more than an untrained lab tech until she had completed several successful RA jobs. Including her dives for Scripps, she survived five short-term RA assignments. She wrote her first book, *Lady with a Spear,* describing two of those experiences, diving in the South Pacific and the Red Sea. That book so impressed the owners of the Cape Haze Marine Laboratory that they offered Eugenie the position of director. She had been working and studying for 15 years when this first big professional break was offered to her.

As the director of a major research facility, Clark got to exercise the project control she had longed for as a lowly research assistant. Now she was responsible for project, boat, tank, and lab schedules, for assistant and staff tasking, and especially for funding—funding for every research project, funding for every lab facility, even funding for boat maintenance and gasoline.

Clark spent six months writing proposals and begging for funding for her most famous study to measure shark intelligence. It occurred to her that humans' irrational fear of sharks might be dispelled if she could show that they were fellow intelligent creatures. Her plan was simple: Capture a group of adult sharks and see if she could train them to perform specific behaviors to obtain food.

Catching sharks in the shark-infested Florida Straits was easy but dangerous. The easy part was luring sharks to a diver's location with hunks of tuna. The dangerous part was having to get close enough to spray a strong tranquilizer down the shark's throat. Clark handled the shark collection because she didn't fear the sharks and had experience handling them in the wild.

With half a dozen lemon sharks successfully relocated into the Cape Haze shark pen, the experiment consisted of feeding the sharks only after they performed a preliminary set of behaviors. At first tuna was attached directly on an underwater target board. To get the tuna a shark had to nose the target board and ring an attached bell.

After a week, the tuna was moved behind a metal grate *next* to the target board. Sharks could see and smell the tuna but couldn't reach it. To be fed, a shark had to learn to nose the target board and ring the bell as it had during the previous week. For two days the sharks hammered the metal grate, tails thrashing, to get the tuna.

One shark, named Rosie, hesitated in the middle of the spacious tank, as if pondering. Rosie swam at the tuna but turned and nosed the target board instead. The bell rang. Waiting RAs lifted the metal grate. Rosie was fed. The entire research team cheered. Twenty-four hours a day, team members sat above the shark pen recording the time and identities both of the sharks that attempted to reach food without first performing the prescribed behaviors and those that performed the prescribed behavior first.

Eugenie Clark's study proved that sharks were far more intelligent than previously thought. Her work was called "revolutionary." It redirected the way in which marine researchers approached intelligence assessments of aquatic species. Her studies have left a permanent mark on the world of marine biological research.

## Key Dates

| | |
|---|---|
| 1922 | Born in New York City on May 4 |
| 1923 | Father died; Eugenie was raised by a single, working mother |
| 1942 | Received B.A. in zoology from Hunter College |
| 1946 | Received M.S. in marine biology from New York University |
| 1946 | Worked as marine ichthyology research assistant for Scripps Institute cataloging coastal fish |
| 1947– 1950 | Worked at temporary jobs at the New York Zoological Society and American Museum of Natural History |
| 1950 | Received Ph.D. from New York University |
| 1950 | Obtained two-year fellowship to study Red Sea fish |
| 1953 | Published *Lady with a Spear* |
| 1955 | Appointed director of Cape Haze Marine Lab in Florida |

1967    Worked as professor of marine biology at City University of
        New York

1969    Worked as professor of biology at the University of Maryland

1969    Published her most popular book, *The Lady and the Sharks*

1984–   Appointed distinguished professor of biology at University
present    of Maryland

## Advice

*Eugenie Clark often advised youth to develop the qualities of curiosity, persistence, patience, and observation. Eugenie also advised new graduates to jump at every opportunity, to live and breathe what excites their passion, and to build a wide general knowledge before specializing.*

*During high school and college take a range of general science, biology, and oceanography courses. Start general, then specialize after graduation as opportunities present themselves. Involve yourself in extracurricular, ocean-related activities, such as SCUBA, biology clubs, local aquarium, and specimen collecting.*

## References

Clark, Eugenie. *The Lady and the Sharks.* New York: Harper & Row, 1969.

———. *Lady with a Spear.* New York: Harper & Row, 1953.

Facklam, Margery. *Wild Animals, Gentle Women.* New York: Harcourt Brace Jovanovich, 1978.

Harley, Sir Alister. *The Open Sea; Its Natural History.* Boston: Houghton Mifflin, 1970.

McGovern, Ann. *Shark Lady.* New York: Four Winds, 1978.

Ward, Ritchie. *Introduction to the Ocean World: The Biology of the Sea.* New York: Alfred Knopf, 1984.

Yount, Lisa. *Contemporary Women Scientists.* New York: Facts on File, 1994.

# Albert Claude

*"The Founder of Modern Cell Biology"*          Biology

## Career Highlights

- Awarded the Nobel Prize for Physiology and Medicine, 1974
- Credited as founder of modern cell biology
- Awarded the Louisa Gross Horwitz Prize by Columbia University, 1970
- Voted an honorary member of the American Academy of Arts and Sciences, 1975

## Important Contributions

Albert Claude was the first scientist to develop procedures for isolating and studying individual structures within a cell. He is the one who mapped the inner organization and activity of a cell and its many components. He is rightly called the founder of modern cell biology.

Although he never graduated from high school, Dr. Claude pioneered the use of centrifuge techniques and the electron microscope for the study of living cells. He discovered a dozen key components of cells, identified the function of other cell sub-structures, and laid the groundwork for a whole new field of biology.

## Career Path

With a third-grade education and his only work experience being as an apprentice in a steel mill, 16-year-old Albert Claude had little hope of fulfilling his dream to become a doctor. Had it not been for the horrors of World War I, he never would have made it.

Albert was born in the small Belgian town of Longlier to American parents living in Europe. His mother died of cancer when he was seven years old. The family scraped by until the European depression forced them to move to the manufacturing city of Athus to seek work in 1909.

Albert, whose three years of meager education had been in a one-room country school house, was thereafter self-taught. To help the family survive, he begged a job at a steel mill, first as an apprentice and later as a draftsman.

When the hard-working boy was 13, his uncle in Longlier suffered a cerebral hemorrhage. Albert returned to help his aging aunt and became close friends with the family physician, who made frequent house calls. The doctor impressed the boy with his depth of knowledge and common sense. Albert began dreaming of becoming a doctor.

Then World War I interrupted all plans and dreams. Albert, though barely 16, volunteered to serve in the British Intelligence Service on dangerous reconnaissance and spy missions and was later cited by Winston Churchill for his bravery on the battlefield.

After the war Albert's "doctor" dream resurfaced. But he had only a third-grade education and no high school diploma, a mandatory prerequisite for college. In the European post-war chaos there was no time to consider the special talents or circumstances of one eager boy. He felt trapped in the life of a steel worker.

In 1922 the Belgian government decreed that war veterans could attend a university even if they had no high school diploma. Twenty-three-year-old Albert Claude was one of the first to enroll in the School of Medicine at the University of Liege, which was less than eager to accept an illiterate country soldier.

College was hard for a young man with no school and studying experience. But Claude was a dedicated worker with a great natural intelligence and a flare for medicine. His most vivid memory of his university days was his preoccupation with powerful microscopes. He recalled "spending hours turning endlessly the micrometer screw, gazing at the blurred boundary of a cell which concealed the secret mechanisms of cell life inside."

Unable to obtain microscopes powerful enough to isolate and study the tiny granules inside a cell's cytoplasm for his dissertation, he wrote instead about the effects of grafting mouse tumor cells onto rats. This seemingly unimportant switch wound up directing his research career.

Claude's dissertation won him a government scholarship for post-graduate study at the Cancer Institute in Berlin in 1928. The institute director maintained that cancer was caused by bacteria because the bacterial samples he injected into mice caused cancerous tumors to grow. The young research scientist was skeptical and showed that the samples used by the lab director had been contaminated by cancerous cells. Conflict flared between them and

Claude was fired. He finished his scholarship studies at the nearby Kaiser Wilhelm Institute.

While pursuing his studies, Claude submitted a lengthy research proposal to the Rockefeller Institute for Medical Research in New York. It was accepted and he emigrated to America in 1930.

Having established that the bacterial theory of the origins of cancer was invalid, Claude proposed to study live cancer cells and discover how the disease really was transmitted. His proposal called for him to separate cells into different components for individual study, something that had never been tried before. There were no established procedures or equipment for such an operation. He had to scrounge crude equipment from machine and butcher shops, using commercial meat grinders to pulverize samples of chicken cancerous tumors, which he suspended in a liquid medium. He used a high-speed centrifuge to separate the ground-up cells into their various sub-parts—heaviest on the bottom, lightest on top. He called the procedure cell *fractionation.*

Claude now had test tubes filled with layers of goo and mud. Because no one had ever separated cell sub-parts before, it took the dedicated scientist several years of study and practice to determine what each isolated layer was and to learn how to successfully isolate the tumor agent from the rest of the cell.

In 1933 Claude succeeded in isolating the cancer agent. Chemical analysis showed this agent to be a ribonucleic acid (RNA), a known constituent of viruses. This was the first evidence that cancer was caused by a virus. He decided to continue using cell fractionation to study healthy cells. Working full-time in his laboratory over the next six years using a centrifuge and a high-powered microscope, he was able to isolate and describe the cell nucleus (the structure that houses the chromosomes), organelles (specialized microscopic elements that act like organs), mitochondria (tiny rod-shaped granules where respiration and energy production actually happen), and ribosomes (the sites within cells where proteins are formed).

Claude was mapping a new world that had only been guessed at before. Still, his view was limited by the power of his microscope. In 1942 the Rockefeller Institute was able to borrow the only electron microscope in New York, used by physicists attempting to probe inside an atom. This scope was capable of magnifying objects one million times their original size.

However, the scope also bombarded a sample with a powerful beam of electrons to create an image. Such an electron stream destroyed fragile living tissue. Eighteen months of testing were required to develop successful methods to prepare and protect cell samples to withstand the rigors of the electron microscope. By mid-1943 Claude had obtained the first actual images of the internal structure of a cell, images previously unthinkable. By

1945 he had published a catalog of dozens of new cell structures and activity never before identified.

Claude's successful efforts to penetrate the mysterious interior of a cell earned him the Nobel Prize for Physiology and Medicine in 1974.

The names of the scientists who broke the barrier of the atom and discovered what lay inside (such as Curie, Born, Bohr, Fermi, and Heisenberg) are well-known and revered. Albert Claude single-handedly broke through the barrier of the cell wall to discover and document a universe of sub-parts and activity inside. Like the most famous of explorers, he led science to places it had never gone before and opened a new world for study and understanding.

## Key Dates

| | |
|---|---|
| 1899 | Born in Longlier, Belgium, on August 23 |
| 1909 | Moved to Athus; landed job at a steel mill |
| 1912 | Returned to Longlier to help care for an uncle |
| 1916–1920 | Served as British Intelligence agent during WW I |
| 1928 | Received Ph.D. in medicine and surgery from the University of Liege |
| 1928–1929 | Pursued post-graduate study at the Cancer Institute in Berlin |
| 1929–1930 | Studied at the Kaiser Wilhelm Institute |
| 1930–1950 | Worked as research scientist at the Rockefeller Institute in New York |
| 1950 | Appointed director of the Jules Bordet Institute in Belgium |
| 1971 | Joined the faculty at Catholic University in London |
| 1972 | Named director of the Catholic University's Laboratory of Cellular Biology and Oncology |
| 1974 | Won Nobel Prize for Physiology and Medicine |
| 1983 | Died on May 22 |

## Advice

*Albert Claude would advise you to get as much schooling as you can as early as possible. Rigorous schooling lays a foundation for how to learn and how to study. With a solid foundation the individual scientist can study any specialty area.Cell biology is dependent on high technology and on sophisticated equipment. Learn the effective use of technology. Practice all you can on equipment. Discoveries require a scientist to mix theory with practical experimentation. Don't let a lack of knowledge of the available equipment slow your discoveries.*

## References

Daintith, John, et al., eds. *Biographical Encyclopedia of Scientists.* 2d ed. Philadelphia, Pa.: Institute of Physics Publishing, 1994. (Good biographical summary.)

Devine, Elizabeth, ed. *The Annual Obituary, 1978.* Chicago: St. James Press, 1979. (Good biographical summary.)

Kordon, Claude. *The Language of the Cell.* New York: McGraw-Hill, 1992. (Review of the field.)

Rensberger, Boyce. *Life Itself: Exploring the Realm of the Living Cell.* New York: Oxford University Press, 1997. (Good review of the field.)

Wasson, Tyler, ed. *Nobel Prize Winners.* New York: H. W. Wilson, 1987. (Good summary of his work.)

# Jewel Plummer Cobb

*"The Best Pathway"*

## Cell Biology and Education

California State University, Los Angeles

## Career Highlights

- Elected to the National Academy of Sciences, Institute of Medicine
- Is National Science Foundation member
- Chosen National Cancer Institute fellow
- Received 20 honorary degrees

## Important Contributions

Jewel Plummer Cobb made important contributions to our understanding of skin cancer. She developed techniques for growing cancer cells in tissue cultures so that scientists could more closely observe how cells grow and multiply. Her research helped lay the groundwork for future researchers in the ongoing battle against cancer. In addition, Cobb worked as an educator and college administrator, where she significantly contributed to the improvement of educational opportunities for women and minorities.

# Career Path

It was in high school that Jewel's love of science began. As a sophomore, she looked through a microscope for the first time and was astonished. "It was really awe-inspiring," she said. "Here's a world that I never even knew about!" She decided then and there that she wanted to become a biologist and explore unseen worlds. She read Paul Dekruif's *The Microbe Hunters,* a book about the pioneers in the study of bacteria, which further fueled her desire to become a biologist. The young girl crammed extra biology courses into her full high school class load to ensure that she would qualify for college.

This was the early 1940s in urban America, and racial discrimination was still a very painful reality. Jewel had been born into a well-to-do black American family, but that didn't free her from the chains of prejudice and favoritism. Her parents believed that education was the most essential element in improving the quality of life for African Americans. They set high educational standards for their only child. Not wanting to disappoint them, she threw herself into school work to make sure she would have her pick of colleges.

Jewel enrolled in the University of Michigan because many of her friends were going there and she knew blacks would be accepted. Once she arrived she realized it had not been a wise choice. The dorms were still segregated, with all the African American students living in one large building. Discrimination was rampant. After three semesters, she transferred to Talladega College in Alabama, a black college. Because Talladega did not accept credits from other colleges, she had to begin again. Nevertheless, she still managed to graduate by 1944, completing four years of university work in only three.

Jewel Plummer applied to New York University (NYU) for graduate school and for a teaching fellowship to defray expenses and help pay her tuition. She was accepted as a student but not offered a fellowship. Desperately needing the financial support, she traveled to New York City to plead her case directly with campus officials. They were so impressed with her presentation that they changed their minds and gave her a teaching fellowship, which she held for the five years of her graduate studies.

At NYU, Plummer developed new methods of growing cells in the laboratory so that she could study how cells grow and multiply. Dressed in operating room garb, with surgical hat, mask, and gloves, she cut tiny pieces of skin from mice and studied the development and growth of skin cells. She stored the cells in covered glass containers, nourished them with special food, then recorded their size, configuration, and shape as they grew and divided.

In doing so, she isolated different types of cells and cataloged the growth patterns and behavior of each.

Plummer was recruited by Jane Wright at the Cancer Research Foundation of Harlem Hospital in New York City to join her study of the effects of various anti-cancer drugs on human cancer cells. She grew the cells in tissue culture, keeping them in test tube flasks, and also made time-lapse movies to show how the cells changed after being given doses of various drugs.

Wright and Plummer hoped to develop a simple test procedure to allow doctors to test different drugs on a few cells from a patient's cancer and pinpoint the most effective drug for that particular patient without having to administer drugs in a hit-or-miss manner. The concept was ambitious and noble. Unfortunately, it was never realized. Their cell experiments could not consistently predict which drug would work for which patient. But their two years of research were not wasted; their experiments helped future researchers better understand the behavior and growth of cancerous cells.

Leaving the Cancer Research Foundation in 1952, Plummer taught at the University of Illinois for two years and then at New York University. There she married Roy Cobb, adding his name to hers, and began to research cells that contain a dark pigment called melanin. Melanin determines human skin color. People with dark skin, such as African Americans, usually have large amounts of melanin in their skin. Skin moles contain concentrations of melanin.

Jewel Cobb found that radiation (including ultraviolet radiation from the sun) damages the nucleic acids in cells, sometimes causing cancer, and that melanin can protect the nucleus of skin cells from radiation damage. She theorized that humans evolved with darker skins in the sunnier areas of the world partly to protect people against skin cancer.

Knowing the value of melanin, Cobb compared normal melanin-containing cells with cells from malignant melanomas, a very serious type of skin cancer that produces dark, melanin-rich tumors. She grew large colonies of both types of cells in her laboratory so that she could study the effects of new chemotherapeutic agents on those cells. She also studied the factors that control cell growth and the relationship of melanin to cell growth. Again, her work produced no major breakthroughs, but did create a large and valuable body of data other researchers are using to further develop her ideas.

Cobb maintained a full teaching load while she conducted research. After teaching for two years at the University of Illinois medical school and six years at New York University, she served as a professor of biology at Sarah Lawrence College for nine years. She then moved into administration. In 1976 she became dean of Douglass College, the women's college of Rutgers University in New Jersey. In 1981, she became the president of California

State University at Fullerton. She was the first African American woman to become president of a major public university on the West Coast.

In all of her administrative positions, Jewell Cobb developed programs to encourage women and minorities to enter the science and medical fields. Even though she retired from the presidency of Fullerton in 1990, she still heads a center that develops pre-college programs aimed at increasing the number of minority students interested in math and science. She firmly believes that "education is still the best pathway" for minorities to achieve equality.

## Key Dates

| | |
|---|---|
| 1924 | Born in Chicago, Illinois, on January 17 |
| 1944 | Received B.A. from Talladega College, Alabama |
| 1947 | Received M.S. from New York University |
| 1950 | Received Ph.D. from New York University |
| 1952–1954 | Taught at University of Illinois medical school |
| 1954–1960 | Taught at New York University medical school |
| 1960–1969 | Worked as professor of biology at Sarah Lawrence College |
| 1969–1976 | Worked as dean and professor of zoology at Connecticut College |
| 1976–1981 | Worked as dean and professor of biological sciences at Douglass College of Rutgers University |
| 1981–1990 | Appointed president of California State University at Fullerton |
| 1990–present | Is emeritus president, professor of biology, and trustee professor at CSU Fullerton |

## Advice

*If you are considering a career in cell biology, Jewel Cobb would advise you to take biology, chemistry, math, and physics courses, as well as specialized courses in genetics and endocrinology. More important, stay focused on what each class is trying to teach you. Do and redo the assignments until you fully understand the principles they demonstrate. Don't be afraid to ask questions, and seek help when you need it. Finally, Cobb would advise you to set your personal and career goals high—higher than you think you have any chance of reaching. Goals are what drive us forward.*

## References

Alberts, Bruce, et al., eds. *Essential Cell Biology: An Introduction to the Molecular Biology of the Cell.* New York: Garland, 1997.

Baserqa, Renato. *The Biology of Cell Reproduction.* Cambridge, Mass.: Harvard University Press, 1985.

Stille, Darlene R. *Extraordinary Women Scientists.* Chicago: Children's Press, 1995.

Thomas, Lewis. *The Lives of a Cell: Notes of a Biology Watcher.* New York: Penguin, 1995. (Collection of well-written, poetical essays on the natural world.)

Yount, Lisa. *American Profiles: Contemporary Women Scientists.* New York: Facts on File, 1994.

# Stanley Cohen

*"Factoring the Growth of Cells"*               Biochemistry

## Career Highlights

- Awarded Nobel Prize for Physiology and Medicine, 1986
- Awarded the Franklin Medal by the Franklin Institute, 1987
- Awarded the National Medal of Science, 1986
- Awarded the Albert Michelson Award by the Association of Science and Industry, 1987
- Awarded the H. P. Robertson Memorial Award of the National Academy of Sciences, 1981

## Important Contributions

We know that plants, animals, and humans grow. But how? What makes the cells divide and specialize? What signals direct that process? These are questions at the very foundation of our understanding of life, questions Stanley Cohen answered.

In his work at Washington University in St. Louis and then at Vanderbilt University in Nashville, Cohen isolated and analyzed two chemical agents that stimulate growth. NGF (nerve growth factor) stimulates growth and development of nerve tissue. EGF (epidermal growth factor) stimulates growth of skin and corneal cells. By isolating these agents and by identifying the chain of nucleic acids that each comprises, he gave medical researchers specific tools to understand and control tissue growth. His 1986 Nobel Prize was awarded "in recognition of his discoveries which are of fundamental importance for our understanding of the mechanisms which regulate cell and organ growth."

## Career Path

It was a bad way to start a life, a way that should have dragged it down rather than lifted it up to scientific heights. Stanley Cohen was born in the Flatbush section of Brooklyn to Russian Jewish immigrants. The family struggled even in good times. During the Great Depression, a period of severe economic hardship that lasted from 1929 to 1935, they barely hung on.

Stanley developed polio as a child and was bedridden for over a year. The disease left him with a permanent limp and also left a profound emotional impact. He increasingly turned inward toward intellectual pursuits. By junior high school he had developed a lasting devotion to science and classical music. He learned the clarinet but knew he didn't have the talent to develop into an orchestral player. That left only science, and the young boy hoped he possessed the classical curiosity of a scientist.

Stanley entered local Brooklyn College, the only school the family could afford. He studied chemistry and zoology, graduating with a B.A. in 1943 and earned a full scholarship to Oberlin College in Ohio for two years of graduate study. In 1945 he graduated with an M.A. in zoology.

Wanting to continue his studies, Cohen sent applications to a number of universities and received an offer to study as a teaching fellow in biochemistry at the University of Michigan at Ann Arbor. He taught and studied for three years and obtained his Ph.D. in 1948. His dissertation was on metabolic functions in earthworms.

Throughout his early days at Ann Arbor, Stanley Cohen had only a vague idea what he wanted to do. His chief interests wavered between zoology and chemistry. Yet neither seemed sufficiently exciting. His only goal had been to create a career in science. Now, he realized, that career needed a focus. By the time he had completed the research for his dissertation, Stanley had ruled out zoology. Animals would not be his focus. Again he seemed left with only one choice. Luckily, chemistry included an idea that tugged at his scientific curiosity: the biochemical study of fundamental metabolism, or growth, in humans.

Cohen spent the next four years in the department of biochemistry and pediatrics at the University of Colorado School of Medicine researching the metabolism of creatinine, a substance found in premature and newborn babies. His work was well regarded, although it produced no significant new findings. It did, however, afford him a chance to concentrate on developing his medical laboratory research techniques.

In 1952, at the age of 30, Cohen transferred to Washington University in St. Louis. Here he split his time between teaching and research that continued to focus on the biochemistry of the growth process. Here he also teamed with

Rita Levi-Montalcini, who was already studying the growth process in nerve cells.

Levi-Montalcini had isolated a substance in mice tumors that could dramatically enhance the growth of the nervous system in chick embryos. She had named the active ingredient in this substance nerve growth factor (NGF). Cohen helped her isolate this growth factor and chemically decoded its atomic structure. After a year of chemical tests and analysis, he was able to identify this growth factor as a protein with looping chains of nucleic acids.

However, the concentrated substance was highly gelatinous and difficult to further separate. Cohen needed to liquefy the goo to continue his investigation of the NGF protein. He added a neural snake venom known to destroy nucleic acids, hoping it would break down the gelatinous bonds. To his surprise, the snake venom showed more NGF activity than had the concentrated NGF extracted from mouse tumors. This discovery shocked the research community, which had believed that NGF was an isolated property of tumors. Now NGF might be anywhere. Research projects were launched at a dozen institutions to locate other sources of NGF. The hunt was on through tissue samples of a limitless variety of creatures.

Three years later, Cohen discovered a rich source of NGF in the salivary glands of adult male mice. He was able to isolate purified samples of NGF, to complete his chemical analysis of this complex substance (it included looped chains of 118 amino acids), and also to develop antibodies to NGF.

This discovery, culled from six years of intense laboratory analysis, was of immense value to neurobiological research because it provided a now well-understood agent to stimulate nerve growth, and one to inhibit it.

In 1959 Cohen was offered a position at Vanderbilt University in Nashville. He planned to continue his growth factor research but also to branch out from his tightly focused study of NGF. He noticed that newborn mice injected with extracts from adult male mouse salivary glands opened their eyes in one week instead of the normal two and developed functioning teeth surprisingly early.

Cohen suspected that another growth factor was at work, since NGF affected only nerve tissue. Unlocking the secrets to physiological development excited him because "we were learning in a few short years how to control and alter a process nature had spent millions of years perfecting."

By the mid-1960s Cohen had isolated a second growth factor that affected epithelial cells (the coverings of internal organs and external body surfaces). He named this new factor epidermal growth factor (EGF). By 1972 he was able to isolate large quantities of EGF and determine its chemical structure—a sequence of 53 amino acids twisted back on itself to form three closed loops. The discovery represented thousands of laboratory hours testing hundreds of different extracts from countless lab specimens. The analysis of EGF's structure represented additional thousands of hours of work in a chemical lab.

Cohen's discovery of EGF opened the floodgates for other researchers to isolate other growth factors and to study the link between growth factors and a variety of diseases. NGF has been shown effective in repairing nerve damage. EGF is effective in healing wounds and also appears to play a significant role in controlling the development of some cancers. The discovery of EGF and NGF earned Cohen the Nobel Prize for Physiology and Medicine in 1986.

Stanley Cohen's work is classed as fundamental research. His discoveries did not directly produce valuable consumer products. Rather, they created the basic understanding other researchers needed to move forward on hundreds of follow-on developments. We now benefit from hundreds of medical techniques and products made possible by this scientist's groundwork. In the future that number will greatly expand. Cures for cancer, the scarring of burn victims, corneal cuts, and a vast range of other ailments will all owe their successful treatment to the careful and diligent fundamental laboratory research of Stanley Cohen.

## Key Dates

| | |
|---|---|
| 1922 | Born in Brooklyn, New York, on November 17 |
| 1943 | Received B.A. from Brooklyn College |
| 1945 | Received M.A. from Oberlin College, Ohio |
| 1946–1948 | Worked as teaching fellow, department of biochemistry, University of Michigan |
| 1948 | Received Ph.D. in biochemistry from University of Michigan |
| 1948–1952 | Worked as instructor at the University of Colorado School of Medicine |
| 1952–1953 | Worked as research fellow, Washington University, St. Louis, Missouri |
| 1953–1959 | Worked as associate professor, Washington University |
| 1959 | Worked as associate professor of biochemistry at Vanderbilt University |

1968–     Works as professor of chemistry, Vanderbilt University
present

1986      Received Nobel Prize for Physiology and Medicine

## Advice

*If you are considering a career in biochemistry, Stanley Cohen would advise you to take as much coursework in chemistry and biology as possible. You can never get too much school or too much practical lab experience. Start with basic physical sciences (physics and chemistry) and with general biology courses. From this foundation build toward specialty courses in areas that interest you.*

*True understanding and discovery take time and great quantities of hands-on work. Learn lab work as well as theoretical work. Don't expect instant answers to fundamental questions. Expect, rather, to spend years nibbling away at the corners of questions trying to gain the first inklings of insights into how the wonders of nature work.*

## References

Alberts, B, ed. *Molecular Biology of the Cell.* New York: Garland, 1983. (Detailed review of cellular biochemistry.)

Cohen, Stanley. *Chemical Mediators of Inflammation and Immunity.* New York: Academic Press, 1986. (Technical description of much of the biochemical work Cohen was involved with.)

Kordon, Claude. *The Language of the Cell.* New York: McGraw-Hill, 1992. (Review of the field of cell management and communication.)

Tanor, Joseph, ed. *McGraw-Hill Modern Men of Science.* New York: McGraw-Hill, 1986. (Strong summary of Cohen's work.)

Wasson, Tyler, ed. *Nobel Prize Winners.* New York: H. W. Wilson, 1987. (Good summary of Cohen's work.)

# Barry Commoner

*"The Paul Revere of Ecology"*

Biology and Ecology

Washington University Photographic Service

## Career Highlights

- Is a "founding father" of the contemporary environmental movement
- Is a fellow of the American Association for the Advancement of Science and was chairman of the committee on science in the promotion of human welfare, 1960–1966
- Won the First International Humanist Award, 1970
- Received the International Prize for Safeguarding the Environment (Italy), 1973

## Important Contributions

Barry Commoner made important contributions to our understanding of viruses and advanced the development of early detection techniques for cancer. But that was only half of his career. Commoner was also one of the "founding fathers" of the environmental movement. He, along with Paul Ehrlich, Jacques Cousteau, Rachel Carson, and others, helped publicize serious ecological problems facing this world—along with recommendations for solving those problems.

## Career Path

During August 1956, only a few summer grad students and faculty populated the Washington University chemistry labs in St. Louis. Banks of overhead fluorescent lights dangled on metal bars. Slow fans moved the muggy air. Hot and stuffy though it was, the faculty liked summer better because they got more research done. Lanky Barry Commoner, wearing a white lab coat and thick-rimmed glasses, and two grad students completed an experiment in a small side lab that held some of the university's most expensive test equipment. The students were chemically testing plant membranes for the presence of TMV, the tobacco mosaic virus. Each student confirmed the presence of high levels of TMV.

With those results, the experiment was completed and declared a success. "Success" meant that three days earlier Barry Commoner had created life. He had not used gigawatt electric generators and lightning bolts. He had not created monstrous humanoids, or even the precursors of humans. He chemically recombined select proteins with RNA (two lifeless organic chemical chains) to create a simple tobacco virus. But he had created a virile, active virus that had successfully invaded two test plants. He had created life. Interestingly, creating life—as monumental as that might seem—was not this man's goal. It was only one step toward understanding human viral infections like encephalitis and hepatitis.

Barry Commoner grew up a city boy in Brooklyn, New York, but he loved nature and spent much of his free time roaming through parks collecting specimens to study under his boyhood microscope. His was not an easy childhood. His parents lost their savings during the Great Depression, a period of severe economic hardship in the 1930s, and his father (a tailor) had to stop working when he went blind.

After graduating from high school, Barry enrolled at Columbia University. He only had enough money for one semester; after that, he had to work his way through college, struggling to earn enough to pay for every class and book as he went. He graduated from Columbia in 1937 and transferred to Harvard on a fellowship. There he received a Ph.D. in biology in 1941. During World War II, he served in the U.S. Navy, attaining the rank of lieutenant. After the war, he joined the faculty of Washington University in St. Louis as an associate professor of physiology, where he taught until 1981.

Most of Commoner's early research focused on viruses, especially TMV. His early experiments indicated that TMV is, basically, a parasite that multiplies when injected into a healthy plant by appropriating the synthesizing mechanism of the host plant. For these findings, he was awarded the Newcomb Cleveland Prize, given annually to a young scientist who makes an outstanding contribution in the field of science.

Commoner believed that by understanding a virus like TMV he could come to understand more complicated and serious viral diseases such as encephalitis and hepatitis. In 1955, he succeeded in separating the basic components of TMV: proteins and ribonucleic acid (RNA). He found that RNA influenced reproduction in the cell and transmitted the cell's chemistry to successive generations. When he successfully recombined these lifeless components in the summer of 1956, he made compounds that were alive, infectious, and similar to the original virus. This led to his suggestion that the proper synthesis of protein and nucleic acid would form artificial hybrids that could form protective antibodies in humans and aid in immunization.

By the late 1950s and early 1960s, Commoner had formed a collaboration with Dr. George E. Pake, a physicist, to test a hypothesis advanced in 1930 by Leonor Michaelis that the oxidation of one organic compound by another involved a flow of electrons, moving at fantastic speeds, singly instead of in pairs, from one molecule to the next. Molecules containing these unpaired electrons are called free radicals. Commoner believed that free radicals released the energy for cell metabolism. His experiments with free radicals indicated that they were present in cells and played an important role in cell functions.

To study free radicals more clearly, Commoner asked physicist Dr. Jonathan Townsend to join them and build a highly sensitive electron spin resonance spectrometer (ESR) that would respond to very small amounts of free radicals in living cells. In 1954, the team detected the presence of free radicals in living tissue and verified that these molecules played a role in the transfer of energy in plant and animal cells. Later, the team demonstrated that free radicals were involved in photosynthesis.

In 1965, Commoner's research team found that cancer in laboratory rats was indicated by the presence of abnormal free radicals. In 1969, his team discovered free radicals in cancerous tissue samples, an important step in the development of early detection techniques for cancer.

In later years, Commoner turned his attention to ecology. He felt that scientists had a moral obligation to keep people well informed of the dangers that technology and science could pose to humankind's habitat. He helped found the St. Louis Committee for Nuclear Information and served as its president from 1958 to 1965. The committee helped promote the nuclear test-ban treaty of 1963.

Barry Commoner especially concerned himself with the pollution of air and water by excessive use of chemical fertilizers, detergents, insecticides, and other harmful substances. "There is now simply not enough air, water, and soil on earth to absorb man-made poisons without effect," he said, as quoted in *Time* (August 15, 1968). "If we continue in our reckless way, this planet before long will become an unsuitable place for human habitation."

In 1970 at a meeting of the American Association for the Advancement of Science, Commoner warned that by the year 2000, the world would contain between six and eight billion people (he was right), and he warned that that was the maximum number of people its food system could support. His belief in the seriousness of the problems of overpopulation and pollution—and the inability of our politicians to address the problems—even led him to run (unsuccessfully) for president of the United States in 1980.

## Key Dates

| | |
|---|---|
| 1917 | Born in Brooklyn, New York, on May 28 |
| 1933 | Graduated from James Madison High School; entered Columbia University |
| 1937 | Received B.A. in zoology with honors from Columbia; entered Harvard University |
| 1940–1942 | Taught biology at Queens College in New York City |
| 1941 | Received Ph.D. in cellular physiology from Harvard |
| 1942 | Entered the United States Naval Reserve |
| 1946–1947 | Worked as associate editor with *Science Illustrated* |
| 1947–1981 | Worked as associate professor of physiology at Washington University in St. Louis (promoted to full professor in 1953) |
| 1965–1969 | Served as chairman of botany department at Washington University |

1966    Served as director of Washington University's Center for the Biology of Natural Systems; published *Science and Survival*

1972    Worked as professor at Colgate University

1980    Ran for president on his own ticket, the Citizens Party

1981    Accepted a position at Queens College

1988    Worked as professor at St. Lawrence University

1992–present    Works as professor at Connecticut College

# Advice

*Biology is a wide and diverse field. Barry Commoner would advise anyone planning to enter the field to begin with a wide overview of biology and related fields before deciding to specialize. Also study technology and resource economics because those forces have the greatest impact on biology in modern times. Finally, include advanced studies of ecology so that you gain an understanding of living organisms within the context of their physical and chemical environments.*

# References

Caldwell, Lynton Keith. *Between Two Worlds: Science, the Environmental Movement, and Policy Choice.* Cambridge Studies in Environmental Policy. Cambridge, England: Cambridge University Press, 1992. (An integrated analysis of science, the environmental movement, and public policy; reveals the interactive roles of environmentalism and science in policy generation.)

Chisholm, Anne. *Philosophers of the Earth.* New York: Dutton, 1972.

Commoner, Barry. *Making Peace with the Planet.* San Francisco: New Press, Peter Smith Publications, 1992.

———. *The Politics of Energy.* New York: Alfred A. Knopf, 1979.

———. *Science and Survival.* New York: Viking Press, 1966.

DeLeon, David. "Barry Commoner," in *Leaders from the 1960s.* Westport, Conn.: Greenwood, 1990.

Stefoff, Rebecca. *The American Environmental Movement.* Social Reform Movements. New York: Facts on File, 1995. (Good discussion of prominent figures and incidents in the environmental movement.)

Strong, Dennis H. *Dreamers and Defenders: American Conservationists.* 2d ed. Lincoln: University of Nebraska Press, 1988: 221–245.

# Gerty Radnitz Cori

## *"Lifting Nature's Veil"*     Biochemistry

Copyright © The Nobel Foundation

## Career Highlights

- Was first American woman to win the Nobel Prize for Medicine or Physiology, 1947
- Discovered the chemical structure of glycogen and identified the biochemical defects that cause glycogen-storage disease
- Received the Garvan Medal of the American Chemical Society, 1948
- Elected to the National Academy of Sciences

## Important Contributions

Gerty Cori, together with her husband, Carl Cori, laid the foundation for our understanding of how cells use food and convert it into energy. They were pioneers in the fields of enzyme and hormone studies, and their discoveries greatly increased our understanding of diabetes and diseases caused by enzyme deficiencies.

The work they started continues; their lab has produced eight Nobel Prize-winning scientists, including the Coris themselves.

## Career Path

Family collaboration. America seemed to be obsessed with preventing family collaboration. By 1930 Gerty Cori hated the sound of those words almost as much as she had hated the sound of the word antisemitism in the early 1920s while still living in Austria. Gerty had the necessary education, she had excellent technical skills in the lab, she had valuable ideas, and she had produced important results in the lab. Yet, just because she and her husband were in the same field, because they preferred working together on research projects, the hated words, family collaboration, were whispered behind their backs while heads wagged and faces sneered.

Lab administrators said it was un-American for a woman to work with her husband and take a job that another man could use to support a family. University officials warned that she was holding back her husband's advancement by insisting on working with him. Lucrative offers arrived for her husband with the proviso that he stop working with his wife. But Gerty Cori knew they were engaged in important work and that they did it better when they did it together. She would not quietly withdraw from the work she loved and did so well.

Gerty Radnitz had been raised in Prague and educated by tutors until she went to a private girls' school at age 10. At age 16, she decided to study medicine, being influenced by an uncle who was a professor of pediatrics. Because she lacked the necessary training in mathematics and Latin, she enrolled at the *Realgymnasium* in Tetschen. In two years, she completed eight years of Latin and five years of mathematics, physics, and chemistry. She then took and passed the entrance examinations to the Medical School of the German University of Prague.

In medical school, Gerty met her husband-to-be and lifelong career partner, Carl Cori. They were married in 1920, the year they both graduated with their doctorates, and she added his name to hers.

For two years Gerty Cori worked at the Karolinen Children's Hospital in Vienna, where the quality of the food was so poor that she developed a vitamin A deficiency. The atmosphere in Vienna—indeed in most of Europe—was growing increasingly hostile. When the Coris became convinced that the increase of antisemitism would soon put Europe into another war, they decided to leave.

Carl accepted a position at the New York State Institute for the Study of Malignant Diseases in Buffalo. Gerty did not join him for six more months, until he had secured a position for her as an assistant pathologist at the Institute.

For their first few years in Buffalo, they were free to study what they wished, and Gerty focused on the effects of X-rays on the skin and on the metabolism of body organs. Then the Coris became interested in how human bodies send energy from one place to another. Very little was known about how a body maintained a constant supply of energy. Scientists knew that the liver and the muscles contained a starch-like substance called glycogen, "the sugar maker." But what scientists didn't understand—and what the Coris discovered—was the role glycogen played in providing usable energy.

The research pair tracked tiny amounts of sugar, glycogen, and two controlling hormones in lab animals. After six years of research, they were able to explain how mammals get their energy for heavy exercise. Energy moves in a cycle from muscle to liver then back to muscle again. During a burst of exercise, glycogen in muscles is converted to sugar, which the muscles use as energy. However, some energy is left unused in the form of lactic acid. Lactic acid is sent to the liver where, with oxygen from panting, it is converted back into sugar. Sugar returns to the muscle where it is converted back into glycogen for storage. They called this process "the cycle of carbohydrates," but everyone else called it "The Cori Cycle," and it had a major effect on the treatment of diabetes.

In 1931, the Washington University School of Medicine in St. Louis, Missouri offered Carl a professorship. They grudgingly offered Gerty a position as a mere "lab technician." Despite the fact that she was considered the "lab genius," many of the job offers that came to Carl pointedly omitted Gerty. The pair accepted the offer from St. Louis because they were ready to leave the cancer center, and it was the only offer that had included Gerty.

At Washington University, the Coris continued their metabolic studies, focusing on enzymes and sugar metabolism. At one point, in what they hoped would illuminate the biochemical changes glycogen and glucose went through in the carbohydrate cycle, they chopped up some frog muscle tissue, rinsed it with distilled water, and studied the biochemicals that remained. They found new enzymes and a compound of glucose, which they called *Cori ester.*

This *Cori ester* later enabled them to make one of their most important discoveries. In the late 1930s, they found that an enzyme called phosphorylase converts glycogen to glucose and back again. When they mixed *Cori ester* with phosphorylase, they were able to create the first synthesis of glycogen in the test tube.

For their studies on the role and formation of glycogen, the Coris won the Nobel Prize for Medicine in 1947. That same year, Gerty was finally offered a teaching position instead of the meagerly paid lab technician position she had previously held. Hugo Theorell, upon presenting them with their Nobel Prize, stated that their astonishing feat of synthesizing glycogen in a test tube is "one of the most brilliant achievements of modern biochemistry."

The year the Coris won the Nobel Prize brought the best news and the worst: they were notified of winning the Nobel, and they were notified that Gerty was suffering from a fatal type of anemia. (Later, scientists speculated that the work she had done with X-rays may have caused her illness.) She lived and worked for 10 more years, finally succumbing to the disease on October 26, 1957, when she died at home, alone with Carl.

## Key Dates

| | |
|---|---|
| 1896 | Born in Prague, Austria (now The Czech Republic), August 15 |
| 1920 | Received M.D. from German University; married Carl Cori |
| 1920–1922 | Moved to Vienna and worked as an assistant at the Karolinen Children's Hospital |
| 1922–1925 | Worked as an assistant pathologist at the Institute for the Study of Malignant Diseases, Buffalo, New York |
| 1925–1931 | Worked as assistant biochemist at the Institute |
| 1931–1943 | Moved to St. Louis to work as lab technician in pharmacology at the Washington University School of Medicine |
| 1943–1947 | Worked as research associate of biochemistry at Washington University |
| 1947 | Worked as full professor at Washington University |
| 1957 | Died October 26 in Missouri |

## Advice

*Friends said that Gerty Cori loved her work with an emotional intensity that was almost stunning. Gerty herself once described the rewards she found in her work: "For a research worker, the unforgotten moments of his life are those rare ones, which come after years of plodding work, when the veil over nature's secret seems suddenly to lift and when what is dark and chaotic appears in a clear and beautiful light and pattern." Cori would advise anyone considering chemical research to bring abundant and intense enthusiasm and energy. Then apply that energy to every class and project. You never know which will later be the most important in defining your career. Don't wait for your junior and senior years to take lab classes. Take them early and take as many as you can, even if you have to audit some. There is no substitute for excellent lab technique.*

## References

Gilbert, Hiram F. *Basic Concepts in Biochemistry: A Student's Survival Guide.* New York: McGraw-Hill, 1991.

McGrayne, Sharon Bertsch. *Nobel Prize Women in Science: Their Lives, Struggles, and Momentous Discoveries.* New York: Carol Publishing, A Birch Lane Press Book, 1993.

Stille, Darlene R. *Extraordinary Women Scientists.* Chicago: Children's Press, 1995.

Stryer, Lubert. *Biochemistry.* 4th ed. New York: W. H. Freeman, 1995. (Comprehensive but difficult reading.)

Yost, Edna. *Women of Modern Science.* Westport, Conn.: Greenwood, 1984.

# Jacques Cousteau

*"Studying the Drowned Museum"*　　　Marine Biology

## Career Highlights

- Was world's best-known aquatic explorer
- Invented the Aqua-Lung and developed a one-man jet-propelled submarine
- Created the Conshelf I, II, and III (the first manned undersea colonies)
- Awarded the Medal of Freedom by the United States, 1985

## Important Contributions

Two-thirds of our planet is underwater and, before Jacques Cousteau came along, it was unviewable, unknowable. Cousteau changed all that by introducing the world to the marvels of what lay beneath the seas. He made tremendous technological advancements in underwater exploration (such as inventing the Aqua-Lung, or SCUBA), but he will be most remembered for bringing the oceans into our living rooms.

## Career Path

In March 1936, a sullen 26-year-old French naval officer waded into the turquoise waters of the small Mediterranean bay at Toulon, France, just 30 kilometers east of Marseilles. Knee-high waves lapped at the shore and sighed as they washed across the beach. The man scowled as he rubbed his thin, stiff arms. He felt that his career and his useful life were over.

The man had been assigned to this dead-end naval post to recover, but he was tired of recovering from handicaps. He had been sickly as a youth, and doctors had warned him not to engage in strenuous activity. But he overcame his weakness by learning to swim. He had a hard time in school and was expelled for throwing rocks and breaking 17 school windows. But he overcame his problems and not only qualified to enter the French Naval Academy, but graduated second in his class. He was less than a week from graduating from Navy flight school when an auto accident broke both his arms. When the casts finally came off, his arms were stiff, thin, and weak. He was assigned to Toulon to recover, but he knew that he would never fly nor advance into Naval command.

After a final stretch, the man adjusted the straps on his new underwater goggles. He had seen island pearl divers use them when his sea duty took him through the South Pacific. He thought they might keep his eyes from stinging while he swam to recuperate, so he had ordered a pair. He took a breath and dove forward to begin his exercise swim. An hour later this same man emerged from the warm Mediterranean, exhilarated, amazed, and with a new, radiant purpose to his life.

The man was Jacques Cousteau. His new purpose was to explore the wondrous and hidden realm beneath the sea. Those goggles gave him his first magical glimpse of the mysterious underwater world. He later wrote, "I was astounded by what I saw. . . . I was in a jungle never seen by those who floated on the opaque roof. Sometimes we are lucky enough to know that our lives have been changed, to discard the old, embrace the new, and run headlong down an immutable course. It happened to me at [Toulon] on that summer's day, when my eyes were opened on the sea."

Jacques Cousteau brought a flare for engineering and design as well as new-found enthusiasm to his underwater studies. At 11 years of age, he had built a four-foot working model of a 200-ton marine crane. Two years later, he built a three-foot battery-powered automobile. He majored in engineering in college and at the Naval Academy.

Cousteau's engineering skills were essential, because in those days, methods of underwater exploration were quite limited. The only alternative to skin diving, helmet or "hard-hat" diving, was clumsy and awkward. Divers were attached to a ship with an air hose like an umbilical cord; they wore heavy copper helmets and were weighted down with lead-soled boots. Cousteau wanted to find a way to dive underwater and stay submerged for long periods of time without all the encumbrances of helmet diving.

In 1939, World War II interrupted his work. Yet even as he served as a gunnery officer during the war, he focused much of his energies on the world beneath the sea. He made his first two underwater films during this time and continued his work to find a way to breathe underwater.

Cousteau knew what he wanted: self-contained, compressed-air cylinders with a valve that would feed air on the inhale and at the ambient pressure of the surrounding sea, and which would then shut off the flow of air on the exhale. Such a valve just didn't exist.

In 1942, Cousteau brought his idea to engineer Emile Gagnon, who showed him a Bakelite valve and said, "Something like this?" Cousteau was astonished—it was exactly what he needed.

Together they worked on the design and created a spring-loaded diaphragm open to the sea. The diaphragm regulator ensured that air would always be delivered at a pressure equal to the surrounding water so that the diver could breathe comfortably. He called his invention the Aqua-Lung (the United States Navy would later call it SCUBA: self-contained underwater breathing apparatus). When he tested the Aqua-Lung in 1943 in the French Riviera, it worked! His dream of flying free under water had materialized. He could swim horizontally like a fish, weightless, easily maneuvering in all directions. It was an epic-making invention that redefined how we could explore our world.

In 1944 Cousteau then founded and became head of the Undersea Research Group, which cleared Mediterranean ports of German mines after the war. He prepared underwater films that showed the processes of laying mines and firing torpedoes. He studied the effect of underwater explosions and even helped recover art treasures from a Roman vessel sunk in 100 feet of water off the Tunisian coast. While engaged on this work, Cousteau improved and perfected his techniques and equipment.

In 1950, Cousteau acquired *Calypso,* a 360-ton YMS-class minesweeper, and converted it into a well-equipped, oceanographic research vessel. He produced the world's first color film at a depth of 150 feet underwater. In 1956, after a four-year oceanographic expedition, he took a picture of the ocean bottom at a depth of four and one-half miles. He wrote of these experiences in his book *The Silent World* (1953), which became an instant hit, selling 5,000,000 copies. His film by the same name won the Grand Prize at the Cannes Film Festival in 1956 and an academy award in 1957.

In 1957, Cousteau directed the Conshelf Saturation Dive Program, in which people lived and worked for extended periods underwater along the continental shelves. He even envisioned semi-permanent stations, where people could live indefinitely underwater.

By 1960, Cousteau realized that the quality of the earth's oceans had dramatically decreased in the years that he had been studying the "drowned museum." Once clear waters were now murky. Once richly laden ocean bottoms were now devoid of life. Cousteau the explorer then became Cousteau the environmentalist. He used his fame and influence to protect and preserve the ecology of the world's oceans. He began educating the world, for he believed people would be incapable of destroying that which they loved. In 1968, the first of over 50 television films about his work appeared on ABC-TV. "The Undersea World of Jacques Cousteau" would become the highest-rated documentary series in broadcasting history.

Until his death in 1997, Jacques Cousteau used his platform as the world's best-known underwater explorer to lobby for greater awareness of the ecological problems facing the world's oceans.

## Key Dates

| | |
|---|---|
| 1910 | Born in Saint André-de-Cubza, France, on June 11 |
| 1930 | Graduated from the College Stanislas in Paris; entered Brest Naval Aacademy |
| 1933 | Graduated from Brest Naval Academy |
| 1942 | Developed the Aqua-Lung |
| 1944–1945 | Set up Underwater Research Group in Toulon |
| 1950 | Purchased and equipped *Calypso* |
| 1951 | Created the Centre d'Etudes Marines Avancees, a company designed to develop underwater equipment |
| 1953 | Published *The Silent World* |
| 1957 | Became director of the Oceanographic Museum at Monaco |
| 1959 | Invented the Diving Saucer, a highly maneuverable submarine |
| 1960 | Was influential in preventing French atomic wastes being dumped into the Mediterranean Sea |
| 1962 | Developed the Conshelf experiments |
| 1968 | Broadcast his first television film on ABC-TV |
| 1973 | Founded the Cousteau Society |
| 1997 | Died in Paris on June 25 |

## Advice

Jacques Cousteau's formal schooling was in engineering. Marine biology was, for him, a self-taught subject. From his own experience, Cousteau would advise you to do three things: (1) include general engineering courses in your oceanographic studies; (2) study physical and chemical oceanography as intently as biological oceanography, because these three fields are tightly interrelated; and (3) don't wait for college to become familiar with the marine environment. Oceans are not discovered through books and lectures, but through swimming, snorkeling, and diving in the sea. Experience the sea as often, as early, and as deeply as possible. Then academic learning will have more meaning and value.

## References

Cousteau, Jacques. *The Silent World.* New York: Harper & Brothers, 1953.

Cousteau, Jacques, and James Dugan. *The Living Sea.* New York: Harper & Row, 1962.

Dugan, James. *Undersea Explorer: The Story of Captain Cousteau.* New York: HarperCollins, 1957.

Guberlet, Muriel L. *Explorers of the Sea: Famous Oceanographic Expeditions.* Ann Arbor, Mich.: Books on Demand, 1984.

Madsen, Axel. *Cousteau: An Unauthorized Biography.* New York: Beaufort Books, 1987.

# Francis Crick

*"The Most Significant Discovery of the Century"*

Molecular Biology

## Career Highlights

- Awarded the Nobel Prize for Medicine (shared with James Watson), 1962
- Awarded Royal Medal by the Royal Society of England, 1972
- Voted foreign member, American National Academy of Sciences, 1969
- Voted honorary member, American Academy of Arts and Sciences, 1972

## Important Contributions

British biochemist Francis Crick, and his American partner, James Watson, created the first accurate model of the molecular structure of deoxyribonucleic acid, or DNA, the master code to heredity in all living organisms. That discovery has been called by many "the most significant discovery of the century."

Francis Crick also made important discoveries about the genetic code carried by the DNA molecule. He identified the molecule, called transfer RNA, by which genetic direction is communicated by the DNA molecule. He formulated the central dogma of molecular genetics: the passage of genetic information is from DNA to RNA to protein.

Crick's discoveries relating to DNA structure and function reshaped the study of genetics, virtually created the field of molecular biology, and gave new direction to a host of endeavors in various fields of medicine.

## Career Path

The room looked like a tinker toy party gone berserk, like the play room of over-active second grade boys. Complex mobiles of wire, colored beads, strips of sheet metal, cardboard cutouts, wooden dowels, and wooden balls dangled from the ceiling like a forest of psychedelic stalactites slowly twirling in the breeze from the fan. Construction supplies, scissors, and tin snips were strewn about the desks and floor, as were pages of complex equations, stacks of scientific papers, and photographic sheets of fuzzy X-ray crystallography images.

The room was really a second-floor office shared by graduate students Francis Crick and James Watson in a 300-year-old building on the campus of Cambridge University. The mobiles were not the idle toys of students with too much free time. Rather, they were a frantic effort to win the worldwide race to unravel the very core of life and decipher the shape of the DNA molecule. For Watson, it was a minor sidelight to his biology focus. For Crick, this race represented the culmination of his core beliefs.

Always described as an "inquisitive lad," Francis Crick was fascinated by science topics and decided early to pursue "one of the sciences." He entered University College in London and received a B.S. in physics in 1937. He stayed at the graduate school of University College for an M.S. in physics, which he received in 1939.

England was then deeply involved in World War II. Crick joined a team of scientists at the Admiralty Research Laboratory and was assigned to the mine design department. He spent the war designing new ocean mines powerful enough to destroy German warships and sophisticated enough to avoid detection.

In the summer of 1944, Crick read a book at his desk at the Admiralty Lab, titled *What is Life?*, written by a German physicist, Erwin Schroedinger. In it Schroedinger postulated that the basic principles of biology could be analyzed in the precise terms of physics and chemistry.

Schroedinger's theories appealed to Crick in part because of his physics orientation and, in part, because of his atheistic beliefs. He thought it a foolish illusion to believe that life was a divine gift that could not be explained by physical laws. The idea of disproving that belief greatly appealed to him and turned his interest toward the emerging field of molecular biology, which used insights gained from physics and chemistry to probe the fundamental structures of living organisms. He applied for a position at the Medical Research Council at Cambridge University, stating that his specific area of interest was "the dividing line between living and non-living."

In 1949 Crick accepted a research position at the Cavendish Laboratory, Cambridge University, while he continued his studies. By this time biochemists had already deduced that DNA in a cell's nucleus carried genetic information. The key mystery was how the huge DNA molecule reproduces itself to physically pass this information to a new cell, a new organism, and a new generation. The most popular theory was that protein molecules held the key to this understanding. Crick believed that the DNA molecule, itself, held the key.

At Cambridge, he teamed up with American biologist James Watson. The two found that they had a great intellectual affinity and agreed to pool their efforts to construct a model of the DNA molecule while they pursued their separate studies and thesis research.

By 1951 bits and pieces of information about the DNA molecule were emerging from across the globe. Erwin Chargaff discovered that a definite ratio of nucleotide sequences could be detected in the DNA bases, suggesting a paired relationship. Oswald Avery conducted experiments on bacteria DNA showing that DNA carried genetic information. Linus Pauling conceptualized the alpha helix configuration for certain polypeptide chains of proteins. Finally, Rosalind Franklin used X-ray crystallography to create two-dimensional images of the DNA molecule, which were critically important to Crick's development.

Crick and Watson attempted to combine these disparate clues into a single physical structure. Using bits of wire, colored beads, sheet metal, and cardboard cutouts, the two scientists hung possible spiral models across their shared office. They correctly surmised that a linking chain of sugar and phosphate formed the backbone of the DNA spiral. They correctly linked base pairs of peptides. Still the model did not fit with available atomic data.

It was not until early 1953 that stolen X-rays of Rosalind Franklin's latest work allowed Crick to hit upon the idea of a "double helix," two intertwined spiral chains, like a spiral staircase with hydrogen bonds between paired nitrogen bases as steps. Upon viewing the double helix model hanging from ceiling to floor of their office, Watson quipped, "It was too pretty not to be true."

The discovery of the structure of DNA earned Crick and Watson instant worldwide recognition and a Nobel Prize. Crick completed his Ph.D. work in 1953, and then continued to study the DNA molecule and the chemical mechanisms it uses to exert its genetic will over each cell in the body for an additional 18 years. During that time he made at least four additional important discoveries, including an identification of the genetic codes that control the synthesis of proteins, the cellular compounds responsible for basic biological functions.

In 1971, at the age of 61, Crick accepted a position at the Salk Institute in San Diego, California, to allow him to shift his research focus to two new fields that had always fascinated him: brain research and the origins of life.

He developed the theory, presented in his second book, *Life Itself,* that life in the form of microscopic organisms had to have been sent to, or placed on, earth by some advanced extraterrestrial civilization. DNA was too complex to have any reasonable probability of developing on its own.

Francis Crick combined the luck of finding himself in the right field at the right time with the insight and tenacity to fit the jigsaw pieces into a unified whole image and make the phenomenal discovery of DNA structure. That one discovery has had an impact on the fields of biology similar to the impact on physics created by Einstein's theory of relativity. Molecular biology has been forever changed by his work.

## Key Dates

| | |
|---|---|
| 1916 | Born in Northampton, England, on June 8 |
| 1937 | Received B.S. in physics from University College, London |
| 1939 | Received M.S. from University College |
| 1940 | Worked as research scientist for British Admiralty |
| 1947 | Was graduate student at Strangeways Research Laboratory, Cambridge, England |
| 1949 | Shifted to the Cavendish Laboratory, Cambridge University |
| 1953 | Discovered the DNA double helix; received Ph.D. from Cambridge University |
| 1962 | Won Nobel Prize for Medicine |
| 1977 | Accepted professorship at Salk Institute in San Diego, California |
| 1984–present | Retired |

# Advice

*If you are considering a career in molecular biology, Francis Crick would advise you to combine related fields in your studies. Don't over-specialize. Many fields relate to each other and can contribute to understanding in any one field. Start with a broad base: physics, chemistry, organic chemistry, and biology. Then pick several related fields to specialize in. Search for connections between fields and for ways in which knowledge of other fields can further the study of your own specialty.*

# References

Crick, Francis. *Life Itself: Its Origins and Nature.* New York: Simon & Shuster, 1981. (Crick's novel theories on the origins of life on earth.)

———. *Of Molecules and Men.* Washington, D.C.: Washington University Press, 1966. (Autobiographical review of the discovery of the structure and function of the DNA molecule.)

Judson, Horace. *The Eighth Day of Creation: Makers of the Revolution in Biology.* London: S & S Trade Books, 1979. (Discoveries in molecular biology from 1930 to 1970.)

More, Ruth. *The Coil of Life: The Story of the Great Discoveries of the Life Sciences.* New York: Alfred A. Knopf, 1961. (Discusses the discoveries related to the chemical basis of heredity. Includes sections on Crick.)

Olby, Robert. *The Path to the Double Helix.* Seattle: University of Washington Press, 1984. (History of molecular biology.)

Watson, James. *The Double Helix: A Personal Account of the Discovery of the Structure of DNA.* New York: Atheneum, 1985. (Autobiographical account by Crick's partner.)

# Marie Curie

*"A New Age of Science"*

Physics and
Radiochemistry

## Career Highlights

Courtesy of the Archives, California Institute of Technology

- Was first to identify that smaller particles existed within an atom and thus opened the door to the atomic age
- Discovered radium and polonium
- Awarded Nobel Prize for Physics, 1903
- Awarded Nobel Prize for Chemistry, 1911

## Important Contributions

Marie Curie's discovery of two naturally radioactive elements, polonium and radium, made headline news, but her real discovery was that radioactivity had to be the result of something happening within the atom itself. She discovered that atoms were not small solid balls and that there must be even smaller particles inside them. This opened the door to all atomic research and even to the splitting of the atom.

Curie carried out her research in appalling conditions, with little or no physical comforts and a never-ending lack of money and recognition, and she worked hands-on with radioactive elements at a time when the dangers of radioactivity were not understood, so that she suffered from ill-health (radiation sickness) for most of her adult life. Indeed, for many years after her death, her notebooks and seat were still highly radioactive. For her pains and efforts, Marie Curie won two Nobel Prizes and opened the door to a "New Age of Science," the nuclear age.

# Career Path

As a gray Paris afternoon faded into damp February twilight in 1901, a growing line of eager university professors and students once again snaked across the frozen campus grass. Was it dark enough yet? Could the daily tour begin?

At the front of this expectant line stood a dumpy, dilapidated shack. For three years it had been the laboratory of graduate student Marie Curie and her professor husband, Pierre. Everyone at the university knew by now that Marie had found some new metal. And this metal glowed—all on its own, even at night, a soft, ethereal, fairy-like glow. She had hung test tubes of the stuff from the ceiling of her shack to brighten it up.

As darkness fell each evening, an anxious procession of visitors marched through the shack, faces and hands bathed in warm pastel glows from the radium and polonium salts. Yellow from one test tube, a faint pink from the next, luminescent green from a third. Gasps of wonder and delight rose from each person passing slowly through the shed in enchanted awe as Marie and Pierre stood proudly by the door. No one knew that the glowing light she had found was concentrated, deadly radioactivity.

Marya Sklodowska was born in 1867 in Warsaw, Poland (she changed her name to "Marie" as a student in France). In a locked glass-fronted cabinet in the parlor, her father kept various instruments of physics—pipes, tubes, crystals, scales—all of which fascinated the young girl and helped develop her passion for studying physics. From her father, Marie inherited logic and precision; from her mother she inherited a sense of duty, honor, the virtue of hard work, and the ability to make a little go a long way.

All of her siblings were smart, but Marie was especially brilliant. She read fluently at age four and was always at the top of her class in school, even though the Russian professors at her secondary school treated Polish students as enemies. Because no Polish universities accepted women, she wanted to go abroad for higher education to the Sorbonne University in Paris, which did accept women, but her family could not afford to send her.

Marie and her sister decided they would support each other through school. Marie would work as a governess to support her sister Bronya while Bronya studied medicine in Paris. When Bronya qualified as a doctor, she could support Marie while she studied science.

For three years Marie supported Bronya. Then Bronya married and left Marie to support herself through school. When she finally made it to Paris in 1891, Marie found herself a cheap attic room near the university, where she did nothing but study and sleep. She often forgot to eat. She was very frugal, yet still had difficulty surviving; sometimes she had to choose between food and warmth. But her perseverance paid off. When she took exams for her master's degree in physics in the summer of 1893, she was first in the class. The next year, she took a second degree, in mathematics.

In 1894 Marie met Pierre Curie, the laboratory director of the Municipal School of Industrial Physics and Chemistry in Paris. She was immediately charmed by this idealistic dreamer who spoke mesmerizingly about physics and social issues. She gave him her address the day they met (considered shocking at the time), and in 1895 they were married without rings, blessings, or priests.

Two years after their marriage, right after their daughter Irene was born, Marie Curie decided to complete her doctoral dissertation in a totally new field: radiation. Scientists knew that electrically charged radiation flooded the air around uranium, but not much else was known. She used a device Pierre had invented to detect electric charges around mineral samples. She named this process radioactivity and concluded that it was emitted from inside a uranium atom.

This so intrigued Pierre that he dropped his own projects and began to work exclusively with his wife. For their laboratory, the Curies used an abandoned wooden shed, which had been a dissecting room for the medical school but was in such a state of disrepair that no one even considered it fit for cadavers. It was unbearably hot in the summer and freezing cold in the winter, with a few wooden tables and chairs and a rusty stove.

In 1898, Madame Curie was given a puzzling uranium mineral ore called pitchblende, which her tests showed gave off more radioactive emissions than expected from the amount of uranium it contained. She concluded that there must be another substance inside pitchblende that gave off the extra radiation. Since chemists had analyzed pitchblende but missed this, she concluded it had to be something present only in tiny amounts but with enormous energy.

Marie began each test of the substance with three and one-half ounces of pitchblende—she planned to remove all of the known metals so that ultimately all that would be left would be this new, highly active element. She ground the ore with mortar and pestle, passed it through a sieve, dissolved it in acid, boiled off the liquid, filtered it, distilled it, then electrolyzed it. Oddly, each time she removed more of the known elements, what was left was always *more* active than before.

It took four years, but, finally, in March 1902, she produced a tiny sample of pure radium salt. It weighed .0035 ounces—less than the weight of a potato chip—but it was a million times more radioactive than uranium!

In the dark, with a light rain pattering onto the roof, the Curies stood in their shed, silently gazing in amazement at the softly glowing radium they had discovered. It was beautiful! It brought a catch to Marie's throat, and she later commented that she was "stirred with new emotion and enchantment" as she gazed at the glowing tube of pure radium salt. This discovery of the subatomic world merited the 1903 Nobel Prize for Physics.

Because the dangers of radiation were not yet understood, the two scientists took no precautions and were plagued with health troubles. Aches and pains. Ulcer-covered hands. Continuous bouts of serious illnesses like pneumonia. Never-ending exhaustion. Still, they refused to believe that their ill health came from anything except working so many hours on their research.

Finally, the radiation she had studied all her life killed Marie Curie. But Marie Curie's studies rank as one of the great turning points of science. Just as Newton and Einstein changed the direction and focus of physics with their theories, so, too, did Marie Curie. Physics after her was completely different than before and focused on the undiscovered subatomic world. She cracked open a door that penetrated inside the atom and has led to most of the greatest advances of twentieth-century science.

## Key Dates

| | |
|---|---|
| 1867 | Born in Warsaw, Poland, on November 7 |
| 1893 | Received M.S in physics from the Sorbonne University |
| 1894 | Received degree in mathematics |
| 1901 | Discovered radium, her second new element |
| 1903 | Awarded Doctor of Science, the first woman in Europe to receive such a degree |
| 1903 | Awarded Nobel Prize for Physics |
| 1906 | Took over Pierre's work at the Sorbonne after he was killed by a heavy horsedrawn cart; became first woman ever to teach there |
| 1911 | Awarded Nobel Prize for Chemistry for discovery of radium and polonium; first time anyone had won two Nobel prizes |
| 1934 | Died July 6 |

## Advice

*Marie Curie believed in "hands-on" science. She was not a theoretician, but an experimenter. If you are considering a career in physics, Marie Curie would encourage you to adopt a similar outlook. On your own, learn to carefully and critically observe everything. Perfect experimental technique. Nothing is proven until substantiated experimental results are obtained. Look for physics and chemistry courses that emphasize experimentation and lab work. Let them and math be the backbone of your studies.*

## References

Boorse, Henry, and Lloyd Motz. *The Atomic Scientist, A Biographical History.* New York: John Wiley, 1989.

Born, Max. *Atomic Physics.* New York: Dover, 1979.

Dunn, Andrew. *Pioneers of Science, Marie Curie.* New York: Bookwright Press, 1991.

Keller, Mollie. *Marie Curie, An Impact Biography.* New York: Franklin Watts, 1982.

McGrayne, Sharon Bertsch. *Nobel Prize Women in Science: Their Lives, Struggles, and Momentous Discoveries.* New York: Carol Publishing, A Birch Lane Press Book, 1993.

McKown, Robin. *Marie Curie.* New York: G. P. Putnam's Sons, 1971.

Parker, Steve. *Science Discoveries: Marie Curie and Radium.* New York: HarperCollins, 1992.

# Jean Dausset

*"Typing Tissues"*                                        Physiology

## Career Highlights

- Discovered antigens and the system used for tissue compatibility typing
- Awarded the Nobel Prize for Medicine, 1980
- Awarded the Robert Kock Prize, 1978
- Awarded the Wolf Foundation Prize in Medicine, 1978

## Important Contributions

The human immune system is a complex and wondrous defense mechanism. But its very complexity made it extremely difficult to uncover how it performs its deadly job. The first step was made by physician Karl Landsteiner in 1897, when he discovered that the compatibility of blood samples was determined by specific factors, which he called blood types. His discovery instantly made transfusions tenfold safer and more successful.

The next giant step was made by Jean Dausset, and earned him the Nobel Prize. Dausset discovered the existence of a complex set of antigens that control the body's response to transplanted and grafted tissue. He developed ways to "type" tissue samples just as Landsteiner had developed ways to type blood samples.

Using Dausset's work, physicians were able to predetermine the genetic compatibility of transplant tissue and organs before attempting an operation. The success rate of transplants took an instant leap forward. His work uncovered the base functioning of the immune system and led researchers to understand immune system diseases and to explain the susceptibility of many individuals to disease, infection, and tumors.

## Career Path

Sand was everywhere. Flat plains of it stretched away in every direction in the shimmering heat of Tunisia, Africa. Occasionally the sand mounded into a sea of rolling brown waves. But a lowly French Army medic, like Jean Dausset, had little time for—or interest in—gazing at the hellish landscape. His sole focus was the shattered French, English, and American soldiers who flowed in a steady stream through the tent hospital while the African campaign of World War II was in full swing.

Dausset's job was mind-numbingly simple: confirm patient blood type and begin intravenous blood transfusions. In 1939 he was drafted out of the university while half-way through medical school, given a crash course in military medical techniques, and hustled to the boiling African front.

Jean Dausset noticed a curious thing as he administered his endless line of transfusions. Even though all blood supplies were tested and matched before transfusions, still many transfusions produced severe reactions in the patient, reactions that weren't supposed to happen with matched blood types.

The researcher began to suspect that elements of human blood beyond the red blood cell characteristics used for blood typing were responsible for the reactions. But he had little time to conduct studies and no test equipment in the scorching desert. In the back of his mind he knew he was seeing something important, but couldn't step back from his crushing load of wounded long enough to figure out exactly what it was.

By the time Dausset was transferred back to France to participate in the Normandy campaign (1944), he strongly suspected that an antigen called the anti-A antibody was causing the immune system of the blood recipients to reject the new blood. But the suspicions of one medic were of little interest to the French Army, desperate to reclaim their homeland.

By early 1945, Dausset had found time for preliminary tests, which supported his theory: The immune systems of some soldiers given diphtheria and tetanus vaccinations produced anti-A antigens, which altered the compatibility of donor and recipient blood. The reaction of antibodies against foreign antigens caused a given blood type to reject even its own type of donated blood.

This discovery was important, but it seemed to him like the tiniest tip of a very large iceberg. The important thing he had sensed in Africa was still just beyond his grasp. How many other significant antigens were there? How many forms of compatibility should be checked?

In late 1945 Dausset was discharged from the Army, completed his schooling for a medical degree, and was appointed to head the laboratories of the French National Blood Transfusion Center. Here he continued to focus on the problems of abnormal transfusion reactions. His goal was to catalog all such reactions and obtain blood samples from each donor and recipient for detailed study. In the midst of this prolonged work, he received a fellowship in hematology at Harvard University and spent two years in the United States.

Upon his return to Paris in 1950, Dausset continued his work armed with new theoretical tools learned in the Unites States. By 1951 he had tightened his focus to the study of white blood cells. (Landsteiner had focused exclusively on red blood cells to create his blood types.)

Some patients who had received many transfusions, or who had been treated with certain groups of drugs, developed reactions against the white cells in donated blood. This observation was hopeful, but still confusing. Some—but not all—patients created antibodies to a specific antigen in donor blood even though they did not produce an antibody to the same antigen in their own blood. Dausset realized that more data were needed about the characteristics of these antigens in the general population.

In 1958, the same year Dausset joined the faculty of the medical school at the University of Paris, he was finally able to identify and isolate a trait of white-cell antigens that had gone unnoticed before. He observed that most of the population possessed one variant of this trait, but a substantial minority possessed the opposite variant. He named this variant MAC (for the first letter of the last names of the first three patients in whose blood he detected it). Anti-MAC antibodies were formed when a MAC-negative person received blood from a MAC-positive donor.

The medical world instantly saw the potential value of Dausset's discovery. If these white-cell antigen variations explained why so many tissue transplants were rejected and failed, it would be the most important medical discovery in decades.

Dausset and a host of other researchers attacked white blood cell antigens with incredible energy and discovered a blizzard of other variants that would affect tissue compatibility. In 1965 Dausset proposed that all of these antigens and their variants formed a single system, which he called the major histocompatibility complex (MHC). Within a year he had isolated a simple blood test that would type compatible MHC groups. Now the theory had to be tested.

Over a three-year period, Dausset collected blood samples from recipients and donors for over a thousand tissue and organ transplant operations. Using his blood test, he predicted which would be successful and which would be rejected and fail. After his thousand-sample test, he was able to show that in virtually every case, his theory and blood test successfully predicted the compatibility of the donated tissue to its new host.

This study made Jean Dausset an instant worldwide hero and earned him a Nobel Prize. Over the next 18 years, before his retirement from research in

1987, Dausset continued to explore the relationship between MHC and a variety of diseases and disorders. He also wrote six technical reference and text books on immunology and on blood and organ compatibility for transplantation and over 300 articles describing his work. But he will be best remembered for the millions of lives he saved and for how his meticulous detective work over a 20-year period produced a simple blood test that made consistently successful tissue and organ transplantation a common reality.

## Key Dates

| | |
|---|---|
| 1916 | Born in Toulouse, France, on October 19 |
| 1939– 1945 | Served in French Army medical corps during World War II |
| 1943– 1963 | Named director of the laboratories of the National Blood Transfusion Center |
| 1945 | Received M.D. from University of Paris |
| 1946– 1950 | Served internship at St. Louis and St. Antoine hospitals in Paris |
| 1948 | Awarded fellowship in hematology and received M.D. from Harvard Medical School |
| 1958 | Worked as professor of hematology at the University of Paris |
| 1968 | Appointed professor of immunohematology |
| 1969 | Appointed director of the Research Unit in Immunogenetics for the National Institute for Scientific Research |
| 1977– 1987 | Worked as professor of experimental medicine by the College of France |
| 1980 | Won Nobel Prize for Medicine |
| 1987– 1994 | Worked as professor of immunohematology, Center Etude Polymorphime Humain, Paris, France |
| 1994– present | Retired |

# Advice

*If you are considering a career in medical research, Jean Dausset would advise you to start by forming a detailed dream of what you want. Dausset's motto was vouloir pour valoir, which translates as "to achieve any worthy goal you must wish it hard enough." Visualize your goal and then refuse to accept any other outcome than what you have wished for. Success is a function of undaunted determination and perseverance.*

*Most pre-med and medical schools have relatively fixed curricula. You will have little choice in classes. Any practical experience will have to be gained outside of school. Try to find summer jobs in research labs or with a coroner's office in the pathology lab. Gain practical experience to balance your academic learning.*

# References

Desowitz, Robert. *The Thorn in the Starfish: How the Human Immune System Works.* New York: W. W. Norton, 1995. (Good review of the development of immunology.)

Hall, Stephen. *A Commotion in the Blood: Life, Death and the Immune System.* New York: Henry Holt, 1997. (Good review of the development of immunology.)

Moritz, Charles, ed. *Current Biography Yearbook, 1990.* New York: H. W. Wilson, 1991. (Good review of Dausset's work.)

Tanor, Joseph, ed. *McGraw-Hill Modern Men of Science.* New York: McGraw-Hill, 1986. (Strong summary of Dausset's work.)

Wasson, Tyler, ed. *Nobel Prize Winners.* New York: H. W. Wilson, 1987. (Good summary of Dausset's work.)

# Paul Dirac

*"Quantum Mathematics"*                    Physics

## Career Highlights

- Awarded Nobel Prize for Physics (shared with Schrodinger), 1933
- Awarded Royal Medal of the Royal Society, 1939
- Helped to launch the field of quantum mechanics
- Elected to the Lucasian Professor Chair (Newton's chair) at Cambridge, 1939

## Important Contributions

Paul Dirac is considered by many to be the greatest British theoretical physicist since Newton. His eloquent contributions to the formation and the mathematical explanation of quantum mechanics and his quantum theory of the emission and absorption of radiation resolved several major contradictions in quantum calculations and launched the field of quantum electrodynamics.

Dirac was the first to predict the necessary existence of positrons and anti-protons, or anti-matter. He also made major contributions toward the development of a unified field theory, a single theory that would connect the macro-world (the forces governing the motion and action of stars, galaxies, and the universe) to the micro-world (forces governing the motion and action of subatomic particles). His work has become the theoretical framework of modern particle physics. Modern cosmologists and physicists are able to extend and apply the precepts of quantum physics, quantum electrodynamics, and quantum mechanics in large part because of Dirac's work.

# Career Path

Silence becomes a friend as well as a prison when it is enforced over a long period of time. Paul Dirac, born in 1902 in Bristol, England, was raised in a strict home environment. His father, Charles, was an émigré from Switzerland and taught French at a local college. Professor Dirac received neither visitors nor friends at home; neither did he allow either his wife or his children to receive any. Silence was enforced during meal times and in the evenings. Necessary conversation in the house was restricted to French, more to keep the children quiet than to teach them to speak a second language.

As a result of this severe upbringing, Paul grew up a loner, preferring long walks, gardening, and the contemplation of nature to social events and school activities. As an adult he was inclined neither to collaborate nor to consult with others and did his best thinking and work alone.

The lonely young man graduated from high school with no specific career goals and entered Merchant Venturer's Technical College, where his father taught. After two years of school, he transferred to Bristol University. Throughout these years of undergraduate study, Dirac found that he first neglected, and then intentionally ignored, literary, arts, and humanities courses and gravitated instead toward explicit, numerical engineering courses.

By his junior year Dirac had settled into electrical engineering, expecting to make it a career. He later believed that this engineering background strongly influenced his approach to physics. It taught him to solve problems step-by-step, and to tolerate approximations, in fact to constructively rely on approximations, when trying to describe the physical world.

Dirac graduated with a B.S. in 1921. But in the post-World War I depressed economy, it was impossible for a shy, silent graduate to find a job. Desperate for something to do, he accepted an offer for two years of free tuition if he continued his studies in mathematics at Bristol University. His heart wasn't in these studies even though he found the work mildly interesting.

During this two-year period Dirac came under the influence of two dynamic professors and finally found a focus for his talent and a purpose for his intellect and energies. The first influence was Peter Fraser, mathematics professor, who instilled an appreciation for rigor and exactness into Dirac's lackluster approach to mathematical calculations.

The second influence was Charlie Dunbar, who taught philosophy of science courses and offered the aspiring mathematician a sweeping overview of the flow, purpose, and majesty of science. By 1923, Dirac had found the enthusiasm he had previously lacked and decided to continue his schooling and specialize in physics.

Dirac transferred to St. John's College at Cambridge University and was assigned Ralph Fowler as a graduate advisor. Fowler, a preeminent specialist in statistical mechanics and quantum theoretical research, exposed Dirac to the latest subatomic theories of Bohr, Born, and Heisenberg as well as to the then-familiar methods of quantum mechanics and general relativity.

Shy, retiring, and secretive by nature, Dirac seemed distant and uncommunicative to his advisor. But as Dirac gained an appreciation for the beauty in mathematical physics, Fowler developed a grudging appreciation for his tremendous mental abilities and insights.

By 1923 the theories of relativity and quantum mechanics were well-established, but their limits and the exact implications and meaning of the theories were not. The theories had not been fully generalized to establish the range of situations they described. Quantum mechanics, the study of systems so small that Newtonian physics breaks down, is based on the assumption that subatomic matter acts both like particle and wave. The contradictions and paradoxical implications of this assumption and the mathematics used to try to describe it were drawing physics toward a crisis point.

Through a series of cunning research efforts and precise, articulate papers, Dirac began to chip away at these inconsistencies, bringing clarity and reason to what had previously seemed to be chaotic uncertainty. He refined the methods to calculate a particle's speed as defined by Eddington's equations. He resolved the discrepancies of the covariance of Bohr's frequency condition.

Still as a graduate student, Dirac published five important papers and turned his attention to the more general problem of uniting quantum mechanics (the laws governing the micro-world of elementary particles) and relativity (the laws governing the macro-world of planetary and universal gravitation). To this work he brought his engineer's ability to accept and use approximations when exact calculations were not possible and where exact measurements did not exist. This talent allowed Dirac to venture into new areas of analysis whose inexactitude had stopped previous researchers.

During completion of his doctoral work and throughout the first five years of his work as a researcher at Cambridge, Dirac struggled to resolve the apparent incompatibility of these two major systems of thought and analysis. By 1929 he had concluded from his calculations that several subatomic particles had to exist that had never been detected. Protons and neutrons were known. He also concluded that a negatively charged particle of equivalent mass must also exist. The existence of this anti-proton, or anti-matter, was confirmed more than 25 years later.

Similarly, Dirac concluded that if an electron existed, positively and neutrally charged particles of similar mass (positron and neutrino respectively) must also exist. The existence of positrons was confirmed two years later, in 1932. Neutrinos were positively identified in the mid-1970s, but their mass was not confirmed until recent (1998) work by Japanese researchers.

Following this breakthrough work in the early 1930s, which earned him a Nobel Prize, Dirac made a series of significant contributions in the field of quantum electrodynamics and quantum physics. He searched for relationships between the structure of the universe and that of an atom. He solved more than a dozen significant problems that had held up progress in subatomic physics. He published over 60 major papers and three books.

Uncomfortable with people to the end of his life, Paul Dirac accepted few students and rarely conferred with the other scientists leading the fight to unearth the secrets of quantum and cosmic physics. He worked alone with his thoughts and his calculations and, in so doing, made more contributions to the advancement of subatomic physics and quantum mechanics than any other single researcher of the twentieth century.

## Key Dates

| | |
|---|---|
| 1902 | Born in Bristol, England, on August 8 |
| 1921 | Received B.S. in electrical engineering from Bristol University |
| 1926 | Received Ph.D. in physics from St. John's College, Cambridge University |
| 1927 | Worked as instructor of mathematics, Cambridge |
| 1932–1969 | Was Lucasian Professor of Mathematics, Cambridge |
| 1969 | Was professor emeritus, Cambridge |
| 1971–1984 | Worked as professor of physics, Florida State University |
| 1984 | Died on October 20 |

## Advice

*Paul Dirac was a shy loner and reticent to advise others. Still, he consistently acknowledged the value of his study in engineering, both electrical and mechanical, before he turned to the study of hard sciences. Engineering trained him to be practical and pragmatic and to approach complex problems in a straightforward, step-by-step manner.*

## References

Daintith, John, et al., eds. *Biographical Encyclopedia of Scientists.* 2d ed. Vol. 1. Philadelphia, Pa: Institute of Physics Publishing, 1994. (Summary entry on Dirac's work.)

Devine, Elizabeth, ed. *The Annual Obituary, 1983.* Chicago: St. James Press, 1990. (Good biographical summary.)

Dirac, Paul. *The General Theory of Relativity.* New York: John Wiley, 1975. (Good review of mathematical quantum mechanics and relativity.)

————. *The Principles of Quantum Mechanics.* London: Cambridge University Press, 1958. (Good review of Dirac's work.)

Kragh, Helge. *Dirac: A Scientific Bibliography.* London: Cambridge University Press, 1990. (Complete bibliography.)

Wasson, Tyler, ed. *Nobel Prize Winners.* New York: H. W. Wilson, 1987. (Excellent summary of Dirac's work.)

# Benjamin Duggar

*"The Wonder Drug"*                    Plant Pathology

Archives of National Academy of Sciences

## Career Highlights

- Discovered aureomycin, the first of the tetracycline antibiotics, by isolating the fungus *Streptomyces aureofaciens* and then extracting and purifying the compound chlortetracycline
- Founded the American Society of Agronomy, 1907; founded the American Phytopathological Society, 1908
- Served as president of the American Botanical Society, 1923
- Served as president of the American Society of Plant Physiologists, 1947

## Important Contributions

Benjamin Duggar's research in plant pathology helped make commercial mushroom farming possible in the first half of the twentieth century. His related research into viral plant diseases (a research field Duggar pioneered) led to his greatest discovery: aureomycin, the first of the tetracycline antibiotics. Aureomycin, an antibiotic used to treat pneumonia and other diseases caused by bacteria and viruses, was hailed as the first "wonder drug" since penicillin and saved countless millions of lives. Discovering aureomycin was a milestone in the story of humanity's attempt to conquer pathogenic bacteria.

## Career Path

In the summer of 1943 Benjamin Duggar decided that 55 years of life in university campuses was enough; that at the age of 70, retired life would be good, especially since he was retiring as a professor emeritus from the University of Wisconsin. Now he was free to relax at home, catch up on his reading, and still putter about campus and his office whenever he felt restless. He had already turned down several lucrative consulting offers, and didn't want the pressure and the hassles. Playing the part of beloved, dottering ex-professor suited him just fine.

Then he read a short article about his retirement in a popular scholarly journal. In summary it said, "Dr. Duggar will best be remembered for his noteworthy inquiry into the physiology of mushrooms." Duggar stared at that sentence for a long while. It seemed to sum up the accomplishments of an insignificant life. Surely he had amounted to more than a few insights about mushrooms. Despair turned to indignation. He swore that his final epitaph would describe deeds of more importance than mushrooms. He decided to shed his fledgling retirement and accept the consulting job with Lederle Laboratories to do independent research. Millions of people are glad he did.

Benjamin Duggar was raised in rural Alabama. One of his father's friends, Charles Mohr, was a druggist in nearby Mobile. Mohr frequently stayed at the Duggar home, scouring the countryside for flora to make drugs for his business. Young Benjamin accompanied the chemist on these scavenger hunts, pawing through the fields, marshes, and woods of Alabama and listening to tales of the plant extracts Mohr could sell to cure virtually any known ailment. During these trips, the boy became increasingly fascinated with the complexity and potential of plant life.

Benjamin was schooled by private tutors and enrolled in the University of Alabama shortly before his fifteenth birthday. His fascination with agricultural science led him to switch to Mississippi Agricultural and Mechanical College (now Mississippi State) after two years. From there he graduated with a B.S. with highest honors in 1891. He received his M.S. in 1892 from Alabama Polytechnic Institute.

Clearly Benjamin loved university life. As soon as he graduated from Alabama, he went to Harvard on a medical scholarship, receiving the equivalent of a medical master's degree in 1895. With his second master's degree in hand, Duggar entered a doctoral program at Cornell University, working as a botany instructor while he studied. His Ph.D. work specialized in crop diseases. Rather than seeking immediate employment, he spent the 18 months after completing his degree studying at four European universities, spending most of his time studying plant physiology.

With 13 years of university-level study under his belt, Duggar returned from Europe in 1900 to Cornell to a position as a professor of plant physiology. He left that position after a year to become plant physiologist at the Bureau of Plant Industry with the U.S. Department of Agriculture. While there he studied cotton diseases in the South and developed new methods of both insect and fungal disease control. By this time he had studied plant disease and plant physiology as much as anyone in the country and had become a recognized expert.

In 1902, Duggar founded the botany department at the University of Missouri. There he focused on a study of methods of mushroom culture. His efforts marked the first time scientific methods and experimentation had been applied to mushrooms. He made possible the development of a commercial mushroom-growing industry in this country. In 1904 he was awarded a grand prize for his exhibit of mushroom and other fungi at the St. Louis Fair.

Duggar left the University of Missouri after five years and returned to Cornell as a professor of plant physiology. He stayed there for five years, then left again to go to Washington University in Saint Louis as a research professor of plant physiology. In 1927, he switched to the University of Wisconsin, where he combined research with teaching for 16 years until his one-month retirement in 1943.

After accepting the position with Lederle Labs, he began an extensive and systematic search for molds. Penicillin, the first mold-based wonder drug, had already saved thousands of lives. The major pharmaceutical companies wanted to see if other molds would prove as useful and as profitable. In a spacious lab he grew molds from thousands of fungus samples collected from all over the country. One full-time assistant was needed just to keep up with the book work to track each sample and the molds grown from it.

Each mold was tested on a wide variety of viruses and bacteria to see if the mold would prove lethal to these disease-causing agents. Month after month, using tray after tray of petri dish samples, Duggar and his assistants cultivated and tested molds.

In September 1945, Duggar isolated and tested a new mold species, *Streptomyces aureofaciens,* grown from a parasitic fungus collected in central Missouri. From this mold he obtained the drug aureomycin, the first of the tetracycline antibiotics. He tested aureomycin for two years, studying how to grow the mold and what concentrations would have what effect on which viruses and bacteria. In 1947 aureomycin was given for the first time to human patients at the Harlem Hospital in New York City. By December 1948, aureomycin was available to physicians.

Aureomycin was hailed as a "wonder drug," and the *Lancet* reported that it had the widest application of any known antibacterial and anti-viral substance. Aureomycin was particularly effective at reducing high fevers quickly. Surgeons used it after operations to reduce the risk of infections.

By the time he died in 1956, Benjamin Duggar had published over 100 articles and several books. While his research into mushrooms and into cotton and tobacco viruses advanced the field of commercial agriculture, it is for his discovery of aureomycin antibiotics that he will always be thankfully remembered.

**\*   \*   \***

## Key Dates

| | |
|---|---|
| 1872 | Born in Gallion, Alabama, on September 1 |
| 1887–1889 | Attended the University of Alabama |
| 1892 | Recived B.S. and M.S. from the Mississippi Agricultural and Mechanical College |
| 1895 | Received medical degree from Harvard University |
| 1898 | Received Ph.D. from Cornell University |
| 1899–1900 | Did post-graduate studies in Europe |
| 1902–1907 | Founded the botany department at the University of Missouri |
| 1907–1912 | Was professor of plant physiology at Cornell |
| 1907 | Founded the American Society of Agronomy |
| 1908 | Founded the American Phytopathological Society |
| 1917–1919 | Worked as professor of biological chemistry, Washington University, St. Louis, Missouri |
| 1927–1943 | Worked as professor of plant physiology at the University of Wisconsin. Retired as professor emeritus |
| 1944–1956 | Worked as consultant with Lederle Laboratories |
| 1956 | Died September 10 in New Haven, Connecticut |

## Advice

*Benjamin Duggar believed fervently in education. He believed it was impossible to study and learn too much. Pick a field that interests you and then take all the related classes you can from all the teachers you can for as long as you can. Don't be in a rush to "graduate and get a job." It may take a dozen years of study to even find the questions you want your career to answer. If you rush the learning process, you may never find those questions at all.*

## References

Abraham, Edward. *Launching the Antibiotic Era.* New York: Rockefeller University Press, 1987. (Historical overview of the field.)

Garraty, John, ed. *Dictionary of American Biography, Supplement Six, 1956-1960.* New York: Charles Scribner's Sons, 1980. (Good entry on Duggar's life.)

Gillispie, Charles, ed. *Dictionary of Scientific Biography.* Vol. IV. New York: Charles Scribner's Sons, 1971. (Good entry on Duggar's life.)

Gotlieb, D., ed. *Antibiotics: Their History and Development.* New York: Springer-Verlag, 1987. (Good technical review of the field.)

Rothe, Anna, and Evelyn Lohr. *Current Biography: Who's News and Why, 1952.* New York: H. W. Wilson, 1952. (Good entry on Duggar's life.)

# Paul Ehrlich

| *"Breeding Ourselves into Oblivion"* | Population Biology and Education |

## Career Highlights

Stanford University

- Authored *The Population Bomb,* 1968, which received the Best Seller's Paperback of the Year Award in 1970
- Founded Zero Population Growth (president, 1969–1970)
- Was National Science Foundation fellow at University of Sydney, 1965–1966
- Won the John Muir Award (Sierra Club)

## Important Contributions

Stanford University professor Paul Ehrlich authored the groundbreaking 1968 book *The Population Bomb,* which helped trigger the ecological movement of the 1970s. He believes that, unchecked, population will grow faster than the Earth's capacity to support it, that we will "breed ourselves into oblivion." In the years since his book was published, the world's population has soared from 4 billion to almost 6 billion people—and 300 million people have died of starvation.

Ehrlich specialized in more than just the problem of human overpopulation. He also conducted a 35-year study of the checkerspot butterfly, writing over 37 books and conducting research on every continent of the world.

Despite his noted advancements in insect biology, however, he will be remembered for bringing the human population problem to the world's attention.

## Career Path

"One stinking hot night in Delhi (in 1966), my wife and daughter and I were returning to our hotel in an ancient taxi," recalled Paul Ehrlich. "The streets seemed alive with people. People eating, people washing, people sleeping. People visiting, arguing and screaming. People thrusting their hands through the taxi window, begging. People defecating and urinating. People clinging to buses. People herding animals. People, people, people, people. As we moved slowly through the mob, hand horn squawking, the dust, noise, heat, and cooking fires gave the scene a hellish aspect."

The true horror and importance of that scene hit Ehrlich as he realized that this was no special event, rather just a very ordinary night in Delhi. The streets were jammed with massed humanity *every* night and *every* day. The realization that human populations everywhere could easily expand to this overcrowded nightmare shook Ehrlich to the core of his being. That was his second wake-up call, a call so powerful it completely altered the focus of his career and life.

Paul Ehrlich was born in 1932 in Philadelphia, Pennsylvania, but grew up in Maplewood, New Jersey, where his most vivid memories were of chasing butterflies and dissecting frogs. There was never a time when insects and zoology weren't his central interest. In high school, he read William Vogt's pioneering book about the population-food problem, *Road to Survival.* That was his first wake-up call. The book bothered him, but he was too young to know what to do about it.

Paul enrolled at the University of Pennsylvania, where he studied zoology. During the summers, he worked as a field officer on the Northern Insect Survey. Among other projects, he studied biting flies on the Bering Sea and insects in the Canadian Arctic and Subarctic.

After graduation, Ehrlich applied to the University of Kansas for a master's and doctorate in zoology. While pursuing his studies, he investigated the genetics and behavior of parasitic mites, funded by a fellowship from the National Institutes of Health. But most of his field work was conducted in Stanford's Jasper Ridge Biological Experimental Area and in the Rocky Mountain Biological Laboratory at Crested Butte, Colorado. He was especially interested in controlling butterfly caterpillars with ants (a natural enemy) rather than with pesticides.

In 1959, the young zoologist joined the faculty at Stanford University as an assistant professor of biology. By 1966 he had been promoted to full professor of biology, and he spent the rest of his academic career at Stanford, splitting his time between teaching and research.

While Ehrlich worked on insect biology, the human population problem festered within him. He knew it was a major problem; he knew it was serious. He understood all that intellectually, but the problem did not hit him with emotional force until that visit to India in 1966. The densely packed sea of humanity in India was a wake-up call that he could not ignore any longer. He had to do something about it.

Ehrlich began compiling extensive data banks of information. He wrote articles and lectured about the population explosion, which culminated in his book, *The Population Bomb.* In it, he argued forcefully that if the birth rate is not brought into line with the death rate, we will breed ourselves into extinction. He likened the uncontrolled multiplication of people to the uncontrolled multiplication of cancer cells. He argued that we must shift our attention from the symptoms of the cancer (food shortage, environmental deterioration, and so forth) and focus our attention on the cause of the cancer (a population spiraling out of control).

The book cited frightening statistics that pointed out that the world's population continues to double more and more quickly. It took centuries (until 1850) for the world's population to reach one billion. It took only 80 more years (1930) to reach two billion. It took less than 40 years for the population to double again, to four billion. We are now at almost six billion. Ehrlich pointed out that the planet cannot sustain this rate of population growth. He saw two kinds of solutions to this problem: one is a "birth rate solution," in which we find ways to lower the birth rate; the other is a "death rate solution," in which ways to raise the world's death rate (famine, disease, and so forth) will find us.

After *The Population Bomb* was released, Johnny Carson interviewed Ehrlich for a full hour on the *Tonight Show.* Tall, intense, and fit, with piercing blue eyes and an even sharper tongue, the author was a hit. His appearance drew an amazing response: NBC received more than 5,000 letters, virtually all in support of Ehrlich. The American public had seen the future through his eyes, and they were frightened by what they saw. They were ready for action.

Ehrlich founded Zero Population Growth, a political action organization, and he served as its president for a couple of years. Zero Population Growth aims to help aid the passage of legislation that will reduce overpopulation and seeks to promote political candidates who are dedicated to saving the environment.

While many of Paul Ehrlich's doomsday predictions about the planet have been correct, he hasn't always been right. In 1990, he lost a $1,000 bet with "techno-optimist" Julian Simon. Simon argued that advances in technology will keep the earth plentiful; he argued that Ehrlich's approach discounts the "only real resource," the human mind. In 1980, Simon bet Ehrlich that over the course of 10 years, the price of five metals would *decrease,* thus proving that resources are *not* finite and we are not running out. Simon was right. This bet earned Ehrlich the nickname "Dr. Doom" and Simon the nickname "Dr. Boom."

Although some might view this "lost bet" as a setback to Ehrlich's theories, most people recognize how serious the world population problem is. As a leader in the international crusade for population control and ecological awareness, Paul Ehrlich has focused national and world attention on the problems of overpopulation. He has done for ecology what Rachel Carson did for environmental protection.

## Key Dates

| | |
|---|---|
| 1932 | Born in Philadelphia, Pennsylvania, on May 29 |
| 1949 | Graduated from Columbia High School in Maplewood, New Jersey |
| 1953 | Received B.A. in zoology from University of Pennsylvania |
| 1955 | Received M.A. from University of Kansas |
| 1957 | Received Ph.D. from University of Kansas |
| 1959–1966 | Worked as assistant professor and associate professor, Stanford University |
| 1966–present | Is professor at Stanford University; editor in population biology at McGraw-Hill Book Co. |
| 1969–present | Is president of Zero Population Growth |

## Advice

*Human population biology is a complex field of study because it involves biology, ecology, economics, and psychology. Paul Ehrlich would advise you to start with general science, with an emphasis on biology, math, and resource economics. Take classes in other fields as your individual course of study requires them. However, many of the real lessons of resource management and conservation are learned in the street rather than in the classroom. Recycle, reuse, conserve. Join local clubs and organizations that promote recycling and conservation and see the real-life problems they confront every day. Stop thinking like frontiersmen and begin thinking like astronauts. Don't think of the planet as a frontier to be exploited; instead, think of it as a spaceship with strictly limited carrying capacity.*

## References

Baumber, Ernest. *Paul Ehrlich: Scientist for Life*. New York: Holmes & Meier, 1984.

Cox, Donald W. *Pioneers of Ecology*. Maplewood, N.J.: Hammond, 1971.

Ehrlich, Paul. *The Population Bomb*. New York: Amereon Ltd., 1976.

————. *The Population Explosion*. New York: Simon & Schuster, 1991. (Thoroughly researched update to *The Population Bomb*.)

Ehrlich, Paul, with Carl Sagan, Donald Kennedy, and Walter Orr Roberts. *The Cold and the Dark: The World After Nuclear War*. New York: W. W. Norton, 1984.

# Albert Einstein

*"The Troubled Amateur"*                    Physics

## Career Highlights

Courtesy of the Archives, California Institute of Technology.

- Created theory of relativity, revolutionized thinking about physics, established the relationship between matter and energy, and first proposed that light is both wave and particle
- Awarded the Nobel Prize for Physics, 1921
- Awarded Copley Medal, Royal Society of London, 1923
- Awarded Gold Medal, Royal Astronomical Society, 1926

## Important Contributions

Albert Einstein is one of only three or four scientists in history who have changed the fundamental ways in which humans view the universe. He proposed two theories in 1905 that rank as the greatest discoveries of the twentieth century. First, Einstein's theory of relativity changed humankind's fundamental assumptions about the nature of the universe and of Earth's and humans' place in it.

Second, he established the relationship between matter and energy by creating one of the two most famous equations in the history of humankind, $E=mc^2$. (The other is the Pythagorean Theorem for a right triangle, $A^2 + B^2 = C^2$)

The twentieth century's developments in technology, science, and math owe their foundation to this unassuming scientist in a deep and fundamental way. He has touched our lives probably more than any other scientist in history. But for the first 26 years of his life, no one thought he had any chance of entering the world of science at all.

## Career Path

It was while riding on a Berne, Switzerland, trolley car one afternoon in the spring of 1904 that the image first flashed across Albert Einstein's mind. It was an image of a man in an elevator that was falling from a great height. Einstein realized immediately that the images of this "thought experiment" could bring focus to a problem that had been plaguing him (and other scientists) for years.

Einstein understood that the man in the elevator would not know he was falling because, relative to his surroundings (the elevator), he wasn't falling. The man would not be able to detect that he was caught in a gravitational field. If a light beam entered the side of the elevator, it would strike the far wall higher up because the elevator had dropped while the light beam crossed. To the man, it would appear that the light beam bent upwards. From our perspective, gravitational fields bend light. Light not only could be, but routinely was, bent by the gravitational fields of stars and planets.

It was a revolutionary concept worthy of one of the world's greatest scientific minds. It is amazing that, in 1904, Albert Einstein hadn't completely given up thinking about science even though he had failed his science entrance exams, been thrown out of school twice, been refused any job in science, and repeatedly been told that he would never qualify to work in a scientific field at all.

In 1904 the first third of Einstein's life was ending, a third that had been filled with struggle, frustration, and bitter rejection. The middle third of his life, from 1905 through 1929, held unrestrained triumph, fame, and world-wide acclaim. During the final third of his life he faced the frustration of seeing scientific developments pass him by.

Albert Einstein, raised in Munich, Germany, showed no early signs of genius. He was described as a dull child who didn't play well with other children. Grammar school teachers called him irksome and disruptive. They said he didn't pay attention, argued incessantly, and failed to complete assignments. At 16 he was expelled from school. As a high school washout, he was ineligible to enter German universities or to hope for advanced training in the sciences.

But Albert was vitally interested in math and science, just not interested in school. The young man was a dreamer. He developed an early sense of wonder and curiosity, neither of which was satisfied by tightly formatted German schools.

When Albert's father's business failed, the family moved to Milan, Italy, to start over. The boy stayed behind until he was expelled from school. His father encouraged him to apply to the Polytechnic Institute in Zurich, Switzerland, and learn a trade to help support the family. A high school diploma was not needed to enter that Swiss school.

Albert traveled to Zurich but failed the entrance exam. A school administrator, however, was impressed with his math abilities and arranged for him to complete high school in nearby Aarua, Switzerland. At 17, Albert passed the Polytechnic entrance exam and transferred to Zurich.

There he showed promise in math and science, but piled up far too many discipline reports. He was free with his opinions whether they offended or not. Albert cut most lectures and studied privately with his girlfriend, Mileva Maric. His teachers gave him bad reports, one of them calling him "a lazy dog."

At Zurich, Einstein realized he was, by nature, a theoretical physicist rather than a mathematician. Of his schooling, he later wrote, "It is nothing short of a miracle that modern methods of teaching have not entirely strangled the sacred spirit of curiosity and inquiry."

Einstein planned to teach after graduation but his grades weren't good enough for him to find a teaching post. He dropped out of science in disgust and supported himself with odd jobs for almost two years. Then in 1902 he landed a job as a clerk in the Swiss Patent Office, assigned to check the technical correctness of patent applications. It was as far from the world of science as he could get. It appeared that all doors leading to a science career had been firmly closed.

Still, Einstein was content at the Patent Office in Berne. The work was easy and provided enough money to marginally support his new wife and former study companion, Mileva. On evenings and Sundays (he worked six days a week), his mind was free to pursue his passion for the study of fundamental and universal physical relationships.

Einstein used imaginative "thought experiments" to shed light on complex questions of general principles. It was a new and unique way to approach the study of physics and led him to write a series of four papers, which he submitted to a science journal in 1905. Impressed, the journal's editor published all four papers in a single issue. One of those four papers presented the special theory of relativity (relativity principles applied to bodies either moving at a steady velocity or at rest). Another presented his theory of the relationship between matter and energy.

The papers from this "amateur" mathematician had a deep, instant, and profound impact on the scientific community. One article was accepted by

Zurich University as a doctoral thesis. The university granted Einstein a Ph.D, and the papers earned him a Nobel Prize.

In 1909 Einstein was offered a professorship. The world of science literally beat a path to his door. He was offered more and more prestigious positions at university after university. Virtually all physicists shifted their studies to focus on his theories.

In 1916, as the world plunged into world war, Einstein published his general theory of relativity, which described relativity theory applied to objects moving in more complex ways with non-linear acceleration. The whole world applauded.

When the great theorist turned 50 in 1929, his world began to crumble. His attempts to expand his theory of relativity into a unified field theory describing the relationship between electromagnetism and gravity failed. The world of physics had swept past him into quantum mechanics. He was unable and unwilling to grasp its fundamental concepts, even though they were based on his theories. Family and political problems disrupted his ordered life.

In 1933 Einstein fled Germany to Princeton, New Jersey. Although he lived the final third of his life working at Princeton University as a revered elder statesman of science, his contributions to science had ended. His unified field theory never developed. His years of prominence had passed, but his mark was stamped permanently into the fabric of our lives.

## Key Dates

| | |
|---|---|
| 1879 | Born in Ulm, Germany, on March 14 |
| 1995 | Expelled from high school; failed the entrance exam for Zurich Technical College |
| 1901 | Received B.S. from Polytechnic Institute of Zurich |
| 1902 | Abandoned science, took job as clerk in the Swiss Patent Office |
| 1905 | Published a bundle of four small papers—one in particular, his special theory of relativity, revolutionized physics |
| 1905 | Received Ph.D. from University of Zurich |
| 1909 | Offered assistant professorship at University of Zurich |
| 1914 | Worked as professor at the University of Berlin |
| 1916 | Completed research on and development of his general theory of relativity |

| | |
|---|---|
| 1922 | Received 1921 Nobel Prize for Physics |
| 1933 | Emigrated to United States; offered professorship at Princeton University |
| 1940 | Became naturalized citizen of United States |
| 1955 | Died on April 18 in Princeton, New Jersey |

## Advice

*Albert Einstein, more than any other notable scientist, relied on imagination and mental constructs to understand complex problems. In a world eager to find quantitative methods and instant computer solutions, he would advise you not to overlook the power of your own imagination. Practice and develop your mental powers: dream, imagine, and wonder. Take the time to let your mind wander through a problem. Einstein believed that learning is the servant of imagination, and that curiosity and inquiry are the foundation of learning. He also would advise you to get used to teaching yourself. Investigate, read, probe through the areas that stir your passions. University classes are valuable but can never be custom designed for your specific needs as can your own studies.*

## References

Einstein, Albert. *Einstein on Peace.* Edited by Otto Nathan. New York: Simon & Shuster, 1960.

————. *The Evolution of Physics.* Edited by Leopold Infield. New York: Simon & Shuster, 1961.

————. *Relativity: The Special and the General Theory Book.* Rev. ed. Edited by E. Baird. New York: Penguin, 1998.

Goldsmith, Maurice, ed. *Einstein: The First Hundred Years.* New York: Pergamon Press, 1980.

Lightman, Alan P. *Einstein's Dreams.* New York: Warner Books, 1994. (Reprint edition.)

Pais, Abraham. *Subtle Is the Lord: The Science and Life of Albert Einstein.* London: Oxford University Press, 1982.

Parker, Barry. *Einstein's Dream: The Search for a Unified Theory of the Universe.* New York: Plenum Press, 1986.

# Loren Eiseley

*"The Gift of Tongues"*      Anthropology and
Writing

## Career Highlights

- Attracted popular and critical acclaim with the reflective, poetic style of his 11 books
- Elected to the National Institute of Arts and Letters in 1971, a rare achievement among scientists
- Won many of the major literary awards and received over 35 honorary degrees

## Important Contributions

As chairman of the department of anthropology and provost of the University of Pennsylvania, Loren Eiseley was one of the world's leading authorities on the works of Darwin and others who helped develop the theory of evolution. Perhaps what is most interesting about him, however, is that in addition to his distinguished academic career and the contributions he made to anthropology, he is best known for distinguishing himself as a writer.

Loren Eiseley did for anthropology and evolution what Rachel Carson did for the environment, what Isaac Asimov did for space: He made it immediate, accessible, understandable, and important to ordinary citizens. His books are a vivid blend of anthropology, archaeology, natural history, and the history of science written in a dramatic, forceful, and sometimes mystic way. Indeed, writer Ray Bradbury once said that "to read Eiseley is to fall in love."

# Career Path

Loren Eiseley's life revolved around two lifelong passions: a love of books and a fascination with the natural world. He developed both as a boy growing up in Lincoln, Nebraska. Loren spent whole days exploring the salt flats and ponds around his home and the Lincoln area, frequently bringing home snakes, turtles, and other pond life that he put in a homemade aquarium. He marveled at the mammoth bones on display at the University of Nebraska campus. He even created his own museum at home, with bones and skulls that he made of baked clay.

The young boy also read virtually every day of his childhood. Children's books, science books, history books, cultural books, books of early man, poetry—if it lay inside the covers of a book, he was unstoppably drawn to it. He grew to love the sound, tone, and pattern of well-written language as well as the images and ideas contained in the words.

Loren entered the University of Nebraska to study anthropology in 1929, receiving his B.A. in 1933. He was fond of writing poems, stories, and reviews, and when his college fraternity, Sigma Upsilon, founded a "little magazine" called *Prairie Schooner,* he became one of the editors and contributors. His flair for writing did not go unnoticed, and one edition of the magazine described him as "one of America's most promising young poets." He continued publishing in the *Prairie Schooner* even after he left the university, and his writing started to appear in other magazines, both general circulation and scholarly anthropological journals.

After graduation, Eiseley hunted for avenues to further develop the ideas of his anthropology training. During the 1930s, he joined several expeditions to various parts of the West to seek evidences of early human habitation and culture. Eiseley was especially interested in the fields of human evolution and paleo-archaeology and actively searched for evidence of post-glacial man. From 1931 to 1933, he was a member of the Morrill paleontological expedition, which combed parts of Colorado and New Mexico. He joined the University of Pennsylvania and Carnegie Institute expedition to the Southwest in 1934 and the Smithsonian Institution trek to northern Colorado in 1935. During the course of each of these expeditions, he developed insights into the evolutionary relationship between man and his natural surroundings.

Following this series of expeditions, Eiseley worked as an assistant sociologist and then, as a recipient of a Harrison Fellowship, returned to the University of Pennsylvania to get a Ph.D. in anthropology in 1937. In that same year, he was appointed to his first major academic position as assistant professor of anthropology and sociology at the University of Kansas in Lawrence. He held a number of academic positions during his career, moving from assistant professorship to associate professorship, to chairmanship, to provost, and spent many summers as a visiting lecturer at such prestigious universities as the University of California at Berkeley, Columbia, and Harvard University.

In 1953, Eiseley compiled a comprehensive bibliography to shed light on Darwin's correspondence, and a few years later he edited a volume of papers for the American Philosophical Society's centennial on Darwin. He became recognized as an expert on the works and theories of Darwin.

When he wasn't teaching, preparing for class, or attending meetings, Eiseley was usually writing. Writing was a way to join his two loves, books and science. His first book, *The Immense Journey,* was a collection of essays that told the story of living organisms since they first appeared on Earth. It was published in 1957 and won high praise from literary critics and scientists alike. His next book, *Darwin's Century,* reviewed the development of the theory of evolution, and won a Phi Beta Kappa Science Award. *The Firmament of Time* (1960) was honored by the John Burroughs Association.

Without a doubt, Loren Eiseley will be most remembered for his writings—he had a gift for merging facts, science, beauty and wonder that made virtually everyone, from scientist to lay reader, understand and appreciate the significance of the natural world. His unique talent lay in his ability to write movingly about subjects that had hitherto been described in mostly dry, stiff passages. For example, in his essay "How Flowers Changed the World," he writes:

> Once upon a time there were no flowers at all . . . Wherever one might have looked, from the poles to the equator, one would have seen only the cold dark monotonous green of a world whose plant life possessed no other color.
>
> Somewhere, just a short time before the close of the Age of Reptiles, there occurred a soundless, violent explosion. It lasted millions of years, but it was an explosion, nevertheless. It marked the emergence of the angiosperms—the flowering plants . . . [which] changed the face of the planet.
>
> [Before flowers,] it was a world in slow motion, a cold-blooded world whose occupants were most active at noonday but torpid on chill nights, their brains damped by a slower metabolism than any known today. . . . Creatures without a high metabolic rate are slaves to weather. Insects in the first frosts of autumn all run down like little clocks. Yet if you pick one up and breathe warmly upon it, it will begin to move about once more.
>
> A high metabolic rate, however, means a heavy intake of energy in order to sustain body warmth and efficiency. . . . The agile brain of the warm-blooded birds and mammals demands a high oxygen consumption and food in concentrated forms, or the creatures cannot long sustain themselves. It was the rise

of the flowering plants [via seeds] that provided that energy and changed the nature of the living world." *

Loren Eiseley's ability to captivate us with his eloquent prose marks him as a truly gifted educator. As admirer Ray Bradbury once wrote of him, "The gift of tongues is absent among most modern writers. . . . If all the people ran as beautifully as Eiseley writes, the world would be full of gazelles."

## Key Dates

| | |
|---|---|
| 1907 | Born in Lincoln, Nebraska, on September 3 |
| 1933 | Received B.A. from University of Nebraska |
| 1935 | Received M.A. from University of Pennsylvania |
| 1937 | Received Ph.D. from University of Pennsylvania |
| 1958 | Published *Darwin's Century* (which in 1959 won the Phi Beta Kappa Science Prize) |
| 1962 | Published *Francis Bacon and the Modern Dilemma* |
| 1969 | Published *The Unexpected Universe* |
| 1970 | Published *The Invisible Pyramid* |
| 1971 | Published *Night Country* |
| 1977 | Died July 9 in Philadelphia, Pennsylvania |

---

* Loren Eiseley, "How Flowers Changed the World," in *The Star Thrower,* pages 67–69, published by Harvest/HBJ Edition by arrangement with Times Books, 1978. Copyright © 1946, 1950, 1951, 1953, 1955, 1956, 1957 by Loren Eiseley. Reprinted by permission.

## Advice

*Loren Eiseley believed that too often science separates people from the world we live in by using barbarous jargon. Don't allow yourself to experience that sense of separation. Eiseley would advise anyone considering the field of anthropology to study archaeology, natural history, and the history of science as well as subjects classically allied with anthropology. Build bridges between the frontiers of science and the everyday world. Don't limit yourself to one branch of science—don't even limit yourself to science itself. The key is to find ways to relate science to the human mind and spirit.*

## References

Bernard, Russell H. *Research Methods in Anthropology: Qualitative & Quantitative Approaches.* Thousand Oaks, Calif.: Sage Publications, 1994.

Carlisle, Fred E. *Loren Eiseley: The Development of a Writer.* Urbana: University of Illinois Press, 1983.

Eiseley, Loren. *The Immense Journey.* New York: Random House, 1959.

———. *The Star Thrower.* New York: Times Books, 1978.

Heidtmann, Peter. *Loren Eiseley: A Modern Ishmael.* Northhaven, Conn.: Archon Books, 1991.

# Gertrude Elion

*"The Real Reward"*                    Biochemistry

Photo by Clara Hawley

## Career Highlights

- Awarded the Nobel Prize for Physiology or Medicine (together with George H. Hitchings and Sir James Black), 1988
- Developed (with Hitchings) the first effective chemotherapy to fight leukemia
- Developed chemotherapies to inhibit nucleic acid formation in diseased cells without damaging normal cells, which led to many advances in drug research, including the development of the drug AZT, which is used today to fight AIDS
- Received the National Medal of Science, 1991
- Received the Medal of Honor from the American Cancer Society, 1990

## Important Contributions

Gertrude Elion's and George Hitchings's investigations and research into the chemistry of purines and pyrimidines (components of DNA) created major advances in chemical therapies. As a result of their work, the world now has drugs active against leukemia, malaria, gout, kidney stones, herpes, and even AIDS (with the drug AZT). Elion's work revolutionized drug making and medicine; her research made organ transplants possible.

## Career Path

In 1933, when Gertrude Elion was 15 years old, her beloved grandfather lay shriveled and pasty white, dying of stomach cancer. He had lived with her family since she was three and had been her growing-up companion. To Gertrude, it was a stranger lying in the bed. His skin was almost translucent and so fragile looking she barely dared touch him. The robust laughter she loved had been replaced by raspy whispers and a face etched in permanent pain. The body had shrunk in on the bones, looking more like a corpse than a vital being.

The terrible sight of what cancer had done to her grandfather, more than anything else, made Gertrude choose her career. She later said it was her turning point: "It was as though the signal was there: 'This is the disease you're going to have to work against.'" Suddenly nothing else mattered, not a lack of money, not sex discrimination, not a desperate lack of financial resources. She vowed that she would become a chemistry major and fight cancer.

When Gertrude Elion was 11, the stock market crash of October 1929 had ruined her family financially. Until then, it had been a given that she would continue her education after high school. Higher education was a tradition in her family; she was good at school; she loved it; she was the first born. Although her father's bankruptcy drastically limited her options, the City College of New York was free. Since her grades were excellent, she was accepted by Hunter College, the women's section of the university. That was just after her beloved grandfather died of stomach cancer and the young girl had set her sights on chemical research.

After graduation from Hunter, Elion applied for financial aid to graduate schools across the country so that she could pursue a doctorate. Not one offered her a graduate fellowship or assistantship. The underlying reason for their refusal was sex discrimination. She was a woman, and there simply were no jobs or fellowships for women chemists. Bitterly discouraged, she enrolled at a secretarial school so that she could support herself while she worked on her master's degree at New York University.

For seven years, Elion worked at marginal and temporary jobs, teaching biochemistry to nursing students, working at a chemist's lab for free so she could learn, working as a doctor's receptionist, working as a substitute teacher. The only time she could work on her master's degree was at nights and on weekends at the NYU lab. The university turned down the heat on nights and weekends, so it was cold work. She wore heavy coats and warmed her hands over Bunsen burners.

When the United States entered World War II, positions were suddenly available to women. Elion was offered her first real job as a chemist, testing food products for A&P grocery stores. As soon as she had learned everything she could there, she moved to a research position with Johnson and Johnson. That unit closed six months later, and, in search of a new job, she telephoned Burroughs Wellcome Company, a drug company whose research laboratory was hiring.

That Saturday she put on her best suit and went to her first interview at Burroughs Wellcome. Luckily, senior chemist George Hitchings was working that Saturday. Hitchings had already hired one woman, Elvira Falco, who thought Elion looked too elegant to be a real chemist. But Hitchings disagreed. She had a top-notch academic record, and he liked her verve. He hired her, and they became an excellent research team. Elion would stay at Burroughs Wellcome for the rest of her career.

When Hitchings and Elion began working together, little was known about nucleic acids. Scientists had just discovered that DNA was the carrier of genetic information. Hitchings assigned her to study purines, the building blocks of DNA and RNA.

Hitchings was trying to develop drugs by imitating natural compounds. In the past, drugs had been developed by trial-and-error, but he thought it should be possible to develop a rational, scientific approach based on a knowledge of cell growth. He hoped to fool harmful cells into taking in a synthetic compound that was similar to a natural compound the cell needed for growth. This, then, would kill the harmful or defective cell. Hitchings was hoping to create false building blocks that cancerous cells would use when replicating. The false building blocks would kill the cancerous cells without harming normal cells.

While Elion worked on Burroughs's research during the day, she spent her evenings trying to earn a Ph.D. from the Brooklyn Polytechnic Institute. After two years of studies, the dean of the school told her she could no longer work on her doctorate part-time. She would have to quit her job. But she loved her job and she refused to give it up. The dean concluded that this meant she was simply not serious about her education. She was forced to abandon her dream of getting a Ph.D.

In 1950, Elion made a major breakthrough. She developed not one but two anti-cancer drugs, thioguanine and 6-MP, which, when taken with other anticancer drugs, cured childhood leukemia. Now, 80 percent of children with leukemia survive, thanks mostly to Elion's research.

Scientists found in 1958 that 6-MP could suppress the body's immune system, thereby allowing organ transplants. Up until this time, organ transplants rarely worked because the body's immune system would attack any foreign (transplanted) organ. Then researchers found that with a relative of 6-MP called imuran, doctors could suppress the immune system long enough so that the organ transplant would be successful.

In 1968, Elion shifted to working on viruses. Hitchings had retired the year before, so this was her chance to prove what she could do on her own. She hoped to find a drug treatment for the herpes virus infections, which cause chicken pox, shingles, cold sores, and genital sores. For years, she and her team of researchers studied the enzymes specific to particular viruses. Finally they announced the creation of acyclovir, which basically makes the virus commit suicide. It later won FDA approval as Zovirax. This was Elion's "final jewel . . . a real breakthrough in antiviral research." Zovirax is Burrough Wellcome's largest-selling product.

After Elion retired in 1983 and became a consultant to the company, her former unit used her approach to create azidothymidine, or AZT, which is used to treat AIDS. Elion and Hitchings received the Nobel Prize in 1988 for their work in demonstrating the differences in metabolism between normal cells and cancer cells. While the $390,000 prize is certainly an honor, both scientists have repeatedly stated that the real prize has been helping people, curing people. As Elion once observed, "When you meet someone who has lived for twenty-five years with a kidney graft, there's your reward."

## Key Dates

| | |
|---|---|
| 1918 | Born in New York City on January 23 |
| 1937 | Received B.A. from Hunter College with highest honors |
| 1941 | Received master's degree from New York University |
| 1944 | Joined laboratory staff of Burroughs Wellcome in Tuckahoe, New York |
| 1967–1983 | Served as Head of Experimental Therapy at Burroughs Wellcome |
| 1983 | Was emeritus scientist at Burroughs Wellcome |
| 1984–1990 | Served on National Cancer Advisory Board |
| 1988 | Awarded the Nobel Prize for Physiology or Medicine (together with George H. Hitchings and Sir James Black) |
| 1990–1993 | Worked as professor, Ohio State University |
| 1993–1999 | Served on Science and Technology Commission, World Health Organization |
| 1999 | Died February 21 |

## Advice

*If you are considering a career in biochemistry, Gertrude Elion would advise you to work under top leaders in the field to absorb their different philosophies and viewpoints. Extensive anatomy and pre-med courses are valuable along with your complement of chemistry classes. While learning and later while working, constantly ask yourself "What does it mean?" and "Why did it happen?" Science is an iterative process of deduction, intuition, trial-and-error, and back-to-the-drawing-board for a revised deduction—and always more questions.*

## References

Gilbert, Hiram F. *Basic Concepts in Biochemistry: A Student's Survival Guide.* New York: McGraw-Hill, 1991.

McGrayne, Sharon Bertsch. *Nobel Prize Women in Science: Their Lives, Struggles, and Momentous Discoveries.* New York: Carol Publishing, A Birch Lane Press Book, 1993.

Stille, Darlene R. *Extraordinary Women Scientists.* Chicago: Children's Press, 1995.

Stryer, Lubert. *Biochemistry.* 4th ed. New York: W. H. Freeman, 1995. (Comprehensive but difficult reading.)

# Philo T. Farnsworth

*"Father of Television"*

Engineer and
Inventor

## Career Highlights

- Invented the basic components in electronic television
- Registered over 300 domestic and foreign patents

## Important Contributions

Philo Farnsworth lacked advanced formal education but he was filled with innovative ideas, unending persistence, and boundless energy and enthusiasm. With no financial backing or laboratory resources, he envisioned the design of working electronic television transmission and reception systems: He invented television. Just as the Wright brothers were the first to fly a controlled, motorized airplane, Farnsworth was the first to make a television system work. He created the worldwide phenomenon that has influenced billions of people and changed the life and commerce of the world.

## Career Path

The rented living room of a modest San Francisco row house was darkened with heavy curtains even though it was mid-afternoon. It was also quiet except for the hum from stacks of electronic equipment crammed into the spaces where furniture should have been and spilling over into what should have been the dining room. Eight men stood in the room staring— some expectantly, some skeptically—at a small screen, which glowed with hissing static. In rolled-up shirt sleeves and bow tie, Philo Farnsworth flipped the power switches on the camera, amplifiers, and transmitter. Wavy lines rolled across the screen and slowly resolved into the image of a dollar bill, which faded into a short clip of a Gene Tunney boxing match. The picture was fuzzy, flickering, and had too much contrast. But it was there. Television had been born and Philo Farnsworth, a most unlikely inventor for such a high-technology system, was its creator.

Philo was raised in Utah, spending his early years occasionally attending school and more often working on the family farm. When Philo was 13 years old, the family moved to Rigby, Idaho. In their new house he found back issues of various science and technical journals. He studied these periodicals, applying what he learned to repair and improve family farm machinery.

When he first encountered electricity in the form of a Delco generator system, Philo immediately understood how it worked and applied electricity to his mother's hand-cranked washing machine. The next year the boy won a national electronics contest by inventing a magnetized, burglarproof lock for automobiles. He had found his lifelong passion: electricity. Especially, he was fascinated by how light could be converted into electricity and how electricity could be converted back into light.

By this time a German scientist, Dr. Paul Nipkow, had created a mechanical system for electrically transmitting pictures. His system used metal disks with 24 rectangular holes punched in each. Spinning at high speeds, the disks allowed light from various small parts of a total picture to pass through to light-sensitive plates during any given fraction of a second. The problem was that the image quality was poor and viewers tended to develop nauseating headaches.

American Charles Jenkins and British inventor John Baird were struggling to modify and improve the Nipkow system, but with agonizingly slow success.

As a 15-year-old high school student, Philo Farnsworth read the papers on Nipkow's system and decided that a mechanical system could never work. He envisioned performing the whole operation electronically. His idea was to divide an image into thousands of small parts whose light values could be individually sensed by a moving electron beam and transmitted to a distant site where they would be restored to reproduce the image. He explained his idea to his science teacher at Rigby High School, who was staggered by the young boy's ingenuity. This invention would become Farnsworth's consuming preoccupation for most of his life.

In 1923, Farnsworth enrolled at Brigham Young University, but could not afford to stay more than a semester. While working in a United Way office to make ends meet, still a thin, frail-looking teenager, he met two professional fund-raisers, George Everson and Leslie Gorell. They agreed to finance the development of Farnsworth's television design if he would move his lab to California.

First in Los Angeles and then in San Francisco, Farnsworth worked non-stop in his rented apartment lab. Always intense and high-strung, he worked with the shades drawn both for secrecy and to control light in his "studio." The work was made more difficult because he worked alone on new technologies. Most of the pieces of equipment he needed did not exist and had to be scrounged or fabricated from what parts he could find. Vacuum tubes were a constant expense. In one afternoon, he burned up over 50 of them when he forgot to connect the surge protector on his power grid. The giant cathode ray tubes and image dissector tubes had to be made of specially ordered hand-blown glass. He had to design electric pre-heating ovens for several circuits and to construct his own magnetic lenses to control the electron beams.

A constant procession of odd-looking boxes and jars of supplies flowed into the lab. The strange deliveries and the inventor's secretive behavior led, on one occasion, to a police raid. It was Prohibition, a period in the 1920s and 1930s when it was illegal to produce, sell, or own alcoholic beverages in the United States, and they expected to find him making his own alcohol.

By mid-1927, Farnsworth had transmitted his first successful images, a dollar sign, clips from a boxing match, and a movie clip of Mary Pickford combing her hair. One amazed observer claimed that the images, "Jumped out at us from the screen." In 1928, after another year of system improvements, he held press conferences in his laboratory and displayed television images of movie stars and famous scientists to declare his success to the world.

Several national companies (especially Philco, General Electric, and Radio Corporation of American, RCA) were working on their own systems. By late 1928 they all acknowledged the advantages of Farnsworth's system and offered to hire him and purchase his inventions. However, he wished to retain his independence. RCA challenged him in court. They sought to discredit him and his patents, even charging that his patent application infringed on work being conducted by RCA.

Farnsworth stood his ground. But his small company lacked the financial resources to fight giant RCA. Citing financial difficulties, in 1931 he signed a deal with Philco Corporation whereby they would supply financial backing to his company in exchange for his help in designing a television for Philco.

In 1934, Farnsworth quit Philco to bring his invention directly to the public. The next year, he opened his own television station, W3XPF. But any real commercial success depended on developing an agreement with RCA. The president of RCA, David Sarnoff, felt that Farnsworth held too much control, too many crucial patents. Finally, in 1939, RCA purchased Farnsworth's patents and agreed to pay him royalties.

While the agreement benefited Farnsworth personally and financially, it also removed him from active research in the field, and RCA became the leader in developing television. In 1949, Farnsworth Radio and Television began making televisions, but when it encountered financial difficulties, it became a division of International Telephone and Telegraph. The inventor spent the rest of his life wrestling with health problems and focusing on atomic fusion. He died in Salt Lake City, Utah, in 1971.

Americans now watch over 250 billion hours of television each year. Many homes have access to over 100 channels. While others can claim to have invented some of the components of the modern television system, it was independent Philo Farnsworth, working alone with no corporate backing, who made television work.

## Key Dates

| | |
|---|---|
| 1906 | Born in Beaver, Utah, on August 19 |
| 1919 | Moved to Rigby, Idaho |
| 1922 | Earned an electrician's license; moved to Provo, Utah |
| 1923–1924 | Studied at Brigham Young University |
| 1927 | Successfully transmitted television images electronically |
| 1928 | Demonstrated his "image dissector" camera |
| 1929 | Formed Television, Inc. |
| 1934 | Displayed his invention to the public at the Franklin Institute |
| 1935 | Opened his own station, W3XPF, in Philadelphia |
| 1937 | Signed patent-sharing agreement with American Telephone and Telegraph |
| 1938 | Established Farnsworth Radio and Television |
| 1939 | Acquired a manufacturing plant in Fort Wayne, Indiana, to start producing televisions |
| 1949 | Sold his Farnsworth Television & Radio Corporation to the International Telephone & Telegraph Company (ITT) to be a research division |
| 1971 | Died in Salt Lake City on March 11 |

## Advice

*Philo Farnsworth's lack of education made his work slower and harder because he had to struggle on his own to understand the terms and concepts others used in describing electronics developments. He would offer two pieces of advice to anyone considering a career in electronic video technology. First, use university study to learn what others have done and are doing. Discover as much as you can about the thinking and developments of others in your field. Second, don't let academic thinking or the work of others limit your dreams and visions. In May 1990, when a statue of Philo Farnsworth was unveiled in the Capitol in Washington, D.C., his son, Pem Farnsworth, declared, "If Phil were here, he would say, 'Follow your dreams, because nothing is impossible.'"*

## References

Aaseng, Nathan. *American Profiles: Twentieth-Century Inventors.* New York: Facts on File, 1991. (Chapter on Farnsworth.)

Barnouw, Erik. *Tube of Plenty: The Evolution of American Television.* New York: Oxford University Press, 1994. (Review of the development of television.)

Everson, George. *The Story of Television: The Life of Philo T. Farnsworth.* New York: Arno Press, 1974. (Biography of Farnsworth.)

Farnsworth, Philo. "Electron Multiplier Tubes and Their Uses, " *Journal of the Franklin Institute* (1934): 218.

Hofer, Stephen. *Philo Farnsworth: The Quiet Contributor to Television.* Bowling Green, Ky.: Bowling Green University Press, 1977.

McPherson, Stephanie Sammartino. *TV's Forgotten Hero: The Story of Philo Farnsworth.* Minneapolis, Minn.: Carolrhoda Books, 1996.

# Enrico Fermi

*"Navigating into a New World"*

## Nuclear Physics

Lawrence Berkeley National Laboratory

## Career Highlights

- Awarded the Nobel Prize for Physics, 1938
- Served on General Advisory Committee of Atomic Energy Commission by presidential appointment, 1946–1950
- Had major annual prize of the Atomic Energy Commission named in his honor and was the first recipient
- Received the Congressional Medal of Merit, 1946

## Important Contributions

Enrico Fermi is credited with many major discoveries in the field of atomic physics. He developed a new statistical model of electrons, neutrons, protons, and the beta decay process. He discovered and named neutrinos and discovered the "Weak Force," one of the four basic forces of nature.

But Fermi is most famous for creating the world's first self-sustained nuclear reaction. He opened the door to nuclear power.

## Career Path

At 2:20 P.M. on December 2, 1942, Enrico Fermi flipped the switch that would raise hundreds of neutron-absorbing cadmium control rods out of mounds of graphite blocks laced with several tons of uranium oxide pellets. He had stacked 42,000 graphite blocks in an underground squash court situated under the west bleachers of Stagg's field, the University of Chicago football field. No one on campus knew exactly what Fermi was attempting to do in that squash court.

Theory said that a nuclear reaction in the water-filled tank would become a controlled and self-sustaining nuclear reactor once the rods were removed. But theories were often wrong. Nothing might happen, or the entire south side of Chicago might vaporize in a blinding explosion. Students 20 feet above hurried past in the bitter-cold wind without being aware that their lives depended on the theories and calculations of one man, Enrico Fermi. He had built the world's first nuclear reactor. As the cadmium rods withdrew he would either become an international hero and usher in the nuclear age, a failure, or vaporized.

By the time Enrico Fermi reached the age of 13, he had amazed his teachers in Rome, Italy, with his ability to learn complex subjects. He won a fellowship to the University of Piza, where he completed both undergraduate and graduate programs in just four years, graduating magna cum laude in 1922 with a Ph.D. in physics. He was invited to the University of Göttingen in Germany for post-graduate studies with Max Born, and then to the University of Leiden in the Netherlands.

By the age of 23, Fermi had already established a solid international reputation and returned home to create Italy's first modern school of physics at the University of Rome.

The 1932 discovery of neutrons (neutrally charged particles about the same mass as a proton) shifted Fermi's focus into the core of an atom. As a leading physics experimenter, he recognized that neutrons could solve a problem of subatomic physics. Physicists had been trying to smash both electrons and protons into the nucleus of an atom to see if the effort would reveal new secrets of atomic structure. But electrons and protons had to be accelerated to near light speed to overpower the repulsive force of an atom's shells of electrons for an invading electron, or that of the nucleus for an invading proton. Accelerators were giant, expensive, and temperamental pieces of equipment.

Fermi realized that if he bombarded atoms with uncharged neutrons, he wouldn't need a massive accelerator because neutrons would not be repulsed. Using high-powered magnets, his team planned to direct a stream of slower neutrons into a target substance. They hoped the target nuclei would capture these free neutrons and transform the target substance into a new, radioactive isotope.

The scientists' first target was fluorine. They flooded free neutrons at a gaseous fluorine sample. Fermi succeeded in measuring radioactivity from the resulting gas with crude Geiger counters. Slow-moving neutrons *were* absorbed by target nuclei.

Bombarding every element on the periodic table with streams of neutrons, he created over a hundred new, radioactive substances as he tested his way down the periodic chart. Each created substance was chemically tested to establish its new identity and characteristics.

For his work in creating these new substances and for discovering the concept of slow-neutron bombardment, Fermi was awarded the 1938 Nobel Prize for Physics. That same summer, he fled Italy to escape the new Fascist regime and arrived at Columbia University in New York.

In 1940, Fermi, along with many other leading physicists, turned to the potential of fission. If a uranium atom could be persuaded both to split *and* to release several free neutrons when it was struck, then those neutrons could strike other uranium atoms. A chain reaction could be created, releasing incredible amounts of energy.

But a world of questions and incredible dangers stood between that "could" and the reality of a controlled nuclear chain reaction. Even though he was officially an enemy alien (the United States *was* at war with Italy), Fermi was given responsibility for the U.S. government's program to create a nuclear chain reaction. He was the only enemy alien allowed near this top secret effort.

The year 1942 was marked by a string of frantic experiments and discoveries. $U^{235}$ fissioned better than $U^{238}$. The heavier isotope tended to absorb neutrons instead of fracturing when struck. But $U^{235}$ was rare and hard to isolate. Any impurities tended to absorb too many free neutrons and jeopardize the reaction. Graphite blocks successfully slowed neutrons to a speed ideal for $U^{235}$ fission reaction. Cadmium absorbed neutrons and would be a good control substance. Each simple finding entailed weeks of grueling effort.

Fermi's research took him from Columbia to the University of Chicago in early November 1942. His task was to build the world's first working nuclear reactor. He had only one month to do it. He was given an underground squash court to use. One month later, at 2:20 P.M. on December 2, the world entered a new era. His reactor worked. The world's first self-sustained nuclear reaction boiled the cooling water around it for 28 minutes before being shut down by the reinserted cadmium rods.

Observer Arthur Compton said of this historic event, "The Italian navigator has just landed in the new world."

Managing director of the project, John Cockcroft, said, "It was clear that Fermi had unlocked the door to the atomic age."

Fermi continued to refine his efforts to uncloak the mysteries of an atom's nucleus until he died in 1954 of cancer, undoubtedly caused by years of exposure to radioactivity.

In the 50 years that he lived, Enrico Fermi's discoveries and experiments changed not only every field of physical science but also the patterns of our everyday life. During the second quarter of the twentieth century, he was one of the most creative and productive scientists in the world, writing over 270 significant papers. He has rightly been called the greatest Italian scientist since Galileo, the greatest Italian navigator into new worlds since Columbus.

## Key Dates

| | |
|---|---|
| 1901 | Born in Rome, Italy, on September 29 |
| 1922 | Received Ph.D. from University of Piza |
| 1924–1927 | Taught mathematical physics and mechanics at University of Florence |
| 1927–1938 | Founded Theoretical Physics Department at University of Rome |
| 1938 | Fled Italy to escape Mussolini; took professorship at Columbia University |
| 1938 | Awarded Nobel Prize for Physics |
| 1942 | Created the first controlled nuclear reaction at University of Chicago |
| 1942–1945 | Worked on Manhattan Project to develop first atomic bomb |
| 1946–1954 | Served as director of the Institute of Nuclear Studies in Chicago |
| 1954 | Died on November 30 |

# Advice

*If you are considering a career in physics, Enrico Fermi would advise you not to specialize. Specialization limits your ability to creatively advance your work and solve problems. Explore the basics of different fields of science and how those fields interact and affect each other. Include chemistry, nuclear chemistry, thermodynamics, and electronics as well as math and physics courses in your studies.*

# References

Daintith, John, et al., eds. *Biographical Encyclopedia of Scientists.* 2d ed. Vol. 1. Philadelphia, Pa.: Institute of Physics Publishing, 1994. (Summary entry on Fermi's work.)

Dear, Pamela, ed. *Contemporary Authors.* Vol. 157. Detroit: Gale Research, 1995. (Good biographical summary and summary of Fermi's writings.)

Gillispie, Charles, ed. *Dictionary of Scientific Biography.* Vol. XV. New York: Charles Scribner's Sons, 1978. (Good summary of Fermi's work.)

Serge, Emilio. *Enrico Fermi: Physicist.* Chicago: University of Chicago Press, 1970.

Tanor, Joseph, ed. *McGraw-Hill Modern Men of Science.* New York: McGraw-Hill, 1986. (Strong summary of Fermi's work.)

Wasson, Tyler, ed. *Nobel Prize Winners.* New York: H. W. Wilson, 1987. (Excellent summary of Fermi's work.)

# Richard P. Feynman

*"The Most Brilliant Young Physicist"*                    Physics

## Career Highlights

- Redefined the entire field of quantum electrodynamics
- Awarded the Nobel Prize for Physics, 1965
- Received the Albert Einstein Award of the Lewis and Rosa Strauss Memorial Fund, 1954
- Received the Ernest Orlando Lawrence Memorial Award for Physics of the U.S. Atomic Energy Commission, 1962
- Served on a 12-member special commission to investigate the explosion of the space shuttle *Challenger*

## Important Contributions

Copernicus discovered that all the "correction factors" early astronomers had to use resulted from a fundamental theoretical flaw: The Earth was not the center of the universe. The sun was. Richard Feynman accomplished for the field of quantum electrodynamics what Copernicus accomplished for astronomy. He discovered that the prevailing basic assumptions about the behavior of individual particles (electrons, positrons, photons, and so forth) were incorrect.

Feynman created a new theory based on the probability of various possible events actually occurring. His theory led to a great advance in the accuracy with which the behavior of the electron could be computed, and in our understanding of electron interactions. He was also the first to predict the existence of quarks (the building blocks of protons and neutrons) and he made significant contributions to the theory of superconductivity.

# Career Path

In a frustrated and depressed state from months of fruitless struggle, professor Richard Feynman sat in the Cornell University cafeteria and watched a student toss a plate into the air. The plate spun like a Frisbee® and wobbled as the students tossed it from person to person. He was fascinated by the relationship between the plate's spin rate and its wobble. There at his cafeteria table he began to scratch out the equations to describe this relationship.

Admittedly, plate wobble seemingly had nothing to do with electron-photon interactions. But while solving the plate wobble equations, Feynman was struck with a new approach to solving the fundamental problem in quantum electrodynamics (QED), which had tormented him for several years. The solution he devised created a new theoretical understanding that now occupies a central position in physics. It not only restructured the field of quantum electrodynamics, but also earned for Feynman the Nobel Prize. He once wrote that the "whole business I got the Nobel Prize for came from that piddling around with that wobbling plate."

Even as a toddler, Richard Feynman showed great aptitude for mathematics. He was especially good at solving puzzles. He learned how to visualize a problem as a whole, thus dispensing with many computational steps. As a young child, he put on magic shows using simple chemistry principles; in high school, he made extra money by repairing radios. By the end of high school, he had taught himself calculus.

Following undergraduate work at the Massachusetts Institute of Technology (MIT), Feynman began post-graduate studies at Princeton in 1939. After he received a doctorate in 1942, he joined the Manhattan Project, America's secret program to produce the atomic bomb. There he led the team assigned to calculate implosions and he computed the formula for nuclear weapon energy yield—a calculation that is still classified.

Following the war, Feynman accepted an associate professorship of theoretical physics at Cornell University, where he investigated problems in the field of quantum electrodynamics (QED), a sub-field of quantum mechanics that studies the interaction of electrons and photons. Simplifications in the general QED theory (such as that an electron was a point charge instead of an actual particle with volume and mass) had been made to make the resulting equations manageable. While the equations were now solvable, they often produced absurd results (such as that the electrical charge of an electron at its own surface was infinite).

To correct these absurdities and force calculations to match observable realities, physicists introduced a series of normalizing terms into the equations. Soon basic equations stretched over three and four chalk boards. It reminded Feynman of what astronomers did to correct the errors in their predictions of star motion before Copernicus discovered that the errors came from the assumption that the Earth was the center of the universe instead of the sun. Once the general theory was corrected, the need for "fudge-factors" disappeared.

Feynman decided that QED was unintelligible as it currently existed and that someone had to find and correct the theory's fundamental errors and reinvent the field. He decided to take on the job himself, even though the task was daunting. He suffered from a lack of necessary data. Apparatus to allow him to actually see the interactions of electrons and photons did not exist. There seemed to be no worthwhile clues to follow, no reliable data on which to base his calculations. Soon he had reached mental stagnation. Every analysis led to a dead end. Every new idea looped back into the same tired and unproductive concepts.

It was in this frustrated and depressed state that Feynman sat in the Cornell cafeteria and watched students toss that plate into the air. For a diversion, he began to derive equations to describe the plate's spin rate and wobble. In the midst of his second page of equations, he conceived of a new way to solve QED problems.

The results of Feynman's new approach were a series of diagrams that measured the probability of various possible events actually occurring. The diagrams, called "Feynman diagrams," made it possible for him to solve any equation in quantum electrodynamics and to develop a precise picture of the collisions of electrons, positrons, and photons in matter. For this work, he was awarded the Nobel Prize in 1965.

Feynman also studied the relationship between superconductivity and particle physics. This work led him to realize that protons and neutrons were not the most fundamental particles, and he predicted that both were composed of smaller particles. In 1958 he proposed the existence of a new nuclear particle, the "quark." Twenty years later quarks were discovered and, as he had predicted, found to be the building blocks of protons and neutrons.

The physicist's research focus shifted temporarily in 1986 when he was asked to serve on a presidential commission to investigate the explosion of the space shuttle *Challenger*. He brought to the investigation his hard-driving critical intellect and his ability to devote many hours to intense intellectual concentration. As a physicist, he had devoted his life to a grueling intellectual study of the truth; he brought that same attitude to the investigation but found that some co-members on the commission were less interested in truth and more interested in an acceptable story to present to Washington, NASA, and the American people.

At one point during the hearings, a suggestion was made that the shuttle's explosion might have been triggered by a failure of the "O rings." O rings are rubber seals around the valves of the fuel tanks. It was thought that when chilled (launch-time temperatures were well below freezing), O rings might fail and allow volatile fuel vapors to seep into dangerous parts of the rocket booster. Since NASA had been warned of this danger prior to takeoff, a NASA official responded with a lengthy explanation of how difficult it is to test such a theory.

Feynman immediately called for a glass of ice water, took some of the rubbery O ring material, placed it in the cold water, and upon removing it from the glass demonstrated that the rubber had suffered a phase change and grown temporarily stiff.

Richard Feynman's exacting and relentless drive for ultimate truth led not only to a clearer understanding of the *Challenger* disaster, but also, in a more general sense, to the entire field of quantum mechanics. Specifically, his brilliant mind drafted the hypothesis that proved to be a turning point in the development of quantum electrodynamics. Indeed, Robert Oppenheimer, in reviewing the incredible wealth of talent amassed for the Manhattan Project, called him "the most brilliant young physicist here."

## Key Dates

| | |
|---|---|
| 1918 | Born in New York City on May 11 |
| 1939 | Received B.S. from Massachusetts Institute of Technology |
| 1941–1942 | Worked as a physicist at Princeton University |
| 1942 | Received Ph.D. in theoretical physics from Princeton University |
| 1941–1945 | Worked as a physicist on the Manhattan Project at Los Alamos, New Mexico |
| 1945–1951 | Worked as associate professor of pysics at Cornell University |
| 1951–1988 | Worked as professor of theoretical physics at California Institute of Technology |
| 1965 | Won Nobel Prize for Physics |
| 1986 | Appointed to presidential commission to study the explosion of the space shuttle *Challenger* |
| 1988 | Died of abdominal cancer February 15 in Los Angeles, California |

## Advice

*A cornerstone of Richard Feynman's beliefs was that each scientist was responsible to question and challenge theory. No field can develop without rigorous, constant challenge to its hypotheses and assumptions. Above all else, he would advise students to first ground themselves in math and logic. Master all forms of math and their orderly application because mathematics is the language of science. Also learn the skills of reasoning, logic, and analysis. They will guide your questioning. Begin serious studies with physics, thermodynamics, and chemistry before advancing to particle physics and nuclear physics. Finally, open your mind to unexpected sources and ideas. All the world is a science textbook and the ideas you need could be lurking around any street corner, not just in textbooks, science journals, and labs.*

## References

Feynman, Richard P. *Feynman Lectures on Physics.* 3 vols. Boston: Addison-Wesley, 1989.

———. *QED: The Strange Theory of Light and Matter.* Princeton, N.J.: Princeton University Press, 1985.

Feynman, Richard P., and Ralph Leighton. *"Surely You're Joking, Mr. Feynman!": Adventures of a Curious Character.* New York: W. W. Norton, 1985.

———. *"What Do You Care What Other People Think?": Further Adventures of a Curious Character.* New York: W. W. Norton, 1988.

Gianocoli, Douglas C. *Physics Principles: with Applications.* 3d ed. New York: Prentice Hall Press, 1991.

Gleick, James. *Genius: The Life and Science of Richard Feynman.* New York: Pantheon Books, 1992.

# Dian Fossey

*"The Old Lady Who Lives in the Forest"*　　　　　Zoology

## Career Highlights

- Was one of the world's leading authorities on mountain gorillas
- Received the Franklin Burr Award from National Geographic Society, 1973
- Awarded the Joseph Wood Krutch Medal from the Humane Society of the United States, 1984
- Authored *Gorillas in the Mist*, 1983

## Important Contributions

Dian Fossey spent 18 years studying African mountain gorillas in the wild. The data she collected on these shy primates (who do not survive in captivity) has been considered invaluable by naturalists, and she became recognized as the world's leading authority on gorillas. In dense mountain rainforests she studied gorilla habits, social structure, and communication patterns; she even became recognized and accepted by the local gorilla population. She dedicated her life to the study of the gorillas and became a champion for their preservation. Without her untiring efforts to study and preserve this dwindling species, the mountain gorilla would surely be extinct by now.

## Career Path

It was not a promising beginning. When Dian Fossey first met famed anthropologist Louis Leakey at his archaeological excavation in Tanzania in 1963, she broke her ankle running down a hillside and then vomited all over the important fossil his team had just unearthed. She had come to impress

Leakey. Without his help she feared she would not get to see and to experience mountain gorillas in the wild. This was not the first impression she had hoped to create.

Still, when Fossey hobbled off on crutches two weeks later to meet a guide she had hired to lead her into gorilla country, Leakey was very impressed with her courage, fortitude, and determination.

Dian Fossey had been raised in San Francisco, California, where, even as a small child, she loved animals. Her parents did not allow her to have pets, however, other than a goldfish—and she later commented that "Goldie's" death was the first trauma of her life. After high school, she studied pre-veterinary medicine at the University of California, Davis, then transferred to San Jose State College, where she graduated with a degree in occupational therapy.

In 1956, Fossey moved to Kentucky as director of the occupational therapy department at a hospital for crippled children. She enjoyed her work and felt it was important. But neither her work nor the abundant horses she loved to ride could quell a lifelong longing. To her it felt like destiny, a rumbling urge that would not go away: She wanted to go to Africa—*needed* to go to Africa—and especially, she longed to see a gorilla in the wild. It wasn't a dream based on logic. It wasn't something she had worked toward. Just the opposite. She had steadfastly ignored it. But the longing for a journey to Africa would not disappear.

Fossey's parents and friends found her dream dismaying; she found it glorious. In 1963, she decided to make her dream happen and took out an $8,000 loan for a seven-week safari trip to Africa.

During Fossey's first week in Africa she sought out anthropologist Louis Leakey. Leakey was impressed with her as she hobbled off, unwilling to let calamity shatter her plans. After her safari—and her first brief meeting with "the greatest of the great apes," the gorilla—she returned to Kentucky and continued her work with handicapped children. She feared her brief taste of Africa was all she would ever get, although it did not quench her deep thirst for more.

Three years later, Leakey visited Fossey in Louisville and invited her to conduct long-term research on the mountain gorilla. She eagerly accepted despite her lack of zoological, biological, or ecological education or experience. To test her resolve, Leakey told her that if she really wanted to conduct research in Africa, she should have her appendix removed (hers was a completely healthy appendix). She did so, and after the surgery he sent her a note explaining that he was just testing her determination.

By late 1966, Fossey was back in Africa. After paying a brief visit to Jane Goodall to learn fieldwork techniques and the best methods for data collection, she struck out on her own, setting up her base camp in the Republic of the Congo (now Zaire). Six months later, the area fell under civil war. She was placed under "protective arrest," but escaped and fled to Rwanda with two chickens, an old Land Rover, and a pistol hidden in a box of tissues. She was warned that if she ever returned to Zaire, she would be shot on sight.

Fossey established her new camp—two tents—between two extinct volcanoes of the Virunga Mountains in Rwanda. She called the camp the Karisoke Research Center.

The fieldwork was extraordinarily challenging. Because the gorillas were intensely shy of strangers, and inhabited dense, high-altitude mountain rain forests, they were extremely difficult to observe.

Over time, Fossey gradually befriended the gorillas by copying their behavior. She learned to knuckle-walk and to announce her approach by imitating the gorillas' "contentment vocalizations." She pretended to eat the gorillas' favorite foods, and she imitated their grooming practices.

This new approach to field research was effective—although not without its dangers. For many months, Fossey had imitated the gorillas by slapping her hands against her thighs, mimicking the rhythm of their chestbeats. It got the gorillas' attention but, she realized later, was sending the signal for alarm!

Hers was lonely work, filled with great personal discomfort. Still, Fossey thought herself one of the luckiest people on earth. She amassed huge quantities of information about the gorillas and their behavior that had never been observed before. She found the gorillas to be pacific, charging only when threatened or when approached without warning. She found that they had strong family units, often tenderly nursing hurt or ill members of their group. She found that an entire family would fight to the death to prevent even one infant from being harmed or captured. She recounted one such horror story about a park warden who sold two young gorillas to a German zoo. To capture the two infants, the warden and his staff killed 18 adult gorillas. He then brought the two infants, who were near death, to Fossey for medical care. When one of them, Coco, was released from her traveling cage, she climbed onto a ledge to look out the window. When she saw the mountain forest from which she had been taken, she began to cry. Coco and the other gorilla both died a few years later in captivity.

Fossey recorded her study of the gorillas in the autobiographical book, *Gorillas in the Mist.* The purpose of her book was to convey an understanding of the gorillas—and help ensure their conservation and survival. In her book she included scientific analyses (autopsy reports, dung analyses, kinship studies, spectrographic charts, and so forth) along with her personal accounts.

In 1970 Fossey realized that she would need assistance: The gorillas were at increasing danger from poachers. When Digit, her favorite silverback (a dominant male), was killed in 1978, she publicized the poaching problem, recruited student volunteers, and set up anti-poacher patrols. Her efforts to stop poachers, however, made enemies of the local people. There were rumors of her intimidating locals with black magic and interrogations. Once she supposedly kidnapped the child of a local couple who had trapped a gorilla for sale; Fossey apparently held the child until the gorilla was released.

The locals called her *Nyiramachabelli,* "the old lady who lives in the forest without a man." The tension between her and the locals increased until December 27, 1985, when she was murdered in her camp—hacked to death with a machete. According to her wishes, she was buried in the cemetery she had established for gorillas killed by poachers. She left behind two old tents, a few personal effects, and a mountain of compelling, detailed information on the most misunderstood and endangered of all the great apes.

## Key Dates

| | |
|---|---|
| 1932 | Born in San Francisco, California, on January 16 |
| 1954 | Received B.A. from San Jose State College (now San Jose State University) |
| 1955–1966 | Worked as an occupational therapist with crippled children |
| 1967–1980 & 1983–1985 | Served as scientific director of the Karisoke Research Center, Ruhengeri, Rwanda |
| 1976 | Received Ph.D. from Cambridge University |
| 1978 | Served as president of Digit Fund, Ithaca, N.Y. |
| 1980–1983 | Served as project coordinator of the Karisoke Research Center, Ruhengeri, Rwanda |
| 1980–1982 | Was visiting professor at Cornell University |
| 1985 | Died December 27 in Mont Visoke, Rwanda, Africa |

# Advice

*Dian Fossey lacked training in zoology and in general biological field studies, which made her work more difficult. She made up for her technical shortcomings with commitment, enthusiasm, and passion. She would advise someone considering a career in field zoology to first obtain a solid foundation in zoology, general biology, and ecology to learn about a variety of species and how they interact with their environments. Organic chemistry and pre-veterinary courses will also be helpful. But remember that academic knowledge will not be enough to sustain your career. Find fields and studies that stir your passions. Let your dreams guide your direction. Let your coursework support it.*

# References

Clutton-Brock, T. H., [ed.]. *Primate Ecology: Studies of Feeding and Ranging Behaviour in Lemurs, Monkeys, and Apes.* London: Academic Press, 1977.

Fossey, Dian. *Gorillas in the Mist.* Boston: Houghton Mifflin, 1984.

Graham, C. E., [ed.]. *Reproductive Biology of the Great Apes.* New York: Academic Press, 1980.

Roberts, Jack. *The Importance of Dian Fossey.* San Diego, Calif.: Lucent Books, 1995.

# Rosalind Franklin

*"The Outsider"*

Molecular Biology
and X-Ray
Crystallography

## Career Highlights

- Supplied the key information to determine the structure of DNA
- Considered one of the founders of biomolecular science
- Helped found the science of high-strength carbon fibers through her research into coals and charcoals and was recognized authority in industrial chemistry

Department of Crystallography, Birkbeck College, University of London

## Important Contributions

Using X-ray crystallography, Rosalind Franklin established the key information to decipher the structure of DNA. Her research was essential to the work of James Watson and Francis Crick, who are credited with the discovery. Indeed, without Franklin's work, it is clear that Watson and Crick could not have made their momentous discovery. Unfortunately, Watson and Crick beat her to the Nobel Prize by using her data without her knowledge and without crediting her. As more of the facts about Rosalind's life and work have surfaced, she is finally receiving some of the recognition due her for so long.

## Career Path

Rosalind Franklin's childhood should have been ideal, with all the advantages of wealth and position. Her life should have been one of leisure and carefree joy. Rosalind was born in 1920 into a wealthy London banking family and spent her childhood moving between a luxurious home in London and a country home and spending winters along the Mediterranean. The family had plenty of English servants to make their lives comfortable.

But Rosalind never sought what her privilege could provide. She seemed destined for a path of confrontation, conflict, and disappointment. In many ways, this path made for a bitter and disappointing life. In other ways it led to a life of discovery, quiet triumph, and satisfaction that her parents' money could not buy.

As a child, Rosalind's conservative parents could not understand or support her interest in truth, scientific proofs, reasons, and facts. She did not play like other girls her age—she did not like dolls, did not like "let's pretend," and was keenly interested in building things. Her quiet, analytical mind drew no praise from her parents—indeed, it worried them.

At age eight, Rosalind caught a series of colds and flu and was sent on a doctor's recommendation to a convalescent boarding school near the sea. She hated the school and resented that year away from home, and she also learned an unfortunate lesson there. She learned it was safer to ignore illness and pain. At one point, instead of seeking help from the school, she walked alone for blocks in excruciating pain to seek treatment at a hospital for a needle stuck deep in her knee joint. Later, in her thirties, she ignored the first pains of cancer until it was too late to save her.

When she returned home, Rosalind attended St. Paul's Girls School in London, which offered excellent classes in physics and chemistry. By age 15, she had decided to be a scientist. She took and passed the entrance examinations for chemistry at Cambridge, but her father refused to pay her tuition. Although he had once himself thought to have a science career and would have been proud to have a son in a scientific career, he strongly disapproved of university education for women.

Rosalind's Aunt Alice was angered by her brother's refusal and announced that she would pay to send her to Cambridge. Rosalind's mother added her support and said that she, too, would pay for her education out of her own family money. Rosalind's father grudgingly relented, but she never forgave him for opposing her education.

Franklin graduated in 1941 from Newnham College, a women's college at Cambridge University. Because World War II was underway, her first job was with a British government agency studying ways of using coal more efficiently. The papers that she wrote on this subject are still extensively quoted today, and the research she did there supported her Ph.D., which she received in 1945.

In 1947, through a friend, Franklin found a job in Paris at the Laboratoire Central des Services Chimiques de l'Etat. There she worked on X-ray crystallography, firing X-rays through a crystal. When the X-rays strike atoms in the crystal, they bounce off at angles (refract) and form patterns on photographic film. Crystallographers can then decipher how the atoms in a molecule are arranged by studying the X-ray light patterns on film.

In 1951, Franklin returned to England to take up a position as a researcher at Kings College, London. There, scientists led by physicist John Randall were taking X-ray photographs of DNA molecules. John hired her to analyze the photographs. Unfortunately, a breach of communication occurred. She understood that the project was hers and hers alone to lead. But when John's second in command, Maurice Wilkins, returned from an absence, he assumed she was to work for him as a high-class technical assistant. Their conflict never righted itself; in the end they would hardly speak to one another and Wilkins would betray her work to a competitor.

With only a graduate student to assist her, Franklin made better and better X-ray images of DNA molecules. Two scientists at Cambridge, James Watson and Francis Crick, were also working to unravel the structure of the DNA molecule. They attended one of Rosalind Franklin's colloquium talks but remembered her data incorrectly when they used it to construct a model of the DNA molecule. She pointed out the mistakes in their model in her brusque, no-nonsense style. Watson resented being told he was wrong by a woman, especially when she was right. Any thoughts of collaboration or cooperation between Franklin and Watson/Crick instantly evaporated.

This was not an easy time to be an independent woman in science. Women were outsiders. They were resented, ignored, and passed over. In 1952 Franklin made a now-famous X-ray crystallography image of DNA that showed an "X" shape, suggesting a twisted, or helical shape. When she wrote of these findings to American Nobel Prize-winning chemist Linus Pauling and suggested a partnership (he was also working on DNA), he never even wrote back. Instead, he collaborated with Watson and Crick, despite the fact that Watson and Crick were way behind Franklin in DNA research.

Then, in a stroke of very bad luck for Franklin, Maurice Wilkins secretly showed James Watson some of her prize work, including the famous X-shape image. It is clear now that her contribution (given away without her knowledge by Wilkins) was key to solving the puzzle.

Armed with Pauling's manuscript and Franklin's X-shape image, Watson and ·Crick, for the first time, had more information on DNA than Franklin. In March 1953, they announced that they had solved the DNA puzzle. For this work, they later shared the Nobel Prize. Of the 98 references they cited in their Nobel lectures, none was to the work of Rosalind Franklin—even though her work enabled them to make the discovery.

Franklin left Kings College for a position as head of a research group at Birkbeck College. She used her knowledge of X-ray crystallography to study viruses made of RNA, hoping to determine how simple strands of protein and genetic material reproduce and cause illness. She actually worked with Crick and Watson later, eventually becoming friends with Crick (but never Watson, whom she called "the horrible American").

Rosalind Franklin's life ended much as she had lived it. She quietly contracted cancer when 36, stoically lived with it in silence for many months, and died prematurely at 38. A great mind and determined spirit were lost before any of the credit or recognition she deserved were given to her.

Once the structure of DNA was understood, the field of molecular biology exploded, becoming probably the most important rapidly developing field of the late twentieth century. Bioengineering or the use of recombinant DNA is likely to be the most important technology of the twenty-first century. Rosalind Franklin helped get us there.

## Key Dates

| | |
|---|---|
| 1920 | Born in London, England, on July 25 |
| 1938 | Enrolled in Newnham College, a women's college in Cambridge University |
| 1941 | Graduated from Cambridge |
| 1945 | Received Ph.D. |
| 1947–1950 | Worked on X-ray crystallography in Paris at the Laboratoire Central des Services Chimiques de l'Etat |
| 1951 | Worked as researcher at Kings College, London |
| 1952 | Created the image of the X-shape of DNA |
| 1953 | Crick and Watson announced that they had solved the DNA puzzle |
| 1953 | Joined Birkbeck College |
| 1958 | Died of ovarian cancer on April 16 |

# Advice

*The field of X-ray crystallography involves extensive use of laboratory experiments. Rosalind Franklin believed the development of exceptional lab and experimental skills was the most important element of a successful career. Take great pains with the precision of your experiments. Be keenly observant, be precise in your work, and don't take for granted how much easier it is now than it was in the 1950s. In school, focus on molecular biology and courses that allow you to develop lab and experimental skills.*

# References

Bloss, Donald F. *Crystallography & Crystal Chemistry: An Introduction.* Columbus, Ohio: Ceramic Books & Literature, 1989.

McGrayne, Sharon Bertsch. *Nobel Prize Women in Science: Their Lives, Struggles, and Momentous Discoveries.* New York: Carol Publishing, A Birch Lane Press Book, 1993.

Sayre, Anne. *Rosalind Franklin and DNA.* New York: W. W. Norton, 1975.

Stille, Darlene R. *Extraordinary Women Scientists.* Chicago: Children's Press, 1995.

Wood, Elizabeth A. *Crystals & Light: An Introduction to Optical Crystallography.* Mineola, N.Y.: Dover, 1977.

# Dennis Gabor

*"My Luckiest Find Yet"*

Physics and
Electrical
Engineering

## Career Highlights

- Invented holography and patented more than 100 other inventions
- Received Nobel Prize for Physics, 1971
- Won the Albert Michelson Medal of the Franklin Institute, 1968
- Received the Medal of Honor of the Institute of Electrical and Electronics Engineers, 1970

## Important Contributions

Dennis Gabor is best known for his invention of holography, a photographic method of reproducing three-dimensional images without using a lens. The hologram looks like an unrecognizable pattern of shapes and swirls until it is lit by a special light (such as a laser beam), which creates a three-dimensional representation of the original object. The process has a wide range of applications from medical imaging, map making, information storage and computing, to art and diagnosing faults in high-speed equipment.

Gabor also worked on high-speed oscilloscopes, communication theory, physical optics, and television. He took out more than 100 patents for his inventions and became renowned as an outstanding engineer and physicist of the twentieth century.

## Career Path

On a cool spring day in April 1947, Dennis Gabor sat on a bench at his tennis club in London. He hadn't come to play, but to escape the frustrations of work and to sit and feel sorry for himself. His mind filled with vague and discontented grumblings as he listened to the steady thwack of rackets and watched yellow balls race back and forth across the nets on six courts.

Gabor played tennis but not well, so he was excluded from the club's center court. But then, he was used to being excluded. Physicists snubbed him because his degree was in mechanical engineering, even though he always considered himself a physicist. He was excluded from all sensitive and classified work because he had been born in Hungary and was therefore technically an enemy alien during those war years. At that moment his life and his career—which should have held such promise—looked like an endless row of closed doors and exclusive barriers.

Then, as he watched the tennis balls, an idea popped into Gabor's head, an idea he had been searching for all his life, and an idea that solved problems he had struggled with for 15 years. His career was saved and holography was born.

Dennis Gabor was born and raised in Budapest, Hungary. By the time he was in high school, Dennis was demonstrating an amazing understanding of physics. In fact at home, he and his brother would repeat experiments they had only read about in school.

After a short stint in the army during World War I, Gabor signed up for a four-year course in mechanical engineering at the Budapest Technical University. Although his passion was for physics, there were too few professional positions in physics. Engineering seemed more flexible and practical. In his third year, he was once again called up for military service. Because he opposed the monarchy that had come to power in 1920, he fled to Germany and received his diploma in engineering from Berlin Technical University in 1924. He received his doctorate there in 1927. While working on his doctorate, Gabor invented a fast-response cathode-ray oscilloscope. His invention replaced the conventional long-focusing solenoid with a short coil encased in iron. Without realizing it, he had built a crude magnetic electron lens, the forerunner of the electron microscope. But he was too focused on his doctoral work to give much thought to it. Within two years, two other scientists, Ernst Ruska and Max Knoll, developed a two-stage electron microscope, which proved to be one of the most important technological advancements of the twentieth century.

Gabor remained in Berlin after graduation to work in the physics laboratory of Siemens and Halske Company, where he was assigned to study lamp technology. There he invented the quartz mercury lamp, still popular today. In 1933, under the restrictive policies of the newly elected Nazi regime, his contract was terminated because he was not German, and he returned to Hungary. Working without a salary, he invented a new kind of fluorescent lamp, which he called the plasma lamp, at the Tungsram Electron

Tube Research Institute in Budapest. He tried, unsuccessfully, to patent his lamp in Hungary. During the following year he emigrated to England to try to sell his new lamp there. While it was never a success, his plasma lamp helped him get a job at the British Thomson-Houston Company (BTH). At BTH Gabor was assigned to improve the resolution power of the electron microscope—the very machine he had conceived in 1926, but had not pursued and developed, a machine that had swept the world as a revolutionary new device. The electron microscope had improved resolution a hundredfold over light microscopes, but it still did not allow scientists to see atomic lattices. The image was distorted either through fuzziness (like an out-of-focus camera) or through sphericity (like looking through a dew drop). Improving one worsened the other, and vice versa. Gabor hoped to produce an instrument that could "see" individual atoms.

During the war years, Gabor's research didn't go well. As an expatriate Hungarian, he was excluded from classified work at BTH, because only British citizens were allowed to do that type of work, and was cut off from most scientific literature. He couldn't find a way to improve the electron microscope on his own, and he couldn't interest others in working with him on the project. He was seriously considering moving to the United States.

In 1947, as he sat on that bench at the local tennis club, a brilliant idea came to him in what he called "my luckiest find yet." Why not take a bad electron picture, but one which contains the whole information, and correct it by optical means? Why not use light to magnify and read a picture taken with electron beams? Gabor's idea was the beginning of holography. He coined the term hologram from the Greek *holos,* meaning whole, and *gram,* meaning message.

Gabor envisioned splitting an electron beam in two, sending one beam to the object, the other to a mirror. Both would initially have the same wavelength and be in phase. The beam reflected from the mirror would be unchanged, but the beam reflected from the object would contain all the irregularities imposed upon it by that object. When the two beams met at a photographic plate, the interference pattern that resulted could be captured on film. When light was shone through this film, it would take on the interference pattern and produce a three-dimensional image of the object.

In July 1947, Gabor, using a mercury vapor lamp as the light source, produced the interference photographs of simple two-dimensional images. Less than a year later, he introduced a three-dimensional "hologram" to the world.

Unfortunately, Gabor's best holograms were still hazy images, which severely limited their usefulness. His theory was sound, but because the only light sources at the time were conventional, filtered light sources, the only holograms he could create were imprecise. It was not until the invention of laser beams around 1960 that commercial holograms became feasible and the full potential of his invention became realized. Nevertheless, he received the Nobel Prize for his creation of holograms in 1971.

During the final 30 years of his life, Gabor taught and dabbled in a wide range of research projects. His inventions during this period included the flat television tube and speech compression. But it was through his creation of the hologram that Dennis Gabor made a lasting impression on physics, medical science, art, and the lives of all modern Americans.

## Key Dates

| | |
|---|---|
| 1900 | Born in Budapest, Hungary, on June 5 |
| 1924 | Received engineering degree from Berlin Technical University |
| 1927 | Received Ph.D. in engineering from Berlin Technical University |
| 1933 | Returned to Hungary and developed the plasma lamp |
| 1933 | Emigrated to England |
| 1934–1948 | Worked at British Thomson-Houston Company (BTH) |
| 1948 | Became a reader in electronics for Imperial College, London |
| 1958–1967 | Worked as Professor of applied electron physics for Imperial College, London |
| 1967 | Was senior research fellow for Imperial College, London |
| 1971 | Won Nobel Prize for Physics |
| 1974 | Suffered debilitating stroke, which left him unable to read or write |
| 1979 | Died February 9 in London |

## Advice

*If you are considering a career in physics, Dennis Gabor would advise you to consider adding mechanical, electrical, and chemical engineering classes to your physics curriculum. Engineering approaches offer practical perspectives to the complex and theoretical problems of physics. Engineering courses also create a problem-solving orientation that is invaluable in the world of physics.*

## References

Cosslett, Vernon Ellis, and P. Brederoo, eds. *Electron Microscopy*. Vol. 3. New York: Elsevier Science, 1981.

Greguss, Pal, and Tung H. Jeong, eds. *Holography: Commemorating the 90th Anniversary of the Birth of Dennis Gabor*. London: Society of Photo Optical, 1991.

Kasper, Joseph E. *The Complete Book of Holograms: How They Work and How to Make Them*. Contributions by Steven Feller. New York: John Wiley, 1987. (Reprint edition.)

Kock, Winston E. *Lasers and Holography: An Introduction to Coherent Optics*. New York: Dover, 1981.

Talbot, Michael. *The Holographic Universe*. New York: Harperperennial Library, 1992. (Reprint edition.)

# William Gates

Computer Programming

Microsoft Corp.

## Career Highlights

- Invented DOS and Microsoft Windows computer operating systems
- Founded Microsoft Corporation
- Received the National Medal of Technology Award from President Bush, 1992

## Important Contributions

The career of Bill Gates is the ultimate self-made-hero story, the supreme "local-boy-makes-good." He started out as a smart kid who liked to play around on computers. He went from computer hacker, to computer programmer, to business tycoon and multi-billionaire—all within a few short years.

Gates invented DOS and Windows operating systems, founded Microsoft Corporation, and led his company to become the largest and most powerful software manufacturer on the globe. While he himself is an excellent programmer and highly intelligent, his greatest asset might well be his tough entrepreneurial spirit and his business sense.

# Career Path

On a Saturday morning in 1971 two high-school boys sat in the darkened offices of C-Cubed, a small computer manufacturing company, pounding on adjacent keyboards. As a manufacturing plant, the room featured long steel-braced construction tables covered with scattered tools and soldering irons, circuit components, and the skeletons of partially assembled machines.

Each boy chuckled when he created a devilishly difficult series of commands and then groaned when the computer successfully followed. Bill Gates, the thin boy with glasses and bushy blond hair, cheered when an error message flashed across his screen. Then the screen froze and the computer crashed. A printer across the room whined to life as it printed a record of the crash and the keystrokes that led to it. It was Bill Gates's third crash of the morning. The high-schoolers had been hired to search for errors in the computer's code and crash the system.

Four years later, that same young computer hacker, Bill Gates, sat at a conference table in Albuquerque, New Mexico, opposed by the senior lawyers for Pertac Corporation, a $100 million company that claimed all rights to his operating program for the Altair 8800 computer. If he agreed to their demands during this high-pressure big-business meeting, he and his fledgling company would be secure but would always be minor suppliers to larger companies. If he refused, he faced a major court battle he couldn't afford and the risky future of an under-funded independent in the ruthless, capital-intensive computer development industry. Gates refused to settle, won the court case, and Microsoft was set free. It was a meteoric rise for the hacker turned millionaire entrepreneur.

Even as a young child Bill Gates had been fascinated by the possibilities of science and technology. He was an avid reader of science fiction, especially the works of Isaac Asimov, Robert Heinlein, and Arthur C. Clarke.

Gates also possessed a fierce determination, which he brought to bear on all projects. Once, the minister of his family's church challenged anyone in the congregation to a free dinner atop the Space Needle for those who could memorize and recite the Sermon on the Mount (a 20-minute speech). Young Bill memorized the sermon in less than two weeks and received his dinner.

Despite his obvious intelligence, Bill Gates didn't perform well in school. He was bored and prone to pranks. Finally his parents enrolled him in a private school, Lakeside School, a decision which, more than anything else, affected his career. Right after Bill arrived on campus in 1968, Lakeside leased a computer.

Bill was fascinated by the computer, but because none of the teachers knew much about them, they offered no classes on computers. He and several other kids played around on the computer, teaching themselves to use it.

Computer time was expensive, however, and was quickly using up the school's budget.

Beginning in 1970, a local computer company, C-Cubed, offered Bill and his friends free computer time in exchange for testing their computers for bugs. For the young computer whiz, it was a dream come true. However, he soon grew bored with crashing the computer and focused on programming. Using BASIC, he wrote a war game for the C-Cubed computer, which he never finished. He kept adding more elaborate features, having more fun designing the product than finishing it. His grades improved as his interest increased.

When C-Cubed went out of business in Bill's junior year, he and his friends formed the Lakeside Programmers Group. A company asked the group to write a payroll program in COBOL, a language none of them knew. Bill agreed and when the project was finished, Lakeside Programmers was paid with $10,000 worth of computer time, to be used in less than a year.

The Lakeside School offered the group a $4,200 contract to develop a scheduling program for the school. When their overseeing teacher was killed in a plane crash, Gates and a friend, Steve Evans, worked alone on the project. Then, Evans was killed in a mountain-climbing fall. Gates recruited Paul Allen, an original Lakeside member, to take his place, and when the project was finished, Gates had earned $4,200.

TRW, a defense contractor, hired Gates and Allen in 1973 to write software. Allen dropped out of college to work on the project, and Gates got approval from his Lakeside teachers to miss the last trimester of his senior year to work on the project. He returned in time to take his final exams, graduating with honors.

In fall 1973, Gates arrived at Harvard and quickly became known as an excellent programmer and hacker. In January 1975, the cover of *Popular Electronics* magazine announced that a company called MITS had made the world's first minicomputer, the Altair 8800. However, the 8800 lacked a working operating system and couldn't *do* anything. Gates and Allen decided to write the operating code for the new mini. They spent a month working day and night to design an Altair 8800 operating code, which they sold to MITS.

Problems soon surfaced, however. Gates had sold the software's licensing rights to MITS, but because MITS made more money selling the hardware than the software, they were not motivated to sell the software, nor were they motivated to stop the pirating of the software.

Harvard administrators were also unhappy that Gates had used university equipment (and allowed a non-student, Paul Allen, to use school equipment) for personal profit. The maverick student had been growing more and more disillusioned with Harvard life. This was the final straw. He quit college and set out on his own.

Gates and Allen formed Microsoft in the summer of 1975. They recruited some of their hacker friends from Lakeside and Harvard and moved the company to Albuquerque, where they continued to write and test code for MITS.

With his next product, a version of Microsoft BASIC, Gates refused to sell the rights to MITS. He insisted on a non-exclusive licensing agreement, which meant that he would receive a fee whenever the program went out "bundled" with a MITS computer. But Microsoft was also free to sell the program elsewhere. And sell they did. Gates traveled the country, and the name Microsoft became known in the computer industry.

When Pertac Computer Corporation bought MITS, trouble hit. Pertac insisted Microsoft had no right to license software to any other company and claimed all rights to the BASIC code written for the 8800. Gates refused to stop outside marketing. Pertac, with revenues of $100 million, filed suit against the upstarts. But the courts held that Microsoft was free to sell the 8800 source code to anyone. Microsoft had broken free of its chains to MITS. In January 1978, Microsoft moved to Washington.

On July 21, 1980, Bill Gates received a phone call that would change his company's future. IBM had finally decided to enter the microcomputer market, and they wanted to purchase Microsoft's BASIC for their new microcomputer. They also wanted Microsoft to develop the operating system. Eventually, Microsoft would write DOS for IBM, as well as programs for Apple.

Microsoft's Windows 3.0 and Windows 95 cemented the Windows phenomenon, as well as Bill Gates's fortune. Indeed, in 1994, *Forbes* magazine listed him, with a personal fortune of $9.35 billion, as the richest person in America. In 1998, he was worth more than $100 billion and had been named the richest person in the world.

## Key Dates

| | |
|---|---|
| 1955 | Born in Seattle, Washington, on October 28 |
| 1967 | Attended Lakeside School |
| 1973 | Worked for TRW; graduated from Lakeside and enrolled at Harvard |
| 1975 | Wrote BASIC for the Altair 8800; formed Microsoft |

1976    Began selling BASIC to computer manufacturers
1980    Agreed to develop BASIC and an operating system (DOS)
           for IBM
1981    His DOS 1.0 released with IBM PC
1985    Released Microsoft Windows1986
1986    Became world's youngest billionaire
1990    Released Microsoft Windows 3.0 on May 22
1995    Released Windows 95
1998    Released Windows 98

## Advice

*Bill Gates never finished college, yet the engineers and scientists he now hires routinely possess advanced electrical engineering and physics degrees. If you are considering a career in computer technology, Bill Gates would advise you to pursue studies that include mechanical engineering, chemistry, and physics classes in addition to computer science and electrical engineering. Gates would also say that the computer field is driven by consumer needs. The best ideas are those that fill the most basic needs. Develop not just programming skills, but also the ability to recognize needs and create new ideas.*

## References

Boyd, Aaron. *SMART MONEY: The Story of Bill Gates.* Greensboro, N. C.: Morgan Reynolds, 1995.

Gates, Bill, Nathan Myhrvold, and Peter M. Rinearson. *The Road Ahead.* New York: Penguin, 1996.

Herz, J. C. *Joystick Nation: How Videogames Ate Our Quarters, Won Our Hearts, and Rewired Our Minds.* Boston: Little, Brown, 1997.

Lowe, Janet C. *Bill Gates Speaks: Insight from the World's Greatest Entrepreneur.* New York: John Wiley, 1998.

Manes, Stephen, and Paul Andrews. *GATES: How Microsoft's Mogul Reinvented an Industry—and Made Himself the Richest Man in America.* New York: Doubleday, 1993.

Wallace, James, and Jim Erickson. *Hard Drive: Bill Gates and the Making of the Microsoft Empire.* New York: John Wiley, 1992.

# Hans Geiger

*"Mister Counter"*                                    Physics

## Career Highlights

- Invented the Geiger counter for measuring radioactivity
- Awarded the Hughes Medal by the Royal Society, 1929
- Awarded the Duddell Medal by the Physical Society of London, 1938

## Important Contributions

Hans Geiger is best known as the inventor of the Geiger counter. But that device was far more important than just a hand-held tool to use while tromping through the hills searching for trace deposits of uranium. Geiger's counter was the first quantitative meter to measure either the amount of radioactivity or the intensity of radioactive energy. It was the first twentieth-century effort in atomic science instrumentation. Geiger's counter made precise measurements of invisible subatomic phenomena possible and allowed physicists to quantitatively test the prevailing theories of subatomic structure and function.

While the whole world has heard of the Geiger counter, what is not well known is that Hans Geiger also made significant contributions to early basic research on radioactive decay products, alpha and beta particles, and the nature of radioactive decay, or disintegration. Finally, he turned out to be an excellent and inspiring teacher who trained many of the brightest and best German physicists of the rocket and nuclear ages of the 1940s, 1950s, and 1960s.

## Career Path

In 1908 the University of Manchester, England, was one of the world's leading research centers for the new atomic physics, and Hans Geiger was one of the university's newest physics recruits. But after a year of research, he was bitterly dismayed. How could he make any significant discoveries about radioactivity when he had no solid data to use?

What shocked perfectionist Hans Geiger even more was that other researchers, even famed Ernest Rutherford, seemed perfectly comfortable using approximations and surrogate measures for radioactivity. When he claimed that the physics data must either be exact and reliable or thrown away as trash, Geiger backed himself into a corner. If he could not find a way to create accurate measurements of radioactivity, he would have to abandon his hopes of a physics career.

In 1901 Hans Geiger had signed up to take the German *Abitur* test (the placement test that determines a student's eligibility for college education) when he was first eligible. He easily passed and, after a brief period of required military service, entered the Erlangen University to study physics. A determined, studious worker, he transferred to the University of Munich and completed his undergraduate studies in 1904. Two years later he defended his dissertation and received a doctorate in physics.

The world of physics was expanding rapidly in the early 1900s. Electrons, protons, alpha and beta particles, and the entire wondrous subatomic world had just been discovered. The discovery of X-rays was only a dozen years old. Far more questions than answers flooded the new field of atomic physics. What *was* radioactivity? What radiated from an atom? How? Why? What drove alpha and beta particles from inside an atom? Why were there two kinds of radiation?

Most frustrating of all was that there was virtually no available test equipment to measure and analyze atomic radiation. Everyone wanted to study radiation. But it was like researching blindfolded.

Universities across the world were scrambling to develop preeminent research departments in this new atomic physics and were hungrily searching for young, well-trained physicists they could hire to assist in research. Geiger had his pick of job offers and chose a position at the University of Manchester as research assistant to Arthur Schuster.

The young physicist began his research at Manchester as other researchers did, using approximate and surrogate measures for radioactivity. Maybe because he was such a staunch perfectionist, the process bothered him more than most. After one year he shifted to assisting Ernest Rutherford, another prominent Manchester professor. Geiger was assigned to study the nature and charge of alpha particles, but found his progress halted by the galling lack of available equipment to even accurately count the particles, let alone measure their electrical characteristics.

Geiger set to work to remedy the situation. His perfectionist nature would not allow him to continue the study without adequate, accurate measurement. The first of his studies for Rutherford had been to assess the electrical charge of alpha particles. While he was not able to measure the charge, he was able to establish that an alpha particle had one.

Using this information, Geiger designed a low-pressure ionization chamber through which a thin wire was stretched. A small entrance window to admit alpha particles was fixed in one end of the chamber. When a strong electric charge was fed to the wire, the natural charge of any alpha particles entering the ion chamber would cause a cascade reaction through the ion gas that would amplify the particle's charge a thousand fold and make it detectable on a sensitive electrometer.

Geiger was not only able to count alpha particles (estimating that $3.4 \times 10^{10}$ particles were emitted per second from one gram of radium in equilibrium) but also to establish that alpha particles were double charged, confirming T. Royd's theory that alpha particles were double-charged helium atoms.

Moving back to Germany in 1912 to work as the director of the laboratory of radium research at the Physikalisch-Technische Reichsanstalt in Berlin, Geiger revised his counter to a needle-based detector system to allow him to detect beta particles and other types of radiation as well as alpha particles. This was the first counter to provide any measurement of beta particles. He found that this new design could not only detect the presence of a particle, but also measure the intensity of its incident radiation.

Throughout four years as a front-line artillery officer during World War I and during his research and teaching positions after the war, Geiger continued to improve his radiation counter, never satisfied with a design or a result. For every improvement he made, new research demands would identify some new desirable trait or function, new research results would uncover some new information about radiation particles he had not known or considered. By 1928 he had improved his counter's sensitivity to the point where he could make the first-ever measurements of background radiation; he had improved the amplification so that it could trigger an ordinary needle dial; and he had improved the function so that the unit could now be carried in one hand.

This 1928 counter, the result of 19 years of testing and refinement, was the one first marketed as a Geiger counter and marked the first introduction of modern electrical devices into radiation research. For this great accomplishment alone, Geiger is worth remembering. But he also left a legacy of first-rate original experimental research on the nature of radiation particles. He also left his mark as a teacher, being described as one of the most effective and inspiring physics teachers of his generation. Hans Geiger was certainly worth counting.

\* \* \*

## Key Dates

| | |
|---|---|
| 1882 | Born in Neustadt an der Haardt, Germany, on September 30 |
| 1904 | Received B.S. from University of Munich in physics |
| 1906 | Received Ph.D. in physics from University of Erlangen |
| 1906 | Worked as research assistant to Arthur Schuster at University of Manchester |
| 1907 | Worked as assistant to Ernest Rutherford at University of Manchester |
| 1908 | Developed earliest prototype of the Geiger counter |
| 1912–1925 | Served as director of the laboratory for radium research in Berlin |
| 1915–1919 | Served as front-line artillery officer during World War I |
| 1925 | Accepted first teaching position as professor of physics at Kiel University |
| 1929 | Worked as physics professor at the University of Tübingen and as director of their Institute of Physics |
| 1936 | Appointed chair of physics at the Technische Hochschule in Berlin |
| 1942 | Retired |
| 1945 | Died on September 24 |

# Advice

*Hans Geiger was well trained in classic physics, but suffered from a lack of engineering knowledge. He would advise anyone considering a career in physics to integrate engineering skills into a physics curriculum. Geiger also believed that science is a world of exactness and precision and would encourage you to work toward exactness in all you do. Make precision a habit. There is little room for, or value in, unnecessary approximation.*

# References

Daintith, John, et al., eds. *Biographical Encyclopedia of Scientists.* 2d ed. Vol. 1. Philadelphia, Pa.: Institute of Physics Publishing, 1994. (Summary entry on Geiger's work.)

Gianocoli, Douglas C. *Physics Principles: With Applications.* 3d ed. New York: Prentice Hall Press, 1991.

Gillispie, Charles, ed. *Dictionary of Scientific Biography.* Vol. XV. New York: Charles Scribner's Sons, 1978. (Good summary of Geiger's work.)

Healea, M. "Geiger and Proportional Counters," *Nucleonics* 1 (December 1957): 68–75. (An extensive biography with additional references.)

Kuhn, T., ed. *Sources for History of Quantum Physics.* Philadelphia, Pa.: Franklin Institute, 1967. (A review of the development of quantum physics including Geiger's early work.)

Lerner, I. *Radioactivity Science in Its Historical and Social Context.* Bristol, England: Taylor & Francis, 1989. (Good historical overview.)

# Robert Hutchings Goddard

*"The Moon-Rocket Man"*          Physics and
                                 Rocketry

## Career Highlights

- Was one of the founders of modern rocketry and the science of aeronautics
- Received a Congressional Gold Medal for his "pioneering research in rocket propulsion"
- Received the Langley Medal, the highest award for contributions in aerodynamics
- Named for him were the NASA Goddard Space Flight Center and the Goddard Power Plant at Indian Head, Maryland

## Important Contributions

In 1920, a *New York Times* editorial ridiculed Robert Goddard's claim that rockets could fly through a vacuum to the moon. Almost 50 years later, in 1969, while the *Apollo XI* astronauts orbited the moon, the *Times* printed a formal retraction of their earlier criticism, but Goddard never saw it. The retraction came 24 years after his death.

Robert Goddard was a visionary, a dreamer who matched his boundless imagination with practical experimentation. He invented the multi-stage rocket and the liquid fueled rocket and held over 200 patents on rocket system components. He launched the first American rocket and the first rocket to rise more than a mile from Earth. In so doing, he became the father of American rocketry.

# Career Path

On October 19, 1899, 17-year-old Robert Goddard experienced a mystical vision of space flight. He saw a rocket ship blasting into space, soaring beyond the confines of the atmosphere to the moon. With pointed nose and three stabilizing fins in back and two liquid fuel pods strapped to its side, the rocket belched fire and smoke, leaving a thick black trail across the sky as its thunder shook the ground. For years the vision fascinated Robert. He would always remember October 19 as "Anniversary Day." Goddard's lifelong problem was that dreams can't attract funding for research and experiments. He never escaped from the struggle to convert dreams into steel and rumbling propulsion before skeptical peers, a ridiculing press, and reluctant funders doused his slim chances for success.

Robert Goddard was born in a farmhouse near Worcester, Massachusetts, in 1882. Physically frail from his earliest youth, he suffered from pulmonary tuberculosis. He missed so much school due to his illness that he did not graduate from high school until age 21. He did read a great deal, however, especially science fiction. H. G. Wells's *The War of the Worlds* first sparked Robert's lifelong interest in rocketry.

In 1904, Robert enrolled in Worcester Polytechnic Institute and received a degree in physics in 1908. Through graduate studies at Clark University, he earned a master's degree in 1910 and a Ph.D. in 1911. He was hired by Princeton's Palmer Physical Laboratory as a research fellow, where he developed a vacuum-tube oscillator that he later patented. In 1913, his health declined again and he left the lab. While recuperating from tuberculosis, he organized his rocket research data and ideas into patent applications.

On July 7, 1914, Robert Goddard received his first patent, number 1,102,653, which clearly identified the concept of multistaging of rockets, without which it is impossible to land on the moon or send probes to Mars and Venus. One week later, on July 14, 1914, he received his second patent, number 1,103,503, in which he established the foundation of modern rocket design. In that patent he described the rocket casing as having two tanks filled with combustible material, such as gasoline and liquefied nitrous oxide, which, when ignited, would produce an exceedingly rapid but constant combustion.

When his health improved later in 1914, Goddard joined the Clark University faculty as a part-time teacher and researcher. Working on his own, with very little funding and equipment, he tirelessly pursued his rocketry projects.

In 1917, Goddard received a $5,000 grant from the Smithsonian Institution to build a rocket to reach "extreme altitudes." When the United States entered World War I, the U. S. Army Signal Corps provided the Smithsonian with $20,000 to fund Goddard's continued research.

Goddard moved his research to the Mount Wilson Observatory in California, where he experimented with solid-propellant rockets as weapons. In 1918, he demonstrated a rocket that could be fired by an individual soldier (the forerunner of World War II's bazooka). One observer commented that this invention would "revolutionize warfare." The U.S. Army promised him a grant to develop a six-inch rocket. However, four days later, Germany agreed to an armistice ending the war. With the war over, the Army lost all interest in his rocket, and the grant never materialized.

Goddard published a paper, *A Method of Reaching Extreme Altitudes,* in the Smithsonian Miscellaneous Collections. Reporters got hold of the article and newspapers ran headlines about the "moon-rocket man." When it became clear that he had not yet built such a rocket and was only theorizing, he was criticized and called a dreamer. The already shy Goddard grew even more distrustful of publicity.

Abandoning all other work, he began experimenting with liquid-fuel rockets. With grants from the Smithsonian, he developed a rocket motor that would run on gasoline and liquid oxygen. When the pumps caused difficulty, he switched to pressurized gas to force fuel and oxidizer into the combustion chamber.

On March 16, 1926, Goddard achieved the world's first liquid-fuel rocket flight from a farm near Auburn, Massachusetts. The rocket only flew for two and one-half seconds, rising 41 feet and traveling 184 feet laterally. Two years later, he repeated the experiment with a larger, more sophisticated model that reached twice the 1926 altitude before crashing in flames.

Neighbors called the authorities at the sound of the explosions, and Goddard was ordered not to launch any more rockets in Massachusetts. Fortunately, Charles Lindbergh was so impressed with Goddard's achievements that he persuaded the philanthropist Daniel Guggenheim to provide him with a $50,000 grant for a two-year program.

Goddard used this money to rent a farm near Roswell, New Mexico, where he could conduct further experiments. He made consistent progress; his rockets reached a height of 2,000 feet in 1930; 4,000 feet in March 1935; and 7,500 feet in May. By 1937, he had achieved a height of 9,000 feet. It was not a thundering flight to the moon, but it *was* a headline-grabbing world record.

The rocket scientist continued to file patents as he made progress. He patented a method of protecting the thin walls of the combustion chamber with a spray of liquid fuel. He patented a stabilizing method that consisted of gyroscopically controlled vanes in the rocket's exhaust system. He developed high-speed, lightweight aluminum pumps driven by liquid-oxygen gas generators to replace the pressurized gas-fuel systems.

In 1941, Goddard received a small contract from the Army Air Corps and the Navy to develop a liquid-propellant jet-assist-takeoff rocket for aircraft. While his experiments were technically successful, when he attempted to demonstrate the motor on an actual aircraft, the plane exploded and was lost. The military lost interest and returned to cheaper and more dependable solid-fuel units.

Goddard's day had passed. He spent his last few years working for Curtiss-Wright and filing for patents, adding 35 patents to the 48 he already had. After his death on August 10, 1945, his widow applied for another 131 patents.

More than any other single person, Robert Goddard gave American rocketry its beginnings. Indeed, his 214 patents so thoroughly covered the whole range of rocketry development that it was virtually impossible to build a rocket without infringing on one or more of them. In 1960, the government paid Mrs. Goddard $1,000,000 for an infringement claim and for acquired rights to use her husband's inventions in rockets, guided missiles, and space exploration.

## Key Dates

| | |
|---|---|
| 1882 | Born near Worcester, Massachusetts, on October 5 |
| 1908 | Received B.S. in physics from Worcester Polytechnic Institute |
| 1910 | Received M.S. from Clark University |
| 1911 | Received Ph.D. from Clark |
| 1912 | Worked as research fellow with the Palmer Physical Laboratory of Princeton University |
| 1914 | Granted patent for concept of multistaging rockets; granted patent establishing foundations of modern rocket design |
| 1917 | Awarded $5,000 grant by the Smithsonian |
| 1918 | Received $20,000 from the U. S. Army Signal Corps through the Smithsonian for research into applied rocketry; moved to Mt. Wilson Observatory in California |
| 1926 | Launched first liquid-propellant rocket on March 16 |
| 1930–1942 | Launched the first rockets with gyroscopic stabilizers |

1941    Received contract with U. S. Army Air Corps and Navy to develop a liquid-propellant jet-assist-takeoff rocket for aircraft

1945    Died August 10 in Baltimore, Maryland

## Advice

*If you are considering a career in physics and rocketry, Robert Goddard would advise you to base your studies on math, physics, and chemistry. Then add thermodynamics and electrical and mechanical engineering. Goddard would also say that, if you're lucky enough to have a vision, follow through with it, no matter what others think. When Goddard's own vision was criticized, he responded with, "Every vision is a joke until the first man accomplishes it."*

## References

Goddard, Esther C., and G. Edward Pendray, eds. *The Papers of Robert H. Goddard, 1898–1945.* 3 vols. New York: McGraw-Hill, 1970.

Ordway, Frederick I., III, ed. *History of Rocketry and Astronautics.* San Diego: Univelt, 1989.

Stine, G. Harry. *Living in Space: A Handbook for Work & Exploration Stations Beyond the Earth's Atmosphere.* New York: M. Evans, 1997.

Streissguth, Thomas. *Rocket Man: The Story of Robert Goddard.* Minneapolis, Minn.: Lerner, 1995.

Sutton, George P. *Rocket Propulsion Elements: An Introduction to the Engineering of Rockets.* New York: John Wiley, 1986.

# Jane Goodall

## "The White-Skinned Ape"    Zoology and Ethology

Photo courtesy of Michael Neugebauer

## Career Highlights

- Is world's foremost authority on chimpanzees and one of the world's leading authorities in the study of animal behavior
- Received J. Paul Getty Wildlife Conservation Prize, 1984
- Awarded Gold Medal for conservation from San Diego Zoological Society and the conservation award from New York Zoological Society
- Won two Franklin Burr prizes from National Geographic Society

## Important Contributions

Jane Goodall revolutionized long-term field biological studies by directly interacting with the subjects of her study, chimpanzees in the Gombe Stream Game Preserve in Africa. She communicated with them, played with them, and virtually lived with them, and thereby obtained access to their daily lives in a way no other researcher had been able to do. Her studies completely rewrote the manual for the successful conduct of biological field studies.

Goodall also revolutionized our understanding of these, the most intelligent of the great apes. She documented a complex family and social structure and learned that humans are not the only creatures capable of making tools.

## Career Path

One day in 1961, Jane Goodall was sitting in a forest in East Africa with a wild chimpanzee whom she called David Graybeard. She saw on the ground a red palm nut that she thought David would like. She picked it up and offered it to him on her open palm. At first he turned his head away. When she moved her hand closer, he looked at it, then at her. Finally he took the nut, gently holding her hand in his own.

In those brief moments of interspecies connectedness, Goodall fulfilled a personal, lifelong dream.

Jane's family moved to the English coast when she was five. She did well in her studies, although she preferred learning about animals, insects, and the outdoors more than academic subjects. Her love of chimpanzees started early, when her mother gave her a stuffed chimpanzee at the age of two. She graduated from secondary school at 18 and began working a series of odd jobs: first as a secretary at Oxford University, then as an assistant editor in a film studio, finally as a waitress. She was saving money for passage to Kenya, where a friend from school had invited her to visit.

At the age of 23, Jane Goodall made her long-awaited trek to Africa. After visiting her friend, she set off for Nairobi to look for Louis Leakey, the famous paleontologist who was searching for fossils of ancient man in the Olduvai Gorge. She asked Leakey for a job to "get closer to animals." He sensed that her love of animals was not just a passing fancy and hired her as an assistant secretary.

It did not matter to Leakey that Goodall had no degree and little experience. In fact, he preferred it that way. He wanted someone whose mind was uncluttered by theories—and someone who had endless patience. Goodall was perfect.

Leakey secured enough funding to pay for Goodall to conduct a six-month preliminary study of chimpanzees at Gombe Stream Game Reserve. But because authorities would not allow a 24-year-old Englishwoman to live alone in the African wild, she convinced her author mother to accompany her.

Researchers warned Goodall that she would not be successful. No one could get close to chimpanzees in the wild. They encouraged her to abandon the excursion and return to school. Indeed, despite the fact that she rose every morning before dawn and stumbled off through the forest with an African game scout, week after week passed without more than a glimpse of the chimpanzees. She could hear their hooting and screeching in the distance, but they always fled at her approach. It appeared that she would fail.

Two months after her arrival, she found a 1,000-foot clearing above Lake Tanganyika, which she called "The Peak." From this location she had an unobstructed view of the surrounding area. With strong binoculars she could routinely observe the chimps through the forest below.

One of Goodall's first discoveries about chimpanzees was that they were not the vicious, violent animals they were thought to be, but rather affectionate, gentle creatures. She noted that chimpanzees often greet one another with hugs and kisses. They hold hands as they walk. She once saw a male chimp greet a female by pulling her hand to his lips and kissing it gently. The chimps seemed to need long periods of close contact with each other, often grooming each other, combing through their partner's hair to remove dirt, seeds, and ticks. She also discovered that chimpanzees were meat eaters and that chimps make sleeping platforms by weaving smaller branches into a sturdy forked branch. She even saw them use a clump of leafy twigs as a "pillow."

Then Goodall made a discovery that rocked the scientific world. One day she observed a chimp hunting for termites. He picked up a twig and pulled off all of its leaves, then poked this tool into a termite mound. When he withdrew the twig, it was covered with termites, which he ate. He had *made* a tool.

Until that moment, we humans had defined ourselves as being different from the animal kingdom because of our ability to make tools. When Leakey learned of her discovery, he wrote that science either had to (1) define chimpanzees as human, (2) redefine what it means to be human, or ( 3) redefine what we call tools.

In the spring of 1961, Goodall decided to follow the chimps into the forest. Challenging her, a male chimpanzee grabbed a branch of vegetation and shook it, raining down twigs, leaves, and raindrops on her head. He uttered an eerie alarm call; other chimps surrounded her and took up the call and also began shaking the vegetation. She later wrote in *The Chimpanzees of Gombe,* "All around me branches were swayed and shaken, and there was a sound of thudding feet and crashing vegetation. My instincts urged me to get up and leave; my scientific interest, my pride, and an intuitive feeling that the whole intimidating performance was a bluff kept me where I was."

Goodall feigned indifference and pretended to chew up leaves and stems. The chimps ceased their cries and melted back into the forest. After almost six months of the "intimidation display," they started allowing her to follow them into the forest. They had lost their fear of her. She watched them search for food, play, nurse their young, and groom one another. David Graybeard even seemed to wait for her if she got lost following the group.

In the 1970s, the chimpanzee community she had watched for so long began to divide. Suddenly, the gentle beasts were at war among themselves. This change in their behavior was very hard for Goodall to accept. After a nearly four-year "war," one group had almost entirely annihilated the other group.

It took years for Goodall to reconcile herself with this dark side of chimpanzee behavior, which she wrote about in her book, *Through a Window: My Thirty Years with the Chimpanzees of Gombe.* At the time, her methods were criticized: She got too close to the chimps; she named them instead of numbering them; she recorded too many anecdotes and not enough scientific data. Indeed, her advisors at Cambridge kept trying to "correct" her methods. She would listen to them, then go back and do it "her way."

And it is fortunate that she did. Later, Goodall's credentials were vindicated. Her research methods became the standard. "Her way" gave the world a better understanding of the social, biological, and cultural interactions among the species most closely related to humankind.

## Key Dates

1934    Born in London, England, on April 3

1957    Traveled to Mombasa, East Africa; asked Louis Leakey for a job

1960    Arrived at Gombe Stream Research Centre as ethologist and assistant secretary to Dr. Leakey; served as assistant curator of National Museum of Natural History, Nairobi

1965    Received Ph.D. from Cambridge University; began writing career

1970–    Worked as visiting professor of psychiatry and human
1975        biology at Stanford University

1971 Published *In the Shadow of Man*

1972 Was honorary visiting professor of zoology at University of Dar Es Salaam, Tanzania

1974 Witnessed an outbreak of war within a chimpanzee community

1990 Published *Through a Window*

1995–present Moved back to United States; is fighting animal abuse, especially in zoos

## Advice

*Jane Goodall had no relevant college education, which meant that she had to conduct her study and also learn about the ecosystem, the species, and the process of study all at the same time. She was lucky in that her lack of foreknowledge did not detrimentally affect her work. Still, she would advise anyone considering a career in field biology or zoology to use college time to learn about what has been learned and tried in the past. Study successful field techniques in a wide variety of ecosystems and situations. Also include ecology studies with biology and zoology classes to gain a wider appreciation for the interaction of each species with its broader environment.*

## References

Goodall, Jane. *The Chimpanzees of Gombe: Patterns of Behavior.* Bridgewater: Replica Books, 1997. (Technical account of her 25 years of work with chimpanzees.)

———. *Through a Window: My Thirty Years with the Chimpanzees of Gombe.* Boston: Houghton Mifflin, 1990. (Shows darker side of chimpanzees.)

Montgomery, Sy. *Walking with the Great Apes: Jane Goodall, Dian Fossey, and Birute Galdikas.* Boston: Houghton Mifflin, 1992.

Van Lawick-Goodall, Jane. *In the Shadow of Man.* New York: Houghton Mifflin, 1971. (Somewhat idealized portrayal of chimpanzee society.)

# Gordon Gould

*"A Flash of Insight"*

Physics and Invention

Courtesy of Gordon Gould

## Career Highlights

- Invented the laser
- Named Inventor of the Year by the Patent Office Association for the Advancement of Invention and Innovation, 1978

## Important Contributions

Gordon Gould conceived of and invented the laser. When the flash of inspiration hit, he wrote down all the concepts behind his invention, had his notebooks notarized, then got some bad advice. He was told that he had to have a working model to receive a patent, and while he was trying to make such a model to submit to the Patent Office, another inventor filed the patent and received the credit (including a Nobel Prize) for inventing the laser.

After more than 20 years of legal battles, Gould was finally declared the rightful creator of one of the most spectacular and versatile innovations in history. Only now is he beginning to earn some of the fame—and fortune—which should have been his a long time ago.

**226**

# Career Path

Flanked by three armed military police, two sheriff's deputies apologetically served the federal court order when 39-year-old Gordon Gould opened the door to his suburban Long Island, New York, home in late 1959. Dumbfounded, he protested, argued, yelled, and ultimately had to simply watch in disbelief, as the MPs rifled through his study, bookshelves, and desk. Every notebook, article, and scribbled drawing that had anything to do with laser design was stamped "Secret" and filed in a storage box to be carted outside to the waiting military van. It didn't matter that they were his own notes and notebooks. It didn't matter that the sheriff repeatedly apologized and said how sorry he was. The National Security machinery had just barred Gordon Gould from working on his own project.

Raised in New York City, Gordon Gould was a born builder and tinkerer. He began to play with erector sets at the age of three. While still in elementary school he was already building or fixing clocks and other mechanical instruments. By the time he was in high school, he knew he wanted to be an inventor.

Because of his driving need to know how things worked, Gordon was fascinated by physics and felt that it was a good starting point for becoming an inventor. After graduating with a degree in physics from Union College in Schenectady, New York, he went to work for Western Electric, quickly growing discouraged that all the important positions were held by much older men. Gould did not want to waste years climbing the corporate ladder, so he quit work and went to Yale University for post-graduate coursework, where he studied the relationship between light and energy.

After receiving his master's degree in 1943, Gould worked on the Manhattan Project, the U.S. secret project to build an atomic bomb, for almost two years. Around this time he and his first wife joined a study group that focused on the works of Karl Marx, whose ideas formed the basis for Russia's communist revolution. Gould soon lost interest in Marxism, but that innocent dalliance would come back to haunt him later.

To get his Ph.D, Gordon Gould enrolled at Columbia University, a very exciting place in the early 1950s. Six Nobel Prize winners worked at the university, including Charles Townes, who invented the maser (Microwave Amplification by Stimulated Emission of Radiation), which made very short electromagnetic waves more powerful.

Gould incorporated maser theory into his studies of energy waves and light waves. Thirty years before, Einstein had shown that light could stimulate atoms into an excited state and cause them to absorb light energy. Gould also knew that Einstein had predicted that the opposite was possible: that light could stimulate excited atoms into giving off light energy, which would be very powerful because it would be coherent (all of one wavelength and in phase), concentrated light.

The problem was that no one knew how to stimulate light emissions, much less amplify and focus them. On the night of November 11, 1957, as Gould was lying in bed, unable to sleep, the answer popped into his head. He saw how to build a laser. He was "electrified." He spent the next day writing down all his thoughts, ideas, and sketches about his new invention, which he called a laser (Light Amplification by Stimulated Emission of Radiation). The following day, he had his notebooks notarized to help prevent anyone from stealing his discovery.

Then the young inventor received some bad legal advice. He was told that he could not file a patent for his device until he had a working model. Since he knew that the professor he worked under at Columbia would not support some wild foray into the invention of a laser, he decided to leave college in 1958 to build the laser.

Gould joined Technical Research Group (TRG) in New York because he needed both technical and financial assistance to successfully build a laser. While he was working on his invention, Townes and Schawlow beat him to the patent office. They filed their first laser patent in late 1958; Gould did not enter his until the next year, which was too late. His application was rejected for having too much overlap with the Townes and Schawlow patent.

Bitterly disappointed, but still enthusiastic about the potential of his laser design, Gould sought funding to continue its development. Recognizing the implications of a laser as a weapon, he prepared a proposal for TRG to take to the U.S. Department of Defense. The armed forces not only accepted the proposal, but tripled the funding! Unfortunately, however, because of Gould's brief flirtation with communism, he was considered a security risk and was not allowed to work on the project. Even his notebooks were considered secret and he was not allowed to see his own work. As described earlier, the government seized all his materials related to the laser. It was a devastating setback.

While Gould was deadlocked, other people moved ahead, receiving recognition and financial rewards for the invention of the laser. TRG merged into Control Data Corporation in 1965, and two years later Gould left Control Data to work as a professor at the Polytechnic Institute of New York. In 1970, Control Data pulled out of the laser business and returned all their laser patent rights to him. This meant that the legal battle to establish that Gould had actually invented the laser became important for financial reasons as well as reasons of pride.

In 1973, 16 years after he first conceived of the laser, a court ruled that the Townes-Schawlow laser patents did not contain enough information to show how to build a laser. Four years later Gould was granted his first laser patent for his laser optic pump. But the legal battles continued until, in 1986, the U.S. Patent Office Appeals Board overruled all previous objections to his patents. It took 28 years, but he had finally won.

Interestingly enough, Gould himself got to benefit in one more way from his invention. He had two eye operations performed by lasers. Without those operations, he would have lost his sight. Even if he had never conceived of the laser, it is obvious that Townes and Schawlow and others would have. Still, it is important that the record be corrected. There is a distinction in being first, and Gould deserves that distinction.

## Key Dates

| | |
|---|---|
| 1920 | Born in New York City on July 17 |
| 1941 | Received B.S. in physics from Union College in Schenectady, New York |
| 1943 | Received M.S. in physics from Yale University |
| 1943–1945 | Worked on the Manhattan Project |
| 1945–1954 | Worked as professor at City College of New York |
| 1954 | Enrolled at Columbia University; Charles Townes developed the maser |
| 1957 | Discovered a way to build a laser, November 11 |
| 1958 | Left Columbia to work full-time on laser; joined Technical Research Group |
| 1967 | Worked as professor at Polytechnic Institute in Brooklyn, New York |
| 1974 | Was vice president and co-founder of Optelecom, a Maryland-based research and development firm and manufacturer of fiber-optic equipment |
| 1977 | Obtained first patent for optical pump |
| 1985–present | Retired from Optelecom |
| 1986 | Gained clear patent rights to major laser components |

## Advice

*If you are considering a career in physics, laser technology, or invention, Gordon Gould would advise you to base yourself in the physics or atomic physics department but to make many forays into the chemistry and mechanical engineering areas. Custom-build your curriculum to develop a broad base of knowledge and skills that best supports your interests without worrying about department boundaries. He would also remind you not to expect to have a flash of inspiration without first laying the groundwork. His flash of insight for the laser could not have happened without the 20 years of studying he had done in physics and optics.*

## References

Aaseng, Nathan. *American Profiles: Twentieth-Century Inventors.* New York: Facts on File, 1991.

Brown, Kenneth A. *Inventors at Work: Interviews with 16 Notable American Inventors.* Redmond, Wash.: Microsoft Press, 1988.

Duffner, Robert W., and Hans Mark. *Airborne Laser: Bullets of Light.* New York: Plenum Press, 1997.

Flatow, Ira. *They All Laughed: From Light Bulbs to Lasers: The Fascinating Stories Behind the Great Inventions That Have Changed Our Lives.* New York: HarperCollins, 1993.

# Stephen Jay Gould

## *"A New Explanation"* — Paleontology

Harvard News Office

## Career Highlights

- Founded the punctuated equilibrium school of evolution
- Received the Schuchert Award by the Paleontological Society, 1975
- Received a Notable Book citation from the American Library Association, 1980, and an American Book Award in science, 1981, for *The Panda's Thumb*
- Received the National Book Critics Circle Award for general nonfiction, 1981, and American Book Award nomination in science, 1982, for *The Mismeasure of Man*

## Important Contributions

In his award-winning books on evolution and biological determinism, Stephen Gould translated difficult scientific theories into understandable terms, and he managed to popularize his subjects without trivializing them. He challenged traditional views of natural selection by proposing a theory of evolution, called punctured equilibrium, that suggests that many species have a series of rapid evolutions followed by a long period of stagnation. It is for this new theoretical explanation of evolution that Stephen Gould will most be remembered.

## Career Path

Half a thumb. Hundreds of thousands of dollars had been spent hunting for the fossil of a panda with half a thumb. Paleontologists had combed the fossil record for decades searching for it. Early pandas had no thumb; modern pandas did. If Darwinian evolution was correct, there should have been a substantial period when transition species (partial-thumbed pandas) existed. Yet none had ever been found.

It suddenly occurred to Stephen Gould in his office in the geology department of Harvard University that the problem might not be with paleontologists' skill in digging, it might be with the theory. It occurred to Gould that his hero, Charles Darwin, might not have been quite right. The question was: Could Gould prove what he was thinking to a skeptical scientific community, and how would they react to something that would sound like heresy to most researchers in the field?

As a very young child in New York City, Stephen Gould wanted to be a garbage collector because of the "rattling of cans and the whir of the compressor." In some ways, he got his wish—instead of rattling cans, however, he rattled the conventional wisdom and set into motion a whir of controversy.

At age five, Stephen went with his father to the National Museum of Natural History in Manhattan, where he saw a reconstruction of a tyrannosaurus rex. He was so impressed by the 20-foot beast that upon leaving he announced he would be a paleontologist when he grew up. His parents nurtured this goal, and they helped him look for dinosaur bones and the fossils of marine life. The young boy read G. G. Simpson's *Meaning of Evolution* when he was only 11 years old, and it helped him make sense of "all those bodies of bone."

Stephen had hoped to study evolution in his high school biology class, but the fundamentalist religious movement, which preached the biblical explanation of the creation of the Earth, had virtually eliminated the treatment of evolution in his high school's textbooks. Still, Darwin remained his hero, and he continued to study Darwin's works on his own.

Gould received his B.A. in paleontology from Antioch College in 1963. He completed post-graduate studies at Columbia University and, by 1967, had become an assistant professor of geology at Harvard. By 1973, he was a full professor.

During this period, Gould began to notice a pattern of gaps in the fossil record. For species after species, transition fossils were missing from the discovered record. It seemed to him more than an unfortunate coincidence. He teamed with Niles Eldredge to begin a systematic search of the records for a wide variety of species. Their research ranged from the Irish elk (a giant fossil deer from the Pleistocene epoch), to the Caribbean land snails (where Gould not only gathered the information he needed but also contributed to our understanding of that species), to the famous question of the panda's thumb.

In total, Gould and Eldredge studied the fossil record for over 100 species from diverse ecosystems and parts of the world. They concluded that science was "missing the forest for the trees." By blindly assuming that Darwin's gradual evolution theory was correct, and by specializing in only one or two species, no one had noticed that the critical transition fossils were missing for *most* species.

The two scientists proposed a new theory, termed punctured equilibrium, which challenged Darwin's claim that all forms of life evolved from simple, common beginnings over a long period of time through slow, gradual, steady transformations by means of natural selection. Gould pointed out that the "infinitely numerous transitional links" that should connect ancestral and descendant forms rarely show up in the fossil record.

The two researchers claimed that the fossil record actually shows that most species remain relatively stable for a long period of time, until a new species arises rapidly and suddenly (which, in geological time, would be over a period of tens of thousands of years). The heart of their theory was *rapid* change in *small* groups. Evolution was not a gradual process such as Darwin had proposed. Instead, Gould argued that new species arise by the splitting off of small groups, a matter of rapid changes followed by long periods of stability.

The example of the panda's thumb became the lightning rod test case for the swirling controversy Gould and Eldredge's theory sparked. The panda's "thumb" is not a thumb at all, it is actually an enlarged wristbone that enables the panda to strip leaves from bamboo shoots. Gould claimed that it demonstrated the way evolution worked: not in incremental stages, but in leaps. He argued that such a transformation must have occurred all at once or it would not have been preserved by natural selection (half a "thumb," not having any functioning ability, would serve no useful purpose and so would have died off through natural selection).

Gould reasoned that this genetic mutation, as do most, must have occurred almost instantaneously, which would explain why scientists have not been able to find evidence of transitional forms in the fossil record. He argued that those transitional forms simply don't exist.

Criticism from all sides of the scientific community came sharp and swift. The theory was dismissed as wild speculation. Gould and Eldredge were attacked professionally and personally. Only a steady flow of continually mounting supportive evidence from researchers around the world, who began to search for and test evidence of Gould's theory, helped them weather the storm. A decade after making his radical proposal, this evidence was found to be conclusive, and Stephen Gould emerged as the creator of a reputable, supportable theory, the first successful revision of Darwinism since its inception 150 years ago.

In the mid-1960s, Gould turned his attention to the use of physical characteristics (such as skull size or forehead shape) to prejudicially predetermine human potential and intelligence. As he studied human fossil records he concluded that all such divisions serve only to support racial prejudice and are not buoyed by factual evidence.

Gould presented his arguments against such practices in his book, *The Mismeasure of Man,* which exposed the misinterpretations, frauds, and miscalculations that scientists had used to promote this justification of prejudice. *The Mismeasure of Man* won the National Book Critics Circle Award.

Since 1967 Gould has taught biology, geology, and the history of science at Harvard and has authored many columns and essays published by large-circulation magazines. He continues to be one of the country's most successful science popularizers, using books and articles to present complex scientific concepts in easily understood language. His book, *The Panda's Thumb,* actually became a best seller. The quality of Gould's research has enabled him to continue to be a major influence on the development of evolution science. He has served on the advisory boards for Children's Television Workshop and "Nova" and has edited the professional journal *Evolution.*

Gould's ability to make science come alive for the general public—and his passion for the value of science—has made him an articulate spokesperson for the many branches of science that he examines. This alone would be a significant contribution to science. Combined with his important theory on evolution, it marks Steven Gould as a unique and noteworthy leader in the world of science.

## Key Dates

| | |
|---|---|
| 1941 | Born in New York City on September 10 |
| 1963 | Received B.A. from Antioch College |
| 1966 | Worked as assistant professor of geology at Antioch College |
| 1967 | Received Ph.D. from Columbia University |

1967–
1971     Worked as assistant professor at Harvard University

1971–
1973     Worked as associate professor at Harvard University

1973–
present   Works as full professor of geology at Harvard University

## Advice

*If you are considering a career in paleontology, Stephen Gould would advise you to begin working in the field before you begin serious work in the classroom. Study fossils in museums. Volunteer to go on paleontological digs. Join local clubs. In school, broaden your horizons with history, archaeology, geology, and ecology classes.*

*Gould would also caution you to always critically examine theory and belief. Compare it to what you actually see. Stay open to the possibility of finding something new, even if it goes against the grain of conventional thought: "If we ever begin to suppress our search to understand nature to quench our own intellectual excitement in a misguided effort to present a united front . . . then we are truly lost."*

## References

Gould, Stephen Jay. *The Mismeasure of Man.* New York: W. W. Norton, 1983.

———. *The Panda's Thumb: More Reflections in Natural History.* New York: W. W. Norton, 1982.

Moritz, Charles. "Stephen Jay Gould," in *Current Biography Yearbook.* New York: H. W. Wilson, 1982: 126–130.

Rudwick, Martin J. S. *The Meaning of Fossils: Episodes in the History of Paleontology.* Chicago: University of Chicago Press, 1985.

Sternberg, Charles H. *The Life of a Fossil Hunter.* Bloomington: Indiana University Press, 1990.

# George Hale

*"Bigger Is Better"* Astronomy

## Career Highlights

Archives of National Academy of Sciences

- Designed and supervised the construction of the Yerkes, Mount Wilson, and Mount Palomar Observatories, each the largest reflecting telescope on earth at the time of its construction
- Awarded over a dozen honorary doctoral degrees even though he never studied beyond a B.S. degree
- Awarded Nobel Medal by City of Pasadena, 1927

## Important Contributions

When we think of George Hale, we think of a legacy of mammoth telescopes that he constructed for the world to use. He designed and supervised the construction of four giant reflecting telescopes, each the largest in the world at the time of its construction. The 40-inch telescope at Yerkes Observatory in Lake Geneva, Wisconsin, was Hale's first. Then he designed and built 60-inch and 100-inch telescopes on California's Mount Wilson. Finally, he built the greatest of all, California's Mount Palomar telescope, a 200-inch giant, which remains the largest in the world.

But optical telescopes are only a small part of the legacy George Hale left. He wrote six books on deep space and on solar phenomena and published over 450 articles. He discovered the magnetic fields of the sun and helped found both the California Institute of Technology and the Huntington

Library. He also helped found and organize the National Academy of Sciences and the International Astronomers Union in 1919. A great portion of the discoveries about outer space in the first two-thirds of this century owe their origins to George Hale.

## Career Path

*Bigger is better. Just think of the amazing things we'll see when we build the world's largest telescope—our personal window to the great universe beyond!*

Twenty-four-year-old George Hale strolled across the University of Chicago campus with wealthy Charles Yerkes. Although pale and frail looking, he gushed power and enthusiasm when discussing a new observatory. It was a sales pitch he would use successfully four times in his career.

*Just imagine the amazing discoveries we'll make—discoveries that will all have to be named after some . . . benefactor. Why this grand facility, itself, will be named for the generous man who funds its construction. Just think, the Yerkes observatory could go down in history!*

Charles Yerkes nodded appreciatively. Within an hour he had agreed to fund the observatory. Within a day Hale had quit his brand-new teaching post and packed up for the move to Yerkes's home state, Wisconsin, to begin plans and construction. At such times, George Hale sounded more like a flim-flam salesman than a serious scientist. It was a problem that plagued his professional credibility all his life.

George Hale was raised in the Chicago suburb of Hyde Park, where his father built a workshop for George and encouraged him to become interested in tools and machinery. However, the young boy suffered from intestinal ailments and typhoid and spent much time in bed.

Even during these long periods of convalescence, George's first love was always astronomy. When the nine-year-old boy struggled unsuccessfully for six weeks to build a telescope, his father finally bought him a four-inch Clark telescope as a reward for his effort, and the boy used it constantly. As a young teenager, he read about spectrography, the process of photographing the spectral lines of refracted light from the sun (or other star). He tried for three years to build his own small spectrographic setup before his father funded and built a spectrographic lab based on George's own design.

Eighteen-year-old George entered the Massachusetts Institute of Technology (MIT). He majored in physics but found most courses as dull and uninspiring as his high school classes had been. He much preferred to work in his own lab on his own projects. His attendance at class was spotty and he was never considered a "good" student. Later he wrote, "I never enjoyed the confinements and the fixed duties of school life. Born a free lance, with a thirst for personal adventure, I preferred to work at tasks of my own selection."

Hale's greatest joy during his time at MIT came when he persuaded the college observatory director to let him work there as a volunteer assistant. His fascination with spectroscopic analysis was intense, as was his fascination with the sun, the only star close enough to allow detailed observation. However, it was impossible to photograph solar prominences and the solar corona because the sun they surrounded was too bright.

During his senior year, Hale conceived of an instrument that would solve the problems of solar phenomena photography. He was allowed to develop and test his idea at the MIT observatory. The resulting photographs became the core of his senior thesis, "Photography of Solar Prominences," and stand as the first visual documentation of solar phenomena.

After graduation, Hale's father wanted him to either come to work in the family's manufacturing business or continue his studies for a doctorate degree. However, the young man was only interested in his solar experiments. He used his unique sales pitch to persuade his father to fund a small but complete observatory behind their house in suburban Chicago. During the next year he produced the first-ever photographic record of a number of important solar phenomena.

Hale's work drew the attention of the University of Chicago. They waived the requirement for an advanced degree in order to lure him into a teaching post. Although he accepted, Hale had no interest in teaching. He had been bitten by the telescopic bug. He knew what a 12-inch telescope could record and now hungered to know what could be seen through larger optics.

Three weeks before classes were to begin, Hale met wealthy Charles Yerkes. Within a week, Yerkes had agreed to fund an observatory that would bear his name and feature a 40-inch reflecting telescope, the largest and most powerful instrument in the world.

Hale quit his university post before teaching his first class and moved to Wisconsin, where the Yerkes observatory and physical laboratory would be built. It would be the world's first facility combining observatory and laboratory research space.

For just over a decade Hale managed the Yerkes Observatory and compiled a wealth of data on solar activity and phenomena. One particular accomplishment during this period was his use of a spectroheliograph to identify and measure the magnetic field of the sun. This measurement marked the first time magnetic activity had been detected outside the Earth's atmosphere.

By 1904 Hale itched for more optic power and convinced the new Carnegie Institute that a bigger, more powerful telescope—it would be the largest in the world—to be located above the distortions of the lower atmosphere, was needed to expand human knowledge of the universe. The Institute agreed to fund the construction of an observatory on 8,000-foot Mount Wilson in southern California.

Hale hustled his family up to the 8,000-foot level on the rugged slopes of Mount Wilson. For the first six months supplies had to be hauled in on mules. They lived in tents like pioneers. But within four years the observatory was functioning. By 1917 a monstrous, 100-inch reflecting telescope was in operation on Mount Wilson.

Despite his recurring health problems, George Hale was a tireless and dedicated astronomer and advocate for astronomy. He wrote six books, published over 450 articles (an astounding number), and helped edit three astronomy journals. He founded three astronomical societies and compiled more solar data and photographed more solar phenomena than anyone in the world.

George Hale advanced the science of optical telescope astronomy, left the world a richer, better place, and firmly established the preeminence of western United States optical astronomy throughout the twentieth century. He may truly be said to be the father of modern solar observational astronomy.

## Key Dates

| | |
|---|---|
| 1868 | Born in Chicago, Illinois, on June 29 |
| 1889 | Invented his first telescope, the spectroheliograph |
| 1890 | Received B.S. from Massachusetts Institute of Technology |
| 1891 | Built his first observatory, the Kenwood Observatory in Chicago, with a 12-inch reflector |
| 1892 | Appointed associate professor of astrophysics at the University of Chicago |
| 1897 | Completed Yerkes Observatory; it was dedicated that year |
| 1904 | Moved to California to start work on Mt. Wilson observatory |
| 1908 | Brought 60-inch reflecting telescope into operation on Mt. Wilson |
| 1917 | Brought 100-inch reflecting telescope into operation on Mt. Wilson |

1928    Received approval and funding for 200-inch reflecting telescope for Palomar Observatory

1938    Died in Pasadena, California, on February 21

## Advice

*George Hale never taught or worked with students. His regular advice to assistants was to "do." Get out of the classroom and "do" the activity of your field of science. Learn the machinery; learn the experimental processes. Academic learning is valuable but requires the perspective and context of a working knowledge of the practical processes of science to be useful.*

## References

Asimov, Isaac. *Asimov's Biographical Encyclopedia of Science and Technology.* Garden City, N.Y.: Doubleday, 1964. (Good review of Hale's work.)

Gillispie, Charles, ed. *Dictionary of Scientific Biography.* Vol. XV. New York: Charles Scribner's Sons, 1978. (Good summary of Hale's work.)

Osterbrock, Donald E. *Pauper & Prince: Ritchey, Hale, & Big American Telescopes.* Phoenix: University of Arizona Press, 1993. (Biography of George Ritchey, the builder of the first large, successful American reflecting telescopes, and his relationship with George Hale.)

Van Doren, Charles, ed. *Webster's American Biographies.* Springfield, Mass.: G & G Merriam, 1974. (Good review of Hale's work.)

Wright, Helen, and Henry Wright. *Explorer of the Universe: A Biography of George Ellery Hale.* History of Modern Physics and Astronomy, Vol 14. Philadelphia, Pa.: American Institute of Physics, 1994. (Reprint of the 1966 edition; biography of Hale and the development of modern astrophysics.)

# Alice Hamilton

*"Exploring the*
*Dangerous Trades"*

Industrial Medicine

Harvard University Archives

## Career Highlights

- Wrote the first authoritative text on industrial poisons
- Served as representative of the League of Nations Health Committee, 1924–1930
- Appointed to the Harvard University faculty (first woman ever)
- Elected president of National Consumers League

## Important Contributions

Dr. Alice Hamilton was a pioneer in the field of occupational diseases: those diseases that develop as a result of a person's occupation. Because of her long, careful studies, the world became aware of the dangers of carbon monoxide, lead, and mercury. Her books are considered classics, and the results of her surveys eventually led to the passage of workers' compensation laws.

## Career Path

Fire like liquid lava and clouds of sulfurous fumes belched from a row of five steel blast furnaces. Heat rolled from the open furnaces in heavy waves so strong they made it difficult to stand. Men trudged through this blast furnace room in sweat-soaked, ragged T-shirts with bandanas tied around their faces to block the worst of the heat and fumes from the sores around their mouths and noses that the acidic fumes had caused.

Only one person seemed eager to be in the hellish environment of this turn-of-the-century Chicago steel mill. She was 30-year-old Alice Hamilton, standing straight-backed, wearing a floor-length dark dress with a high, starched collar. Dr. Hamilton strode with true purpose across the cavernous cement floor, sample jars rattling in a satchel over one shoulder, notebook and stethoscope in hand. In this forbidding mill, she had found the purpose she had sought for 15 years.

Alice Hamilton was born in 1869 in New York City. After studying the classics as a child at home, Alice completed two years at a girls' finishing school. When she announced that she wanted a medical degree—No, she didn't want to practice as a doctor; she just wanted the degree—her skeptical father demanded that she prove she was serious before he would pay for her to attend a top-notch medical school. She took and easily completed the required preparatory classes at Fort Wayne College of Medicine. Duly impressed, her father enrolled her in the University of Michigan Medical School, where she received her M.D. degree in 1893, only 30 years after the first woman, Elizabeth Blackwell, graduated from an American medical school.

Hamilton had a degree, but no purpose or plans for what to do with it. She spent a year abroad, studying at the universities of Leipzig and Munich. Because women were usually barred from higher education there, school officials only allowed her to be there on condition that she make herself inconspicuous. It was very difficult being the only female student in the German universities. She found the Germans belligerent, racist, and chauvinistic, and she was happy to return to the United States.

After doing more research at Johns Hopkins Medical School, Alice Hamilton became the first woman professor at the Woman's Medical School of Northwestern University in 1897. While this was important work, teaching never felt like enough to her and she longed for soemthing to sink her teeth into. She moved into Jane Addams's Hull House, the pioneer community settlement house and mecca for many of Chicago's visitors at the time. Hull House residents were required to do some social work, so she began bathing neighborhood babies in the basement on Saturday mornings. This was the beginning of Chicago's first well-baby clinic. While she derived some satisfaction from the bathings, Hamilton also felt that this work was far from adequate. She was filled with a vague sense of dissatisfaction.

In 1902, Chicago was ravaged by a serious epidemic of typhoid fever. In addition to caring for the flocks of sick that congregated at the Hull House treatment center, Hamilton investigated the cause of the epidemic's severity. What she found was inept management and poor policy enforcement on the part of the city's Health Department. She set out to solve these problems, and because of her efforts, the Health Department was completely reorganized. But still she was dissatisfied. She wanted to help people in a real and enduring way. She wanted to leave behind some "definite achievement, something really lasting . . . to make the world better." Much to her dismay, she could not even stop the sale of cocaine on the streets outside Hull House.

This concern over not being enough, not doing enough, consumed much of Hamilton's energy. Just when she began to think that she would never achieve any significant success in science, she read Sir Thomas Oliver's *Dangerous Trades.*

Hamilton was horrified to learn that workers in industry were at constant risk due to the poisons that permeated their workplaces. Many immigrant workers had been made incurable invalids because of the toxic fumes they breathed in the steel mills. At the time, the only protection employers offered was to keep "turning over" the labor force, so that no one person would be exposed for too long.

Dr. Hamilton also learned that whereas Europe had laws protecting workers, the United States did not. She realized that the medical profession itself was only vaguely aware of the health problems caused by industrial toxins. She took up the cause as her own. It sparked her passion. It became her focus. The problems of industrial toxins became her lifelong study.

The more she investigated industrial diseases, the more Hamilton became known and respected as an authority on the subject. She forced her way into steel mills, munitions plants, and other heavy manufacturing facilities. She collected and analyzed air and water samples and examined workers. She became the managing director of the Illinois Occupational Disease Commission and oversaw an investigation into the causes of toxic substances and their consequences for employees.

The doctor first concentrated on lead, the most insidious—and widely used—industrial heavy metal. She insisted on interviewing and examining workers herself, often in their own homes. She followed up on every rumor, searched hospital records, and studied the workplaces, even if it meant climbing up ladders and scaling catwalks—in a floor-length dress! A direct result of her investigations was passage of the Illinois workers' compensation laws, the first milestone in a campaign to improve industrial conditions.

In 1919, Harvard University Medical School offered Hamilton a faculty position as assistant professor of industrial medicine. She accepted, becoming Harvard's first female professor. In hiring her, Harvard was not trying to be progressive: She was simply the "only candidate available." Discrimination was still the norm: she was barred from the Harvard club; she could not march in commencement; she was "politely" reminded that female faculty members were not seated at Harvard's graduation exercises. Nevertheless, she taught there for 17 years, retiring in 1935.

Hamilton continued her industrial work even after her "retirement." In 1938 she completed a detailed study of the rayon industry, demonstrating the toxic nature of the industry and prompting passage of Pennsylvania's first workers' compensation law for occupational diseases. In 1943 she wrote her autobiography, *Exploring the Dangerous Trades,* and in 1949 she published a revised edition of her 1934 textbook, *Industrial Toxicology.*

To her career in industrial medicine, Dr. Hamilton added concerns for the poor on Chicago's South Side and international peace efforts. This is not too surprising, considering she went into medicine because, "as a doctor I could go anywhere I pleased, to far-off lands or to city slums, and be quite sure that I could be of use anywhere." She inspired students, instructed colleagues, and influenced industrial practices and laws—and, indeed, was of use anywhere she went.

## Key Dates

| | |
|---|---|
| 1869 | Born in New York City on February 27 |
| 1893 | Graduated from the University of Michigan Medical School |
| 1897 | Became first woman professor at the Women's Medical School of Northwestern University; moved to Jane Addams's Hull House settlement |
| 1902 | Researched bacteriology under pathologist Ludvig Hektoen at Rush Medical School |
| 1910 | Was appointed the first managing director of the Illinois Commission on Occupational Diseases |

| | |
|---|---|
| 1913 | Joined staff of the U.S. Department of Labor |
| 1919–1935 | Was first woman professor at Harvard University |
| 1925 | Published *Industrial Poisons in the United States* |
| 1934 | Published *Industrial Toxicology* |
| 1935 | Retired from Harvard |
| 1937–1938 | Studied poisoning in the rayon industry |
| 1940 | Studied silicosis among miners |
| 1943 | Published her autobiography, *Exploring the Dangerous Trades* |
| 1970 | Died on September 22 |

## Advice

*Alice Hamilton benefited from extensive early education in a wide range of subjects and would advise anyone considering a career in industrial toxicology to do the same. Study as much as you can afford to, and study broadly. Include the classics, history, languages, economics, environmental studies, and physics as well as industrial medicine and chemistry. After undergraduate studies, alternate practical work and further study to prepare for specialization in a field where you feel you can make a contribution. At age 88, Alice said, "For me the satisfaction is that things are better now, and I had some part in it."*

## References

Hamilton, Alice. *Exploring the Dangerous Trades: The Autobiography of Alice, M.D.* Boston: Northeastern University Press, 1985.

———. *Hamilton & Hardy's Industrial Toxicology.* St. Louis: Mosby-Year Book, 1998.

———. "Nineteen Years in the Poisonous Trades," *Harper's* (October 1929): 46–53.

Sammartino McPherson, Stephanie. *The Worker's Detective: A Story About Dr. Alice Hamilton.* Minneapolis, Minn.: Carolrhoda Books, 1992.

# Wesley Harris

## Career Highlights

Courtesy of Dr. Wesley L. Harris

- Elected a fellow to the American Institute for Aeronautics and Astronauts, 1992
- Founded offices of minority education on four university campuses including MIT and the University of Connecticut
- Awarded Meritorious Medal by the American Physical Society, 1992
- Awarded American Institute of Astronautics Gold Award, 1964

## Important Contributions

There are different opinions about what Wesley Harris's most important contribution to science has been. Some would say it has been his long years of distinguished and important research on transonic turbulent air flow and related supersonic air foil design, which led to his appointment by NASA to head the research and design program for their new generation of supersonic transport planes.

Some would say it has been his dedication and service as an inspirational and demanding university teacher.

Still others would say it has been his role as a pioneer in minority opportunities for academic appointments and his tireless efforts to promote minority education. Harris created offices of minority education on four university campuses and regularly used his sabbatical and leave time to assist inner-city minority youths working towards and preparing for college education. In all three areas Wesley Harris stands as a shining example of what can be achieved through dedicated and sustained effort.

## Career Path

A stooped, middle-aged black man stood with his three children just outside the fence at the end of the Richmond, Virginia, airport runway in the summer of 1946. Two of the children romped through the grass playing tag. Six-year-old Wesley Harris stood glued to the fence, memorizing every line of every plane.

A four-engine prop circled to the end of the field and swooped low overhead on its landing approach. The other two children paused to glance up. Wesley stared, hardly breathing, his hands grasping an imaginary control stick, mimicking every necessary pilot maneuver, as if he were landing the plane, himself. On the way home, he announced that he would become a test pilot.

No one doubted his sincerity. Wesley had always loved planes and hadn't minded the teasing from siblings and friends because he spent so much free time building balsa wood and plastic model airplanes. In fourth grade he won a state essay contest about career goals with a description of how and why he wanted to be a test pilot.

But Wesley Harris was born to poor black parents, neither of whom had more than a partial high school education and who worked at minimum wage jobs in Richmond's tobacco factories. He could dream all he wanted. But the adults knew that a poor, black, southern boy wasn't going to fly a plane.

While Wesley played with airplanes, his grandmother believed that an education was the only way he would escape the Richmond slums. She made sure his homework was done every day and that he studied hard for every test and quiz.

Young Wesley was fortunate in another way as well. He had two inspirational teachers during his high school years. Segregation was still enforced in Virginia. Black educators, even those with advanced degrees and extensive experience, could not teach in white universities or public schools. They often settled for teaching positions in black high schools for which they were overqualified. One such teacher taught math at Wesley's school. Another taught him to appreciate the wonders of physics.

The influence of these two teachers combined with one final nudge to convince Wesley to pursue college, something no one in his family had ever done. A year before he graduated, the Soviet Union launched the world's first satellite, *Sputnik I*. The U.S. government responded in part by increasing funding for science education and by expanding science-related programs in aeronautics, astronautics, and avionics. The young student was convinced that these expanding opportunities meant that he could make a place for himself as a test pilot and maybe as an astronaut if he had the appropriate science degrees.

Wesley was admitted to the University of Virginia in Charlottesville in 1960. He wanted to study physics because it would be the most versatile field of study for his later career. But African Americans were not allowed to major in the classical sciences. The closest he was permitted to get was a program in aeronautical engineering.

There were only six other blacks on campus. The campus and town were still segregated. Harris was denied access to many on-campus facilities and activities. There were even restricted hours for his use of the library. The struggling student was now married and trying both to support a wife and, under an unfair set of prejudicial limits, to gain an education.

At the beginning of his senior year, Harris received a needed boost. For his senior research project, he demonstrated the conditions under which air flow over a subsonic wing becomes turbulent and the effect of this turbulence on lift. This research received an award from the American Institute of Aeronautic and Astronautics and attracted the attention of the government body that would soon become NASA.

But by the time Harris graduated in 1964, hard reality had set in. He didn't have, and probably never would have, the money for flying lessons. Without a private license, he would never have the opportunity to pursue a flying career. He shifted his dream to being a university professor in the field of astronautics. That meant graduate school. Both of the professors who had most inspired him at college had received doctorates from Princeton. So he applied to, and was accepted by, Princeton University.

By the time Harris had endured discrimination on another campus and received his Ph.D. in 1968, he had added a second pillar to his plan: teach astronautics *and* work to improve minority opportunities in education. He accepted a position at the University of Virginia partly because it made him the first African American to receive a professorship at that university.

Over the next 25 years, at four different universities, Wesley Harris lived his revised personal dream. He founded offices of minority education on four university campuses, beginning with MIT in 1975. He then used these offices to create and promote programs for minority inner-city youths to increase their opportunities for higher education, to expand minority access to all facets of university life, and to publicize the need for national support of minority education.

Harris also maintained a constant stream of important research in turbulent air flow. Becoming a specialist in supersonic turbulent air flow, he provided essential data to NASA and the aeronautics industry on air foil design and transonic wing design. He authored over 80 journal articles detailing his discoveries and developments.

Harris's current research includes material, chemical, and wind-tunnels studies for new technologies to develop reduced-turbulence supersonic transport planes and an aero-space plane, capable of self-powered flight from the ground through the atmosphere and into space.

Powered flight began with the Wright Brothers as this century opened. The next generation of flying machines to open the twenty-first century will depend in significant part upon the research and discoveries of Wesley Harris.

## Key Dates

| | |
|---|---|
| 1941 | Born in Richmond, Virginia, on October 29 |
| 1964 | Received B.S. in aerospace engineering from the University of Virginia |
| 1964–1966 | Worked as NASA trainee aerospace engineer at Princeton University |
| 1968 | Received Ph.D. in aerospace engineering from Princeton University |
| 1968–1970 | Worked as assistant professor at University of Virginia |
| 1970–1971 | Worked as associate professor of physics at Southern University |
| 1971–1972 | Worked as assistant professor of aerospace engineering at University of Virginia |
| 1972–1981 | Worked as associate professor of aeronautics at MIT |
| 1981–1985 | Worked as professor of aeronautics at MIT |
| 1985–1990 | Served as dean, School of Engineering at University of Connecticut |
| 1990–1993 | Served as vice president and professor at University of Tennessee Space Institute |

1993–
1995      Served as associate dean of NASA Aeronautics Program

1995–
present   Works as professor of aeronautics and astronautics at MIT

## Advice

*Wesley Harris would advise anyone considering a career in aeronautics to use every opportunity and avenue to strengthen and broaden your education. Dr. Harris believes that there is no such thing as too much education or too much learning. Research is a part of study and learning; learning and study are a big part of all research. Those who use their educational opportunities most effectively will be most successful in the future world of science. Good base courses for an undergraduate curriculum include physics, aeronautics, avionics, related engineering courses, and materials courses.*

## References

Hancock, G. J. *An Introduction to the Flight Dynamics of Rigid Aeroplanes.* Englewood Cliffs, N.J.: Prentice-Hall, 1995. (Good review of the engineering in the field.)

Kessler, James, et al. *Distinguished African American Scientists of the 20th Century.* Phoenix, Ariz.: Oryx Press, 1996. (Good biographical and career summary of Harris's work.)

Saltnier, Karla. *Black Engineers in the United States.* Washington, D.C.: Washington University Press, 1985. (Good biographical and career summary of Harris's work.)

Sammons, Vivial. *Blacks in Science and Medicine.* New York: Hemisphere Publishing, 1990. (Biographical summary.)

# Stephen Hawking

*"Finding the Big Bang"*       Physics

## Career Highlights

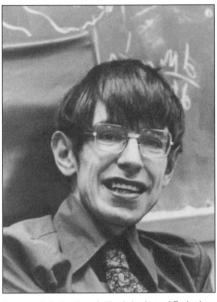

Courtesy of the Archives, California Institute of Technology

- Co-created the Big Bang theory of the origin of the universe
- Developed our theoretical understanding of black holes and other singularities
- Awarded the Paul Dirac Medal and Prize by the Institute for Physics, 1987
- Awarded the Royal Astronomical Society Gold Medal, 1985
- Awarded the Albert Einstein Medal by the Einstein Society, 1979

## Important Contributions

Where did the universe come from? What happened before its beginning? Will it end? What will happen after that? What, then, is the true nature of time? These are the questions that have absorbed theoretical physicist Stephen Hawking, widely regarded as the most brilliant physicist since Albert Einstein, and possibly of all time.

Hawking is the co-founder of the Big Bang theory of the origin of the universe and has developed most of our theoretical understanding of black holes and other space-time singularities, such as cosmic strings and worm holes. In addition, he has inspired millions of people to study the bizarre workings of a relative, curving space-time with his ability to describe almost incomprehensible concepts in a straightforward, lucid style. More than any other individual, Stephen Hawking has both brought the reality of the vast universe into our consciousness and significantly advanced our theoretical understanding of major cosmic events.

## Career Path

*Lou Gehrig's disease.*

The diagnosis, the very words, seemed to hang palpably in the air of 21-year-old Stephen Hawking's graduate school room at Cambridge University. Images raced through his mind of one of baseball's greatest sluggers reduced to a shriveled, helpless invalid in a wheel chair, having to be pushed onto the field to receive the cheers of an adoring crowd, not being able to stand, or wave, or even speak in response.

That was Lou Gehrig's disease. If it could crush the greatest and most fit, how could a slender, young, hopeful scientist keep from being destroyed? How could he ever deliver on the promise of his early career?

Stephen Hawking grew up in St. Albins, a suburb of London near the center where his father headed the division of parasitology for the National Institute for Medical Research. Stephen was a good, but not exceptional, student at St. Albins School. His grades were satisfactory, but he regularly made a nuisance of himself by "always wanting to know how everything worked." Both at home and at school adults complained that Stephen was destructive. He recalls that, "I would take things apart because I *needed* to see how they worked. But they often didn't fit back together."

While he had always been drawn to science, Stephen was never tempted to follow his father into one of the fields of biology because they were "too descriptive and inexact." He felt more comfortable with fields that were less qualitative and more quantitative and precise.

Despite a lackluster high school performance, Hawking won an open scholarship to Oxford. There he studied mathematics his first year and shifted to physics in his second. By the accounts of both his tutors and his own recollection, he sluffed through his undergraduate courses with minimal effort. However, his conceptual and theoretical genius was beginning to be noticed. Robert Berman, his physics tutor, recalled, "Hawking did very little work because anything that was doable he could already do. Once he knew that something could be done, he would do it without looking to see how other people did it."

Hawking graduated with honors in 1962, in part, as one of his professors said, "because the examiners realized they were dealing with someone far cleverer than themselves." He recalls his carefree Oxford days as "a most happy time when I would discuss ideas with friends, attend parties, row for the club, and work very little."

Because he had always been more interested in theory than in observation or experimentation, Hawking shifted to Cambridge for graduate studies in cosmology. Cambridge was the place where scholars were asking the big questions about the universe, questions that soared far beyond our ability to observe but were still within the grasp of the mind.

No sooner had Hawking settled into his studies than tragedy struck. He was diagnosed with Lou Gehrig's disease, an incurable progressive deterioration of the motor neurons of the spinal cord, medulla, and cortex. It disables skeletal muscles, affecting speech, limbs, swallowing, and shoulders, ending in fatal atrophy of the chest muscles.

Depressed by the prospect of physical deterioration and early death, he plodded through his first two years at Cambridge making virtually no progress. Then the disease stabilized. He would survive, albeit disabled. Equally important, he met and married linguistics student Jane Wilde. He felt a new will to live and succeed. He felt a new drive, determination, and enthusiasm for his work. His natural buoyancy returned.

Professional progress started immediately. Hawking and a colleague, Roger Penrose, undertook a rigorous mathematical investigation of the meaning of Einstein's general relativity when applied to black holes. Theory predicted the existence of black holes. But they were still a physical mystery. Black holes are points in space where gravitational forces are so great that not even light can escape. In effect, they disappear from the space-time continuum and cease to be part of our universe, except for their ever-present gravitational well, lurking to snare any nearby object and pull it into the hole's inescapable vortex.

Penrose and Hawking were able to show that in such an "event," space is bent and time ends, or ceases to exist. All known laws of physics break down at a black hole—called a *singularity*—because density and gravity both approach infinity, and volume shrinks toward zero. "This is a great crisis for physics," said Hawking, "because it means one can no longer predict the future. We do not know what will come out of a singularity."

However, Hawking was able to combine known information about a singularity with general relativity and run the cosmic clock backward to show that our universe began as one of these singularity events. He demonstrated that rather than being mere mathematical anomalies, as many physicists suspected, black holes can and certainly do exist, and that, if general relativity is true, then there had to be a beginning to the universe, and that beginning had to occur with a singularity.

With the publication of his first book on these phenomena, *A Brief History of Time*, Hawking became an international celebrity. He was sought out for guest lectures and appearances. However, he accepted few of these offers. For the past 25 years he has been confined to a wheel chair. No longer able to write or talk, most of his communication has been through a computer speech synthesizer. Of this he has said, "It was fortunate that I chose theoretical physics, because that is all in the mind."

Ignoring his physical limitations, Stephen Hawking, still in his prime at 55, daily sets an impish grin on his face and marches ever closer to unraveling the ultimate questions of our universe. He has made more progress than any other theoretician toward the creation of a "grand unification theory" (often jokingly called the "Theory of Everything"), which would combine relativity, classical thermodynamics, and quantum mechanics under a single, all-encompassing descriptive theory. He believes that this theory "will be the ultimate triumph of human reason, for then we would surely know the mind of God."

## Key Dates

| | |
|---|---|
| 1942 | Born in Oxford, England, on January 8 |
| 1962 | Received B.A. from Oxford University |
| 1963 | Diagnosed with Lou Gehrig's disease |
| 1966 | Received Ph.D. from Cambridge University |
| 1966–1968 | Worked as research fellow at Caius College in London |
| 1968–1972 | Became member of the Institute of Theoretical Astronomy |
| 1972–1973 | Worked as research assistant at the Institute of Astronomy |
| 1973–1977 | Worked as research assistant in Department of Theoretical Physics at Cambridge University |
| 1977–present | Works as professor of mathematics at Cambridge University |
| 1988 | Published *A Brief History of Time,* which became an instant best seller |

# Advice

*Stephen Hawking has two pieces of advice for anyone pursuing a career in theoretical cosmology. First, take philosophy as well as physics, nuclear physics, and astrophysics courses. Theory and philosophy are closely related. Second, don't let obstacles stand in your way. They will all crumble if you don't allow them to stand.*

*Finally, Hawking would add that theoretical physics is an area that attempts to answer questions. In choosing a specialty, look first for questions that need to be answered. Fundamental questions should be your long-range career targets. You won't reach answers to them for years. Still, they must interest you and engage your skills and strengths.*

# References

Ferguson, Kitty. *Stephen Hawking: Quest for a Theory of the Universe.* New York: Bantam Books, 1992. (Describes Hawking's role in modern theoretical physics.)

Filkin, David, and Stephen Hawking. *Stephen Hawking's Universe: The Cosmos Explained.* Indianapolis: Basic Books, 1998.

Gribben, John, and Michael White. *Stephen Hawking: A Life in Science.* New York: E. P. Dutton, 1992. (Good biography of Hawking.)

Hawking, Stephen. *Black Holes and Baby Universes.* New York: Bantam Books, 1993. (Explains Hawking's view of the universe and its origin, with special emphasis on the formation and significance of black holes.)

————. *A Brief History of Time.* New York: Bantam Doubleday Dell, 1998. (An excellent, readable review of relativity and astrophysics.)

Lightman, Alan, and Roberta Brawer. *Origins: The Lives and Worlds of Modern Cosmologists.* Cambridge, Mass.: Cambridge University Press, 1990. (Good biographical summary of Hawking's work.)

McDaniel, Melissa. *Stephen Hawking: Physicist.* New York: Chelsea House, 1994. (A good biography of Hawking.)

Strathern, Paul. *Hawking and Black Holes.* Big Idea Series. New York: Doubleday, 1998.

# Werner Heisenberg

## *"The Birth of Uncertainty"*        Physics

## Career Highlights

- Developed the famed Heisenberg "Uncertainty Principle," a cornerstone of quantum mechanics and chaos theory
- Awarded Nobel Prize for Physics, 1932
- Awarded the Max Planck Medal by the German Physics Society, 1933
- Awarded the Niels Bohr International Gold Medal by the Danish Society of Engineers, 1970

## Important Contributions

Werner Heisenberg is famed worldwide for developing his Heisenberg "Uncertainty Principle," which states that it is impossible to determine both the position and momentum of an elementary particle since the effort to determine either would change the other in unpredictable ways. This pivotal theorem marked a fundamental turning point in science. For the first time a limit to scientific observation had been found. It was no longer possible to precisely measure or observe the world. At a certain point, Heisenberg showed, scientists had to step back and take the mathematical equations describing the world on faith.

The Heisenberg "Uncertainty Principle" also undermined the position of cause and effect as a most basic and unassailable foundation block of scientific research, a position it had enjoyed for over 2,500 years. After Heisenberg, at an elementary particle level, every cause had only a fixed probability of creating an anticipated effect.

Interestingly, though, Heisenberg's Nobel Prize was earned for work he completed before he developed the famous "Uncertainly Principle." In earlier work, he had developed a new mathematical approach to quantum mechanics, called matrix mechanics (later renamed wave mechanics). This strange, new mathematical approach to quantum calculations greatly expanded the range and potential of quantum analysis and became part of the foundation of quantum mechanics.

Heisenberg also contributed to basic particle theory, first proposing that neutrons were locked into an atom's nucleus with its protons. Heisenberg also laid many of the early stones along the long path toward the development of an illusive unified field theory. Few have touched physics as deeply or as profoundly as did Werner Heisenberg.

## Career Path

Opening the mail in his Helgoland, Germany, home in the fall of 1926, Werner Heisenberg found a letter from famed physicist Max Planck. The letter glowed with praise for Heisenberg's paper presenting the "matrix mechanics" he had developed. It was his fifth congratulatory letter of the week. He had also received letters from such important figures as Wolfgang Pauli and Max Born.

Every letter hailed Heisenberg's matrix mechanics and talked about its "vast potential." The scientists who sent these letters called it "new and exciting" and "extremely valuable."

But Werner Heisenberg was uneasy, and this feeling was not relieved by this or any of the letters. Buried in his matrix equations, which everyone else lauded as a revolutionary tool for quantum physics, he had detected what he thought was a hard limit to science. If true, it would be the first time science had been told it was impossible to be more precise. A deep dread assailed the foundations of Heisenberg's scientific beliefs. Yet there it was in black and white. If he was right, science had reached an unscaleable wall.

It was a hard reality to face for someone who had given up a budding music career to embrace the promise of an unlimited world in science.

Werner Heisenberg began taking piano lessons when he was five years old. He was performing master-level concerts by the time he was 13. Probably because of his father's academic standing and love of rigorous study and learning, Werner never considered music as a possible career; instead, music remained a lifelong hobby.

Werner's passion was saved for science. He was an eager student who loved school and the process of learning. It was obvious to all that he was exceptionally gifted in mathematics. By the time he graduated from high school in 1919 he had taught himself calculus, had explored advanced elliptical functions, and had written and attempted to publish a paper on number theory.

After working on a farm for three seasons to earn money, Werner entered the University of Munich in 1920, determined to study pure mathematics.

He was a driven student, intent on absorbing everything. He graduated early and obtained his doctorate when only 22 years old.

Graduation did not end Heisenberg's desire for study. He traveled to Göttingen and studied for a year with famed physicist Max Born. He obtained a research fellowship to support him while he traveled to Copenhagen to study with Niels Bohr. Heisenberg's focus throughout these additional three years of study and research was atomic structure and behavior and an attempt to resolve, in a mathematical sense, the work of Max Planck and Albert Einstein.

Having absorbed the thoughts of the best physics minds in the world for six years, Heisenberg returned to Helgoland to recover from a severe attack of hay fever. During his recuperation, a new and comprehensive method for calculating the energy levels of "atomic oscillators" (electrons) "flowed easily" into his mind.

The real debate at that time centered on the image of an atom. Was it a ball of protons surrounded by shells of particle electrons, as Bohr claimed, or were electrons really waves of energy flowing around the central nucleus, as others proposed? It occurred to Heisenberg to forget speculation and begin with what was known: that electrons, whatever they were, became excited and released quanta of energy along specific characteristic frequencies. Heisenberg decided to develop equations to describe and predict the end result, the spectral lines of radiated energy.

Heisenberg turned to matrix analysis to help him derive equations with concepts such as frequency, position, and momentum along with precise ways to mathematically manipulate them. The resulting equations, while yielding good results, seemed strange and unwieldy. Uncertain of their value, Heisenberg almost burned the final paper. Instead he sent a copy to someone he had studied with and trusted, Wolfgang Pauli. Pauli instantly recognized the value of Heisenberg's work and notified Max Born.

Heisenberg's discovery, called matrix mechanics, gained him instant fame and became one of the pillars of quantum mechanics. But he was bothered by something he uncovered during his research. During some of his matrix multiplication he noticed that, because of the matrix nature of the calculations, the value for particle position could affect the value he had to use for momentum and vice versa.

While dealing with imprecision was not at all new to Heisenberg, it was new to realize that the better he knew one concept, the more it would add imprecision to another. The better he knew position, the less he knew about momentum. The more precisely he could determine momentum, the less he would know about position.

Uncertainty was born. In one sweeping revelation the notion of a completely deterministic world was destroyed. Hard limits were placed for the first time on science's ability to measure and observe. For the first time, there were places scientists could not go, events they could never see. Cause and effect became cause and chance-of-effect. At the most fundamental level the very basis of the scientific method was altered. Research was made instantly more complex, and yet new doors and avenues to understanding and progress were opened.

Many scientists, led by Einstein, resisted the notion that statistical probability was now the only way to describe the position and movement of elementary particles. To Einstein, the notion seemed to reduce God's infinitely precise universe to a dice game. But 50 years of rigorous research have consistently confirmed and reinforced Heisenberg's concept. The Heisenberg "Uncertainty Principle" has become a basis of quantum mechanics and a fundamental tenet of the chaos theory developed after Heisenberg's retirement.

Heisenberg also made significant contributions to the theory of nuclear structure and to a unified field theory. He even developed a theory on hydrogen atomic spin that bore practical fruit 40 years later in helping NASA create an improved liquid hydrogen fuel.

Heisenberg's later career was clouded by questions of his participation in the Nazi program to develop an atomic bomb. But it is for the concept of uncertainty—that most profound and fundamental concept of the twentieth century—that Werner Heisenberg will rightly be remembered and revered.

## Key Dates

| | |
|---|---|
| 1901 | Born in Wurzburg, Germany, on December 5 |
| 1923 | Received Ph.D. in mathematics from University of Munich |
| 1924 | Studied at Göttingen with Max Born |
| 1925 | Studied under Neils Bohr |
| 1926 | Offered position as mathematics instructor at University of Munich |
| 1926 | Published "Matrix Mechanics" paper |
| 1927 | Offered professorship at University of Leipzig |
| 1927 | Developed famed "Uncertainty Principle" |
| 1932 | Awarded Nobel Prize |
| 1976 | Died on February 6 |

## Advice

*Werner Heisenberg believed that any study of physics should start with mathematics. Math is the language of science and any scientist should be completely familiar with the concepts and techniques of this language. Heisenberg often advised students to seek out and study under the masters in their particular field. Masters are those who have created the last step in the path of scientific progress. The next step will be taken by those who learned from those taking the current step. Finally, study, study, study. It takes considerable work to reach the forefront of any scientific field. Yet that effort is mandatory for those who expect to achieve.*

## References

Daintith, John, et al., eds. *Biographical Encyclopedia of Scientists.* 2d ed. Vol. 1. Philadelphia, Pa.: Institute of Physics Publishing, 1994. (Summary entry on Heisenberg's work.)

Eggenberger, David, ed. *The McGraw-Hill Encyclopedia of World Biography.* Vol. 5. New York: McGraw-Hill, 1983. (Short entry on Heisenberg's work.)

Gillispie, Charles, ed. *Dictionary of Scientific Biography.* Vol. XV. New York: Charles Scribner's Sons, 1978. (Good summary of Heisenberg's work.)

Hoffman, Banesh. *The Strange Story of the Quantum.* Cambridge, Mass.: Harvard University Press, 1959. (Places Heisenberg's work within the context of the development of quantum theory.)

Rensberger, Boyce. *How the World Works: A Guide to Science's Greatest Discoveries.* New York: William Morrow, 1994. (Good review of Heisenberg's central accomplishments.)

# Warren Henry

*"Leaving His Mark"*　　　Physical Chemistry

## Career Highlights

- Created the Minorities Access to Research Careers (MARC) program to assist minority science-bound undergraduate and graduate students
- Awarded the Carver Award from Tuskegee University, 1978
- Awarded the Meritorious Service Medal for civilian contributions to military technology development, 1970

## Important Contributions

Warren Henry was an excellent and inspiring teacher. But his first love was always scientific research. Even though he carried the load of a full-time university teaching professor, he found time to conduct a continuous stream of physical chemistry research, which produced dozens of important inventions.

Henry invented two new radar systems during World War II that aided both naval and land forces and an ultra-sensitive temperature sensor that proved invaluable in analyzing a wide variety of chemical reactions. He discovered the chemical process behind metal fatigue that greatly improved the performance and safety of new jet aircraft, conducted many of the early superconductivity experiments for the U.S. Navy, and was the first to study the relationship between superconductivity and strong magnetic fields. Henry also invented a breakthrough system for electronic astronomy able to detect and measure outer space magnetic fields. Warren Henry left his mark on a wide range of physical and chemical research areas and on a wide range of students, whom he inspired and assisted toward successful careers in research science.

## Career Path

The life of Warren Henry reads like the profile of a saw blade. The peaks due to hard work and important opportunity were regularly followed by crushing defeats at the hands of poverty and discrimination. Still, his is an all-American story of perseverance and triumph.

Warren Henry was born at home in a farmhouse just outside the tiny village of China, Alabama, during the winter of 1909. Both of his parents were teachers and, as such, were respected members of the community, but they were very poorly paid. The Henrys farmed in the summer to make ends meet.

By modern standards, Warren had a hard childhood. His parents taught at the community school, which Mr. Henry had built with donations from northern churches, and took Warren to school with them each day beginning before his third birthday. The little boy was given toys and books to play with at the back of the room. He liked to pretend that he was a student and would act like he was doing school assignments along with the eight, nine, and ten year olds. He pretended so well that, much to the shock of everyone, he taught himself to read before he turned four years old.

On weekends and during summers, Warren worked the family farm. He was weeding, picking, and planting when he was six. He could run a team of mules to plow the fields when he was nine. He spent his free time picking cotton on neighboring farms to earn money to help with family expenses.

The China community school only went through tenth grade and offered no formal instruction in science. To receive a high school diploma, Warren had to travel to a boarding school in Montgomery. The family could only afford to send him there for one year, so he was instructed to study everything he could and pass his senior tests in the spring.

During that stressful year the young man took his first science course, a chemistry class. And he loved it. He did so well that the teacher made him her lab assistant for the second semester.

Henry's parents encouraged him to continue his education after graduation in the spring of 1927 even though they needed his help on the family farm. He enrolled in Tuskegee Institute, where both of his parents had studied, planning to study chemistry, his first love in the world of science. But school administrators wanted students to obtain a broad, liberal arts background and acquire practical life skills such as carpentry and brick laying. He had to sneak into many of the physics and chemistry classes to get enough exposure to science to satisfy his hunger.

Henry also had to work to support himself through college. For his first year he snatched whatever odd jobs he could find. By his second year he had qualified to be a paid lab assistant for the chemistry courses.

In the summers Henry worked on the Tuskegee experimental farm. They were testing new insecticides and fertilizers to promote cotton growth and control the dangerous boll weevil. It was his first exposure to research. Everything about it fascinated him.

After graduation in 1931, Henry was offered a job as teacher and principal of a small high school in Atmore, Alabama. Throughout his three years of teaching, he longed to continue his studies in chemistry and to return to the world of research. Following a summer refresher science course in which he did very well, Henry was offered a scholarship to enter graduate school. He jumped at this grand opportunity, one he had feared he would never get. He completed his coursework at Atlanta University and then the University of Chicago. To supplement his meager scholarship stipend, he worked as a coat and hat checker, tutored undergraduate students, and conducted door-to-door surveys. But the jobs he sought out and fought for most were research and lab assistant jobs.

Henry's thesis research resulted in his first invention, a device to monitor chemical reactions by measuring minute temperature changes. His device was capable of accurately detecting changes as small as one ten-millionth of a degree.

Henry received his Ph.D. in 1941, but no research positions were available for black chemists. He had to return to teaching. His next great opportunity came in 1943, when the U.S. Army funded the creation of a Radar Systems Research Center at the Massachusetts Institute of Technology (MIT) and Henry was invited to join the staff. Henry's work was on the electrical-chemical interface at the radar operator's scope. In this period before transistors, microprocessors, semiconductors, and computers, he invented a video signal amplifier that filtered the radar signal from background noise, amplified it, and displayed it in a way much easier for operators to identify and interpret. His ground-based and shipboard systems worked perfectly throughout the war.

After the war Henry transferred to the Institute for the Study of Metals at the University of Chicago. There, under contract for the military, he researched the causes of jet aircraft wing failures and crashes. Using his ultra-sensitive temperature sensor, he was able to show that repeated high-speed flexing of the wings caused chemical changes in the molecular bonding of the metal supports, which made them brittle and weak. The phenomenon became known as "metal fatigue." Henry experimented on dozens of metals to develop exact predictions about when and how various alloys would fail.

In 1948 Henry moved to the Naval Research Lab in Washington, D.C. to research the newly discovered phenomenon of superconductivity. From 1945 on, he kept up a full teaching load in addition to his research. It meant long hours and weekend work. But he couldn't imagine giving up either aspect of his career.

Warren Henry received several critically important opportunities during his career. But to a greater extent, his dedication, determination, and continuous hard work earned him each of his golden opportunities. More important, in his view, is that he has spent a great deal of his energy helping minority children gain access to similar opportunities for careers in science and especially in research careers. Henry left his most prized legacy in the successful careers of hundreds of students for whom he opened the door to science.

## Key Dates

| | |
|---|---|
| 1909 | Born in China, Alabama, on February 18 |
| 1931 | Received B.S. in physics from Tuskegee Institute |
| 1931–1934 | Worked as principal at Escambia Country Training School |
| 1934–1936 | Was graduate student at Atlanta University and instructor of physics at Spellman and Morehouse colleges |
| 1936–1938 | Was graduate student and lecture assistant at University of Chicago |
| 1939–1941 | Worked as instructor of chemistry, physics, and radio at Tuskegee Institute |
| 1941 | Received Ph.D. in physical chemistry from the University of Chicago |
| 1941–1943 | Worked as research assistant in physics at MIT |
| 1943–1947 | Was staff member of the Radiation Laboratory at MIT |
| 1947–1948 | Was acting head, department of physics at Morehouse and Clark colleges |
| 1948–1960 | Worked as physicist at the Naval Research Laboratory, Washington, D.C. |
| 1960–1969 | Was engineering group director at the Lockheed Missile and Space Company |
| 1969–1981 | Worked as professor in the School of Engineering at Howard University |

1978    Developed Minorities Access to Research Careers

1981–    Is emeritus professor of physics at Howard University
present

## Advice

*Warren Henry believes that education equals opportunity. Work hard at and for every bit of education you can obtain. Every class and year of schooling is a valuable asset. Even classes far afield from your specialty have lasting value.*

*Warren Henry also believes that the heart of science is research. Learn the methods and techniques of research in your field early and practice them regularly. Remember that advancements and discoveries happen continuously. You must always strive to stay current, no matter how long you have been working in a field. Hard work is the price for the privilege of being a scientist.*

## References

Kessler, James, et al. *Distinguished African American Scientists of the 20th Century*. Phoenix, Ariz.: Oryx Press, 1996. (Good review of Henry's life and work.)

Mayre, Jonathan. *Superconductivity: The Threshold of a New Technology*. Blue Ridge Summit, Pa.: Tab Books, 1988. (Good overview of the field.)

Sammons, Vivial. *Blacks in Science and Medicine*. New York: Hemisphere, 1990. (Biographical summary.)

Schechter, Bruce. *The Path of No Resistance: The Story of the Revolution in Superconductivity*. New York: Simon & Schuster, 1989. (Good review of the field.)

# Matthew Henson

## *"A Special Kind of Scientist"*    Exploration

## Career Highlights

- Was first person to reach the North Pole
- Awarded the Congressional Medal of Honor
- Elected to the Explorers' Club, life membership
- Received honorary master of science degree from Morgan College, 1924

## Important Contributions

On April 6, 1909, Matthew Henson became the first person to reach the North Pole. His co-explorer, Admiral Peary, arrived 45 minutes later. Henson was a self-educated black man who learned three languages of Arctic peoples, became an expert on Arctic survival, and was a leading expert on oceanography, navigation, and sea ice.

Explorers are a special kind of scientist, and whether they are exploring the Arctic wastelands like Matthew Henson, or the oceans, like Jacques Cousteau, they share a hunger for knowing the unknown and a desire for adventure. Matthew Henson not only possessed these traits but also raised himself from the clutches of poverty and discrimination to achieve greatness.

# Career Path

Matthew Henson hunched his back to the howling wind and cupped his gloved hands around the compass dial. He strained to see in the pale light of a sun barely above the distant jags of pack ice even though it was past 10:30 in the morning on April 6, 1909. The compass needle spun idly, seemingly indifferent to the magnetic field of Earth.

Although his exposed face was raw and cracked, Henson was past feeling the numbing −50° F cold. Hundreds of miles of jagged ice and bitter cold stretched off beyond seeing. His eyes searched back down the ragged trail for the second sled. Injury, loss of dogs, and sled damage from the relentless ice had whittled their numbers to these final two sleds. He used an ax to cut ice blocks for a rough igloo to protect himself from the wind while he waited. Wrapped in seal pelts and thick fur, he had survived frostbite, starvation, and bone-chilling cold to get here. Judging from the start Henson got in life, he was the unlikeliest human to be the first to stand at the North Pole even though he had been doggedly struggling to reach this spot for over 18 years.

Matthew Henson was born in rural Maryland less than two years after the end of the Civil War. Like most African Americans of that era, he received no formal education. His mother died when he was two years old, his father when he was eight. At 11 he ran away from his stepmother and her new husband and joined an uncle he had never met.

The orphaned boy lived with his uncle for a couple of years and worked as a dishwasher in a restaurant. At 13, he quit his job and hiked to Baltimore, where he was hired as a cabin boy on a ship bound for Hong Kong. The captain became Matthew's only real teacher. For five years he lived on the ship, learning seamanship, navigation, geography, mathematics, first aid, and how to read and write.

When the captain died, Matthew worked at odd jobs for several years. At age 19, he went to work as a stock boy in a men's clothing store in Washington, D.C. That job changed his life.

One day while Henson was in the back room taking inventory, Robert E. Peary entered the store and asked for a sun hat because he was going to tropical Nicaragua. Henson came out with the hat, they began talking, and the next moment, he agreed to accompany Peary as a field assistant to a canal survey job in Nicaragua.

While working in Nicaragua, Henson learned of Peary's burning desire to cross Greenland and reach the North Pole. It didn't take long for Peary to pass his enthusiasm on to his companion.

In 1891, they left on their first trek across Greenland. Their first goal was to test their ability to navigate the Arctic by sledding across Greenland from the west coast to the east coast. While Peary and a small party made the trek across and back, Henson maintained the base camp and learned Arctic survival from the Eskimos. Peary survived the 1,200-mile round-trip journey but returned exhausted, weakened from exposure, and near starvation. Nevertheless, both men believed they could endure a trip to the North Pole.

Returning to New York, they both believed they'd reach the pole in several years of effort. In fact, it took them two decades. Time after time Peary and Henson arrived in Greenland in late summer, before the ice grew too thick, built forts in which to pass the winter, then set out on foot in the spring. Time after time they were forced back.

Sometimes their ships became locked in ice before they reached the Arctic Ocean. Often their sleighs were destroyed by the unforgiving snow and ice. Usually their food ran short. Once they returned with only one sled dog, 36 having died or been killed for food. Frequently they returned sick and crippled with frostbite. During one winter, Peary's feet froze so badly the doctor had to remove seven of his toes.

But those journeys were not complete failures. Henson and Peary mapped vast reaches of this unknown land; they discovered that Greenland was indeed an island and that the northwest coast was impassable. It was impossible to make an overland trip to the Pole.

The two explorers also discovered three large meteorites, which they brought back to the United States. Each meteorite was placed on display at the Museum of Natural History in New York City (where they still remain). While he recovered his strength from their last attempt, Henson worked from late 1906 to 1908 at the museum because he was recognized as an expert on the Arctic. For two years, he mounted walrus skins, arranged true-to-life exhibits, and presented lectures on the Arctic.

In July 1908, Henson and Peary mounted their ninth expedition to reach the North Pole. They made the west coast of Greenland by August. This time they had designed lighter, broader sleds, which they hoped would navigate the open-ocean pack ice. They also broke camp two months earlier than they had in the past to take advantage of the thick winter ice. After waiting out the winter, Matthew Henson and a small group of Inuit were the first on the trail to the North Pole on February 18, 1909.

Traveling across sea ice was much more difficult than traveling across land ice. The ice shifted into jagged, saw-like mounds or cracked into treacherous crevasses leading into the frigid sea. They used pickaxes to slowly forge ahead. The sleighs broke easily on the rough trail, and fixing them in sub-zero temperatures was difficult at best.

This time, Henson and Peary's group split into rotating teams. One team slept while another forged ahead. Then the other team would catch up along the established trail and forge ahead while the first team slept. For 40 days they continued this grueling schedule.

Temperatures dropped to –50° F and even their brandy froze. All of the "worker" teams were driven back to base camp by hardships and losses. By April 4, the expedition was only 60 miles from the Pole, but down to a dangerously few dogs and only two sleds.

On April 6, Henson broke camp first in a howling wind and threatening sky. At 10:00 in the morning he stopped to build a sheltering igloo and waited for Peary, who caught up 45 minutes later and set up his observational equipment. It only took two minutes to verify that they had made it to the North Pole!

The two men took photographs of the terrain, made observations of the sun, and recorded the depth of the polar sea (greater than 9,000 feet). After 20 years of chasing their dreams with toil and hardship, after losing over 200 sled dogs and 12 men, they had succeeded!

Matthew Henson's efforts helped to extend human knowledge of the Arctic region and he collected a treasure trove of essential data on seasonal variations in Arctic pack ice, weather conditions, and cultural behaviors.

## Key Dates

| | |
|---|---|
| 1867 | Born in Charles County, Maryland, on August 6 |
| 1878 | Ran away to live with an uncle |
| 1880–1886 | Worked on a ship traveling the world |
| 1886 | Worked as a stock boy in a men's clothing store |
| 1887 | Met Robert E. Peary |
| 1891 | Attempted to cross Greenland from west to east with Peary |
| 1893–1897 | Attempted to reach the North Pole through the interior of Greenland with Peary |
| 1898–1902 | Attempted to reach the North Pole with Peary |
| 1905–1906 | Attempted to reach the North Pole with Peary |
| 1908 | Departed New York on July 6 for the North Pole |
| 1909 | Reached the North Pole on April 6, 1909; Peary arrived 45 minutes behind |
| 1955 | Died May 29 |

## Advice

*If you are considering a career as an explorer, Matthew Henson would advise you to prepare yourself by studying mathematics and the earth sciences in depth, especially oceanography, geology, meteorology, and geography. Add in physics, structural engineering, ecology, and cultural studies and language. That curriculum will provide irreplaceable support once in the field. Finally, Henson would say to never give up. Even if it takes 20 years, attaining your goal is always worth fighting for.*

## References

Dolan, Edward F. *Matthew Henson, Black Explorer.* New York: Putnam, 1979.

Hayden, Robert C. *Seven African American Scientists.* Frederick, Md.: Twenty-First Century Books, Henry Holt, 1992.

Henson, Matthew. *Negro Explorer at the North Pole.* New York: Fred A. Stokes, 1912.

May, Julian. *Matthew Henson: Co-Discoverer of the North Pole.* Mankato, Minn.: Creative Education, 1972.

Robinson, Bradley. *Dark Companion: The Official Biography of Matthew Henson.* New York: Widget Magic, 1997.

# Harry Hess

*"Seafloor Spreading"*

## Geology and Oceanography

## Career Highlights

- Developed the theory of ocean-floor spreading, the foundation of plate tectonics
- Awarded (posthumously) the Distinguished Public Service Medal of NASA, 1969
- Served as chairman of the National Research Council's advisory committee to the Atomic Energy Commission on disposal of radioactive waste
- Had Hess Guyot and Hess Deep in the Pacific named after him

Archives of the National Academy of Sciences

## Important Contributions

Internationally known geologist and mineralogist Harry Hess made contributions to geology, oceanography, and space science. He wrote important papers about rock-forming minerals, developed an X-ray system for mineral analysis of rocks, and discovered guyots: submerged, flat-topped summits on the ocean bed. He even developed a Navy method for submarine detection. But most important, Hess gave us the theory of ocean-floor spreading, which helped explain the drifting of continents.

# Career Path

On the deck of a mammoth deep-ocean drilling ship in the mid-Pacific, Navy Commander Harry Hess watched as the crane operator maneuvered the drilling pipe sections from atop the drilling derrick mounted high above the deck. Core sample drilling of the ocean floor had been underway for ten days. They had been retrieving actual bottom core samples for the last three. The seas were calm and drilling conditions were excellent.

A white-coated lab technician forced open a bulkhead door and crossed the wide deck to Commander Hess, handing him the lab report on core sample dating. Test after test showed the ocean bottom age to be less than 100 million years. Two thoughts raced across Hess's mind. The first was indignation that the numbers could be so different than what he had hoped for. The second was the sinking knowledge that he had just disproved all his own theories, that all his work over the past 12 years had been wrong. He would have to start all over. Harry Hess needed a new theory.

Harry Hess had not done well in grade school, graduating with mediocre grades. Still, he performed well enough on college entrance exams to be accepted by Yale University, planning to become an electrical engineer. Early in his junior year, Harry grew bored with engineering and switched to geology, graduating in 1927 with a B.S. After graduation, he spent two years in Rhodesia (now Zambia) as an exploration geologist for Loangwa Concessions, Ltd., searching for exploitable mineral deposits, an experience that gave him a profound respect for field work.

Hess completed his graduate work at Princeton and received his Ph.D. in geology in 1932. While a graduate student, he participated in a U.S. Navy experiment to measure the earth's gravity field aboard a submarine. This voyage was his first exposure to marine geology. Five years later, he went on another expedition for the Navy and was given the rank of lieutenant (j.g.) in the U.S. Naval Reserve. His research during these voyages resulted in his first major papers on the relation of gravity to geology. Hess proposed that the earth's crust buckled downward in places under the oceans, which created gravity anomalies and helped push up arcs of island chains.

As a reserve officer when Japan attacked Pearl Harbor on December 7, 1941, Hess served on active duty for the next five years, during which time he advanced in rank to commander. He first headed an operation charged with detecting enemy submarines in the North Atlantic. By factoring such variables as speed, distance, ocean currents, and fuel capacity, Hess developed a system for estimating and tracking the daily positions of German submarines.

Hess was then given command of the attack transport U.S.S. *Cape Johnson,* operating in the Pacific. Using the Navy sonar systems, Hess made the first systematic echo-sounding surveys of the Pacific Ocean over a two-year period as he steamed back and forth on Navy assignments. He discovered over 100 submerged, flat-topped seamounts 3,000 to 6,000 feet underwater between the Hawaiian and Mariana islands. He described these seamounts as "drowned ancient islands" and named them guyots (to honor Arnold Guyot, a geology professor at Princeton).

In 1946, Hess proposed an inventive hypothesis for the development of guyots. Because they showed no sign of surrounding coral reefs, he argued that the guyots had originally been islands dating back to the Precambrian era, 600 million years ago, a period before coral existed. He believed that by the time lime-secreting organisms emerged, the islands were too far below sea level for the organisms to survive. His argument rested, in part, on his hypothesis that the sea level had risen: Continual deposits of sediment on the sea floor had made the sea level rise.

Hess was not afraid of postulating new hypotheses, or refuting them, even if they were his own. A decade after developing his original hypothesis, he did just that. When, in 1956, Cretaceous fossils (only 100 million years old) were found in the guyots, he knew his explanation of guyots could not be correct. Oceanic core samples taken in 1957 showed that the ocean floor was much younger than the continents and that oceanic sedimentation rates were slower than previously thought. Collected data were not consistent with any part of his theory on the formation of guyots. He realized he needed a new theory.

He then speculated that the guyots had originally been volcanoes that had been eroded to flat tops by wave action. He had to abandon this theory when erosion rate calculations showed that the guyots couldn't have eroded enough to reach their current depth. He continued to struggle with this enigma, searching for new clues and new ideas that could explain the maze of seemingly contradictory data. Finally, he revisited his earlier down-buckling theory and extended it, using established theories on magma convection currents within the mantle. Hess argued that magma rose from the Earth's mantle up through oceanic rifts and spread out laterally across the ocean floor. As the magma cooled, it formed new oceanic crust. He estimated the oceanic crust to be spreading apart along the mid-oceanic ridge by about one to two inches a year.

This theory became known as sea-floor spreading and was the foundation of the plate tectonics revolution in the late 1960s and early 1970s.

Hess was a strong proponent of the "Mohole" project to drill beneath the ocean into the mantle, because he thought it would substantiate his theory. Walter Munk originally suggested the project to him in 1957. Hess got the National Science Foundation to support it from 1958 to 1966. He was in charge of the panel that determined where to drill; they collected the first core sample in 1958. Funding for the project stopped in 1966, but they did succeed in establishing the feasibility of accurately positioning a drilling ship in deep water. Later, this experiment was very important to the deep earth sampling project of the Joint Oceanographic Institution.

Harry Hess's interest in oceanography did not lessen his interest in geology. Indeed, his interests kept broadening, later even including space science. From 1962 until his death, he served as the chairman of the Space Science Board of the National Academy of Sciences. He was a designated NASA principal investigator for the pyroxenes of returned lunar samples. He was also a member of the planetology advisory subcommittee.

Hess had an extraordinary range of research accomplishments. He wrote detailed mineralogical studies about pyroxenes, extensively studied peridotite, and gave us the sea-floor spreading hypothesis. During the years he spent doing research, he remained in the Naval Reserve, and at the time of his death he was a rear admiral.

## Key Dates

| | |
|---|---|
| 1906 | Born in New York City on May 24 |
| 1927 | Received B.S. from Yale University |
| 1928–1929 | Worked as geologist with Loangwa Concessions, Ltd. |
| 1932 | Received Ph.D. from Princeton University |
| 1932–1933 | Worked as instructor at Rutgers University |
| 1933–1934 | Worked as research associate in geophysical laboratory of the Carnegie Institute, Washington, D.C. |
| 1934 | Became an instructor at Princeton |
| 1937 | Was promoted to assistant professor at Princeton |
| 1941–1946 | Served active duty in World War II |
| 1946 | Was promoted to associate professor at Princeton |
| 1948 | Was promoted to professor at Princeton |
| 1949–1950 | Was visiting professor at Cambridge University, England |
| 1964 | Named Blair professor of geology |

| | |
|---|---|
| 1950–1966 | Was chairman of the department of geology at Blair |
| 1969 | Died in Woods Hole, Massachusetts, on August 25 |

## Advice

*Harry Hess would advise anyone considering a career in geology not to limit yourself to one narrow field of study. Embrace all of the fields that appeal to you, and you will find a way to utilize what you learned from each one. Your core courses will be in math and geology, but chemistry and history will be valuable side courses. Don't be afraid to propose a wild theory, and don't be afraid to recant later if you find you were wrong.*

## References

Bermen, Howard, ed. *The National Cyclopedia of American Biography.* Vol. N-63. Clifton, N.J.: James T. White, 1984. (Good review of Hess's career.)

Daintith, John, et al., eds. *Biographical Encyclopedia of Scienctists.* 2d ed. Philadelphia, Pa.: Institute of Physics Publishing, 1994. (Good biographical summary.)

Gillispie, Charles, ed. *Dictionary of Scientific Biography.* New York: Charles Scribner's Sons, 1978. (Good review of Hess's career.)

Hess, Harry. "History of the Ocean Basins," in *Petrological Studies.* Edited by A. Engle and H. James. New York: Harper, 1962. (Excellent review of Hess's ocean-spreading theory.)

Kearey, Philip, and Frederick J. Vine. *Global Tectonics.* Chicago: Bladwell Science, 1996.

Rubey, William. "Harry Hammond Hess," in *Yearbook of the American Philosophical Society (1970).* New York: American Philosophical Society, 1971. (Good biographical review.)

# Ted Hoff

*"The Computer on a Chip"*  **Electronics and Inventions**

## Career Highlights

Intel Corp.

- Invented the microprocessor, 1969
- Named Inventor of the Year by the San Francisco Peninsula Patent Law Association
- Recognized by *The Economist* as one of the seven most influential inventors since the end of World War II

## Important Contributions

In 1969, Ted Hoff revolutionized microelectronics with the invention of the microprocessor. Microprocessor chips are the brains and basic building blocks of virtually every piece of modern electronic equipment. They make your pocket calculator work. They tune in radios, start your car's electronic ignition, and run coffee machines. A microprocessor serves as the "boss" chip in video arcade games, empowering you to make the characters on the screen jump over barrels and pummel enemies. Perhaps most important, microprocessors have made personal computers possible.

Before Hoff's invention, computers were huge mainframes (banks of equipment, often as large as a living room) and very expensive. They were completely unlike the PCs or Macintoshes we use today. The microprocessor put more power into a square inch than previous computers could stuff into a square yard. With this invention, an entire central processing unit (CPU) could now fit on a single, inexpensive silicon chip. This opened up a whole new field in the computer industry. Computers would no longer be limited to large companies, the government, and universities. Within 10 years, Ted Hoff's invention had made the computer business a multi-billion dollar industry in the Silicon Valley in California.

## Career Path

It looked more like a tiny black-and-white smudge than the fitting result of five weeks' work. Ted Hoff held it gently in a pair of small tweezers and slowly turned it as he gazed through a powerful magnifying lens. The one-eighth inch by one-sixth inch blob with tiny wire outcroppings looked insignificant and drew no one else's attention. It was hard to believe this tiny device was one of the most important developments of the twentieth century. It was especially hard for Hoff to believe. He hadn't set out to revolutionize computing, only to fulfill a company contract a little more efficiently. Still, there it sat in his tweezers, and the world would never be the same.

Even as a child, Marcian E. "Ted" Hoff was a problem solver who liked to work puzzles. Later, he realized that working puzzles and solving problems are what inventors do: Finding new ways of doing things is the essence of invention.

Ted's father worked in railway signaling and encouraged his son's interest in electronics. When his company threw out scrap relays and other odds and ends related to aircraft control and railway signaling after World War II, Ted's father brought them home. The young boy played with the relay circuits and discovered that he enjoyed tinkering with electronics.

Ted's uncle was a chemical engineer with Kodak and had many books on chemistry, which the curious boy studied on his own. By the time he was a freshman in high school, Ted knew enough chemistry to pass the New York State Chemistry Regents Exam, without ever having taken a chemistry course.

After high school graduation, Ted Hoff got a summer job at the General Railway Signal Company in New York. He began working with a group of engineers who were building an audio frequency tracking circuit, which used high frequencies and inductance to detect the presence of trains. As an 18-year-old high school graduate, Ted redesigned the receiver circuit, making it more reliable, and developed a method for tuning the system so that it gave a much better defined circuit. His name was one of three that was listed on the patent.

In 1958, Hoff received a B.S. in electrical engineering from Rensselaer Polytechnic Institute and transferred to Stanford University for his graduate work. After receiving a Ph.D. in 1962, he stayed for an additional six years as a research associate before accepting a position with Intel, in the Silicon Valley, as the manager of applications research.

When Intel was approached by Busicom, a Japanese company, to create a set of chips for their new calculator design, Hoff was assigned to work with the Japanese engineers on the project. As he studied the design, he saw flaws and inefficiencies in the chips and circuits. He suggested some adjustments, such as implementing the more complicated steps not in logic but as permanent programs in memory and internally linking logic chips through a central controller. He redrew and improved the architecture and wrote the instruction set to control the mathematical functions. In doing so, he developed one of the most revolutionary inventions of the century: the microprocessor.

Hoff hadn't set out to invent the microprocessor. He hadn't set out to invent anything. His simple goal was to make the electronics of a new calculator work more efficiently. His end result just happened to be revolutionary.

Many scientists had prepared the way for Hoff's discovery. In the 1940s semiconductors—substances through which the flow of electricity could be easily increased or decreased—were discovered. Semiconductors led to the development of the transistor, a sandwich of semiconducting materials. Soon transistors replaced the bulky glass vacuum tubes that controlled electric currents in radios, television sets, and the first computers.

Transistors could move electricity tens of thousands of times faster than vacuum tubes, with far fewer failures. Transistors began to appear in radios, in television sets, and, later, in computers. But the transistor had one failing. It sometimes chipped from its circuit board.

Scientists solved this problem by etching a number of transistors directly onto a slice of silicon and providing the connections between them. That was the birth of the integrated circuit. Scientists at Intel took it a step further. They developed a process that integrated thousands of transistors onto a small chip of silicon. From this large-scale integrated circuit, it was a relatively easy step for Ted Hoff to reach the microprocessor, the so-called computer on a chip.

Hoff's first microprocessor, the Intel 4004, was not much larger than a pencil point, measuring only one-eighth by one-sixth of an inch. A square inch could hold 48 of them. Despite their small size, they held the arithmetic and logic circuitry of a full-sized computer.

When that microprocessor became available to the public in 1971, initial reaction was skeptical and reserved. People didn't quite get it: Computers were now smaller, smarter, more powerful, and cheaper. It didn't seem possible. The public was slow to accept this new computing wonder.

In fact, some people predicted the chips wouldn't be marketable because they were too small and would be difficult to repair. People did not understand the concept that chips don't get repaired. If a chip goes bad, it gets thrown away and replaced. This approach seemed counterintuitive and incomprehensible. When manufacturers finally saw the advantages of microprocessors and began to incorporate them into electronic products, the concept swept across all related fields and geographic regions.

Hoff left Intel in 1982 to become the vice president of research and development at Atari. After a couple of years there, he left Atari to split his time between Teklicon and his private work as a consultant to many different Silicon Valley firms.

Now interested in robotics, Hoff hopes to develop a robot that takes care of the day-to-day chores that people would rather not do, like cleaning. Perhaps he will revolutionize housecleaning the way he revolutionized computers.

## Key Dates

| | |
|---|---|
| 1937 | Born in Rochester, New York, on October 19 |
| 1958 | Received B.S. in electrical engineering from Rensselaer Polytechnic Institute |
| 1959 | Received M.S. from Stanford University |
| 1962 | Received Ph.D. from Stanford University |
| 1968–1983 | Worked as manager of applications research for Intel |
| 1969 | Invented the microprocessor |
| 1982–1984 | Appointed vice president of research and development of Atari, Inc. |
| 1984 | Appointed chief technical officer at Teklicon |
| 1990–present | Is vice president and chief technical officer at Teklicon |

## Advice

*Successful inventors, Ted Hoff believes, are defined by their burning curiosity. "You've got to be curious and keep questioning, 'Why does this work? Why does that happen?' You've got to keep that small-child idea—always wondering why a thing works a certain way or what happens if you put two things together."*

*Hoff commented that too often our educational system forces students into separate, narrow paths: either you're a mathematician or you're an engineer; either you're an electrical engineer or a chemical engineer. Hoff believes you should focus more on blending skills and technologies. Indeed, most of Hoff's inventions have fallen into the "between disciplines" zone. (His analog memory cell that made use of electroplating, for example, was a combination of chemistry and electrical engineering.) Hoff would encourage you to learn as much as you can about as many different fields of interest as you can: "Read as much as possible."*

## References

Brown, Kenneth A. *Inventors at Work: Interviews with 16 Notable American Inventors.* Redmond, Wash.: Tempus, 1988.

Grob, Bernard. *Basic Electronics.* New York: Macmillan/McGraw-Hill, 1996.

Herz, J. C. *Joystick Nation: How Videogames Ate Our Quarters, Won Our Hearts, and Rewired Our Minds.* Boston: Little, Brown, 1997.

Sullivan, George. *Screen Play: The Story of Video Games.* New York: Frederick Warne, Inc., 1983.

Wilson, J. A. Sam, and Joseph Risse. *Introduction to Microprocessor Theory & Operation: A Self-Study Guide with Experiments.* Indianapolis, Ind.: Prompt Publications, 1995.

# Robert Hofstadter

*"Into the Sun: Peering Inside the Nucleus"*                    Physics

## Career Highlights

- Was first scientist to probe into the inner structure of protons and neutrons
- Awarded Nobel Prize for Physics, 1961
- Named California scientist of the year, 1959
- Elected to the National Academy of Sciences, 1958

## Important Contributions

Imagine that an atom is like a solar system. While other mid-twentieth-century researchers were struggling to identify, chart, and count the planet-like electrons and measure the size of the nucleus, or sun, Robert Hofstadter ventured *into* the sun, or nucleus of an atom, to describe not only what was inside that core (protons and neutrons), but also what was inside those particles that were packed inside the nucleus.

Robert Hofstadter won the Nobel Prize for his decade-long effort to probe further inside an atom than any other researcher had ever gone. He was the first to measure the structure of an atom's nucleus. He was the first to actually measure and describe the size, shape, and structure of a proton and a neutron. He was the first to penetrate into the infinitesimal world of the interior of these subatomic particles and describe the composition and inner structure of protons and neutrons. Singlehandedly he took the measurement of subatomic particles to a whole new dimension and greatly enriched our understanding of the physical universe around us.

## Career Path

Robert Hofstadter was a city kid who grew up with no real career plans or interests. He loved the excitement of New York City and never thought much beyond the next weekend. Robert inattentively marched through the public school system as a "slightly better than average" student.

Robert entered City College of New York (CCNY) only because his older brother, Albert, was already studying there. He picked literature and philosophy as a major for the same reason: Albert had picked philosophy. As part of his basic undergraduate requirements, Robert took a physics course in his sophomore year. He found in both the instructor and the subject the first inspirational jolt of his life. He found excitement, far deeper and more powerful than the excitement of Times Square.

The physics teacher told Robert that "the laws of physics could be tested. The laws of philosophy could not." The idea of rigorous accountability appealed to him, and he switched his major to physics at the beginning of the next semester.

Hofstadter graduated in 1935, even winning the school's Kenyon Prize in physics and mathematics, proving both to himself and to his family that he had found the right field. With his Kenyon Prize in hand, he was able to obtain a Cofflin Fellowship from the General Electric Company, which covered his graduate school expenses at Princeton University. He received his Ph.D. in physics in 1938, never regretting his decision to switch to physics.

Through a series of one-year teaching appointments and short-term research positions both in commercial and government laboratories, Hofstadter explored a variety of physics specialties he might pursue. He was a good teacher and a productive researcher. Still, the feeling of excitement began to wear thin. Physics began to feel stale and routine. He itched for the electric thrill and driving compulsion he had felt when he was first exposed to science. His interest in physics began to wane.

Then, in 1950, Hofstadter was invited to join the faculty of Stanford University's physics department, dedicated to unraveling the innermost secrets of the atom. The struggle to understand and define the composition of the material universe has fascinated and frustrated scientists for millennia. Each new century has brought new analytical tools with which to come closer to an answer and an understanding, first probing into a cell, then into an atom, and finally into subatomic particles. At Stanford, Hofstadter was swept up into the excitement of the quest for this most fundamental question of physics. His passion was rekindled.

In 1953 Hofstadter and his team of research assistants used Stanford's mile-long linear accelerator, or "atom smasher," to investigate the structure of an atomic nucleus. He knew he was creating minute subatomic particles that were too small for him to detect, and he began to dream of a machine capable of tracking these infinitesimally small particles.

It took Hofstadter and his team over three years to envision, design, build, and test the barn-sized monstrosity. This "scattering machine" was capable of distinguishing nuclear particles only two one-hundredths of a trillionth of an inch apart and could track individual electrons as they were either refracted by or passed through the nucleus of an atom. The smaller the measurement, it seemed, the bigger and more complex the necessary machines to make the measurement.

After two years of bombarding various nuclei, spending long hours monitoring, maintaining and recalibrating the machinery, and analyzing the resulting scatter diagrams, Hofstadter discovered that protons and neutrons were not evenly packed throughout the nucleus, as had been supposed, but rather were denser in the middle and gradually thinned toward the edges. He calculated that the core of an atom's nucleus is 130 trillion times more dense than water. At that density, a drop of water would weigh two million tons.

Hofstadter spent the next year increasing the power and resolution of his equipment and then attempted to make the world's first actual measurements of a proton and neutron. In 1956 he reported that his team had finally measured the size and shape of a proton. Its diameter was 0.00000000000003 inches, or one 300-trillionth of an inch.

How small is that? It is almost inconceivably tiny. The diameter of a proton is to an inch as an inch is to 900 million miles, or almost 100 times the distance from the earth to the sun. Yet with his high-powered equipment Hofstadter was able to peer not only *at*, but *inside* the tiny proton and discover it had a hard core with a softer outside, like a peach and its pit.

By 1960, Hofstadter was able to describe the layered clouds of mesons (tiny subatomic particles) that made up most of a proton and neutron. He was able to describe the pinpoint of dense matter at the core of a proton, composed of densely packed mesons. He was able to determine that the one real difference between neutrons and protons was that, in a neutron, the clouds of mesons have opposite charges and electrically cancel each other out. For his work uncovering the internal nature of protons and neutrons, Hofstadter received the Nobel Prize for Physics in 1961.

All this work was performed at a scale thousands of times smaller than any researcher had ever been able to study before. Hofstadter was studying entities so small that the finest pinpoint contained more than could ever be counted.

Scores of scientists had worked through the early years of the twentieth century to open the door of the atom and peer inside. Working alone with a small team of assistants, Robert Hofstadter took physics to the next level by opening the door to the wondrous inner workings of protons and neutrons. It was as if, from the confines of another galaxy, he had peered into the inner workings not of our galaxy, not of our tiny solar system, but of the sun itself. Few have ever made so great a contribution to science.

## Key Dates

| | |
|---|---|
| 1915 | Born in New York City on February 5 |
| 1935 | Received B.S. from City College of New York (CCNY) |
| 1938 | Received Ph.D. from Princeton University |
| 1940 | Worked as instructor in physics at the University of Pennsylvania |
| 1941 | Worked as instructor in physics at CCNY |
| 1942– 1943 | Worked as physicist for the National Bureau of Standards |
| 1943– 1946 | Worked as physicist for Norden Laboratories |
| 1946 | Appointed assistant professor of physics at Princeton University |
| 1950 | Appointed associate professor of physics at Stanford University |
| 1955 | Appointed full professor at Stanford University |
| 1971 | Named the Max Stein honorary professor of physics at Stanford University |
| 1990 | Died on November 17 |

## Advice

*Many great scientists have found that it takes more time than they initially imagined to gain the experience and depth of knowledge needed to recognize the questions that are of greatest interest. Certainly, Robert Hofstadter was one of these, not having found his specific niche and scientific focus until 38 years of age. Hofstadter believed that physics is the sum of continual study and exploration. Don't expect one year's worth of classes to give you a fundamental understanding. It takes years of intense study to truly understand a field. Plan for it. Allow for it in your college and graduate school plans.*

## References

Frauenfelder, Hans, and Ernest M. Henley. *Subatomic Physics*. New York: Prentice Hall, 1991. (An explanation of the basic concepts of theoretical and experimental nuclear and particle physics.)

Garraty, John, ed. *Encyclopedia of American Biography*. New York: Harper & Row, 1984. (Detailed summary of Hofstadter's work.)

Hofstadter, Robert, and Robert Herman. *High Energy Electron Scattering*. Palo Alto, Calif.: Stanford University Press, 1960. (Best description of the process of electron scattering research and the associated equipment.)

Schwarz, Cindy, and Sheldon Glashow. *A Tour of the Subatomic Zoo: A Guide to Particle Physics*. Philadelphia, Pa.: American Institute of Physics, 1996.

Tanor, Joseph, ed. *McGraw-Hill Modern Men of Science*. New York: McGraw-Hill, 1986. (Strong summary of Hofstadter's work.)

Wasson, Tyler, ed. *Nobel Prize Winners*. New York: H. W. Wilson, 1987. (Excellent summary of Hofstadter's work.)

Weinberg, Steven. *The Discovery of Subatomic Particles*. New York: W. H. Freeman, 1983. (Good historical review.)

# Arthur Holmes

*"Dating the Age of the Earth"*  Geology

## Career Highlights

- Pioneered geochronology and was the first scientist to accurately estimate the age of the Earth
- Proposed the first quantitative geological time scale
- Awarded the Penrose Medal of the Geological Society of America, 1956
- Awarded the Murchison Medal by the Geological Society of London in 1940 and the Wollaston Medal (their highest honor), 1956

## Important Contributions

Arthur Holmes's career had a profound impact on earth science in at least three areas. First, his research (with Lord Rayleigh) on radiometric dating of rocks led not only to the discovery of the age of the Earth but also to the development of the first time-scale independent of the fossil record.

Second, his new approach to the Earth's thermal history led him to make many important conclusions about convection in the substratum (or mantle) and the resulting migration of the continents. These concepts would become essential to the breakthrough in global tectonics in the 1960s.

Third, his studies of the origins of alkali-rich igneous rocks gave insights into the composition of the mantle. This information was critical to the development of accurate models of the Earth's core and mantle and of the thermal, electrical, and magnetic activity in both core and mantle.

## Career Path

The nine-year-old boy's brow furrowed as he slumped on the family couch in Hebburn, England, in 1890. In one hand he held an article that proclaimed 4004 B.C. as the date of the creation of the world, based on a series of biblical references. In his other hand he held an article describing a controversy between the famed and revered scientist, Lord Kelvin, and the geology community. Kelvin claimed that the earth was 40 million years old. Geologists argued that it had to be much older.

Young Arthur Holmes stared at the two articles. Six thousand years old? Forty million years old? Older? Other children might be confused or bored. Arthur was fascinated. He itched to find out who was right. But how? People could argue about the age of the Earth partly because there was no scientifically established method for measuring or even estimating the Earth's age. Arthur had to tuck the problem away for a decade, but he never forgot it.

Holmes attended Imperial College in London, where he studied under Lord Rayleigh, who had recently discovered a major heat source within the earth. Rayleigh argued that so many radioactive elements existed in the Earth's crust that the Earth could not simply be a cooling globe. He was also pursuing the hypothesis that radioactive minerals might contain a record of the time elapsed since their crystallization and encouraged Holmes to develop a radioactive dating method.

Working with physicists, Holmes was able to detect and measure stable decay rates for key radioactive elements and to then develop chemical lab procedures to measure the concentration of these specific isotopes in rock samples. He then studied geologic records and samples of known age to obtain estimates of initial concentrations of the various elements and isotopes he wanted to track.

Holmes initially tracked radioactive isotopes of all basic metals, concentrating on uranium, thorium, and potassium. The process worked fine in theory but poorly in practice. Most of the known isotopes either had initial concentrations that were too low, or half lives that were too short, to produce sufficient remaining amounts of the isotope in modern samples for testing. After over 500 tests spread out over his last two years of undergraduate studies, he stumbled upon a radioactive isotope of common carbon, $C_{14}$, which perfectly fit his list of requirements: large and predictable initial concentrations and slow decay rate. Using $C_{14}$ and Holmes's radioactive model, Rayleigh was able to overthrow Kelvin's estimate, showing that the world had to be more than a billion years old. This was the beginning of the answer to Holmes's childhood question.

After receiving his B.Sc. degree in physics and mathematics in 1909 and his master's degree in geology in 1910, Holmes spent a year doing field work and geologic exploration in Mozambique. He planned to focus his field research on Pre-Cambrian granites, tertiary lavas, and *inselberg* geomorphology. Unfortunately, he spent most of his time in bed, having contracted malaria and blackwater fever in Mozambique, and was forced to abandon the trip. Because he continued to suffer recurrent attacks of malaria, he was found to be unfit for active service during World War I, although Naval Intelligence still employed him to compile maps and charts for the war effort.

From 1912 to 1920, Holmes taught geology at the Imperial College in London. He wrote three books during that time and published many scientific papers. His first book was a history of all the attempts to date the age of the Earth, ending with his earlier radiation dating methods and estimate, now set at 2 billion years. His other achievements during this period included (1) the demonstration that lead ores were not generated from granitic magmas as had been generally supposed, (2) his detailed studies of Arctic basalts, and (3) the discovery of a previously unknown mineral, kalsilite.

In 1921, Holmes traveled to Burma as chief geologist for an oil company. This expedition failed to locate any commercially attractive deposits, however, and when he returned to England in 1924, he had to sue for his pay. From 1924 to 1943, he headed the geology department of Durham University. From 1943 to 1956 he was regius professor of geology and mineralogy at the University of Edinburgh.

During these years, Holmes returned to his original question: How old is the Earth? He had been an early supporter of Wegener's theory of continental drift, arguing that drift must be produced by strong thermal convection currents in the Earth's mantle. His estimates of how much heat would be generated by radioactive decay in the Earth offered an explanation for continental plate movement. In his book *Principles of Physical Geology,* he included diagrams of the formation of the new ocean floor that uncannily predicted what scientists would later discover once direct measurement and observation of the ocean floor was possible. His studies also revealed how ancient orogenies gradually built up cratonic shields and continental nuclei.

More important, Holmes constructed a Phanerozoic time-scale by plotting radiometric dates, as they became available, against the cumulative maximum thicknesses of the sedimentary systems down to the base of the Cambrian. This was the first quantitative geological time-scale ever created for the Earth. Using these data, Holmes was able to revise his estimate of the age of the Earth to somewhere between 10 and 12 billion years.

Arthur Holmes's work touched nearly every aspect of geology. His *Principles of Physical Geology* is considered a classic and has been called one of the "most successful textbooks ever written." The book won international acclaim and, because of its readability, probably achieved a wider audience than any other geology book of the time. Perhaps most important, Holmes's work gave the world a systematic approach for estimating the Earth's age, thereby giving the world a scientific date for the beginning of Earth.

✳   ✳   ✳

## Key Dates

| | |
|---|---|
| 1890 | Born in Hebburn, England, on January 14 |
| 1909 | Received B.Sc. (physics and mathematics) from Imperial College, London |
| 1910 | Received A.R.C.S. (geology) from Imperial College |
| 1911 | Went on expedition to Mozambique |
| 1917 | Received D.Sc. from Imperial College |
| 1920–1925 | Worked as chief geologist for an oil company in Burma |
| 1924–1943 | Worked as professor of geology at Durham University |
| 1943–1956 | Appointed regius professor of geology at Edinburgh University |
| 1944 | Published *Principles of Physical Geology* (revised edition 1965) |
| 1955 | Elected as foreign associate of the Institut de France |
| 1956 | Resigned from Edinburgh University |
| 1965 | Died on September 20 in London, England |

## Advice

*Arthur Holmes believed that all fields of science relate to the earth and thus can have an influence on geology, the actual study of the Earth and its history. Therefore, bring other fields into your studies besides geology. Become especially familiar with physics, inorganic chemistry, and math in addition to earth sciences and geology.*

*Geology is a field for those who have a compelling need to help unravel the mysteries of the Earth. Don't limit yourself to one branch of geology; the wider your base of study, the more you can draw from other areas of expertise.*

## References

Gohav, Gabrial. *A History of Geology.* New Brunswick, N.J.: Rutgers University Press, 1994.

Greene, Jay E., ed. "Arthur Holmes," in *McGraw-Hill Modern Men of Science.* New York: McGraw-Hill, 1968: 240–242.

Hallam, A. *Great Geological Controversies.* New York: Oxford University Press, 1993.

Harland, W. B., David G. Smith, R. L. Armstrong, A. V. Cox, L. E. Craig, and A. G. Smith. *Geologic Timescale.* New York: Cambridge University Press, 1990.

Holmes, Arthur. *The Age of the Earth.* Darby, England: Darby Books, 1981.

Holmes, Arthur, and Doris L. Holmes. *Holmes Principles of Physical Geology.* New York: Halsted Press, 1978.

# Edwin Hubble

*"Measuring the Stars"*

Astronomy and
Cosmology

## Career Highlights

- Founded modern extragalactic astronomy and was first to provide observational evidence for the expansion of the universe
- Elected to the National Academy of the Sciences, 1927 (after only eight years of professional work)
- Awarded the Barnard Medal of the National Academy of Sciences, 1935
- Received the Franklin Medal of the Franklin Institute of Philadelphia, 1939

## Important Contributions

Edwin Hubble discovered the relationship between the distances of galaxies and their apparent speeds of recession, called Hubble's law, which has been widely considered to be the most significant astronomical discovery of the twentieth century. His work confirmed Einstein's theory of general relativity, giving observational evidence that the universe is expanding. In addition, his work allowed scientists to date the age of the universe.

## Career Path

In mid-1914, John P. Hubble, a prominent Missouri lawyer with a keen, observant eye, began to wonder if his son, Edwin, would ever settle down and pick a career. Fickle indecision was admirable in high school and tolerable in college, but how far beyond graduate school could a young man go without sticking to anything? Edwin was 25 and already starting his fourth career.

While Mr. Hubble worried, Edwin contentedly looked forward to his new career—as always. To Mr. Hubble, it seemed unlikely that his son would ever be able to catch up with youths who had applied themselves and accomplish anything of significance. At the time, Edwin might well have agreed.

Edwin had won a scholarship to the University of Chicago in 1906, where, despite his love of sports, astronomy, and the outdoors, he chose to study law (probably because his father was a lawyer). He supplemented the scholarship by working as a laboratory assistant to Nobel Prize-winning physicist Robert A. Millikan, who so inspired young Hubble that he changed his major to physics.

During summer breaks, Hubble earned tuition money for the next year's school by working as part of a surveying crew in wilderness areas around Lake Superior. The outdoor work and friendly competitions reaffirmed what a good athlete he was and tempted him to become a professional boxer and abandon physics. During his junior year, he came under the influence of astrophysics professor George Hale, who rekindled Hubble's boyhood love of astronomy. Hubble switched majors again and, in 1910, received a combined B.S. in mathematics, physics, and astronomy.

Hubble had changed fields so often that, upon graduation, he had little idea what to do with his degree or future. An exceptional boxer, he was offered the role of "Great White Hope" in a match later that year against the world heavyweight champion, Jack Johnson. Hubble entered training camp to see if he was up to the fight but, although sorely tempted, he finally decided instead to accept the Rhodes scholarship to Oxford University that he had won. Unfortunately, he had applied for the scholarship in his sophomore year when he was studying law, and law was what the scholarship specified that he must study at Oxford. He entered Oxford Law School and in 1912 received his B.A. degree in jurisprudence.

When Hubble returned to America, he was admitted to the bar in Kentucky and practiced law in Louisville for one year. Then, abruptly, he left law to study astronomy. Practicing law had been his father's choice of career; it was not his. He chose instead to become a research assistant at Yerkes Observatory at Williams Bay, Wisconsin.

While Hubble was there, Professor Hale offered him a position in California at the Mount Wilson Observatory, where a 100-inch telescope was under construction. The year was 1917, and the United States had just entered World War I. Hubble received his Ph.D. from the University of Chicago that year and enlisted in the infantry of the U.S. Army. Immediately following his discharge from the service in 1920, he joined Hale at the Mount Wilson Observatory in Pasadena, California.

In the early part of his career, Hubble studied faint nebulae, which looked like fuzzy blobs through a telescope. He theorized that while some were in our galaxy and were simply clouds of luminous gas and dust, others (called spiral nebulae) had to lie beyond the galaxy. As soon as the powerful 100-inch telescope was operational at Mount Wilson, he used it to make some of the most important astronomical discoveries of the twentieth century.

In 1923 Hubble discovered a Cepheid variable star—a pulsating star whose variation in brightness directly relates to its luminosity and whose distance can therefore be accurately determined—in the Andromeda nebula. His discovery demonstrated that Andromeda and other spiral nebulae like it were independent galaxies that lay at vast distances from our own. This discovery settled the problem of the status of spiral nebulae that had puzzled astronomers for 75 years.

Within three years, Hubble had calculated distances for 18 isolated galaxies and for four members of the Virgo cluster, and he used this information to make the most remarkable of all his discoveries. The farther away the galaxies were, the faster they were moving away from the Earth. This fact made no sense, but was consistently true. This remarkable discovery became known as Hubble's law: The velocity of a galaxy's recession is directly proportional to its distance from the Earth. This discovery provided support for earlier work by astronomers Alexander Friedmann and Georges Lemaitre, who claimed that the universe was indeed expanding. Now, the concept of the expanding universe is central to every cosmological model. Hubble's law was also used to develop the Big Bang theory of the origin of the universe.

Hubble also undertook a sky survey of the density and distribution of these nebulae that lie outside our own galaxy. On the basis of this survey he produced the first significant classification of galaxies based on a suggested evolutionary pattern. He divided galaxies into three classes—elliptical, spiral, and other—a classification system still used today. By introducing order into the apparent confusion of nebular forms and showing that galaxies are closely related members of a single family, he accomplished one of the most significant astronomical achievements of the century.

When the United States entered World War II, Hubble once again sought active duty in the army, but he was asked to serve as chief of ballistics and director of the Supersonic Wind Tunnels Laboratory at the Army Proving Grounds in Aberdeen, Maryland. For his services there he was awarded the Medal of Merit.

In 1946, Hubble became chairman of research for the Mount Wilson and Palomar observatories and turned his attention to the development of the famous 200-inch Hale telescope. When the telescope was finally ready in 1949, he was the first person to use it. In the last years of his life he suffered from a heart ailment, and in 1953 he died of coronary thrombosis in San Marino, California.

**\* \* \***

## Key Dates

| | |
|---|---|
| 1889 | Born in Marshfield, Missouri, on November 20 |
| 1910 | Received B.S. from University of Chicago |
| 1910–1913 | Awarded Rhodes scholarship to Oxford University in England; studied law there |
| 1912 | Received B.A. degree in jurisprudence |
| 1913 | Admitted to the bar in Kentucky and practiced law in Louisville |
| 1914 | Left law to study astronomy; was research assistant at Yerkes Observatory |
| 1917 | Received Ph.D. from University of Chicago |
| 1917–1918 | Enlisted in the infantry of the U.S. Army |
| 1919 | Joined staff of the Mount Wilson Observatory in Pasadena, California |
| 1942–1946 | Served as chief of ballistics and director of the Supersonic Wind Tunnels Laboratory at the Army Proving Grounds in Aberdeen, Maryland; awarded Medal of Merit |
| 1946–1953 | Served as chairman of research for Mount Wilson and Palomar observatories |
| 1953 | Died of coronary thrombosis on September 28 in San Marino, California |

## Advice

*Edwin Hubble believed that physics and math were as important as astronomy for astronomy students. The three disciplines are inseparable. Gain a solid foundation in all three areas and then take advanced theory and technique under the top researchers in your particular field or sub-field. Learn their experimental techniques as well as their subject matter.*

## References

Hubble, Edwin. *The Realm of the Nebulae.* New Haven: Yale University Press, 1982.

Sandage, Alan. *The Hubble Atlas of Galaxies.* Washington, D.C.: Carnegie Institution of Washington, 1984. (Collection of photographs of galaxies and Hubble's classification scheme.)

Shapley, Harlow. *Of Stars & Men: Human Response to an Expanding Universe.* Westport, Conn.: Greenwood, 1984.

Sharov, Alexander S., and Igor D. Novikov. *Edwin Hubble: The Discoverer of the Big Bang Universe.* New York: Cambridge University Press, 1993.

Wilson, Robert. *Astronomy Through the Ages: The Story of the Human Attempt to Understand the Universe.* Princeton, N.J.: Princeton University Press, 1998.

# Shirley Jackson

*"Superconductivity and Super Conduct"*                    Physics

Nuclear Regulatory Commission

## Career Highlights

- Was first woman and first African American appointed chair of the Nuclear Regulatory Commission, 1995
- Awarded the Candace Award by the National Coalition of Black Women, 1982
- Was first black woman to receive a Ph.D. from MIT
- Received Outstanding Young Woman of America Award, 1976, 1981

## Important Contributions

Shirley Jackson is a gifted physicist and has made important contributions in the areas of condensed-matter physics, plasma physics, and ceramics as a medium for superconductivity. Her early experiments contributed to the development of liquid crystal technology (used in digital watches, timers, and television and VCR displays as well as in integrated circuits and computers). Her more recent studies have focused on light and electrical conductivity through sandwiches of thin strips of ceramic and metal materials.

But Jackson's greatest contributions have been as an activist in the worlds of science and academia. She has been a powerful voice for both minority and women's access to scientific career opportunities and education and also for better partnership among government, universities, and industry. Through her active involvement in policy formation for a long list of national organizations, she strove to promote equal access for all to the riches of science.

## Career Path

In one respect, Shirley Jackson was one of the lucky ones because she always knew what she wanted to do. She knew she wanted to be a scientist by the time she turned five years old. She knew she wanted to study physics by the time she was seven. Even as a child, the concepts of matter, energy, and motion fascinated her, as did the process of describing those fundamental properties of the universe. The question was never what *Shirley* wanted to do. The question was whether a black, low-income woman would ever be wanted by American science.

While other children in Washington opened fire hydrants and played in the gushing streams of water on sizzling summer days, young Shirley often immersed herself in scientific experiments. She'd trap bees in wide-mouthed mason jars and study how they moved and flew. Then she'd see if their motion changed as a function of what she gave them to eat. Even as a child, science *was* Shirley's version of play.

Court-ordered desegregation reached the Washington, D.C., school system at the beginning of Shirley's third-grade year. She was transferred to Barnard Elementary School in a wealthy suburban neighborhood. Her teachers there recognized the young girl's exceptional aptitude for science and math and gave her extra reading material to develop her skills.

In high school, Shirley took advanced placement math and science courses. She studied Latin in junior high school to learn and understand the scientific names for plants, animals, and parts of the body. She also competed regularly in regional science fairs. She raised mice and studied the relationship between diet and vigor. She repeated her bee experiments and expanded them to include wasps. Although her science-fair projects often centered around animals, her interest always focused on physics: the study of matter and energy.

When Shirley graduated from high school in 1964, she had the best grade record in her class, held half a dozen science fair ribbons, and had already taken four science courses at a local college. She had done everything in her power to embrace science. She nervously waited to see if science would embrace her.

Her impressive high school record gained Shirley two important things she had dreamed of, but had not dared to hope for: admission to the Massachusetts Institute of Technology (MIT), the number-one science school in the nation, and two four-year scholarships to pay for her schooling.

Jackson's feeling of euphoria lasted only until she reached MIT. The highly competitive and unsupportive environment there was a jolt for her. Each space at the school was coveted. Faculty members seemed more willing to replace any student who fell below average than to work with struggling students to improve their grades. An air of competition and isolation lay over the students. Jackson was a solid student but felt overwhelmed by the workload and longed for assistance, support, and guidance. The feeling of isolation was exaggerated by her double-minority status. There were only 43 women in her freshman class and only 20 African American undergraduates on campus. She was the only freshman who fell into both categories. Much of the support that helped her through the difficult undergraduate years came from the tiny Black Student Union (BSU).

Late in her junior year, Jackson needed to choose a topic for her senior research project. She selected the general area of superconductivity. The existence of super-low-temperature conductivity had been known since early in the century. However, little was known about the limits of superconductivity. Could it happen at temperatures as warm as that of liquid nitrogen? Which materials exhibited superconductive qualities? What changes at the atomic and subatomic levels created superconductivity?

Shirley Jackson was excited by these questions. They "stirred [her] passion for knowledge." For her senior project she tried to research the characteristics of different materials that might make them suitable for superconductivity. She made no great breakthroughs (the vast majority of research does not) but did add valuable knowledge to the growing body of related research coming from around the world. More important, superconductivity became a focus for her career and occupied almost all of her subsequent research.

Activism on behalf of minority students became Jackson's other great passion. She grew more active in the BSU. She worked to persuade administrators to do more to recruit and retain minority students. Following graduation in 1968, she stayed at MIT for graduate studies and to continue her activism with the BSU.

Jackson received her Ph.D. in 1973 and continued her research into mathematical descriptions of the subatomic forces surrounding superconductive phenomena for four years, two at the Fermi Laboratory in Illinois, one at the CERN European nuclear research facility in Switzerland, and one at Stanford University in California. From there she accepted a research position at Bell Labs in New Jersey.

Jackson's research assignment centered on condensed-matter physics. Her special projects focused on the electrical and material properties of ceramic material and of plasma gases. Her goal for both studies was to discover high-temperature superconducting materials. Her research compiled a wealth of important information and contributed to several valuable spin-offs, including liquid crystal displays, now routinely used on digital electronic equipment from watches, televisions, and VCRs to integrated circuit controls.

Hundreds of scientists work for years to compile essential background information that leads one individual to take the final step to a major discovery. Progress for Jackson was frustratingly slow; successes seemed inconsequential. Setbacks seemed daunting even though they were an essential part of her progress. The struggle was not to *do* an experiment, but to derive the idea for which experiments would be worth doing. She uncovered no high-temperature superconductor breakthroughs or discoveries, but her research has helped countless other researchers design more productive experiments.

Shirley Jackson also continued to be active in community and professional affairs. She worked tirelessly with university, industry, and government officials to improve opportunities for minorities in science employment and education. She has given her time to over 30 commissions, boards, and associations to actively pursue this goal. The list of associations and activities she has given time to, and her list of accomplishments through those efforts, is unparalleled in modern science. She is a unique and valuable blend of talented research scientist and powerful community activist.

## Key Dates

| | |
|---|---|
| 1946 | Born in Washington, D.C., on August 5 |
| 1959 | Won her first regional science fair blue ribbon |
| 1968 | Received B.S. in physics from MIT |
| 1973 | Received Ph.D. in theoretical solid-state physics from MIT |
| 1973– 1974 | Worked as research associate in theoretical physics at the Fermi National Accelerator Laboratory |
| 1974– 1975 | Was visiting science associate at the European Organization for Nuclear Research (CERN) Laboratory, Geneva, Switzerland |

| | |
|---|---|
| 1975–1976 | Worked as research associate in theoretical physics at the Fermi National Accelerator Laboratory |
| 1976–1977 | Worked as research associate at the Stanford linear accelerator center |
| 1976–1978 | Appointed to technical staff in theoretical physics at the Bell Laboratories |
| 1978–1991 | Worked as senior physicist for scattering and low-energy physics at the Bell Laboratories |
| 1985 | Appointed to the New Jersey Commission on Science and Technology |
| 1991 | Appointed professor of physics at Rutgers University |
| 1995–present | Is head of the Nuclear Regulatory Commission |

## Advice

*Shirley Jackson found that physics is a broad field, probably too broad for any one person to successfully master. She believes anyone considering a career in theoretical physics should study broadly, but always have a specific focus for what you want to do in physics, for what excites you within the general field of physics and stirs your passions. Passions alone, however, produce little. Passions backed by long-term, committed effort produce miracles.*

## References

Buckel, Werner. *Superconductivity: Fundamentals and Applications.* New York: VCH, 1991. (Good overview of the field.)

Hayden, Robert. *Seven African American Scientists.* Frederick, Md.: Twenty-First Century Books, 1980.

Kessler, James, et al. *Distinguished African American Scientists of the 20th Century.* Phoenix, Ariz.: Oryx Press, 1996. (Good review of Jackson's life and work.)

Schechter, Bruce. *The Path of No Resistance: The Story of the Revolution in Superconductivity.* New York: Simon & Schuster, 1989. (Good review of the field.)

Turner, Joseph, ed. *Black Women: Achievements Against Odds.* Washington, D.C.: Smithsonian Institution Press, 1989. (Good biographical entry.)

# Jack Kilby

*"Breaking the Tyranny of Numbers"*     Integrated Circuits

## Career Highlights

Courtesy of Texas Instruments

- Invented the microchip
- Awarded International Engineering Gold Medal, the world's top engineering award, by National Academy of Engineers, 1989
- Awarded National Medal of Technology, 1990
- Inducted into National Inventors Hall of Fame, 1988
- Awarded National Medal of Science, 1970

## Important Contributions

Jack Kilby invented the microchip. More correctly, he invented the monolithic integrated circuit. Monolithic means that the entire device was formed from a single slice of silicone crystal. Integrated means that, for the first time, individual circuit components (transistors, resistors, capacitors, and diodes) were not separately manufactured and then soldered together, but were formed by giving different regions and layers of the silicone different electrical properties.

Kilby's microchip singlehandedly ushered in the Information Age. Computers, video games, car electronics, smart rockets, space shuttles, jet airplanes, stereo systems, microwaves, mail sorting equipment, wristwatches, bar codes and scanners, telephone routing systems, manufacturing, medical technology, smart toasters, and thousands of other products that affect our daily lives owe their existence to the microchip.

## Career Path

*Failed.*

Each letter of the word slammed into 17-year-old Jack Kilby like hammer blows, literally pounding the air from his chest and making it difficult to breathe. How could he have possibly failed his MIT entrance exams? There must be a mistake. Jack was good at science. He had been *committed* to physics and electrical engineering since he was 14 years old and had *known* it was his future. Now MIT had said no, it wasn't. He was not only shaken to his core, for the first time he was unsure that there would ever be a place for him in the field he loved.

Jack Kilby's dad was an electrical engineer for a Kansas power company. When the blizzard of 1937 knocked down power lines and trees across eastern Kansas, Mr. Kilby borrowed a neighbor's ham radio to keep in touch with his company. Fourteen-year-old Jack spent two days with earphones squeezed against his head, rotating the big antenna, tuning the frequency dial, listening to static crackle over faint and distant signals. Recording every word he could decipher, Jack was fascinated by the idea that voices from all around the state and world reached his ears in the livingroom of their rural Kansas house.

It was a magic adventure for the teen-aged boy. He was hooked. He *knew* an important future awaited him in the world of electronics. He started a ham radio club at his high school and studied all the electronics he could.

After graduation in 1941, Jack Kilby confidently applied to MIT, the greatest electrical engineering university in the country. Then he failed the entrance examination and was denied admission. He was devastated. It never occurred to him that he might fail. His father had to scramble to find another university that would accept his son. In September 1941, Jack entered the University of Illinois.

In December the Japanese bombed Pearl harbor. By January, Jack Kilby was a soldier. He spent World War II in a radio repair shop in northern India, fixing and improving radios for use in the Burma campaign. In three years of war, he learned an invaluable engineer's lesson: Take what you've got and find a way to make it work.

After the war Kilby returned to the university and graduated in 1947. He accepted an engineering position with Centralab, a small company manufacturing miniature circuits for hearing aids, radios, and televisions. He took this job because, "of all the applications I sent out, Centralab was the only offer I got back."

The work at Centralab was disappointing. The late 1940s and early 1950s were a wondrous period in the mushrooming field of electronics. Breakthroughs seemed to occur daily. Wild dreams became reality almost before they could be dreamed. Fortunes were there to be made. Momentous discoveries seemed to lurk around every corner.

Designing hearing aid circuits seemed unimportant to the ambitious young man. He felt that he had been shunted onto a sidetrack and would miss the great electronics revolution happening around him.

But this was also a frightfully frustrating period for electrical engineers, champing at the bit to be turned loose into a limitless future. The complex transistorized circuits they were designing often required hundreds of thousands of separate, tiny components: resistors, capacitors, transistors, and diodes. But manufacturing lines could not produce the continual perfection required of these complex circuits. There were too many components and solder points. Some would always fail and the circuit would crash. New ideas in the industry were being held up by this simple tyranny of numbers.

Jack Kilby realized that Centralab was too small to make any real contribution to this struggle. He looked for a bigger company with substantial resources. In May 1958 he landed a job at Texas Instruments (TI) in Dallas.

Two weeks after Kilby arrived, the TI operations virtually closed for mandatory summer vacations. Because he hadn't worked long enough to earn a vacation, he reported—alone—to the vast TI lab every day while everyone else swam, tanned, and played. TI was already a powerhouse in transistors and semiconductors. Vast stores of raw materials and momentarily abandoned sophisticated lab facilities were at his beck and call. He had two weeks to putter in that lab and to follow any whim, with the one proviso: Either come up with some new and important idea or be ready to work in one of the minor production divisions.

During those two weeks of tinkering and pondering, a general concept crept into his mind and onto his notebook pages: Replace separate components with a single chip of silicon, minute sections and layers of which could be altered to mimic any of the standard components.

Soldering would be eliminated. Minute component flaws would be eliminated. But building electrical components into the fabric of a semiconductor crystal was a revolutionary idea. It existed in untested theory only. No one had yet devised a way to demonstrate the theory.

Kilby presented his concept in mid-July. Management was impressed but skeptical. He was given two months to prove that his concept was reliable and inexpensive.

July and August were months of intense, high-pressure work. Kilby experimented day and night with schemes for charging and restructuring minute regions of a silicon chip and with systems for connecting and controlling each region of the chip.

On September 12, 1958, Jack Kilby threw the power switch on the first integrated circuit ever built. While TI executives watched, the green, waving line of a sine wave rolled across an oscilloscope. All that first microchip could do was convert a direct current signal into an alternating current in the shape of a sine wave.

But it did it. Built purely out of shaved slivers of silicon glued together and insulated in a plastic coating, Kilby's invention proved that microchips were possible.

Within a year TI employed photographic etching processes similar to those used in silk screening and lithography to implant hundreds of thousands of electronic components onto a chip the size of a baby's fingernail. Those early microchips were crude and bulky by modern standards, but they were sufficient to revolutionize the world.

Jack Kilby emphatically called himself an engineer rather than a scientist. "A scientist is driven by quest for knowledge, the need to explain something. An engineer's drive is to solve problems."

During his career, Jack Kilby's solutions earned him over 60 patents related to microcircuits, over 40 major awards, and an honored place as one of the pioneering founders of the Information Age.

## Key Dates

| | |
|---|---|
| 1923 | Born in Jefferson City, Missouri, on November 8 |
| 1947 | Received B.S. in electrical engineering from University of Illinois |
| 1947–1958 | Worked as design engineer for Centralab, Milwaukee, Wisconsin |
| 1950 | Received M.S. in electrical engineering from University of Wisconsin |
| 1958–1970 | Worked in Microprocessor Division of Texas Instruments |
| 1958 | Successfully demonstrated first integrated microcircuit on September 12 |

1970– Worked as professor of electrical engineering at Texas
1984    A&M University

1970– Works as freelance consultant and inventor; has registered
present   over 50 electrical patents on integrated circuits

1978– Was Distinguished Professor of Electrical Engineering at
1984    Texas A&M University

## Advice

*Jack Kilby believed that the place to start valuable electrical engineering research is with problems that require solutions. Search first for questions that interest you and then learn the necessary skills and tools to help you solve those problems. The goal of learning for Jack Kilby was to support the joy of problem solving. Key courses to take include physics, electrical engineering, chemistry, math, and thermodynamics. But even these are simply tools for solving problems.*

*Jack Kilby also advised beginning engineers to practice searching for nonobvious solutions. If there were obvious solutions, they would already have been found. Often the ultimately successful "nonobvious" solution is the one that everyone else said was obviously wrong.*

## References

Braunn, Ernest, and Stuart McDonald. *Revolution in Miniature.* Cambridge, Mass.: Cambridge University Press, 1983. (Good review of the development of electronics.)

Desmond, Kevin. *A Timetable of Inventions and Discoveries.* New York: M. Evans, 1986. (Covers both Jack Kilby and microprocessors.)

Haggerty, Patrick. "Electronics Evolution," *Research Management* XII (September 1979): 317–330. (Good section on Jack Kilby's work.)

Kilby, Jack. "Invention of the Integrated Circuit," *IEEE Transactions on Electronic Devices* ED-23 (July 1976): 648–654. (Excellent description of Kilby's invention.)

Reid, T.R. *The Chip: How Two Americans Invented the Microchip and Launched a Revolution.* New York: Simon & Shuster, 1984. (On both Kilby and the chip in general.)

Texas Instruments Incorporated. *25th Anniversary Observance, Transistor Radio and Silicon Transistor.* Dallas: Texas Instruments Incorporated, 1980. (Describes Kilby's work and that of other TI researchers.)

Van Zant, Peter. *Microchip Fabrication: A Practical Guide to Semiconductor Processing.* Chicago: Semiconductor Services, 1996. (Describes to a nontechnical reader the issues, science, processes, and materials involved in manufacturing microchips.)

# Edwin Land

*"Instant Success"*

Physics and
Invention

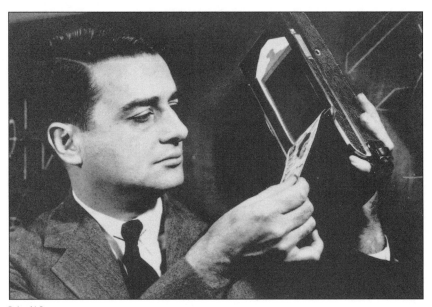

Polaroid Corp.

## Career Highlights

- Invented instant photography
- Awarded the Presidential Medal of Freedom, 1963
- Awarded the National Medal of Technology, 1988
- Awarded the National Medal of Science, 1967
- Elected to the Inventors Hall of Fame, 1977

## Important Contributions

Edwin Land invented what is often referred to as the miracle of instant Polaroid™ photography. We now take for granted that a thin piece of photographic film can be exposed and, before our very eyes, turn itself into a light-tight darkroom, develop itself as a normal photo-negative, convert itself into a photo-positive, and then have the light-tight chemical cover dissolve away to reveal the finished photo in all its brilliant color. This process usually requires a laboratory, specialized equipment, sequential immersion in five separate chemicals, and additional pieces of light-sensitive paper. Because of the research, development, and inventiveness of Edwin Land, the whole process can happen in our hands in 60 seconds.

But Land has other, even more important, scientific contributions to his credit. Land invented the polarization technology used worldwide in commercial and industrial applications. He also conducted research on how the brain perceives and interprets color. But more than anything, Edwin Land permanently changed the way we view film and the photographic process.

## Career Path

It was a typical family driving vacation. The Land family had puttered west from New York in June 1947, stopping repeatedly along the way. In the mountains of New Mexico, Edwin Land, successful developer of polarizing technology, lined up his family for a photo in front of a breathtaking vista. His older daughter, then nine, whined that she was tired of having her picture taken. She had posed for a hundred pictures and hadn't gotten to see one of them yet. Land coaxed her into smiling and standing up straight, but she wouldn't stop whining. What was the point of taking all these pictures if she had to wait weeks after they got home to see any of them? Why couldn't they see them *now*?

Mrs. Land huffed at her daughter to be quiet, but Edwin Land was lost deep in his daughter's complaint. Why *not* see them now? Why *not* see a picture moments after it was taken? His wife had to remind him to snap the picture. He clicked it mechanically and headed back to the car. The next day the family was speeding back to New York. It didn't matter that he had never finished college or that he knew little chemistry. His daughter's words had started him on a quest and such minor impediments were not going to stand in his way.

Edwin Land had been a quiet, studious child with a natural gift for understanding the function and workings of mechanical things. Even his early grade school teachers recognized his talent for science and predicted a successful career in physics.

But Edwin grew restless in school. High school bored him. Light and photography thrilled him. The idea that, with the push of a button, a permanent thing could be created that was "a part of himself and yet completely outside himself" was fascinating. He conducted simple light experiments during his boyhood years "just for fun."

Edwin was admitted to Harvard, even though he had no burning desire for a college degree or any specific career objectives. As a freshman he concentrated more on his private experiments than on class studies.

One drizzly evening while he walked through the glitter of the sparkling lights of New York's Broadway, Land was struck by an idea about one of his chief areas of interest: light polarization. It was known that certain crystals were able to block, or absorb, light waves vibrating along one plane (axis) and transmit those that vibrated along a perpendicular plane. This process was called polarization. But those crystals were expensive, bulky, easily damaged, and difficult to produce and so had not found wide use.

The idea came to Land that evening that a sheet of tiny (cheap) crystals might do as good a job of polarization as one big crystal. He took a leave of absence from his Harvard classes to research his idea. While the idea was simple, the execution proved extraordinarily difficult. He had to learn how to make microscopic herapathite particles (the crystal form he settled on after several months of research), then learn how to mix them into a clear plastic mass, and finally to orient them all in the same direction while forming a smooth, transparent finished sheet.

What Land had thought would take weeks took a year and a half of concerted effort. When he showed his first successful polarized sheets to Harvard administrators, they instantly saw the value of his work and assigned him a large lab space to continue his research. He worked on campus for another year and then took a second leave of absence to develop Polaroid J Sheets (the name of his original polarizer) into a commercial product.

Land never returned to the university, nor did he ever finish his undergraduate degree. He saw a limitless future for his invention in reducing glare from auto headlights, in revolutionizing movie production, in eliminating glare through home and office windows, in glass wear, and so forth. But problems arose. Polaroid sheets broke down too quickly. They couldn't withstand heat. All proceeds from early sales (the first order for 10,000 sheets was made by the Eastman-Kodak Company) were plowed back into research. Sales for sunglasses skyrocketed in the mid-1930s. Polarized camera lenses were a steady seller. But other markets never developed. Revenues from sales never kept pace with Land's new (and often costly) ideas and their expanding research costs.

During that family vacation to New Mexico in 1947, a whining complaint by Land's daughter started him on the hunt for an instant photography system. Experimenters in Europe had already attempted one-step photography systems, but so far none worked.

One of the two breakthroughs Land needed came from Edith Weyde at Agfa film. She developed a method for letting a negative image on one surface transfer silver salts to a second sheet to create a positive image. Land produced the second necessary breakthrough by designing a new kind of receiver (or positive) sheet. It then took a year of playing with the chemistry to develop the right kind and strength of one-step developer to package with each negative and to learn how to deactivate it after the one-minute developing cycle was over. Finally, it took him half a year of experimenting with equipment to figure out how to evenly roll the developer across the negative after it was exposed and how to package the negative and positive sheets so that the image would be properly transferred.

The first Polaroid instant camera system produced sepia tone prints. By 1953 good black and whites were available. By 1963 instant color film had been produced.

Edwin Land revolutionized photography and photographic film. For his work he received international acclaim and over 500 patents relating to cameras, film, and polarizing sheets and films. He also studied brain physiology and contributed greatly to our understanding of how the brain records and interprets color. In many ways Land has been to film and cameras what Carl Benz and Henry Ford were to automotive development. He is a giant, a permanent standard of innovation and achievement for the rest of the industry to measure itself against.

## Key Dates

| | |
|---|---|
| 1909 | Born in Bridgeport, Connecticut, on May 7 |
| 1925–1926 | Attended Harvard University (did not graduate) |
| 1929 | Announced the invention of a polarizer (conceived three years earlier) |
| 1932 | Founded Land-Wheelwright Laboratories with George Wheelwright |
| 1937 | Founded Polaroid Corporation; was chairman and director of research |
| 1947 | Developed Polaroid Land Camera (first instant photography system) |
| 1963 | Invented Polarcolor (first color instant photography system) |

1982    Retired

1991    Died March 1

## Advice

*Although Edwin Land never finished college, he later recognized the value of years of concentrated study. For a career in light-related technology development, take math, the physical sciences, and mechanical engineering. But remember that knowledge is just a tool. Discoveries are made "by the individual who has freed himself from a way of thinking that is held by friends and associates who may be more intelligent, better educated, better disciplined, but who have not mastered the art of taking a fresh, clean look at old knowledge." Then work incessantly, compulsively, wholeheartedly in your field and on your projects. Land often said, "Anything worth doing, is worth doing to excess."*

## References

Devine, Elizabeth, ed. *The Annual Obituary, 1991*. Chicago: St. James Press, 1993. (Good biographical summary.)

Garraty, John, ed. *Encyclopedia of American Biography*. New York: Harper & Row, 1984. (Detailed summary of Land's work.)

McElheny, Victor K. *Insisting on the Impossible: The Life of Edwin Land*. Sloan Technology Series. New York: Perseus Books, 1998.

Olshaker, Mark. *The Instant Image: Edwin Land and the Polaroid Experience*. New York: Facts on File, 1978.

Polaroid Corporation. *Polaroid Corporation: A Chronology*. Cambridge, Mass.: Polaroid Corporation, 1983. (Good review of Land's invention and research.)

Tanor, Joseph, ed. *McGraw-Hill Modern Men of Science*. New York: McGraw-Hill, 1986. (Strong summary of Land's work.)

# Ernest Lawrence

*"Accelerating the Search"*  Nuclear Physics

## Career Highlights

Lawrence Berkeley National Laboratory

- Invented the cyclotron and three transuranic elements
- Awarded Nobel Prize for Physics, 1939
- Awarded the Enrico Fermi Award by the Atomic Energy Commission, 1957
- Awarded the first Sylvanus Thayer Award by the United States Military Academy, 1958
- Had national laboratory complex he developed and the 11th transuranic element named in his honor

## Important Contributions

Ernest Lawrence invented and developed the cyclotron. The cyclotron was the first practical, controllable system for accelerating subatomic particles and for imparting great energy to those particles. With enough energy and speed, electrons, neutrons, and protons could be used to smash apart other atoms. The cyclotron became the standard research tool for high-energy nuclear medicine, physics, transuranic explorations, atomic energy research, and atomic weapons development.

Lawrence also created the first manmade element and created two additional new elements before his death in 1958. One of them, element 103, *lawrencium,* was named after him to honor his great contribution to science, making him one of fewer than a dozen scientists in all history chosen to have an element named after them. The honor signified his vast importance to the development of worldwide nuclear physics.

## Career Path

In 1933, the building looked like a reinforced airplane hangar rising from the hills above the University of California, Berkeley, campus. A cement and metal monstrosity sprawling across its middle looked like the fantasy creation of a science fiction movie. It pulsed and hummed with an ominous intensity. Workers encased in heavy protective clothing had to climb over thick bundles of cable that snaked across the floor. Steam hissed from cooling circuits. Rising almost two stories high, the gargantuan machine looked capable of creating new worlds. Really, it was only capable of speeding up tiny specks smaller than could be measured and lighter than could be weighed. Its inventor was not a mad descendant of Dr. Frankenstein, but mild, bespeckled Ernest Lawrence. The question was, after five years of development and millions of dollars spent, could Lawrence's monstrous cyclotron smash an atom?

By age nine, Ernest was interested in simple electronic devices. By thirteen, he had designed and built wireless communication equipment. However, he thought of electronics as toys and a hobby. His steadfast desire was to study medicine after high school. Ernest pursued that goal for one year at St. Olaf's College and for a second at the University of South Dakota before the influence of two dynamic scientists opened his eyes to the wonders and excitement of the emerging fields of electronics and atomic physics.

Ernest Lawrence's university teachers were impressed, as had been his high school teachers, with his originality of thinking and his knack for successful experimentation. Lawrence craved chances to rummage through the laboratory to find a way to demonstrate and prove theories others were content to simply memorize. By the time he had earned a Ph.D. in 1925, it was clear that Lawrence was one of the most talented experimentalists in the country.

The promising youg man settled into the life of a professor and researcher at Yale University. His graduate work had related to photoelectric effects induced in gaseous vapors, with a particular emphasis on potassium vapor. Yale expected him to continue this research there.

Three years later Lawrence was offered an assistant professorship position at the University of California at Berkeley. Everyone expected him to refuse because Yale was a well-funded, prestigious Eastern university. Who would give that away for an unknown state school in the Far West, a region that had never produced any significant research?

Lawrence accepted, partly to get back to the West, where he had been raised, and partly for the opportunity to help create a new physics department. Robert Oppenheimer had already been hired to work there. Lawrence, at 27, was to assist him in building a new physics mecca.

Upon arriving at Berkeley, Lawrence deliberately abandoned his photoelectric research for the new department's focus: nuclear physics. Berkeley theorists were hard at work deducing the inner workings of an atom. But Lawrence was an experimenter. He needed to *see* inside an atom. To do that he needed some way to penetrate the atom's microscopic shell.

Previous researchers had relied on high-energy subatomic particles created by natural radioactivity, especially by radium, to smash apart other atoms. But radium was expensive and scarce. The emitted alpha particles shot out in uncontrolled directions. Actual desired collisions were rare. The experiments were time consuming and tedious. Lawrence wanted to be able to control the speed and direction of his subatomic probes so that they would always hit his targets.

In 1929, Lawrence read an article about a failed attempt by a Norwegian physicist to use electric currents to accelerate a proton. The article gave Lawrence an idea. He could combine a high-voltage electric field to continuously accelerate an ion with a magnetic field to drive a charged particle in a circular path that would slowly increase as the particle absorbed more and more energy from the electric field and accelerated. If a particle started at the middle of a circular dish and spiraled toward the outside, he could force it to accelerate through thousands of circular orbits, all in a very small space.

The idea of a circular accelerator, or cyclotron, was born. It took Lawrence over a year to design the alternating electric field and magnetic field to work in unison and to accurately aim a charged particle. Equipment shattered during high-stress tests. Parts failed under these new kinds of high-energy loads. Improved parts had to be designed and fabricated.

On January 2, 1931, Lawrence completed the first successful cyclotron test. It used a tiny, four-and-one-half-inch chamber and accelerated particles to 80,000 electronvolts of energy. It was far short of the atom-smashing power he needed, but it was a start. Two years later, with a 34-inch cyclotron and an 85-ton high-energy magnet, Lawrence accelerated particles to over 1 million electronvolts.

The atom smasher had arrived. Scientists could now accelerate any ion to any desired speed and energy level and blast it into any desired target substance. The cyclotron was a turning point in physics and medical research. One of the first applications of cyclotron technology was for cancer research and for the creation of radiation therapy. One of the first test patients of this revolutionary therapy was Lawrence's own mother, successfully treated for cancer in 1937.

In the ensuing years, Lawrence conducted countless experiments on larger and larger cyclotrons. He created new, manmade elements. He isolated the U235 used for research and development of America's atomic bombs in the Manhattan Project during World War II. He studied and revealed the inner workings of the atoms of dozens of elements, and created never-before-available opportunities to study new subatomic particles. For the vast body of subatomic discoveries he made with the cyclotron, Lawrence was awarded the Nobel Prize for Physics in 1939.

By 1950 Lawrence's health had begun to deteriorate. His work grew more sporadic. He faded from the forefront of physics research. Still, he had left an indelible mark. Only one person in many millions has the ability to make a contribution that significantly advances a whole civilization. Ernest Lawrence was such a person. His inventions and discoveries changed the late twentieth century as much as Thomas Edison's discoveries had changed the late nineteenth century.

## Key Dates

| | |
|---|---|
| 1901 | Born in Canton, South Dakota, on August 8 |
| 1922 | Received B.S. from South Dakota State University |
| 1924 | Received M.S. from University of Minnesota |
| 1925 | Received Ph.D. from Yale University; continued as a faculty member |
| 1928 | Moved to University of California, Berkeley, with Robert Oppenheimer |
| 1929 | Conceived the idea for a cyclotron |
| 1931 | Built first cyclotron |
| 1932 | First split an atom with a cyclotron |
| 1939 | Awarded Nobel Prize for Physics |
| 1958 | Died on August 27 |

## Advice

*Ernest Lawrence believed that classroom learning should support laboratory experimental learning. Successful physics careers should begin by learning how to conduct the tests and experiments to validate and extend physics theories. Gather as much hands-on experience as you can with the equipment and process of research. Understand how available test equipment works, how to use it, and how to improve it. Combine this knowledge with a solid understanding of the theory of your field and you will succeed.*

## References

Childs, Herbert. *An American Genius: The Life of Ernest Lawrence.* New York: Sutton, 1968. (A complete biography.)

Davis, Nuel. *Lawrence and Oppenheimer.* New York: Da Capo Press, 1986. (Good review of nuclear physics and the Manhattan Project.)

Heilbron, J. L., and Robert W. Seidel. *Lawrence and His Laboratory: A History of the Lawrence Berkeley Laboratory.* California Studies in the History of Science. Berkeley: University of California Press, 1990. (Gives the history of the science that led to the development of the atomic bomb.)

Livingston, M. Stanley. "History of the Cyclotron," *Physics Today* 12 (October 1959): 18–23. (Excellent history of the development of the cyclotron.)

National Geographic Society. *Those Inventive Americans.* Washington, D.C.: National Geographic Society, 1971. (Good chapter on Lawrence and his significance.)

Shafroth, Stephen M., ed., and James C. Austin, cont. *Accelerator-Based Atomic Physics: Techniques and Applications.* Philadelphia, Pa.: American Institute of Physics, 1997.

# Louis Leakey

*"The Black Man with a White Face"*

Archaeology and Anthropology

## Career Highlights

- Discovered *Homo habilis*, the oldest primate with human characteristics
- Discovered *Proconsul africanus*, considered to be the root stock of all higher primates
- Awarded the Rivers Memorial Medal of the Royal Anthropological Institute, 1952
- Given the Henry Stopes Memorial Medal of the Geological Association, 1955

## Important Contributions

Archaeologist, anthropologist, human paleontologist, zoologist, anatomist, geologist, and teacher: Louis Leakey was a multifaceted scientist. He lectured extensively to large American and European audiences, working tirelessly to share what he had discovered during the 40 years he and his wife had spent excavating the Olduvai Gorge on the eastern Serengeti Plains of Tanzania, even though their colleagues initially told them they were wasting their time. Their colleagues had been wrong. The Leakeys' discoveries of early primate fossils revolutionized twentieth-century theories of human evolution.

## Career Path

Jogging barefoot across the central African plain, wearing a rough woven loincloth, the 48-year-old white man seemed oddly out of place. In this fall of 1950, a merciless sun glistened off his bare shoulders, deeply tanned from years of work in Africa. A hand-ground stone knife was stuffed into a crude, woven belt. In his hands he carried stone throwing axes. The man, Louis Leakey, was in his second day of stalking a gazelle.

Leakey was not a hunter. He did not need the food. He was an anthropologist and archaeologist and needed to see if early man could have successfully hunted with the tools Leakey had found in his Olduvai Gorge digs. Before that second sun set, he had downed a gazelle with his ax and skinned and bled it with his version of a prehistoric stone knife. It might seem to be an extreme way to test his theory, but he always had to prove every point to a very skeptical and unsympathetic audience of colleagues and critics.

Louis Leakey was born near Nairobi, Kenya, where his British missionary parents had settled. Louis befriended boys of the Kikuyu tribe, and he learned to speak the local dialects before he learned English. He was initiated to manhood in a Kikuyu ceremony when he was 13, probably the only white man to have done so. The tribal chief said of Louis, "We call him the black man with a white face because he is more of an African than a European."

Louis was tutored at home until, at 16, he traveled to England for two years of public school. In 1922, he entered St. John's College, Cambridge University. There he suffered a head injury playing rugby, which resulted in blinding headaches. His physicians recommended a leave of absence, a recommendation that led to one of the most important trips of his life: He joined an expedition of the British Museum led by paleontologist W. E. Cutler to search for dinosaur fossils in Tanganyika. On that trip Louis learned skills and techniques that would serve him for the rest of his life.

After qualifying in archaeology and anthropology at Cambridge in 1926 (eventually receiving a Ph.D. in African prehistory), Leakey organized and led his first fossil-hunting expedition to East Africa. He was convinced that humankind had originated in Africa, even though he was virtually alone in that view. His contemporaries believed that early man had originated in Asia. Indeed, his professors at Cambridge told him he was wasting his time with Africa.

But Leakey was steadfast in his belief, despite the fact that his first two expeditions to Africa were largely unsuccessful. On his third expedition his persistence was rewarded. In Kenya, he nearly fell over the edge of a concealed cliff. Carefully looking down, he saw a hand ax sticking out of the side of the cliff. When he excavated the area, he discovered the first living site of the hand-ax man, who lived 200,000 years ago. He had found the Olduvai Gorge, the area he would excavate for over 30 years.

Several million years ago, the Olduvai Gorge was a lake. The 35-mile-long gorge had been channeled by a stream, cutting away 300 feet of sediment to reveal layer after layer of fossils and history. Leakey suspected that primitive man had inhabited the area, and the Olduvai Gorge became the site of some of his most important finds.

While serving as a research fellow at St. John's College following this expedition, Leakey met Mary Nicol, also an archaeologist. Although he was already married, he and Mary fell in love and began an affair that shocked the Cambridge world. When he asked for a divorce from his wife in 1934, the scandal ended any possibility of a further connection with St. John's College or support from Cambridge. Oddly enough, had it not been for this opposition, the Leakeys might never have settled in Kenya, where they made their magnificent discoveries.

The Leakeys returned to Olduvai and settled into excavation life in Africa. Their work was interrupted only by his trips to act as visiting professor and secure more funding and during three years he spent researching and creating a grammar of the Kikuyu tribe for the Rhodes Trustees. World War II also forced him to stop his fossil hunting; from 1939 to 1945, he worked for British Intelligence in Nairobi. When the war was over, Leakey once more began hunting for the origins of man in Africa.

Digging for fossils was not easy work. Most of the time Leakey crawled up and down slopes with his eyes only inches above the ground, often in 110° heat! Once fossils were found, digging had to be conducted with dental picks and brushes more often than with shovels to preserve the delicate remains. But the painstaking work paid off. In 1948, he found *Proconsul africanus,* a creature considered by most authorities to be a common ancestor of man and the apes. In 1962, he and his wife found *Kenyapithecus,* another link between ape and man. In 1959, Mary discovered *Zinjanthropus,* or East Africa man, in the Olduvai Gorge. A year later, the Leakeys discovered the remains of *Homo habilis*, dated at 1.7 million years old. Leakey also discovered the skull of *Homo erectus,* which he felt was on the direct evolutionary line with *Homo sapiens.*

Leakey was also interested in learning about the behavior of chimpanzees and gorillas, because he believed that studying them would yield insights into the nature of early man. It was this belief that led him to enlist Jane Goodall and Dian Fossey to study the great apes.

Before the Leakeys' findings, most experts in the field believed that man's origins were in Asia. But the findings at Olduvai and the dating of *Zinjanthropus* and *Homo habilis* at 1.8 to 1.6 million years old changed all that, leading to a new understanding of how and where humans evolved.

Louis Leakey's contributions to archaeology continue despite his death in 1972. In 1975, Louis's son Richard discovered a 1.6-million-year-old skull of *Homo erectus,* and in 1984 he and another paleontologist discovered a nearly complete skeleton of *Homo erectus.*

\* \* \*

## Key Dates

| | |
|---|---|
| 1903 | Born in Kabete, Kenya, on August 7 |
| 1922 | Enrolled in Weymouth College and St. John's College, Cambridge |
| 1924 | Joined a British Museum East African archaeological expedition to Tanganyika |
| 1926 | Led the first of his own East African archaeological research expeditions; received degrees in archaeology and anthropology |
| 1929 | Discovered first living site of hand-ax man |
| 1929–1934 | Became a fellow at St. John's College, Cambridge |
| 1933–1935 | Became Leverhulme Research Fellow |
| 1936 | Became Munroe Lecturer at the University of Edinburgh |
| 1937–1939 | Researched customs of the Kikuyu tribe for the Rhodes Trustees |
| 1941 | Became honorary part-time curator of the Coryndon Memorial Museum in Nairobi; position became full time in 1945 |
| 1948 | Discovered *Proconsul africanus* |
| 1959 | Mary Leakey discovered *Zinjanthropus (Australopithecus boisei)* |
| 1960 | Discovered skull of *Homo erectus* |
| 1960–1961 | Served as Herbert Spencer lecturer at Oxford University |
| 1961 | Became the Huxley Memorial lecturer at Birmingham University |
| 1962 | Discovered *Kenyapithecus* |
| 1963 | Served as a regents lecturer at the University of California |
| 1963–1964 | Served as The Silliman lecturer at Yale |
| 1972 | Died October 1 in London |

## Advice

*Louis Leakey said that if you want to work in the fields of anthropology and archaeology, you've got to be willing to do the dirty work. Include natural history, anatomy and physiology, and human history in your required curriculum, but don't let your mind get overly cluttered with other people's theories. You need to do enough hands-on research to develop some of your own theories. And don't dismiss an idea just because no one else happens to believe in it yet.*

## References

Leakey, Louis. *By the Evidence: Memoirs, 1932–1951.* New York: Harcourt Brace Jovanovich, 1974.

———. *White African: An Early Autobiography.* Rochester, N.Y.: Schenkman Books, 1966.

Leakey, Mary. *Disclosing the Past.* New York: McGraw-Hill, 1986.

Morell, Virginia. *Ancestral Passions: The Leakey Family and the Quest for Humankind's Beginnings.* Salt Lake City: Touchstone Books, 1996. (Authoritative personal and scientific biography of the Leakey family.)

Phillipson, David W. *African Archaeology.* Cambridge, Mass.: Cambridge University Press, 1985.

Willis, Delta. *The Leakey Family: Leaders in the Search for Human Origins.* Makers of Modern Science Series. New York: Facts on File, 1992. (Good biography of the family.)

# Edward Lorenz

## *"The Butterfly Effect"*　　　　Meteorology

Photo by Donna Coveney

## Career Highlights

- Founded modern chaos theory
- Awarded the Roger Revelle Medal by the American Geophysical Union, 1992
- Awarded the Kyoto Prize by the Inamori Foundation, 1991
- Awarded the Elliott Creson Medal by the Franklin Institute, 1989

## Important Contributions

In the early twentieth century, there was a great push to apply modern scientific methods to the study of the atmosphere and create methods for accurate long-range forecasting. Ed Lorenz was one of the mathematicians drafted into this effort. But instead of neatly packaged forecasting algorithms, Lorenz uncovered a non-linear, complex, interdependent system. While wading through the inherently unpredictable mire of a fickle atmosphere, he discovered not how to make long-range predictions, but rather the forces that make such predictions impossible.

Specifically, Lorenz is linked to three discoveries: the butterfly principle, the Lorenz attractor, and chaos theory. Through the butterfly principle, he showed that atmospheric models are so dependent on initial and boundary conditions that even seemingly infinitesimal changes at either temporal or physical boundaries can create major changes in the system. In other words, when a butterfly flaps its wings over Beijing, the models might well predict that it will change the weather in New York City.

Next Lorenz discovered a chaotic pattern toward which atmospheric solutions are inevitably attracted, just as a swinging pendulum inevitably slows and comes to rest pointing toward the center of the Earth. This end-state chaotic pattern was called the Lorenz attractor and became one of the "strange attractors" first noted by David Ruelle in 1971.

Third, this work opened the door to Lorenz's development of chaos theory itself, or the study of chaotic and unpredictable systems. Scientists are discovering that many natural, biological, and environmental systems are best described and better understood through chaos theory than through traditional forms of analysis.

## Career Path

Having a computer was enough of a novelty in 1958 to entice many MIT faculty and students to make the trip to Ed Lorenz's office just to watch the thing work. But excitement quickly turned to despair as he studied the computer's printouts. He had created a set of equations to act as a mathematical model of atmospheric storm movement and behavior.

Lorenz noticed that tiny changes in the starting conditions of the model soon produced enormous changes in the outcome. Tiny starting differences *amplified* over time, rather than damping, or normalizing out. If the actual atmosphere acted like his models, he had just proved that long-range weather forecasting was impossible because starting conditions were never known with enough precision to prevent chaotic, amplified error. It was an unsettling and sinking feeling to trade the excitement of finding a new research tool for the despair of proving that your field and work were both inherently flawed and impossible.

At an early age, Ed Lorenz had been fascinated by numbers. Before he was two, he could read all the numbers on the houses when his mother took him for a walk. When he learned what multiplication was, he became fond of perfect squares and memorized them from 1 to 1,000. He played mathematical puzzles with his father and enjoyed figuring square and cube roots using the long-hand method. Along with this love of numbers came a love of card games and chess and other numerically based games.

Ed also developed an early fascination with maps and especially with maps that were enlarged sections of other maps. By the time he was seven he was drawing maps and following road maps as the family went on drives or trips. This spatial orientation translated later into a fascination with mountains and astronomy.

When Ed entered Dartmouth College in 1934, he had long made up his mind to be a mathematician. Neither the suggestions of advisors to study something more general nor the early appeal of physics and geology courses changed his decision. He graduated with a bachelor's degree in mathematics in 1938 and entered Harvard University to continue his study of math.

With the outbreak of World War II, it became apparent that Ed Lorenz would not be able to finish his last year of graduate studies. Rather than wait to be drafted, he volunteered for an Army program offering training in meteorology for qualified enlistees, who would then become weather officers for the Army Air Crops. Several months before he had expected to receive a Ph.D. in mathematics from Harvard, Ed moved two miles down the Charles River to attend Army meteorology classes at MIT.

In the mornings, the enlistees attended MIT graduate classes in meteorology theory. In the afternoons they learned to forecast, using historical case studies. Because of Lorenz's mathematical background, he specialized in dynamic meteorology, which views the atmosphere as a large, inhomogeneous mass of gas infused with liquid drops and solid particles, enveloping a spherical earth with an irregular surface. Ed learned to regard the weather as a combination of density, pressure, temperature, three-dimensional wind velocities, and the atmosphere's gaseous, liquid, and solid content. The equations that describe these variables define the current weather conditions. The rates of change in these equations define the changing weather pattern.

What Lorenz was not taught, and only much later discovered, was that no one knew how to use these non-linear dynamic meteorology equations to actually predict weather and that most thought it could not be done. The equations were too complex and required too much initial and boundary data.

Lorenz struggled with the dynamic equations for a year before he was discharged in 1946. He faced a major decision: return to Harvard to complete his mathematics degree, or return to MIT to pursue meteorology. The decision seemed to hang on a perfectly balanced scale, teetering back and forth as his discharge date approached. Then he considered the problems of applying dynamic meteorology: "I saw some fundamental unresolved problems there and thought I could see ways to approach them." The lure of important, unsolved problems swung the scale toward meteorology.

Lorenz returned to MIT and began his work by trying to apply the dynamic equations to predict the motion of storms. Because computers were not commonly available in the early 1950s, most of this work was carried out on blackboards and with slide rules and paper and pencil. Each calculation was tediously time consuming.

In 1958 Lorenz obtained a Royal-McBee LGP-30 computer (about the size of a large desk) to develop his sets of dynamic, non-linear model equations. As a research tool, computers were still almost unused in meteorology, but they were Lorenz's only means for finally resolving the dynamic meteorology he had first worked on for the Army a decade before. The results of those computer simulations showed that tiny initial differences *amplified* over time, rather than damping, or normalizing out. If the model was right, weather was chaotic and inherently unpredictable. Although the equations could be solved, the solution was meaningless because it couldn't account for the system's chaotic behavior.

Several years of atmospheric testing convinced Lorenz and others in his department that he and his model were correct. The atmosphere was a chaotic rather than a predictable system (such as the system of interactions between inorganic chemicals, or the physical pull of gravity). The drive to use a new tool to complete an old project became one of the most profound discoveries in the science of meteorology.

Ed Lorenz continued his research on the behavior of the chaotic atmosphere and, in so doing, developed the whole field of quantitative chaos theory. He has published over 80 articles and one book on his work, which now encompasses both meteorology and chaos. But he will be known as the person who discovered the true nature of the atmosphere and who thereby discovered the limits of the nature of existing forecasting methodology. He will be remembered as the one who showed that a tiny butterfly can change the weather.

## Key Dates

| | |
|---|---|
| 1917 | Born in West Hartford, Connecticut, on May 23 |
| 1938 | Recieved bachelor's degree from Dartmouth College |
| 1940 | Received master's degree from Harvard University |
| 1941–1942 | Was teaching fellow in mathematics at Harvard |
| 1942–1946 | Worked as U.S. Army Air Corps weather forecaster |
| 1946–1955 | Worked as research staff member, MIT Department of Meteorology |
| 1948 | Received Ph.D. in meteorology from MIT |

1955–
1962    Worked as associate professor of meteorology at MIT

1962–
1987    Worked as professor of meteorology at MIT

1987–
present  Is professor emeritus of meteorology, MIT

## Advice

*Ed Lorenz would advise someone considering a career in meteorology to search for three qualities, or characteristics, in yourself and let them guide your career: an intense interest in the subject matter of science (you must feel intensely curious about the phenomena of the world), the ability and tenacity to pursue and eventually discover answers to the questions that intrigue you, and an interest in always searching for explanations other than those that have been commonly disseminated and perhaps commonly accepted. Let these three qualities lead you into the fields, courses, and studies for which you are best suited. Dr. Lorenz believes that the most important single subject to master is mathematics, and that the most important course is algebra, followed by calculus.*

## References

Fuller, John. *Thor's Legions.* Boston: American Meteorological Society, 1990. (Good historical review of meteorological techniques.)

Gleick, James. *Chaos: Making a New Science.* New York: Viking, 1991. (Good review of the field of chaos.)

Lorenz, Ed. *The Essence of Chaos.* Seattle: University of Washington Press, 1993. (Good review of chaos theory and Lorenz's work on it.)

———. "A Scientist by Choice," in *Proceedings of the Kyoto Prize for 1991.* Kyoto, Japan: The Inamori Foundation, 1991. (Excellent autobiographical review.)

Parker, Berry. *Chaos in the Cosmos.* New York: Plenum Press, 1996. (Good review of chaos principles.)

# Shannon Lucid

*"Patient Explorer"*

Chemist and
Astronaut

## Career Highlights

National Aeronautics and Space Administration

- Selected for astronaut program, 1978
- Chosen for Mission Specialist Crew for shuttle mission, 1985
- Chosen for extended duty on the Russian space station, MIR (only American woman)
- Holds the record for longest time in space by a woman and for the longest time in space by an American

## Important Contributions

Shannon Lucid was already a successful senior biochemist, a mother of three, and a competent prop and jet pilot. Then she added record-setting astronaut to her list of credentials. Shannon flew on the *Discovery* shuttle for seven days in July 1985 and on three subsequent missions. She also spent more time on the MIR space station (179 days) than any other American and has spent more time in space than any woman.

Lucid was one of the group of six women accepted into the astronaut training program in 1978. They were the first women to enter the U.S. space program. Collectively they expanded career opportunities for women both in the sciences and in space. Shannon Lucid serves as a model of dedication, persistence, and patience.

## Career Path

It was not a usual beginning for a life: being captured twice at gunpoint and shipped to prison camp before the age of six. Perhaps these trials helped Shannon Lucid visualize unusual goals for her career and life.

Shannon Lucid learned to walk and talk in a Japanese prison camp. She was born Shannon Wells in Shanghai, China, in 1943, where her parents served as Baptist missionaries. When she was only six weeks old, her parents were captured by the advancing Japanese. Shannon spent the first year and a half of her life in a prison camp.

The family was released in late 1944 and returned to the United States. After Japan surrendered and withdrew from China, the Wells family returned to their missionary work in China. When Shannon was six, the family was captured by the advancing Communist Chinese and marched to prison camp again. Rather than being permanently interned, the family was expelled, returned to the United States, and moved to Lubbock, Texas, and later to Bethany, Oklahoma, the family's original home town.

Even as a young child in China, Shannon had been struck vividly by the vastness of space and by a longing to travel into it. She also wanted to fly airplanes: "Other young girls at the mission wanted to play dolls and dress-up. I wanted to fly planes and play space."

By the time Shannon graduated from high school in 1950, reality had settled in like a soggy blanket to quench her fiery plans. There was no U.S. manned space program. Airlines did not hire women pilots. There seemed no prospect of finding work in either of her two long-coveted professions. She would have to be patient and wait for other opportunities.

Shannon was accepted to Wheaton College in Illinois and settled for a major in chemistry, her third choice. She had always been fascinated by science and in particular by the composition, or make-up, of different substances.

To pay for her education, Shannon worked in the student union and cleaned houses. During the summer between her sophomore and junior years, Wheaton raised its fees. She couldn't afford the higher rate and transferred to the University of Oklahoma. She graduated in 1963 with a B.S. in chemistry.

After graduation, Shannon got a job working for the Oklahoma Medical Research Foundation. The salary gave her a chance to pursue one of her dreams. She took flying lessons and got her pilot's license. By the early 1970s, Lucid had logged enough hours to obtain a commercial pilot's license.

Shannon met her future husband, Michael Lucid, also a chemist at the Foundation, when she applied to him for a new research position. He turned her down. It was the first such rejection she had experienced in her life. Eighteen months later, another job opened that Michael thought Shannon was better suited for. He offered it to her and she accepted. Two years later they were married.

In 1970, then with two young daughters, Lucid decided to return to school to get her Ph.D. in biochemistry. A doctorate would open a great array of new career options for her. At the time it never occurred to her that one of those options would be her first passion, an opportunity for space travel. In 1973, just before her son was born, she graduated and returned to work at the Foundation.

In 1977 Lucid's world changed. NASA announced that they were accepting applications for an expanded astronaut corps. Women could compete on an equal footing with men. Although she itched to apply, she made it a family decision. It would, after all, affect them all. With her family's enthusiastic support, Lucid applied in late 1977. So did over 8,000 other men and women. Two hundred were selected for first-round interviews in Houston. Fifteen pilots and twenty mission specialists would be chosen. Lucid was accepted in 1978 as one of six women in the expansion class.

The Lucid family moved to Houston, which would be the base for Shannon's training. Now came the hard part. Crammed into one year, she had to learn every electronic, electrical, and physical system on the shuttle. She had to take classes in flight mechanics, meteorology, rocket propulsion, computer science, upper atmosphere physics, astronomy, astrophysics, and aerodynamics.

In addition to the intense academics, each day included hours of physical training and flight simulation work. Lucid had to learn how to parachute safely and comfortably over both land and water. She had to learn extensive survival skills. All astronauts lift weights and work out every day to keep in top physical condition.

Astronauts also practice flight skills in T-38 high-performance trainer jets. This was Lucid's favorite training element. Even though, as a mission specialist instead of a pilot, she most often had to ride in the back seat and focus on navigation, communications, and flight planning, still she loved every minute spent soaring above the humid Texas plains.

Finally, astronauts must practice weightlessness. They train in large tanks wearing SCUBA gear, where buoyancy compensators allow them to achieve neutral buoyancy, or weightlessness.

While effective as a training vehicle, the tank training had its limits. Water is thick and resists movement. Weightlessness in water feels substantially different than weightlessness in air. NASA has a fleet of KC-135 cargo jets it uses to let astronauts experience true weightlessness. The jet makes a series of arcs through the sky. Each arc begins with a steep climb and ends with a rapid descent. At the top of the arc, the passengers become weightless for 30 seconds, barely enough time for the trainees to practice moving around. Each flight may involve 15 or more arcs and a total of seven or eight minutes of weightlessness. Unfortunately, like an extremely rough roller coaster, the flights also tend to produce motion sickness. Like most astronaut trainees, Lucid eagerly anticipated the flight. Also like most trainees, her dread of the dizziness and stomach churning soon overcame her love of the few seconds of weightlessness.

When Lucid graduated in 1979, she was eager and ready for a shuttle assignment. Along with her entire class, she was assigned to support and research projects while she waited her turn for a mission assignment. In mid-1982, Sally Ride was chosen as the first woman to make a flight into space, with a June 1983 lift-off. Shannon Lucid continued to wait for her turn.

Finally, in June 1985, Lucid flew as part of the crew of the *Discovery* as a mission specialist. Following her shuttle flight, she continued to work for NASA and a decade later was given the chance to spend five months on the Russian space station, MIR. Two delays in the date of her return meant that she, who had had to wait so patiently for her chance to fly, had logged more time in space than any other American astronaut and more than any other woman in the world.

Lucid believes that the opportunity to fulfill her lifelong dream of space travel can be credited to the women's movement of the 1960s and 1970s. The steady push for equal opportunity opened her dream careers, airline pilot and astronaut, both of which were closed to women when she first wanted to enter the programs.

## Key Dates

| | |
|---|---|
| 1943 | Born in Shanghai, China, on February 18 |
| 1963 | Received B.S. in chemistry from University of Oklahoma |
| 1963 | Hired by Oklahoma Medical Research Foundation |

| | |
|---|---|
| 1973 | Received Ph.D. in biochemistry from University of Oklahoma |
| 1978 | Selected for U.S. Astronaut Training Program |
| 1979–present | Is member of NASA Astronaut Corps |
| 1985 | Flew into space on *Discovery* shuttle, mission #51-G |
| 1996 | Spent 179 days aboard Russian space station, MIR |
| 1996–present | Holds an astronaut advisory position at NASA |

## Advice

*Shannon Lucid would recommend a good grounding in math and the physical sciences for anyone considering a career as an astronaut. Then pick one field of science that appeals to you and specialize in it to develop the mission skills you can offer to NASA. Work in "team" situations and develop outside interests. Stay physically active and fit. And learn to fly. In an emergency, any of the astronauts must be able to fly and land a shuttle craft.*

## References

Briggs, Carole. *Women in Space*. Minneapolis, Minn.: CarolRhoda Books, 1988. (Biographical summary.)

Burdett, Gerald, ed. *The Human Quest in Space*. San Diego, Calif.: Univelt, 1987. (Good review of the field.)

Hansen, Rosanna. *Astronauts*. New York: Random House, 1997. (Good review of the field.)

NASA Web site: www.jsc.nasa.gov.

O'Connor, Karen. *Sally Ride and the New Astronauts: Scientists in Space*. New York: Franklin Watts, 1983. (Good review of astronaut training.)

Yenne, Bill. *Astronauts*. New York: Simon & Schuster, 1991. (Good review of the manned space program.)

# Maria Goeppert Mayer

*"The Madonna of the Onion"*          Physics

## Career Highlights

AIP Emilio Segrè Visual Archives, Physics Today Collection

- Was first American woman to receive the Nobel Prize for Physics, 1963
- Was one of the world's leading authorities on the structure of the atomic nucleus
- Elected to the National Academy of Sciences, 1956
- Awarded four honorary doctorates

## Important Contributions

Maria Goeppert Mayer explained the arrangement of particles within the nucleus of an atom. For this discovery, she won the Nobel Prize for Physics in 1963. Her work in nuclear physics and her earlier work led to developments in laser physics, laser isotope separation, and molecular orbital calculation. Despite her brilliant mind and impressive record, for 30 years Mayer worked, researched, taught, and discovered without pay because she was a woman.

## Career Path

The sheer beauty of the new image that danced across 52-year-old Maria Mayer's head made her gasp. For months she had pictured the nucleus of an atom like layers of an onion. This image explained many of the phenomena scientists had observed, but it seemed far too static to mesh with the dynamic forces that dominated an atom and its core.

Then, in a flash of insight, a beautiful new image replaced the onion. Mayer saw a roomful of dancers in her native Germany wearing gowns and tuxedos and twirling through a waltz. From high above she watched all the couples in each circle, or shell, spin in the same direction. The whole circle also turned as couples moved around the dance floor. The dance involved twirling people, but Mayer's image was of spinning couples of protons and neutrons: She had conceived a new model for explaining the behavior of atomic nuclei.

Now Mayer had to do the math to prove her model was consistent with observed measurements. If this model fit with recorded data, it could be her vindication after 30 years of being treated like a second-class citizen. Maybe now she could find a paying job.

When Maria Goeppert Mayer was a child, her father's status as a professor at the University of Göttingen gave the family great prestige. Indeed, the town treated little Maria like a princess. She grew up brimming with headstrong self-confidence, never doubting that she would go to college.

But when Maria's small school closed, she had no way to prepare for the rigorous entrance examinations to German universities. Rather than wait a year and enroll in a new school, the young girl decided to take the entrance exams anyway. Her parents and former teachers warned her against it and reminded her that she would have one chance only. If she failed the exam, the doors to higher education would be forever closed to her in Germany. Maria would not be swayed from her own plan. She took the exams and passed them easily.

When Maria Goeppert entered the University of Göttingen in 1924, she planned to study mathematics. This was at the height of Göttingen's prestige in physics, and she soon found the allure of physics more compelling than that of mathematics. "Mathematics," she said, "began to seem too much like puzzle-solving. . . . Physics is puzzle-solving, too, but of puzzles created by nature, not by the mind of man. . . . Physics was the challenge." She remained at Göttingen to study for a doctorate.

Goeppert found 1930 to be a whirlwind year of change. In January she married fellow physics graduate student, Joseph Mayer, an American from the University of California. In March she completed her thesis and passed her doctoral examination. In April the couple moved to the United States, where Joe had an assistant professorship at Johns Hopkins University. As a woman scientist, Maria knew she could never have a university career in Germany, but she hoped it might be different in America. America was the land of opportunity, and she expected there would be opportunities for her as a professor in an American university. Life in America, she thought, would be perfect.

But Mayer was wrong. Following major financial crises in 1929, the Great Depression had gripped America. Many families had no income. Nobody would give a job to the wife of a professor because no family deserved two incomes. But Maria Mayer loved physics and could not bear to abandon her chosen field. She volunteered to teach and conduct research on campus without pay, assuming that a full-time position would be available when the economy recovered.

However, the idea of two-paycheck families was scorned just as fiercely after the Depression. Most U.S. colleges and universities adopted anti-nepotism rules prohibiting a husband and wife team from being paid by the same university. That meant that although wives could work at the universities that employed their husbands, they could not be paid for their work. Maria Goeppert Mayer so loved physics and science that she continued to work as a volunteer.

For the nine years that Mayer worked without pay at Johns Hopkins University, she taught courses in chemistry and focused her research on the problem of explaining the existence of a stable phase (a liquid) between a state of complete disorder (the gas) and a state of complete geometrical order (the crystal). She and her associates were able to show that there is a temperature at which every crystal breaks down (melts), resulting in a stable liquid phase.

In 1939 the Mayers shifted to Columbia University. Again, while her husband received a paid position as associate professor, Maria Mayer had no official appointment. She taught physics and chemistry and researched the chemical behavior of transuranic elements, all without pay. This work led to her appointment to a team conducting research for the Manhattan Project, the secret U.S. government project to develop an atomic bomb—still with no salary.

In 1945, the Mayers were offered positions at the University of Chicago (she was offered a position of *voluntary* associate professor). A year later, Maria was promoted to full professor (still unpaid) at Chicago and offered a half-time position as research physicist in the theoretical physics division of the new Argonne National Laboratory. She began working with Edward Teller on a theory of the origin of elements. During the course of this research she noticed that certain elements, such as lead and tin, were very stable; they did not break down or decay, thus turning into other elements. She found that those stable elements had very specific numbers of neutrons or protons in their nuclei. She called these "magic numbers." Any element with a magic number's worth of protons or neutrons was very stable.

Mayer wondered if perhaps the atom's nucleus might be arranged in shells, like the layers of an onion (thus earning her the nickname, "The Madonna of the Onion"). Atoms with a magic number's worth of protons or neutrons had an outer orbit or shell that was completely filled; this made it stable. No more protons or neutrons could be added without opening a new shell and using a lot of energy.

Then, in a flash of insight, Mayer realized that particles in an atom's nucleus are like a roomful of spinning waltzers. She was able to mathematically show that this model completely explained the observed behavior of the nucleus.

For her theory of spin-orbit forces in the shell model of atomic nuclei, Mayer won the Nobel Prize in 1963. Almost more important, the University of California San Diego offered Mayer her first paid position as professor of physics. For 30 years, she had worked without pay for the sheer love of physics and had to earn science's highest prize before being honored, respected, and paid for her work.

## Key Dates

1906    Born in Upper Silesia, Germany (now a part of Poland), on June 28

1910    Moved to Göttingen

1924    Entered the University of Göttingen

1930    Received Ph.D. in physics from University of Göttingen; moved to the United States; joined Johns Hopkins University as physics assistant, associate, and research associate

1939–1945    Worked as lecturer at Columbia University

1946–1959    Worked as volunteer professor at University of Chicago

1946–1960    Worked as senior physicist at Argonne National Laboratory

1956    Elected to the National Academy of Sciences

1960    Moved to California, received her first full-time, paid professorship at University of California, San Diego; suffered a debilitating stroke

1963    Won the Nobel Prize for Physics

1972    Died of a pulmonary embolism on February 20

## Advice

*To Maria Mayer science was an activity of passion. She would advise anyone considering a career in physics not to go into science for fame or money. Do it because you feel you must. She would also say that there is hardly a wrong course of study as long as it allows for full mastery of math and the course is rigorously pursued. There are many successful avenues into physics in general and nuclear physics in particular. Not all of them even begin in the physics department. Chemistry or electrical engineering could be launching points for a physics career.*

## References

Boorse, Henry, and Lloyd Motz. *The Atomic Scientist, A Biographical History.* New York: John Wiley, 1989.

Dash, Joan. *A Life of One's Own.* New York: Harper & Row, 1973. (One-third of book is devoted to Mayer.)

Haber, Louis. "Maria Goeppert Mayer," in *Women Pioneers of Science.* New York: Harcourt Brace Jovanovich, 1979: 68–76. (For young adults.)

McGrayne, Sharon Bertsch. *Nobel Prize Women in Science: Their Lives, Struggles, and Momentous Discoveries.* New York: Carol Publishing, A Birch Lane Press Book, 1993.

Shields, Barbara. *Winners: Women and the Nobel Prize.* Minneapolis, Minn.: Dillon Press, 1985. (For young adults; includes a chapter on Mayer.)

# Barbara McClintock

*"Jumpin' Genes"*　　　　Genetics Research

## Career Highlights

- Discovered that genes are not fixed on chromosomes, 1951
- Awarded Nobel Prize for Genetics, 1983
- Awarded Israel's Wolf Foundation Prize, 1981
- Was second woman ever elected to National Academy of Sciences, 1944
- Was first woman president of Genetics Society of America, 1944

## Important Contributions

Working alone in a small, wind-swept cornfield at Cold Springs Harbor, Long Island, Barbara McClintock proved every other genetics scientist in the world wrong.

Carefully studying wild corn, McClintock found that genes not only *can* jump, but regularly *do* jump from one position to another on a chromosome. She found that controlling genes direct these jumping messenger genes to shift position and turn on, or turn off, the genes next to them in their new location.

Genes, complex molecules that carry the encoded genetic information that makes us who we are, were discovered when early twentieth-century scientists began to unravel heredity, or how traits are passed to new generations. Then chromosomes, the long chain-like structures that carried genes, were identified. Every researcher in the world accepted that genes were strung on chromosomes in fixed positions like pearls on a necklace.

It took over 20 years for the rest of the scientific community to understand and accept Barbara McClintock's results. Once they did, her findings were heralded as one of the two greatest genetic discoveries of the century.

## Career Path

In September 1950, Barbara McClintock, a small, wiry woman (barely five feet tall and under 90 pounds), with worn and wrinkled face from long exposure to wind and sun, worked the rows of her small cornfield: weeding and checking for pests and disease that could ruin her experiments. Barbara held a doctorate in genetics and was a senior researcher at the Cold Springs Harbor Research Station.

This was her sixth year of planting and growing the corn plants and studying their genes as they passed from generation to generation.

This solitary woman's world was limited to that half-acre corn plot and a two-room apartment over the garage. She worked alone with scant funding even though she had established an excellent reputation in the field of genetics. In the early 1950s women could *teach* science. But scientific *research* was still considered a "man's field." McClintock was at tiny, out-of-the-way Cold Springs Harbor because "I was a woman and had few options. There was nowhere else for me to go."

How she spent her days depended on the season. In summer, most of her time was spent in the cornfield, nurturing the plants that would produce her data for the year. In the fall she harvested each ear by hand and began her lab analysis of the gene location and structure on the chromosomes of each ear. Her lab consisted of one powerful microscope, chemical lab trays, and stacks of journals to record her findings. This work would consume the long hours through winter.

In spring McClintock split her time between numerical analysis of the previous year's data and field planning and preparation for the next generation of corn plants.

Within a decade, McClintock's careful, methodical work had produced her revolutionary theory of "jumping genes." But her papers and lectures were ignored. She was dismissed as a relic, an "odd duck" who didn't fit in with modern scientific thought.

Barbara grew up feeling that she never fit in. She was born in Hartford, Connecticut, and was raised as the son her father never had. As a child she preferred boxing gloves to dolls. She became a self-proclaimed loner and a "thinker." Even as a child Barbara was drawn to science. She enrolled in

Cornell College because women were allowed to take science classes and because Cornell charged no tuition.

As a junior she took the only course offered in genetics, just because it was a science course. She later said that one course brought her whole life into focus and gave her purpose. In 1983 she described that course as the beginning point of her life. At 20, she had found her field.

McClintock began her career as a teacher at Cornell University. She had done her graduate work in botany because that was the only science department that admitted female graduate students.

Her male colleagues were paid to both teach and conduct research. But the university said research was inappropriate for a woman, so McClintock conducted her own research with no allotted time, budget, or paid assistants. Her genetic research at Cornell focused on studying the genes and chromosomes of wild corn, the colorful ears often used to decorate Thanksgiving tables. She planted and tended her first cornfield there.

From this research, McClintock produced ten major papers (far more than any of her male counterparts). Each was critically acclaimed by the scientific community. Only 32 years old, she was recognized as a leader in the field of genetics. Still, Cornell refused to offer her a permanent position because she was "only a female."

From 1931 to 1936, during the depths of the Great Depression, when the entire country was in bad economic shape, McClintock drifted to wherever she could find even part-time work in her field. In each of these temporary jobs, she made significant genetic discoveries. She unraveled the chromosome structure of corn and she discovered circular or "ring" chromosomes resulting from X-ray mutation.

In 1936 she landed a teaching job at the University of Missouri. She was never a great teacher. In the same year that she published a paper heralded as the cornerstone of experimental genetics (1941), she was forced to resign from the university because of the poor reviews of her classroom presentations.

With no other employment prospects, McClintock accepted the position at little-known Cold Springs Harbor Research Station on Long Island. It was there that she revolutionized the world of genetics research.

Twenty-five years after her discoveries were first announced in 1952, the world caught up to Barbara McClintock and realized what she had discovered. Fame, notoriety, awards, and a stream of photographers followed. In 1983 she was called the greatest genetics field researcher of the century and was awarded the Nobel Prize.

McClintock continued to live in her two-room apartment and to quietly study in her cornfield until forced to retire at the age of 85. Because she was a woman, she never received the same level of support, pay, or prestige as the top 100 male geneticists worldwide. Still, she steadfastly continued the work she loved.

For over 35 years, Barbara McClintock combined careful field research, antiquated equipment, and incredible personal tenacity to make one of the greatest genetic discoveries of the twentieth century. Her patience, persistence, careful documentation, and painstaking analysis are the ideal model for any field researcher to follow.

## Key Dates

| | |
|---|---|
| 1902 | Born in Hartford, Connecticut, on August 20 |
| 1923 | Graduated with B.S. from Cornell College |
| 1927 | Received Ph.D. in genetics from Cornell |
| 1927 | Hired to teach at Cornell as first female science teacher |
| 1927–1931 | Published ten major papers in national journals |
| 1931–1935 | Worked at various part-time positions whenever she could find them |
| 1936–1940 | Worked as assistant professor at University of Missouri at Columbia |
| 1941–1987 | Hired by Carnegie Institute of Washington for their Cold Springs Harbor facility |
| 1951 | Completed research to prove that genes jump and that they are directed by a few "director" genes |
| 1979–1981 | Finally received recognition and awards for her work |
| 1983 | Awarded Nobel Prize for Genetics |
| 1987 | Retired from Cold Springs Harbor |
| 1992 | Died on September 2 |

## Advice

Barbara McClintock's general advice to anyone considering a science career was always to immerse yourself in a field that makes you want to get up early each morning and stick with it. Mastery comes from long years of observation and effort. Don't expect to understand a worthwhile field too quickly.

Rather than list specific courses, McClintock advised genetics students to develop experimental abilities early. Seek research assistant jobs in labs, volunteer on experimental projects, and study under top experimenters. Genetics is a laboratory, or experimental, field. Little progress is possible without good experimental technique. Be curious, observant, persistent, and exacting. All else will fall into place on its own.

## References

Dash, Joan. *The Triumph of Discovery.* New York: Simon & Schuster, 1991.

Keller, Evelyn. *A Feeling for the Organism: The Life and Work of Barbara McClintock.* San Francisco: W. H. Freeman, 1983.

Maranto, Gina. "At Long Last—A Nobel for a Loner," *Discover* (December 1983): 26.

McClintock, Barbara. "Induction of Instability of Selected Loci in Maize," *Genetics* 38 (1953): 579–599.

Opfell, Olga. *The Lady Laureates: Women Who Have Won the Nobel Prize.* Metuchen, N. J.: Scarecrow Press, 1988.

Shields, Barbara. *Winners: Women and the Nobel Prize.* Minneapolis, Minn.: Dillon Press, 1985.

# Margaret Mead

*"Education for Choice"*      Anthropology

## Career Highlights

- Was world's leading authority on fast-disappearing primitive tribes
- Was first anthropologist to study child rearing and women in cross-cultural perspective
- Authored and edited 50 books and numerous articles
- Was president of World Federation for Mental Health, 1956–1957
- Was president of the American Anthropological Association, 1960

## Important Contributions

Anthropologist Margaret Mead is generally acknowledged as having made anthropology understandable to the American people through her interesting and clearly written books. Her writings did more than popularize social anthropology, however: they also made her a national hero.

Mead drew comparisons between so-called primitive peoples and contemporary America, forcing "civilized" society to look at the roots of human behavior. These research projects into native Pacific and Western cultures produced landmark studies in social anthropology and widened the range of anthropological studies to include sociology, psychology, and economics. In addition, Mead redefined the methodology for field research in anthropology and documented several native cultures about to be swallowed up by expanding twentieth-century technology.

## Career Path

As its engine slowed to idle, the small boat drifted through a small bay toward the one rickety pier on Ta'u, an 11-mile-long speck in the Samoan chain of islands. Twenty-four-year-old Margaret Mead fidgeted nervously on the deck as the island closed in around her—lush, green, thick, steamy, and *very* far from everything she had ever known. As soon as she stepped off this Navy shuttle, she would be isolated, cut off from the entire civilized world for eight long months. There would be only Margaret and the small native population she had come to document and study.

The lone woman suddenly felt terribly unprepared. She hadn't finished graduate school; she knew only a few words of the local language. There was no guide for how to conduct prolonged anthropological field studies or how to survive in the jungle when you have lived your whole life in the city. With a very heavy heart, Margaret Mead stepped onto the pier with one suitcase, a typewriter, and two boxes of paper, ribbon, and notebooks. This marked the beginning of modern anthropology.

Most of Margaret's early education was conducted at home by her paternal grandmother, who was probably the most influential person in her life. Her love of writing made her decide to become an English major when she first enrolled in college at DePauw University. But after a year, her love of people influenced her to change to psychology, and she transferred to Barnard College.

In her senior year, Margaret took an anthropology course taught by Franz Boas, which she later claimed was the single most influential event in her life: That class made her decide that she would become an anthropologist. Anthropology allowed her to bring together two of her passions: science and human behavior. And later, by writing about her studies, she brought her third passion—English—into her work as well. Upon graduation, she entered the anthropology department of Columbia University.

Franz Boas *was* the anthropology department at Columbia. He taught every class and had only one assistant, Ruth Benedict. Nevertheless, it was an exciting time to be studying anthropology. The horrors of World War I were still fresh in people's minds, and anthropologists were asking themselves how their knowledge of the nature of humankind might be used to prevent a recurrence of those horrible events. The department was charged with intellectual excitement as whole new perspectives for anthropology opened up.

For Mead's thesis, she wanted to study adolescent females in Samoa. Boas refused to approve the project, saying it was impossible to control or complete such a study. The university said it was too dangerous. Parents and friends said she was unprepared for such a venture. Colleagues advised her to pick a project in America, which would allow her to keep in touch for help should she need it.

Mead bravely insisted and became one of the first women to conduct anthropological field research—and also one of the first anthropologists of her generation to work outside the Americas. Anthropology was her passion now, and she would not be kept from it.

The task Mead set herself was to study the transition of Samoan girls into adulthood. Specifically, she wanted to determine whether problems related to adolescence (such as disruptive behavior) were culturally or biologically determined.

In Samoa, Mead lived in a Samoan household as "one of the girls." She learned their language (one of seven she would eventually master). She discovered that Samoan girls do not experience the tension and angst that American and European girls suffer on entering adulthood, and she recorded the types of social arrangements that made this transition easier for the Samoans. She concluded that cultural conditioning and environment are more vital than biological factors.

Mead described her findings in her most popular book, *Coming of Age in Samoa*. When the book was finished, however, her publisher worried that the book fell into no conventional category. He asked for a chapter on what the work's significance would be to America, and so Mead wrote the final chapter, "Education for Choice," which was a basic theme for much of her lifework. She focused on how the Samoan education differs from our own in the hopes that we would turn a "vividly self-conscious and self-critical" eye on our own system of education. The book enjoyed great popular success and established her reputation as an expert on primitive cultures.

Over the course of her career, Mead conducted 24 major expedition field trips among six South Pacific peoples. She reported the results of her studies in scholarly journals. In addition, she interpreted the results for general audiences. She had a unique ability to write books of scholarly merit that were also popular best sellers.

Mead also used her studies to argue for "responsible social intervention." She believed that an appreciation of other ways of life could help us to reconsider our own lives and the education we give our children. In her autobiography, she noted that "I have spent most of my life studying the lives of other peoples, faraway peoples, so that Americans might better understand themselves."

## Key Dates

1901    Born in Philadelphia, Pennsylvania, on December 16
1919    Entered DePauw University in Indiana as an English major

| | |
|---|---|
| 1920 | Transferred to Barnard College in New York City |
| 1923 | Received B.A. in psychology from Barnard College |
| 1924 | Received M.A. in psychology from Columbia |
| 1925–1926 | Obtained a National Research Council fellowship and embarked on a field trip to the Samoan Islands |
| 1926–1942 | Worked as assistant curator of ethnology at New York's American Museum of Natural History |
| 1928 | Published *Coming of Age in Samoa* |
| 1928–1929 | Made field trip to the Admiralty Islands in the West Pacific |
| 1929 | Received Ph.D. in anthropology from Columbia |
| 1930 | Published *Growing Up in New Guinea* |
| 1935 | Published *Sex and Temperament in Three Primitive Societies* |
| 1936–1939 | Did research in New Guinea and Bali |
| 1942–1964 | Promoted to associate curator of New York's American Museum of Natural History |
| 1949 | Published the widely acclaimed *Male and Female: A Study of the Sexes in a Changing World* |
| 1954 | Became adjunct professor of anthropology at Columbia |
| 1964 | Promoted to curator of New York's American Museum of Natural History |
| 1968 | Named chair of Fordham University's social science division |
| 1970 | Published *Culture and Commitment* |
| 1978 | Died November 15 of pancreatic cancer |

## Advice

*If you are considering a career in anthropology, Margaret Mead would advise you to be thorough and rigorous in your schooling and very flexible in your work. Anthropology involves "not only scientific research but the practice of rugged expedition, tropical medicine, care of children, organization and maintenance of camps in the bush, cultivation of rapport with primitive peoples, and many varieties of writing necessary to record the results."*

*Study culture, language, history, communication, effective writing, ecology, and social organization in school, remembering that there will be no time to dash back for a weekend refresher class once you are in the field. Once in the field, however, don't expect anything to go as planned. Learn how to improvise, substitute, and make do. Your success will depend on it.*

## References

Cassidy, Robert. *Margaret Mead: A Voice for the Century.* New York: Universe Books, 1982.

Freeman, Derek. *Margaret Mead and Samoa: The Making and Unmaking of an Anthropological Myth.* Cambridge, Mass.: Harvard University Press, 1983. (Challenges Mead's accomplishments and charges that she introduced her own biases into her research.)

Howard, Jane. *Margaret Mead: A Life.* New York: Simon & Schuster, 1984. (The definitive biography of Margaret Mead.)

Mark, Joan T. *Margaret Mead.* Oxford Portraits in Science. Oxford: Oxford University Press, 1998. (Inspiring biography told with entertaining tales.)

Mead, Margaret. *Anthropologist at Work.* New York: Avon Books, 1980. (Reprint.) (Written for high school students as vocational guidance.)

———. *Blackberry Winter: My Earlier Years.* New York: William Morrow, 1995. (Reprint.) (Autobiography.)

———. *Coming of Age in Samoa: A Psychological Study of Primitive Youth for Western Civilization.* New York: William Morrow, 1988. (Reprint.)

# Lise Meitner

*"The Discovery of the Century"*　　　　Nuclear Physics

## Career Highlights

Lawrence Berkeley National Laboratory

- Discovered the explanation for splitting of the atomic nucleus; for this experiment, which she initiated and explained, her partner, Otto Hahn, received a Nobel Prize
- Awarded the Planck Medal (shared with Otto Hahn) by the German Physical Society, 1949
- Discovered thorium C (1908) and protactinium (1917) with Otto Hahn
- Had an element (109, meitnerium) named after her, 1992

## Important Contributions

Sometimes it's easy to forget just how far we've come. Not too long ago, women weren't allowed to own property, vote, or even go to high school. Lise Meitner, a brilliant, talented physicist, was one of those women. Despite the extraordinary obstacles facing her, Meitner managed to pursue her passionate study of physics and, in doing so, explained one of the greatest scientific puzzles of this century: nuclear fission. She has been called "the most significant woman scientist of this century."

# Career Path

On a gray, wintry afternoon in 1911 a man and a woman dashed out the door of a basement lab into the bracing Berlin cold. Both were in their thirties and formally dressed, he in tall, stiff collar and tie, she in floor-length dress with high, lace neck. Both pumped up the stone steps to ground level and sprinted across the Kaiser Wilhelm campus toward the Physics Institute over half a mile away. In her bare hands Lise Meitner cradled a precious sample of their laboratory work. Otto Hahn ran interference, shouting for everyone to get out of their way.

The tiny sample was a radioactive isotope of thorium. As often happened after these runs, Meitner's hands would be covered with blisters, burns, and open sores that would take weeks to heal. They would have preferred a lab in the Physics Institute for their work on radioactive isotopes, but Meitner was a woman and a poorly equipped basement lab at the edge of campus was the only place a woman was allowed. In typical fashion, it never occurred to her either to complain or to allow such a formidable roadblock to slow her down.

Lise Meitner, raised in Vienna, Austria, had always been captivated by the marvelous mysteries nature held and by a passion to learn about them. Why did a puddle of water mixed with oil have such beautiful, iridescent colors? Why did sunlight through a crystal create tiny rainbows on the wall? If she worked hard enough, could she understand nature's laws?

However, education for girls in Vienna ended at age 14 and concentrated on how to run a household, raise children, and converse charmingly with a husband. After school ended it was time to think about getting married. But Lise wanted to study physics, even though her dream of becoming a physicist seemed totally unrealistic at the time. There weren't even jobs for male physicists, certainly none for a female physicist.

Lise's father, seeing no future for her in physics, insisted that she spend three years earning a certificate to teach French in girls' finishing schools. Only then would he hire a tutor to prepare her for university entrance examinations. She did, and in two years of tutoring, she completed eight years of school work (including eight years of Latin and six years of Greek). She was one of four women who passed the entrance examinations, and in 1901 she entered the University of Vienna. She received her doctoral degree in 1905, only the fifteenth woman to earn a doctorate from that university since its founding in 1365 and the first to receive one in physics.

Meitner's determination to study physics so impressed her father that he supported her decision (both financially and emotionally) to move to Berlin in 1907 and continue her studies. She worked, studied, and experimented in the only part of Berlin's Chemistry Institute in which she was allowed: the basement laboratory. No women, except cleaning women, were allowed upstairs with the men. Desperate to hear chemistry lectures, she sometimes sneaked upstairs and hid under the seats to listen. There was not even a restroom for her use on campus—she had to use facilities in a restaurant up the street.

In her basement laboratory, Meitner worked and collaborated with her friend and science partner Otto Hahn. They kept their working relationship very formal and proper. For years, they did not call one another by their first names and never socialized outside the laboratory, not even to eat lunch together.

While Hahn discovered, studied, and chemically purified radioactive elements, Meitner studied and measured the radiation they gave off. They often worked with their bare hands to complete their assessments before their radioactive materials disintegrated, getting finger burns that took weeks to heal. Their equipment was crude and dangerous by today's standards, and the work was tedious. To pass the boring hours, they sang together—German folk songs and Meitner's favorite, Brahms's *lieder*.

Because their basement laboratory was so poorly equipped, the pair frequently needed to complete experiments in the Physics Institute, a kilometer away. Indeed, Meitner recalled them "racing out of the Chemistry Institute like bullets from a gun" to bring their specimens to the Physics Institute to be examined before the radioactive materials disintegrated.

Meitner was the "intellectual leader of the team" (although Hahn received more recognition and advancement). It was she who discovered that radioactive thorium decayed into a substance she called "thorium D." And it was she who would later explain their greatest experiment: nuclear fission.

It was also Meitner who was studying the radioactive decay of actinium, radium, and thorium, and she persuaded Hahn to join her. She was studying the possibility of creating artificial elements with an atomic number greater than 92 (transuranic elements) by bombarding uranium with neutrons. But the results of the experiments didn't make sense. Instead of creating elements with greater atomic numbers, the bombardments merely created a bewildering array of subatomic particles.

Hahn suspected that their uranium sample might be converting into radium, with atomic number 88, and that the rest of the uranium's protons and neutrons were being emitted as alpha and beta particles. To test this theory, the partners devised an experiment using non-radioactive barium to separate out and measure radioactive radium. But before they could complete the experiment, Meitner, who was Jewish, was forced to flee Germany in 1938, under threat of Nazi persecution. World War II was upon them.

Although Hahn was in Germany and she was in Sweden, Meitner continued to work with him via letters. Hahn became her "hands" in that he continued with the experiments and would send the results to her for interpretation.

On December 19, 1938, Hahn wrote to Meitner about an experiment that he could not figure out: "Our 'radium isotope' behaves like barium. . . . Perhaps you can propose some fantastic explanation. We know ourselves that it can't decay into barium. . . . Write as soon as you can."

Contemplating this puzzle, Meitner went for a walk in the snow on January 1, 1939, while her nephew Otto Frisch skied along beside her on cross-country skis. As they went along, Meitner began explaining to Frisch about the mysterious experiment. Why hadn't Hahn found radium? All he had found was radioactive barium, an element with an atomic number roughly half that of uranium. What could it mean?

Suddenly, it all fell together. The uranium nucleus had split, forming two light elements: barium with 56 protons and krypton gas with 55 protons. Sitting down on a fallen tree with snow drifts all around them, Meitner and Frisch calculated that at the time the nucleus split, matter in the nucleus was transformed into an enormous amount of energy. Meitner had discovered nuclear fission.

Overnight, Meitner became famous. But despite her undisputed contribution, it was Otto Hahn who won the Nobel Prize for the discovery of nuclear fission.

Today this would not happen. Women in science have come a long way, and we have women like Lise Meitner to thank for it.

## Key Dates

| | |
|---|---|
| 1878 | Born in Vienna, Austria, on November 7, third of eight children |
| 1901 | Entered the University of Vienna |
| 1905 | Received her doctoral degree |
| 1926 | Became Germany's first woman full physics professor |
| 1938 | Fled Germany for Sweden, escaping Nazi persecution |
| 1938 | Realized that Otto Hahn had split atomic nucleus |
| 1939 | Published paper on nuclear fission; World War II began |
| 1944 | Otto Hahn received Nobel Prize for Chemistry for the discovery of nuclear fission |
| 1947 | Officially retired but continued research in Sweden |

1960    Stopped work and moved to England

1968    Died in Cambridge on October 27

## Advice

*Lise Meitner always felt that she suffered because she was barred from many of the lectures, classes, and educational opportunities she wanted. She would advise anyone considering a career in nuclear physics to study as extensively as possible to understand the natural world around you with emphasis in four academic areas: math, chemistry, physics, and nuclear physics. Additionally, Meitner would recommend that you cultivate curiosity. You must have a burning curiosity about the laws of nature, and a willingness to work very hard to understand those laws.*

## References

Boorse, Henry, and Lloyd Motz. *The Atomic Scientist, A Biographical History.* New York: John Wiley, 1989.

Grinstein, Louise S., Rose K. Rose, and Miriam H. Rafailovich. *Women in Chemistry and Physics: A Biobibliographic Sourcebook.* Westport, Conn.: Greenwood, 1993.

Kass-Simon, G., and Patricia Farnes, eds. *Women of Science: Righting the Record.* Bloomington: Indiana University Press, 1990.

McGrayne, Sharon Bertsch. *Nobel Prize Women in Science: Their Lives, Struggles, and Momentous Discoveries.* New York: Carol Publishing, A Birch Lane Press Book, 1993.

Sime, Ruth Lewis. *Lise Meitner: A Life in Physics.* Berkeley: University of California Press, 1996.

Stille, Darlene R. *Extraordinary Women Scientists.* Chicago: Children's Press, 1995.

Yount, Lisa. *Twentieth-Century Women Scientists.* New York: Facts on File, 1996.

# Albert Michelson

*"Faster Than a Speeding Light Beam"*

Physics

## Career Highlights

- Was first to accurately measure the speed of light
- Awarded Nobel Prize for Physics, 1907 (first American to win the prize)
- Awarded the Franklin Medal by the Franklin Institute, 1923
- Elected president of the National Academy of Sciences, 1916
- Awarded 11 honorary doctorates, although he only earned a bachelor's degree himself

Archives of the National Academy of Sciences

## Important Contributions

Albert Michelson is best known for making the first accurate measurements of the speed of light, a project that consumed his energy and resources for 50 years. The problems of measuring a speed faster than any clock's or other machine's ability to measure were enormous. There was no equipment suitable for his purpose. But Michelson was a master of instrumentation, a genius at designing precision equipment.

As he poured his energy into the problem of how to make such a measurement, Michelson invented half a dozen new designs for precision devices. One of them was called an interferometer. He used this elaborate piece of gear, first alone, and then with his long-time associate Edward

Morley, not only to measure the speed of light, but also to disprove the prevailing theory about the nature of light and the universe. The two men's work set the stage for Einstein's special theory of relativity and earned Albert Michelson the first Nobel Prize to be given to an American physicist.

## Career Path

A skinny, scruffy boy with baggy pants cinched tight by a rope belt stood in the dusty street of a bustling California gold rush town in 1856. Hastily thrown-up shacks sprawled out from the one commercial street lined with businesses and bars. The five-year-old boy helped his mother lay out a display of dry goods from their family wagon and then helped his father bark up a sizable crowd of customers, shouting about the amazing values of each of their products. It was a scene the family repeated almost daily as they wandered the gold rush foothills, scratching out a living from their dry goods cart. Albert Michelson, that young hawker, didn't seem a likely candidate to win America's first Nobel Prize for Physics.

Albert's family immigrated to America from a small town along the German-Polish border when he was two years old. The boy traveled California's gold rush country from town to town and camp to camp with his parents, helping to sell dry goods, until he was 11 years old. He loaded and unloaded the family supply cart and did odd chores in the gold-mining camps. Then he was sent to live with relatives in San Francisco to get his first taste of schooling. He wound up boarding with the principal of Boy's High School, who sparked Albert's interest in science.

This principal also helped Albert fix his mind on wanting to attend the U.S. Naval Academy at Annapolis, Maryland. With a supporting letter from his congressman, Albert appealed directly to President Grant, even though all the positions in that year's class had already been filled. The president and school administrators were sufficiently impressed with his persistence that they created an extra slot in the class just for him.

Cadet Albert Michelson graduated in 1873, served on a naval ship as a midshipman for two years, and was assigned back to the Academy as an instructor in physics and chemistry. While teaching physics in 1878, Michelson first became interested in the speed of light. He had demonstrated his single-mindedness and tenacity in his dogged pursuit of an appointment to the Naval Academy. Now he turned that same relentless energy toward the task of finding out the speed of light. He was still struggling to refine and improve his measurements when he died 50 years later.

Needing time to work on attempting to measure this immense speed, Michelson took a leave of absence from the academy. There were no devices at the time capable of detecting or registering so great a speed. All existing measurements of the speed of light were made by indirect inference. Although he was able to improve on existing estimates in this first attempt, he chiefly recorded the need for improved measuring equipment.

Michelson traveled to Europe to study optics for two years. Upon his return he resigned from the Navy to develop a piece of equipment he had conceived of in Europe. He called it an interferometer. The device split a beam of light, sending half in one direction and the other half in a perpendicular direction. At some distance away mirrors reflected both beams back to the origin point, where they were recombined. If the beams traveled either different distances, or at different speeds, the waves would return out of phase with each other and Michelson would detect interference patterns.

Famed Scottish physicist James Maxwell had theorized that light traveled as an electromagnetic wave. A wave needs some physical medium to travel through. So Maxwell claimed that all space must be filled with an invisible ether through which light traveled. Michelson planned to use his interferometer and Maxwell's ether to establish an exact speed of light. If light traveled through the ether at a fixed speed and the Earth also traveled through the ether, then light traveling in the direction of the Earth's motion should seem to travel at a different speed to an observer on Earth than light traveling perpendicular to the Earth's motion, just as the sound of a train whistle seems to change depending on whether the train is moving toward the observer or away.

Michelson set up his interferometer and sent his two beams out over a mile to fixed mirrors. He would have liked to move the mirrors farther back, but existing light production and focusing equipment could not produce a strong enough beam. Light traveling in the direction of the Earth's motion should have appeared on Earth to travel slower and thus arrive behind and out of phase with the other beam.

Although Michelson expected to see interference patterns and, from them, to calculate a more accurate speed for light, he found no interference. Confused, he repeated the experiment. Again the two beams returned in phase. The speed of light was the same no matter which direction it traveled. This was not the answer he expected to find.

With great surprise, Michelson realized that he had disproved Maxwell's theory of light propagation. There was no ether. He created a tumultuous uproar with his announcement, but the undeniable precision of his equipment eventually convinced the world. Still, he wasn't satisfied. Even though he had measured the speed of light at 186,320 miles per second (far more accurate than any previous measurement), he could see limitations in the equipment and shortcomings in his methodology.

Ignoring his sudden fame, Michelson took a job teaching at Case University, where he could design better hardware. There he met Edward Morley, who would become his long-time research partner. There he also met famed gyroscope manufacturer Elmer Sperry. Sperry would take on the job of building the improved lights and precision machines needed to make the measurements more accurate.

Albert Michelson's work represents a turning point in American physics. Michelson instilled a new sense of precision into the process of scientific measurement and experimentation. Science became dependent upon machines capable of seeing and sensing beyond the range of human senses. Michelson set the standard for the development and accuracy of such specialty instruments for scientific measurement.

## Key Dates

| | |
|---|---|
| 1852 | Born in Strelno, Germany, on December 19 |
| 1873 | Graduated from the U.S. Naval Academy |
| 1873–1975 | Served as midshipman |
| 1875–1979 | Appointed instructor of physics and chemistry at the Naval Academy |
| 1880–1882 | Studied optics in Europe |
| 1882–1889 | Appointed physics professor at Case Western School of Applied Science |
| 1889–1893 | Appointed professor of physics at Clark University |
| 1893–1931 | Appointed head of physics department of new University of Chicago |
| 1907 | Won Nobel Prize for Physics |
| 1928 | Made his last and best measurement of the speed of light at Mount Wilson, California |
| 1931 | Died on May 9 |

## Advice

*Albert Michelson believed in a broad, general education at the undergraduate level. Learn literature, history, and how to write. Learn math, physics, chemistry, and engineering. Don't try to specialize until graduate school. But always remember that science requires dedication, tenacity, and exactness. Science is not a field of approximation. When you find your specialty, apply yourself relentlessly in the pursuit of precision, which is the key to science. Know the instruments and apparatus of your field intimately. Know their limits and faults as well as their abilities.*

## References

Daintith, John, et al., eds. *Biographical Encyclopedia of Scientists*. 2d ed. Vol. 1. Philadelphia, Pa.: Institute of Physics Publishing, 1994. (Summary entry on Michelson's work.)

Jaffe, Bernard. *Michelson and the Speed of Light*. New York: Greenwood Press, 1979.

Garraty, John, ed. *Encyclodedia of American Biography*. New York: Harper & Row, 1984. (Detailed summary of Michelson's work.)

Goldberg, Stanley. *The Michelson Era in American Science: 1870–1930*. A I P Conference Proceedings, 179. Edited by Roger H. Stuewer. Philadelphia, Pa.: American Institute of Physics, 1988.

Livingston, Dorothy. *The Master of Light: A Biography of Albert Michelson*. Los Angeles, Calif.: University of California Press, 1979. (Good description of both Michelson's work and the growth of American physics from 1880 to 1930.)

Wasson, Tyler, ed. *Nobel Prize Winners*. New York: H. W. Wilson, 1987. (Excellent summary of Michelson's work.)

# Cynthia Moss

*"The Elephant Bug"*　　　Wildlife Biology/
Journalism

Photo by Martyn Colbeck, African Wildlife Foundation

## Career Highlights

- Awarded the American Book Award for science paperback, 1982
- Was driving force behind the 1990 international moratorium on ivory
- Provided the first in-depth, natural habitat study of the African elephant
- Awarded African Wildlife Leadership Foundation grant, 1975
- Elected to membership in the East African Natural History Society

## Important Contributions

Cynthia Moss studied elephants in the wild for almost 30 years. Documenting the life, behavior, and social structure of any species requires years of dedicated, in-depth, on-site, meticulous, and systematic observation. She not only performed this daunting task with grace and aplomb, she also helped redefine the protocol and standard methodology for conducting long-term field studies.

Moss also acted as an advocate for the African elephants. She successfully lobbied for national and international laws protecting elephants and for a moratorium on the commercial trade in ivory. A philosophy major and freelance writer, Cynthia Moss was bitten by the Africa and elephant bugs, and turned herself into a first-class field biologist. Her work has been described as an "irreplaceable" and "invaluable" contribution to our understanding of elephants and elephant society.

## Career Path

Two towering female elephants shuffled leisurely out of the tall brush toward her. Their lumbering bodies swayed rhythmically with each step. All that separated these mammoths from Cynthia Moss was a small pool of brown mud, the remnants of a rainy season watering hole.

Although twenty feet still separated her from these great beasts, Moss held out her hand as if to touch one. One of the elephants snorted and extended its dust-covered trunk toward her. This electric moment was Moss's first encounter with a wild elephant and instantly rewrote who she thought she was and what she wanted to be.

Cynthia Moss grew up with no particular affinity for or passionate feeling about animals and wildlife. She didn't surround herself with pets. She never dreamed of studying wild game or traipsing across Africa.

However, Cynthia was an avid horsewoman. She loved to ride, especially through wooded, natural areas near her home, and she mourned their gradual loss as they were steadily replaced by encroaching commercial and residential development. "I did love wilderness areas," she recalled later, "and I hated to see it disappear. At the time I just hated seeing houses and strip malls replace the paths I loved to ride along."

Cynthia enrolled in Smith College in western Massachusetts for a philosophy degree even though she had no plans to be a philosopher. Rather, philosophy seemed like a good catch-all title for a general, liberal arts curriculum. Her plan was to follow her father into the world of writing and editing.

During college Moss showed no interest in science or science courses. However, she did prefer the more analytical and rigorous classes to more qualitative classes. Years later she realized that, "I obviously had a scientific mind and didn't know it."

After graduating in 1962, Moss held a series of small, part-time jobs in the newspaper and magazine publishing world until 1964, when she was offered a position on the staff of *Newsweek* as a researcher and reporter in the religion and theater department. It was a plum position for a young college graduate still struggling to establish herself.

In 1966 Moss received a series of "wonderful, beautiful letters" from a college friend who was touring Africa. The graphic descriptions rekindled her longing for wild and open spaces. She itched to see the world's last wilderness places before they disappeared.

In 1967, Moss arranged a leave of absence from *Newsweek* to tour Africa. She quickly realized that what had been planned as a several-month trip would have to become much more. She recalled that "within a week of getting there, I had this overwhelming sense that I had come home . . . that this was where I belonged."

Moss met her first elephant in Lake Manyara National Park, where *Newsweek* had arranged for her to interview British zoologist Iain Douglas-Hamilton, who was conducting a pioneering ecology study. At a very deep level, she "became completely hooked on elephants." She recalled later that she "had never felt that kind of passionate attachment and commitment before in my life."

When Douglas-Hamilton offered her a research assistant position at his camp, the young reporter jumped at the opportunity without thinking of what effect this decision would have on her budding career as a magazine writer. Moss wrote in her journal that "elephants are such impressive, remarkable, and complex creatures that I instantly wanted to devote my life to studying them." The field biologist lurking under the surface burst out with passionate abandon. "I felt that every talent I had could be poured into this one study."

Moss's problem was that she had no background or credentials for biological field work. Still, she bravely decided to settle permanently in East Africa and moved full-time into Douglas-Hamilton's camp for the next eight months, and part-time for the next two years. She made ends meet by assisting on other projects wherever she could: as a veterinary researcher in Nairobi; as a research assistant in a study of eland, wildebeest, and hartebeest; and as an assistant to a University of Nairobi professor studying elephant ecology in Tsavo National Park.

The rug was pulled out from under Moss's delicate coalition of jobs when, in late 1970, Douglas-Hamilton completed his study and left Africa. She still lacked the credentials to obtain her own funding. For the next two years she eked out a living submitting freelance pieces on African wildlife to *Time* and *Life* and by taking over editorship of a small newsletter, *Wildlife News*.

In late 1972 Moss's big break arrived in the personage of David Western, a zoologist based in Kenya who had funding from the New York Zoological Society to set up a long-term study of the elephants in Amboseli National Park, a 150-square-mile park in southern Kenya. He wondered if she would be interested in running the study with another researcher, Harvey Croze.

Moss and Croze spent over a year compiling a photographic "recognition file," or identity record, of all the Amboseli elephants and cataloging the herd's social structure. Croze departed and Moss continued the study on her own with American Wildlife Federation funding. This study was not only the first intensive study of elephants in the wild, but it is now the longest continually running field study of a single species in the world.

Moss documented social relations, family behaviors, and social structure and interaction. She recorded the elephants' interaction with other species and with the Amboseli ecosystem. She cataloged elephant emotional responses and expressions and a wide range of personality traits. She followed them from birth to death, from mating to child-rearing. She wrote about how they greet, how they play, how they threaten, and how they protect. She mapped their migrations and their social hierarchy.

In over a quarter-century of daily observation, Cynthia Moss has led science to truly understand the elephant, its needs, and its role in the African ecosystem. Along the way, she has become one of a handful of modern field researchers who have redefined the protocols and procedures for conducting field studies and has set a new standard for in-depth field studies. She has not only taught us to understand and care for the magnificent elephant, but also a better way to learn.

## Key Dates

| | |
|---|---|
| 1940 | Born in Ossining, New York, on July 24 |
| 1962 | Received B.A. in philosophy from Smith College, Massachusetts |
| 1964–1968 | Worked as reporter and researcher for *Newsweek* Magazine |

1968 Worked as research assistant studying elephant behavior in Tanzania

1969 Worked as research assistant to veterinary researchers in Kenya

1970 Worked as research assistant to environmental physiologist in Kenya

1971–
1972 Worked as freelance nature writer

1972–
1975 Worked as research assistant in Amboseli on study of elephants

1975–
present Assumed directorship of Amboseli study under new AWF funding

1979–
present Is American Wildlife Federation publication editor

## Advice

*Cynthia Moss would advise anyone planning a scientific career to begin with a broad, liberal arts undergraduate program. Don't worry about mastering a single field, or even picking a specific field. Rather, concentrate on learning how to think and learn effectively and critically. Liberal arts programs teach that skill better than quantitatively oriented, technical courses. You can master the technical content of your chosen specialty field on your own or in graduate school. Also learn how to effectively communicate in writing. You will always need to be able to write persuasively about what you have done and, for funding, about what you want to do.*

## References

Dear, Pamela, ed. *Contemporary Authors.* Vol 12. Detroit: Gale Research, 1995. (Excellent biographical summary and summary of Moss's writings.)

DiSilvestro, Roger. *The African Elephant: Twilight of Eden.* New York: John Wiley, 1991. (Good review of elephant ecology.)

Moritz, Charles, ed. *Current Biography Yearbook, 1993.* New York: H. W. Wilson, 1994. (Good review of Moss's work.)

Moss, Cynthia. *Elephant Memories.* New York: Houghton Mifflin, 1988.

———. *Portraits in the Wild: Behavioral Studies of East African Elephants.* New York: Houghton Mifflin, 1975.

Sukumar, Rama. *Elephant Days and Nights.* New York: Oxford University Press, 1994. (Similar on-sight study of Indian elephants.)

# John Muir

## "Father of Our National Parks"

## Geology, Botany, and Ecology

National Park Service

## Career Highlights

- Was foremost leader of the conservation movement
- Authored over 500 published articles, essays, and books
- Discovered living glaciers in Yosemite
- Received honorary degrees from California, Harvard, Wisconsin, and Yale
- Was member of American Association for the Advancement of Science
- Founded the Sierra Club

## Important Contributions

It is to John Muir, more than anyone else, that we are indebted for the preservation of many of America's most beautiful natural wonders. Muir awoke the public's interest in wilderness values through his political activism and his many books, articles, and essays. He spoke for nature, when it could not speak for itself. He escaped to the mountaintops for solitude and rejuvenation, but when he descended, it was to lead a crusade for the protection of the environment.

Yet while nearly everyone has heard of John Muir the naturalist, not everyone knows that he also made contributions to botany and geology. Muir challenged the conventional theories of glacier formation, and his theories of glaciation in Yosemite and the geological record left in the formation of the Sierra landscape established him as an expert and placed him in an elite circle of prominent scientists of his day.

## Career Path

John Muir was born in 1838 in Scotland, the third of eight children, to Daniel Muir, a grain merchant, and Anne Muir. When John was 11 years old, the family immigrated to central Wisconsin. The boy had attended elementary school in Scotland and been taught reading at home. His father, however, was a stern disciplinarian (not at all adverse to corporal punishment) who would not allow his son to "waste" daylight hours on reading. Instead, he required that his son perform the tasks of a man. On their pioneer farm, John split rails, cradled grain, and cleared forests.

But the young boy hungered to learn. So he asked for and was granted permission to read in the early morning hours before daylight. To make sure he could wake up early (at one o'clock in the morning), John built an ingenious alarm clock that actually tilted the bed and dumped him out, a sure-fire way to get his reading started! Reading whenever he could, the hard-working boy educated himself enough to be admitted to the University of Wisconsin in 1860.

John Muir remained at the university for only three years, leaving without a degree. But during that time he met Dr. and Mrs. Ezra Slocum Carr, who would become lifelong friends. Dr. Carr, a geologist, chemist, and professor, introduced him to the world of geology.

By 1865 Muir had decided to try to make a living as an inventor. On the farm he had created a variety of objects out of wood, including a number of clocks that had received a lot of attention at the Wisconsin State Fair. He used his inventive mind to design machinery for a broom handle manufacturer, where he worked for a couple of years. When an eye injury temporarily blinded him, he gave up that line of work.

In September 1867, Muir set out on his first great adventure. Armed with only a bedroll, a journal and pen, and a minimum amount of food, he planned to walk to the Gulf of Mexico and into South America. He fell seriously ill in Florida, however, and decided to go west instead of farther south. By 1868, he had arrived in San Francisco, California, where he worked on a sheep ranch. He soon discovered Yosemite Valley, where he lived for the next six years.

During all of his trips, adventures, and wilderness explorations, Muir kept carefully detailed journals, including drawings. These journals would later become the basis for his books, essays, and articles.

In the course of his explorations of Yosemite, Muir noted rocks grooved with striae, which he reasoned had been caused by glaciers. The deep "U-shaped" valley, the waterfalls, the smooth rock surfaces, Half-Dome, hanging valleys; all these things helped confirm his belief that glacial action had created the Yosemite Valley. The state geologist, Professor Josiah D. Whitney, however, disagreed, claiming that glaciation had not played a part in forming Yosemite Valley. Whitney even called Muir a "sheep-herder. . . . an ignoramus." By 1870 geology professor Joseph LeConte had confirmed that Whitney was wrong and Muir was right. The latter had discovered the only two glacially formed valleys in the contiguous United States, Yosemite and Hetch Hetchy, a parallel valley 10 miles to the north.

During his years of studying and living in the Yosemite Valley, Muir became increasingly alarmed at the devastation caused by lumberjacks and sheep grazers in the region. He began writing and speaking about the need to preserve the forests. In 1892, he founded the Sierra Club, which he considered one of his greatest achievements. He used the club to promote the preservation of the environment for the public good.

While Muir loved Yosemite, he did not limit his studies to that beautiful valley. He traveled to Alaska, where he studied and documented many glaciers (one is now named Muir Glacier). He also traveled to Africa, Australia, and South America to study great forested areas.

In 1889, Muir began campaigning to establish Yosemite National Park, feeling that federal protection was the only hope for salvaging the natural wonder of the area. He published articles on the beauty of Yosemite and on the need for preserving it so that its beauty would be available for other generations. In 1890, Congress passed the Yosemite National Park bill and, in the next 10 years, over 148 million acres of forest became forest reserves, 16 national monuments were added to the system, and national parks were created.

But Muir's last major campaign failed. For six years, he fought to protect the Hetch-Hetchy Valley from being turned into a reservoir. He saw the exploitation of Hetch-Hetchy as the beginning of the end of the parks. Even with the aid of the Sierra Club, Muir lost the battle. Some of Muir's close friends said that the battle to save Hetch-Hetchy so weakened him physically that it contributed to his death.

John Muir devoted his life to the American wilderness. He spent years studying the flora and geology of Yosemite and Alaska, and he even convinced President Theodore Roosevelt to preserve wilderness areas in an extended national park system. To honor Muir's achievements, Roosevelt established the Muir Woods National Monument in California in 1908. Also named in his honor are the John Muir Trail, a 212-mile footpath from Mount Whitney to the Yosemite Valley; Muir Glacier in Glacier Bay National Park;

and the John Muir National Historic Site in Martinez, California, a 17-room mansion where Muir lived in the two decades before his death. But his real monument is the preserved spectacle of Yosemite Valley, available to all generations in its natural glory.

## Key Dates

1838     Born in Dunbar, Scotland, on April 21

1860     Left home to pursue a career as an inventor

1861–    Attended the University of Wisconsin; taught public school
1863

1864–    Took a lengthy botany expedition and worked at a broom
1866       factory in Meaford

1866     Returned to the United States and worked in a carriage
          factory

1867     Temporarily blinded in April; in September began a
          1,000-mile walk to the Gulf of Mexico and South America

1868     Moved to California

1868–    Lived in Yosemite
1873

1873     Began profession as nature writer

1879–    Took first trip to Alaska
1880

1888     Launched lobbying campaigns to create Yosemite, Sequoia,
          and General Grant National Parks

1892     Organized the Sierra Club

1903     Escorted President Theodore Roosevelt on three-day
          camping trip to Yosemite

1905–    Fought to save Hetch-Hetchy Valley
1908

1914     Died on December 24 in Los Angeles

# Advice

*John Muir would advise anyone considering a career in geology or botany to do more than study required courses. Read the works of Ralph Waldo Emerson, Cicero, and Henry David Thoreau. Study history, ecology, and basic biology. Study physics to learn of the basic forces of nature. But most important, gain firsthand knowledge of nature. Hike, camp, explore. Join clubs and groups that conduct expeditions. Spend time in the wilderness and actively study the rocks, landscapes, and vegetation you find.*

# References

Fox, Stephen. *John Muir and His Legacy: The American Conservation Movement.* Boston: Little, Brown, 1981. (Examines the history of the American conservation movement, beginning with Muir's involvement.)

Jones, Holway R. *John Muir and the Sierra Club: The Battle for Yosemite.* San Francisco: Sierra Club, 1965. (Muir's role in the Sierra Club.)

Muir, John. *Mountains of California.* New York: Penguin Books, 1985 (reprint). (Considered by many to be Muir's finest work.)

———. *Stickeen: The Story of a Dog.* Berkeley: Heyday Books, 1981 (reprint). (Best seller about Muir's adventures in Alaska with a small dog.)

Tolan, Sally. *John Muir.* People Who Have Helped the World. New York: Morehouse Publishing, 1990. (Good biography.)

Turner, Frederick. *Rediscovering America: John Muir in His Time and Ours.* New York: Viking Press, 1985. (Well-written overview of Muir's life.)

Young, Samuel Hall. *Alaska Days with John Muir.* Introduction by Richard F. Fleck. Minneapolis: Peregrine Smith, 1991. (Book details two of Muir's discovery journeys, in 1879 and 1880.)

# Bill Nye

"*The Science Guy*"     Science Education

KCTS-TV, Seattle, Washington

## Career Highlights

- Created and starred in the most popular science television program in history
- Awarded the Environmental Media Award, 1996, 1997
- Received the award for Outstanding Achievement in Children's Programming from the Television Critics Association, 1997
- Awarded the Science Society of Presidents Award for improving public understanding and appreciation of science, 1997
- Winner of four Emmys at Daytime Emmy Awards Creative Arts ceremonies, 1997

## Important Contributions

In just five years of national syndication, *Bill Nye the Science Guy* has piled up over 20 major entertainment and educational awards. Rave reviews by scientists, educators, and children alike confirm that Bill Nye has found the key to making science thrilling. His programming helps children see both the joy of science and its central role in our lives and culture. He presents accurate, challenging scientific information in a rapid and continually fascinating format.

Bill Nye is out to change the world's perception of science. Still in his early forties, he is well on his way to achieving that ambitious and noble goal.

# Career Path

The television camera pans past a table of bubbling beakers of colored liquid connected by roller-coaster shaped glass tubes. It settles on a hand pouring baking soda into a flask of vinegar. A balloon is clamped over the flask and inflates and then explodes all on its own. It's the start of another *Bill Nye the Science Guy* program, the nationally syndicated, award-winning television series dedicated to using high-energy, humorous science education as a vehicle for reshaping a generation of children's attitudes toward science.

A sense of humor runs rampant in Bill Nye's family. It always has. "We just get together and laugh," he says. Born in 1955 in Washington, D.C., Bill Nye entered a family where humor and education were both highly prized commodities. As a boy growing up in the 1950s and 1960s, Bill loved the idea of flight and airplanes. "The space program was really important to me as a kid. I still have a photo of Armstrong and Aldrin on the moon in my living room." One of his first childhood memories is throwing a rubberband-powered airplane, the Sky Streak, and figuring out how to make it turn left. "That way I could stay in one place and the plane would come back to me. It was riveting."

As with his rubberband airplane, Bill learned by doing. When shown or told how something worked, he felt compelled to tear it apart and see for himself what made it tick. "My favorite victim was my bike. I spent more time working on it than riding it. I loved seeing how it worked."

In high school Bill discovered two qualities in himself that would later become central to his future. First, he realized that he had an exceptional ability to deeply understand science and math. He didn't just understand how to apply the equations, he could "see" each scientific concept as clearly and plainly as he could his own hand. Second, he discovered that he had a talent and a flare for tutoring; he had a gift for presenting concepts in an enjoyable and comprehensible way. He spent his high school summers demystifying math and science for fellow students who were taking make-up summer classes.

After high school Bill enrolled in Cornell University in Ithaca, New York. He decided to major in mechanical engineering, or the study of how and why things work. In his mind this was not a split from science; to him engineers *are* scientists. They must learn the scientific method and the scientific concepts and principles applicable to their field of engineering. Bill Nye views engineers as applied scientists. Thus mechanical engineering was a practical way to study a broad range of sciences and also to study the links between the sciences and our modern technology.

Never staying strictly within the limits of mechanical engineering courses, Nye stuffed in a great number of seemingly unrelated science courses to get as broad a science background as possible. His favorite of these were his astronomy courses, taught by the great Carl Sagan. Astronomy seemed like an extension of flight.

After graduation in 1977, Nye landed a job as an engineer working for the Boeing Company in Seattle, Washington. He was thrilled to be working on his first love, airplanes and flight. But he spent most of his time writing and debugging software codes for the navigational black boxes on commercial aircraft. This work didn't *feel* like building airplanes and seeing how they work.

In 1979, on a lark, Nye entered and won a Steve Martin look-alike contest. Comedy Clubs were beginning to sprout up across the country, and that win opened the door to occasional stand-up comedy gigs. He had always thought of himself as a "funny guy," and so accepted the challenge. He tried engineering jokes. They fell flat. But he found that wacky science demos and bits consistently worked. Even in the stand-up comedy environment, people were fascinated by strange and funny science bits.

Nye's stand-up routines expanded into a second career, working as an engineer during the day and a science comedian at night. He also expanded his repertoire of wacky science stories and demonstrations to use during his stand-up routines.

In 1983 Nye linked up with a group of Seattle comedians who had formed *Almost Live*, a spin-off television comedy show based on the popular *Saturday Night Live* format. He worked with the *Almost Live* production both as comedy writer and as a performer in the persona of "Bill Nye the Science Guy," playing off the successful science comedy routines he had developed for stand-up.

*Almost Live* was first a great regional success, then syndicated to a national audience. Nye received offers to appear on guest slots on both national and regional talk radio programs to answer science questions from callers. He was invited to appear as "the Science Guy" on the Mickey Mouse Club. He got funding to create several science-based documentaries, including *Fabulous Wetlands* for the Washington State Department of Ecology.

By 1986 Nye was committed to pursuing a career as the next "Mr. Wizard," the hit science children's television show from the 1950s and 1960s. He quit his engineering job to pursue *Bill Nye the Science Guy* full time.

In 1992 Nye was finally able to sell the program to KING-TV, a Seattle television station. The program went into national syndication in 1993. Since then he has ridden a rocketship to the top of the charts. He has served on presidential advisory panels for science education and has been appointed to a special commission by the Secretary of Energy to provide advice on energy education. Bill Nye and his program have received an average of five honors and awards each year and have developed a huge and dedicated following.

Still in his early forties, Bill Nye feels that he is just beginning his career as a science educator. "My modest little goal," he chuckles, "is to change the world." His plan is to foster a new generation of science-literate science enthusiasts. Along the way he has also become an inventor, already holding a patent for a collapsible, water-filled magnifying glass. He has already touched and affected the world. It is possible that, before he is through, he will have altered its course.

## Key Dates

| | |
|---|---|
| 1955 | Born in Washington, D.C., on November 27 |
| 1977 | Received B.S. in mechanical engineering from Cornell University |
| 1977 | Hired as a mechanical engineer by Boeing Aircraft |
| 1979 | Won a Steve Martin look-alike contest and was offered his first stand-up comedy gig |
| 1982 | Shifted from Boeing to Applied Sciences Engineering, a Boeing Contractor |
| 1983 | Began to write and perform for *Almost Live* for KING-TV, a Seattle television station |
| 1986 | Quit his engineering job to pursue full time becoming the next "Mr. Wizard" |
| 1992 | Created *Bill Nye, the Science Guy* television program |
| 1993 | Appeared for first time in syndication around the country |

## Advice

*Bill Nye believes that the first job of anyone who wants to work in science is to get excited about it. Find ways to make science seem fascinating. Science is fascinating, but you'll never be able to work effectively in it unless you see its heart-pounding excitement. Once you have an emotional connection to science, pursue those aspects that seem most amazing to you.*

*Bill Nye would recommend that you also take engineering and math courses. Engineering is the application of science and links science to practical, day-to-day experiences and phenomena. Engineering classes are excellent for establishing rigorous discipline in your pursuit of science. Math is the essential language of science.*

*Perhaps most important of all, learn how to experiment, how to do science. Make trying things a mandatory part of all learning. Question the process until you can make it work for yourself. "One test is worth a thousand expert opinions."*

## References

Buck, Eng. *The History of Science.* London: Science History Publications, 1987. (Good review of the general fields of science.)

California Department of Education. *California Class Project: Classroom Learning Activities for Science.* Sacramento, Calif.: California Department of Education, 1992. (Good review of science education.)

Levenson, Elaine. *Teaching Children About Science.* New York: TAB Books, 1994. (Good review of science education.)

Montgomery, Scott. *Minds for the Making: The Role of Science in American Education, 1750-1990.* New York: Guilford Press, 1994. (Good review of the history of science education.)

Stalon, Hilarie. *Science and Stories: Integrating Science and Literature.* Glenview, Ill.: Goody Year Books, 1994. (Good assessment of science education.)

# Julius Robert Oppenheimer

*"Father of the Bomb"*        Nuclear Physics

## Career Highlights

Archives of the National Academy of Sciences

- Directed the Manhattan Project, which developed the first atomic bomb.
- Was director of the Princeton University Institute for Advanced Studies, 1947–1967
- Received the Enrico Fermi Award, 1963
- Was chair of the General Advisory Committee of the Atomic Energy Commission, 1947–1952

## Important Contributions

Robert Oppenheimer achieved great distinction in three separate areas. As a subatomic theoretical researcher and teacher, he is credited with building the School of Theoretical Physics at U.C. Berkeley into the greatest physics school in the world.

Oppenheimer successfully directed and molded the massive, high-pressure military program, the Manhattan Project, to develop and build the world's first atomic bomb. Finally, as an elder statesman of science, he spoke forcefully and eloquently for control over nuclear expansion and testing following World War II, and he warned of the risks of nuclear energy.

While opinions differ about which arena of his work offered the greatest contribution, it is abundantly clear that Robert Oppenheimer was one of a handful of legendary scientists in the mid-twentieth century who shaped our understanding of, and attitude toward, subatomic physics.

## Career Path

Julius Robert Oppenheimer grew up hating his given name, Julius, and called himself either J. Robert or simply Robert. For most of his life he claimed that the J. didn't stand for anything at all.

Robert was born into a life of wealthy privilege and attended excellent private schools in New York. He was universally described as "precocious in all subject areas" but seemed especially gifted in chemistry and English. He was also described as "high strung and nervous."

Robert entered Harvard in 1922 to pursue a degree in chemistry. He took a maximum load of courses, audited others, and tore through the book stacks at Widener Library as if reading every science-related book were a mandatory activity for all undergraduates. In his senior year it became clear to him that physics, rather than chemistry, was his first love. But it was too late to change majors. He graduated summa cum laude with a B.S. in chemistry in 1925, having crammed four years of coursework into three years.

Then came an offer of a graduate position at Cambridge University in the Cavandish Laboratory for Physics Research. In his two years at Cambridge, Oppenheimer proved two things: first, that he was a brilliant theoretical physicist; and second, that he was lousy at conducting experiments. He was sloppy and imprecise in his lab measurements. Errors crept in. He could do the theoretical work better than virtually all the professors. But he couldn't do the physical, experimental work to back it up.

Believing that his lack of prowess in the laboratory was a death blow to a physics career, Oppenheimer slipped into a deep, year-long depression. That funk was shattered when he received a letter from Max Born inviting him to continue his studies under Born at the University of Göttingen. He rushed to Germany and spent "two glorious years" settling into the role of one of the world's leading theoretical physicists. The work was exciting, it suited him, and it required no experiments. By the time he received his Ph.D. in 1927, he had established a solid international reputation.

In 1929 Oppenheimer accepted academic positions at both U.C. Berkeley and Caltech. For the next 13 years he divided his time between these two institutions and was at the forefront of the most important research in atomic physics. The long list of his papers during this period could serve as an excellent guide to all that was important in theoretical physics. His work provided guidance not only for particle physicists but also for cosmologists, as it illuminated former mysteries in electron-photon showers, neutron star cores, and other wonders of deep space.

Then in late 1941 the publications ceased. To all outward appearances, Oppenheimer's research had halted. It appeared that he no longer asked probing academic questions. In fact, his work had gone underground. He had agreed to head the U.S. Army's massive, high-pressure, top-secret, rush effort to build an atomic bomb, officially called "Manhattan District." It would forever be known as the Manhattan Project.

For security reasons, the project was placed in a new energy research lab in the vast desert near Los Alamos, New Mexico. Enriched uranium would be used for the bomb fuel. Enough was already known about the fission, or splitting, of uranium to let Oppenheimer's task force proceed with their calculations. But huge questions remained. How much uranium was needed to obtain a critical mass to sustain the explosion? How could and should the uranium be detonated? How should it be housed? Shielded? Could workers be protected from radiation?

Oppenheimer was now more a project manager than a scientist. He used his standing in the international physics community to assemble a huge team of scientists and engineers. For two years he was the glue that held the project together. There were constant conflicts within the project.The military demanded tighter security: smaller staff, less outside contact, more extensive security checks, fewer phone calls to family. The scientists demanded the freedom to use whatever resources and expert advice they deemed necessary.

The world's best scientific talents threatened to quit; Oppenheimer's eloquence and scientific stature held them at Los Alamos. The Army threatened to use military managers and supervisors; his persuasive ability held the generals at bay and gave the scientists just enough freedom to get their work done.

Oppenheimer described this two-year whirlwind as "a time of hard work, deep commitment, comradeship and deep happiness—the happiness that comes from intense stimulation and intellectual success."

In July 1945, the world's first atomic bomb was ready for testing. Up to that moment it had existed only in theory, safely contained on paper. Now it was about to become an awesome reality: either a dismal flop or a horrific weapon capable of obliterating every edifice of humankind.

In the shimmering, early-morning heat of the Alamagordo Test Range in New Mexico, the bomb was detonated. A blinding light flashed across the countryside. A stretch of desert dirt half-a-mile across bulged into the air. In the next few seconds, a searing heat wave many thousands of degrees hot tore across the land and evaporated plants, incinerated buildings, and instantly melted steel for miles in every direction. Then the wind and thunderous noise of the shock wave struck. Like a hundred hurricanes, a wall of high-powered wind flattened everything that moved or stood in its path. The noise shattered windows and rattled bodies 20 miles away, sounding like both earth and heaven were being torn apart.

A boiling column of dense smoke and debris rose from the center of this decimated land. The ominous mushroom cloud of seething fury and unopposable force climbed into the early morning sky, boiling brown and gray as it carried tons of New Mexico soil up with its relentless currents.

From a safe distance the science team watched in stunned silence. It was the most awe-inspiring, humbling, and terrifying sight they had ever seen. Each observer was filled with an odd mix of fearful dread and fierce pride. They had accomplished the miracle of the century. They had opened a Pandora's box that could never again be safely closed.

Six months after the Alamagordo blast and the dropping of two A-bombs on Japan, Oppenheimer resigned from the Army's nuclear weapons development program. He spent the remainder of his career and life lecturing and arguing for tighter control of both nuclear energy and nuclear weapons from his new position as director of the Institute for Advanced Studies at Princeton University.

Because of his reluctance to support continued weapons development, Oppenheimer was discredited by the U.S. government and subpoenaed to appear before the Senate's Un-American Activities Committee in 1957. Although he was never convicted of any "un-American" activities, the mere fact that he had been subpoenaed destroyed his professional reputation, and his career never recovered from the cruel and false suspicions of a Communist connection. He was also never able to replace his image as the father of the bomb with his post-war efforts to limit and curtail nuclear expansion.

## Key Dates

| | |
|---|---|
| 1904 | Born in New York City on April 22 |
| 1925 | Received B.S. degree summa cum laude in chemistry from Harvard University |
| 1925–1926 | Pursued graduate studies in Cambridge, England, in physics |
| 1927 | Received Ph.D. in theoretical physics from Göttingen University, Germany |
| 1929–1941 | Held joint teaching appointments at U.C. Berkeley and Caltech. Developed theoretical physics departments on both campuses |
| 1941 | Joined U.S. government program for military applications of atomic energy |
| 1942 | Appointed director of the Manhattan Project |
| 1945 | Exploded first atomic bomb at Alamagordo, New Mexico |

1946     Resigned from atomic weapons development program

1947     Served as director of the Institute for Advanced Studies at Princeton University

1947-     Was chair of the General Advisory Committee of the
1952        Atomic Energy Commission

1953     Had his security clearance revoked; the "Oppenheimer Case" began

1967     Died on February 8

## Advice

*Although he was a university teacher for many years, Robert Oppenheimer was loathe to offer career advice to students. He did, however, believe that it is difficult to know which specific aspect of a general science field you want to pursue and which you are proficient at doing until you have actually attempted to do it. Study and attempt every aspect of physics you can to discover what you do well and what you do poorly. Then mold your career around your strengths. Attend a university where advanced research is actively pursued and where the facilities for state-of-the-art research exist. You will have more opportunities for obtaining practical exposure to a greater variety of science activities at these institutions. Let your interests and talents guide you from a general field (quantum physics, for example) to a specific area of specialty as you advance through your years of schooling.*

## References

Bethe, Hans Albrecht. *The Road from Los Alamos.* Masters of Modern Physics. Philadelphia, Pa.: American Institute of Physics, 1991. (Non-technical essays on weapons research, arms control, and nuclear power.)

Garraty, John, ed. *Encyclopedia of American Biography.* New York: Harper & Row, 1984. (Detailed summary of Oppenheimer's work.)

Goodchild, Peter. *J. Robert Oppenheimer: Shatterer of Worlds.* New York: Fromm International, 1990. (Detailed biography.)

Groves, Leslie. *Now It Can Be Told.* New York: Prentice Hall Press, 1962. (A review of the Manhattan Project.)

Hoddeson, Lillian, Paul W. Henriksen, and Roger A. Meade. *Critical Assembly: A Technical History of Los Alamos During the Oppenheimer Years, 1943–1945.* Edited by Catherine L. Westfall. Cambridge: Cambridge University Press, 1993. (Lucid and accurate history of the technical research that led to the first atomic bombs.)

Serber, Robert. *The Los Alamos Primer: The First Lectures on How to Build an Atomic Bomb.* Edited by Richard Rhodes. Berkeley: University of California Press, 1992. (Serber's annotated lectures from Los Alamos in 1943.)

Stern, P. M. *The Oppenheimer Case: The Trial of a Security System.* New York: Franklin Watts, 1969. (A biographical review.)

# Wolfgang Pauli

*"The Conscience of Physics"*        Physics

## Career Highlights

- Developed the "exclusion principle" and discovered the neutrino
- Awarded Nobel Prize for Physics, 1945
- Awarded the Franklin Medal of the Franklin Institute, 1952
- Awarded the Max Planck Medal of the German Physical Society, 1958

A Courtesy of the Institute for Advanced Study

## Important Contributions

Wolfgang Pauli was a legendary theoretical physicist among his peers for his critical abilities and his stringent standards for rigorous and exact analysis. If Pauli reviewed and accepted a paper or principle, it was accepted as valid throughout the physics community. No physicist since Newton had been held in such high regard.

But it is for his two great contributions to theoretical physics and quantum theory that he is best known. He developed the "exclusion principle," which vastly improved existing models attempting to explain the behavior and motion of electrons orbiting inside an atom. He also discovered an explanation for the apparent "missing energy" in beta decay and in so doing theoretically identified the existence of a new subatomic particle, the neutrino, which was physically discovered 30 years later.

# Career Path

Albert Einstein called it the best analysis of his theories of special and general relativity he ever read. With typical Einstein humor, he quipped that he wished he could have written the original theory half as well as Pauli had written the assessment. Professor Arnold Summerfield called the work masterful. It remains to this day the most clearly stated and technically complete assessment of special and general relativity ever written. The entire European physics community scrambled to discover who had written such a brilliant analysis of Einstein's revolutionary work.

The answer was an unknown, 20-year-old undergraduate student who had written the 250-page analysis as a favor for Professor Sommerfield. The day Wolfgang Pauli turned in that paper, no one had heard of him. Within a year everyone had acknowledged that Pauli was not only a brilliant physicist, but "gloriously artful" in the way he explained complex science. Not bad for someone who was not yet halfway through his undergraduate studies.

Wolfgang Pauli had been a child prodigy. His superior grasp of mathematics and physics was evident from his earliest schooling. As a 12-year-old boy he read and understood Jordon's *Cours d' analysis*, the most comprehensive and advanced treatise on higher math in existence. In high school he became exceedingly bored with math classes and, on his own, read Einstein's papers on the theory of special relativity. He said it was as if a veil had fallen away from his eyes. One day relativity appeared so obvious he wondered why he hadn't known it all along.

Theoretical physics was the obvious melding of Wolfgang's math and physics abilities. There was never any question that that would be his field. Wolfgang enrolled in the University of Munich in 1918 to study under famed physicist Arnold Sommerfield. Werner Heisenberg, who later developed the famed "Uncertainty Principle," was a classmate of Pauli's.

Sommerfield was asked to write a review of Einstein's theory of relativity for a monumental new compilation of the current state of affairs of science. He turned the job over to Pauli, even though he was barely 20 years old and only in his fourth semester at the university.

The 250-page critical assessment Pauli turned back in created an incredible stir in the European physics community. Few, if any, of the long-time professionals could have matched its precision and brilliance. Instantly, the young scientist was launched into the limelight.

Pauli received his Ph.D. in 1921 in the shortest time allowed by university rules and transferred to the University of Göttingen for post-graduate studies under Max Born. A year later he transferred to the University of Copenhagen to serve as an assistant to Neils Bohr. These two years of study introduced Pauli to the emerging field of quantum physics.

The ability of physicists to peer into an atom and explain its inner workings had been extremely limited by available technology. Machines capable of performing the necessary tasks were still 50 years away. All scientists could do was to study the patterns of energy emitted from inside an atom under different conditions. Nothing in classical physics explained what they saw. Atoms did not emit energy continuously over all wavelengths as did the sun, but rather in discrete, narrow bands with vast ranges of wavelengths between which no energy was emitted at all.

Niels Bohr solved the conundrum by proposing that electrons could only travel in several fixed orbits around the nucleus and could only change energy states by jumping from one to another of these allowed neighboring orbits, which would require the electron to either absorb or radiate a fixed quantum of energy.

Mystery solved. Quantum mechanics was born. But by 1922 holes, or at least serious cracks, were being found in Bohr's theory. Not all energy lines were explained by his theory. More serious, the theory didn't explain why electrons didn't collapse back to the lowest possible energy state.

Using strong magnetic fields, Pauli began to study the structure of, and emissions from, a variety of elemental atoms. He detected something, a subtle variation in spectral lines that varied depending on the strength and orientation of his magnetic field.

It seemed to the young physicist that there was a property of electrons that had not been detected and that could account for their as yet unexplained behavior. He called it "spin." Electrons not only orbit the nucleus, they also spin, as does the Earth, giving them both magnetic and physical rotational momentum. Different spin orientations vary slightly in energy level. Pauli could now identify four properties of an electron, which he called its quantum numbers. He noticed that no two electrons within an atom possessed identical quantum numbers.

When Pauli applied his new principle that no two electrons could have the same set of numbers, the results exactly matched experimental results and explained each of the cracks and holes in Bohr's theory. Pauli's concept became known as the "exclusion principle" and was marveled at for its ability to create a clear and complete image of the behavior and motion of orbiting electrons. For this discovery, he was awarded the Nobel Prize.

In the 1930s Pauli took on another mystery of the atom. When a neutron emitted an electron and became a proton (beta decay), the laws of conservation of energy seemed to be violated. A small amount of energy disappeared.

Pauli set up a series of laboratory experiments to find this mysterious beta energy. Although he was one of the finest theoreticians of the early twentieth century, he was not a lab man. He lacked manual dexterity. His mind was easily distracted from the physical task at hand. Progress was slowed by what colleges laughingly called the "Pauli effect." Whenever he entered a lab, accidents and disasters happened.

Still Pauli persisted, searching for symmetries, for clues that would lead him to the missing energy. Finally he detected slight shifts in momentum at the moment of energy disappearance. This led him to conclude that beta decay produced not just an electron, but also a second particle, which had not been detected because it had the same infinitesimally small mass as an electron but no electrical charge. Its momentum accounted for the missing energy. Enrico Fermi later named this particle a "neutrino." Thirty years after Pauli identified it, the neutrino was experimentally detected and proven to exist.

Pauli rarely taught and was, in fact, a lousy teacher. He mumbled. His board writing was small and disorganized. He had a tendency to stop his lectures and think about a topic. His greatness was in the discipline and critical ability of his mind. He possessed unparalleled abilities to review and analyze statements, theories, and arguments. He enforced the highest and most stringent standards for rigorous and exact analysis both on himself and on others. Wolfgang Pauli was truly, as many called him, "the critical conscience of theoretical physics."

# Key Dates

| | |
|---|---|
| 1900 | Born in Vienna, Austria, on April 25 |
| 1921 | Received Ph.D. in theoretical physics from the University of Munich |
| 1921–1922 | Studied at the University of Göttingen under Max Born |
| 1922–1923 | Assisted Neils Bohr in Copenhagen |
| 1923–1928 | Appointed assistant professor of physics at the University of Hamburg |
| 1928–1940 | Worked as instructor at the Federal Institute of Technology, Zurich, Switzerland |
| 1940–1946 | Served as chair of theoretical physics at Princeton's Institute for Advanced Studies |
| 1945 | Won Nobel Prize for Physics |

1946– Was instructor at the Federal Institute of Technology,
1958     Zurich, Switzerland

1958 Died on December 15

## Advice

*Wolfgang Pauli tried to never offer advice to others, believing that each person and career was unique. However, he advocated several principles that he would advise any student to incorporate into his or her early studies and careers. Demand precision and exactness in your own work and in that of others. These are habits that you must teach yourself early in a science career. Study mathematics carefully and learn from its precision and rigor. The value of your science and your science reputation will be measured by the care with which you perform both analyses and computations.*

## References

Asimov, Isaac. *Asimov's Biographical Encyclopedia of Science and Technology.* New York: Doubleday, 1974. (Strong review of Pauli's life and work.)

Fierz, Marcus, and V. F. Weiskoph, eds. *Theoretical Physics in the Twentieth Century: A Memorial Volume to Wolfgang Pauli.* Cambridge, Mass.: Cambridge University Press, 1960. (Comments by 14 prominent scientists on Pauli's life and work.)

Hendry, John. *The Creation of Quantum Mechanics and the Bohr-Pauli Dialogue.* Philadelphia, Pa.: D. Reidel, 1984.

Hermann, A., ed. *Wolfgang Pauli: Scientific Correspondence.* Vols. 1 and 2. Frankfurt: Springer-Verlag, 1979. (Translations of Pauli's correspondence on theoretical physics with other great figures.)

Pauli, Wolfgang. *Theory of Relativity.* Photography by A. Sommerfield. New York: Dover, 1981. (Good reference on historical matters and conceptual questions on special relativity.)

Wasson, Tyler, ed. *Nobel Prize Winners.* New York: H. W. Wilson, 1987. (Summary review of Pauli's important work.)

# Linus Pauling

*"The Unconventional Genius"*    Physics and Chemistry

## Career Highlights

- Won the Nobel Prize for Chemistry, 1954
- Won the Nobel Peace Prize, 1963
- Was first scientific Nobel laureate to also win Nobel Peace prize
- Awarded the Presidential Medal of Merit, 1948

## Important Contributions

From inauspicious beginnings to winning two Nobel prizes, Linus Pauling catapulted himself to the center stage of the scientific community. He was one of the first pioneers to use chemistry, physics, and biology to study the structure of protein. He won the Nobel Prize for Chemistry for his brilliant insights in applying quantum mechanics to complex molecules. His book of essays, *The Nature of the Chemical Bond,* quickly became a classic, and his theory of the chemical bond remains one of the landmarks of modern chemistry.

In addition to his contributions to science, Pauling became an outspoken advocate for peace, even when it made him unpopular. He organized peace petitions. He challenged the government's claims that fallout from nuclear testing was not harmful. While he became an outcast in the scientific realm for his "radical" leanings, he also became a hero with the public.

## Career Path

Professor Carl Selsman of the Oregon State University physics department first cleared the appointment of his new assistant professor with the department chair, then with the Dean of the School of Sciences, and finally with the university president. Each official voiced the same objections: We've never offered assistant professorships to anyone who doesn't hold a doctorate. He hasn't even finished his bachelor's! He's too young. At 18, he'll be younger than most of his students. He just finished taking that course last term, and now he's supposed to teach it?

To each objection Selsman offered the same reply: He's brilliant. He knows the material better than I do and he can communicate it better. And so Linus Pauling completed his undergraduate studies as an assistant professor, the first, last, and only 18-year-old undergraduate assistant professor in the history of the university. It was a whirlwind beginning to a career that would lead to the U.S. government being so afraid of him that they refused to allow him a passport to travel to peace conferences. The star-studded road in between was anything but straight and clear.

As a child, Linus Pauling was a voracious reader. After he had consumed all the books in his house and his neighbors' houses, he even read his father's 692-page *Pharmacopoeia of the United States* and the 1,947-page companion book, *The Dispensatory of the United States of America,* both handbooks for druggists and doctors.

An elderly neighbor taught him Greek, and by the time Linus was 13 years old, he knew some Greek, could count to 100 in Chinese, and was able to speak German passably well. That same year, a friend introduced him to chemistry, and he began to conduct experiments at home using materials from his parents' kitchen.

In high school, Linus proved himself an exceptional student. He graduated in three and a half years and planned to go to Oregon State University (OSU). But his mother did not understand Linus's passionate drive for knowledge. "No one on the street has gone to college," she complained. "Why don't you get a good job instead?" No one in the family saw value in higher education and Linus started college without family support or approval.

At OSU Pauling took the hardest courses he could find, quickly developing a reputation for his brilliant intellect and inquiring mind. In 1919, he accepted the position as assistant professor and, although only 18, proved to be one of the most popular and effective teachers in the department.

Pauling secured a teaching fellowship at the California Institute of Technology (Caltech) for graduate school, which had no rules limiting the number of courses a student could take. He often registered for 60 hours of classes and 20 hours of research, yet still he excelled, receiving his Ph.D. summa cum laude.

At age 26, Pauling accepted an assistant professorship of chemistry at Caltech and became the youngest member of the faculty. It was there that his bright, inquisitive mind fueled the research that would earn him the title "the unconventional genius."

From early research on molecules Pauling concluded that the properties and functions of *all* molecules are determined by their chemical bonds. Thus he began studying the molecules and bonds of human hair, his first move toward studying protein molecules in humans. Through this work, he discovered that sickle-cell anemia was hereditary, caused by a disorder of the hemoglobin molecule.

When World War II began, Pauling put his personal research on hold to contribute to the war effort. He served as a consultant to the government on medical research. During a war, great quantities of blood plasma (the liquid part of blood) are needed for wounded soldiers but are not always available on the battlefield. Pauling experimented until he was able to create a synthetic blood plasma. For this contribution, he was awarded the Presidential Medal of Merit, the highest honor the President of the United States can bestow on a civilian.

After the war, Pauling looked forward to resuming his work on molecular biology, yet he and his family could not forget the tragedy and misery of war. "What good will science do if the world is destroyed, Linus?" his wife asked him. "War is the greatest evil. There must be an end to it. You and I must work toward that end."

Pauling had to concur. He set science aside to become a peace activist. He gave speeches urging peace and exposing the horrors of testing atomic bombs. His actions made him so unpopular with the government that he was actually denied a passport to travel to London in 1952 for a two-day conference at which he was to be the first speaker. Still he persisted, drawing up a petition signed by 2,500 scientists urging a ban on nuclear weapons testing, which he presented to the United Nations. Nothing happened. Pauling sent the petition around the world, and 13,000 scientists signed it. Again the petition was presented to the United Nations. Again nothing happened, and the testing of nuclear weapons continued.

Pauling continued his anti-war efforts despite the fact that doing so earned him the disapproval of Senator McCarthy and the House Un-American Activities Committee, who were investigating supposed Communist infiltration in the United States in the 1950s. Finally, he was subpoenaed by the Senate Internal Security Committee to appear in Washington and give information about his peace petitions. He answered all of the questions except one: He would not reveal the names of the students and friends who had helped him. For this he was held to be in contempt and could have been imprisoned. His stand was supported in newspaper editorials across the country and, with mounting public support for the beleaguered scientist, the committee dropped the inquiry. Pauling would later win the Nobel Peace Prize for his efforts on behalf of world peace.

Later in life, Pauling devoted most of his time to promoting his belief that vitamin C can protect people from flu, colds, mental disorders, and even cancer. Since human beings are one of the few animals that do not manufacture vitamin C, he believed it was necessary to give the body additional doses. His advocacy of large doses of vitamins made him a hero to the alternative health crowd, but shocked and angered most of the scientific world. He was denounced as a crank. He was repeatedly criticized, his credentials were questioned, his opinions dismissed. Traditional Western medicine would not take seriously Pauling's ideas about health, wellness, and vitamins.

Unfortunately, Pauling's "fall" from the scientific pedestal may have occurred because he was simply ahead of his time: In the last years of his life, a national medical conference gave him a standing ovation with the announcement, "Pauling was right all along."

## Key Dates

| | |
|---|---|
| 1901 | Born in Portland, Oregon, February 28 |
| 1917 | Left high school and entered Oregon State University |
| 1919 | Accepted a position as assistant instructor at Oregon State |
| 1922 | Began graduate studies at California Institute of Technology |
| 1925 | Graduated with his Ph.D., summa cum laude |
| 1927 | Worked as sssistant professor of chemistry at Caltech |
| 1931 | Received a prize from the American Chemical Society as the most promising young research chemist in the United States |
| 1937 | Was made head of the chemistry department and director of the Gates and Crellin Laboratories |
| 1939 | Published *The Nature of the Chemical Bond* |
| 1954 | Won Nobel Prize for Chemistry |
| 1963 | Won Nobel Peace Prize |
| 1994 | Died of cancer on August 19 |

## Advice

*Linus Pauling was mostly self-taught and would advise you to read anything and everything you can find that is even tangentially related to your field of interest. Also read everything that is interesting, whether or not it directly relates to your field. All knowledge eventually comes to bear on a scientific career. In undergraduate school, study humanities and philosophy as well as the major physical sciences. Try to read far beyond the recommended reading for every class as if that knowledge were critical to your future success. Who knows? At some point, it might be.*

## References

Atkins, P. W. *Physical Chemistry.* New York: W. H. Freeman, 1997.

Goertzel, Ted, and Ben Goertzel. *Linus Pauling: A Life in Science and Politics.* New York: Basic Books, 1995.

Serafini, Anthony. *Linus Pauling: A Man and His Science.* New York: Paragon House, 1989.

White, Florence Meiman. *Linus Pauling: Scientist and Crusader.* New York: Walker, 1980.

# Roger Penrose

*"The Math Wizard"*

Physics,
Mathematics, and
Cosmology

## Career Highlights

University of Oxford

- Proposed (with Stephen W. Hawking) that the universe was created in a Big Bang
- Awarded Royal Medal from Royal Society, 1985
- Received Wolf Foundation Prize (with Hawking), 1988
- Received Dirac Medal and Prize, Institute of Physics, 1989
- Awarded Albert Einstein Medal, 1990

## Important Contributions

Roger Penrose has tackled several mysteries in mathematics and physics and, in doing so, has made significant contributions to our understanding of the universe. He has developed theorems and methods for use in complex proofs and in the investigation of space and time. He may be more popularly known, however, for his discoveries in recreational mathematics, puzzles, and games, and for his proposing (along with Hawking) the Big Bang theory of the beginning of the universe.

# Career Path

Roger Penrose was almost 30 and couldn't make himself stop playing with math. Math was fun; it was a game, a plaything. His father had told him so when he was a child, grumbling that math was an idle toy people turned to only when they weren't interested in anything else. Roger heard and remembered the part about playing with math, but he missed the implied message that math was a lousy career for anyone with the ability to tackle anything else.

Everyone agreed that Penrose was gifted. But while other noted scientists of the day seriously delved into the mysteries of the cosmos, he toyed with math puzzles. It infuriated many in the science community when his doodlings uncovered monumentally important concepts that had eluded the more serious searchers.

Roger Penrose was not much of a reader as a young child. He preferred to build things, especially geometrical models that he made out of cardboard. His earliest influence other than his father was Fred Hoyle's radio talks on cosmology. The cosmos fascinated Roger from an early age, and even though he began his professional career as a pure mathematician, he had, from childhood, a recurring interest in the mysterious nature of space and time.

Penrose remembers Fred Hoyle saying that galaxies disappear off the edge of the visible universe when they reach the speed of light. As a young man Penrose was both fascinated and puzzled by this concept and drew various pictures to try to explain it. (He was "geometrically minded" and frequently drew pictures to help him understand mathematical concepts.) When he first met Dennis Sciama (a researcher at Cambridge University at the time), Penrose offered an explanation for the "disappearing" galaxies by drawing a picture of his theory. He theorized that the galaxies never actually disappear. Instead, he suggested that their speed and direction relative to Earth placed them outside the light cone for Earth. They are there, but no longer in a place and time where we are able to see them.

Sciama was impressed. When he discussed Penrose's theory with Fred Hoyle, their calculations established that the young man was right. When Penrose later became a student at Cambridge, Sciama took him under his wing and continued to develop his interest in physics.

In 1952, Penrose received his bachelor of science degree at University College, London, and became an assistant lecturer in mathematics at Bedford College. In 1957, he received his Ph.D. from St. John's College, Cambridge, and became a research fellow at Princeton, Syracuse, and Cornell universities. He enjoyed "playing" with mathematics. In the late 1950s, he discovered a now popular illusion called the Penrose Staircase, which is a two-dimensional representation of an impossible three-dimensional object. In this case, it was a staircase that rises, makes four right-angle turns while climbing, then returns to the beginning point in an endless loop.

Another playful application of mathematics came with the simple tiling of a floor. It is fairly simple and easy to tile a floor with triangles, squares, hexagons, and so forth. However, it is much more complicated to tile a floor with pentagons, because they have a five-fold symmetry. Three pentagons fitted together always leave a crack. Penrose found a way to tile a plane with pentagons in non-repeating patterns. Specifically, he constructed two rhombuses by dividing the diagonal of a regular parallelogram by a golden section. These could be combined to cover the plane in such a way as to have an almost five-fold symmetry. Interestingly, this "unnatural" symmetry of his tile pattern has now been discovered in the quasi-crystals of some metal alloys.

Penrose brought his mathematics background and aptitude to a project attempting to expand on Einstein's theory of relativity, especially as it relates to black holes. A black hole is a mass so compact that not even light can escape its intense gravity; thus, from the outside, it appears black. If our sun were compressed to a sphere four miles in diameter, it would become a black hole. Scientists believe that some massive stars, after they exhaust their nuclear fuel, collapse under their own weight to form black holes. Working with Stephen Hawking, Penrose was able to prove one of Einstein's theorems asserting that at the center of a black hole there must evolve a "space-time singularity," where the laws of physics as we know them break down.

Penrose and Hawking collaborated on a second major theoretical discovery. Over the course of several years they attempted to track the universe back to its origin point. Hawking provided the theoretical concept and, as only a mathematical wizard could, Penrose played with the numbers to see where the theory would lead. Ultimately, they arrived at a massive singularity, which had to have exploded in what is now called the Big Bang to begin the universe as we know it. To Penrose, it was just another math puzzle to play with.

In more recent years, Penrose has focused his attention on trying to devise a unified field theory, or quantum theory of gravity. This is an attempt to reconcile the inconsistencies between the general theory of relativity, which describes the interactions of celestial bodies on a large scale, and quantum mechanics, which describes the behavior of subatomic particles on an extremely small scale.

Penrose has also studied the mathematical implications of the relatively new science of artificial intelligence, which is the belief that computers will someday achieve human intelligence and consciousness; they will have minds. In his book, *The Emperor's New Mind: Concerning Computers, Minds, and the Laws of Physics,* he attacked certain aspects of artificial intelligence, arguing that some aspects of the mind will never be duplicated by a "thinking" machine. Penrose proposed that when we humans think, our brains use quantum mechanics to split into millions of parallel brains, all thinking slightly different thoughts at once; thus a human can consider nearly an unlimited number of possibilities in the amount of time it takes a computer to consider one. His forceful argument against computers ever achieving artificial intelligence has made Penrose an outcast in a scientific community enthusiastically behind, and partly funded by, the drive to create artificial intelligence.

Through his books, Roger Penrose has given us a glimpse into the possible future of science. His research and theorems have helped us better understand our universe. Since the mid-1960s, he has been working on a new cosmology based on a complex geometry, and one can only guess at what new directions this might take our thinking about the universe.

## Key Dates

| | |
|---|---|
| 1931 | Born in Colchester, England, on August 8 |
| 1952 | Received B.Sc. from University College, London |
| 1956–1957 | Assistant lecturer in mathematics, Bedford College |
| 1957 | Received Ph.D. from St. John's College, Cambridge University |
| 1957–1960 | Was research fellow at Princeton, Syracuse, and Cornell universities |
| 1959–1961 | Was NATO research fellow at Princeton and Syracuse universities |
| 1961–1963 | Was research associate in mathematics at King's College |
| 1963–1964 | Was visiting associate professor of mathematics and physics at University of Texas |
| 1964–1966 | Was reader in applied mathematics at Birkbeck College, London |
| 1966–1973 | Was professor of applied mathematics at Birkbeck College, London |
| 1973 | Elected Rouse Ball Professor of Mathematics at Oxford University |

1983–
1987     Worked as professor of math at Rice University

1987–
present     Is professor of math at Oxford University

## Advice

*Roger Penrose firmly believes that math lies at the core of science. If you want to pursue a career in physical or theoretical science, first delve into mathematics. Become master of all forms of mathematics. Penrose believes there is a "deep unity between mathematics and physics." Math is the foundation upon which science is built and "once you have put more and more of your physical world into a mathematical structure, you realize how profound and mysterious this mathematical structure is."*

## References

Hawking, Stephen W. *A Brief History of Time: From the Big Bang to Black Holes.* New York: Bantam Books, 1988.

Lightman, Alan, and Roberta Brawer, eds. *Origins: The Lives and Worlds of Modern Cosmologists.* Cambridge, Mass.: Harvard University Press, 1990.

Penrose, Roger. *The Emperor's New Mind: Concerning Computers, Minds, and the Laws of Physics.* New York: Viking Penguin, 1991.

———. *Quantum Concepts in Space and Time.* New York: Oxford University Press, 1986.

Penrose, Roger, and Wolfgang Rindler. *Spinors and Space-Time.* Vol. 2. New York: Cambridge University Press, 1988.

# Max Planck

*"Planck's Constant and the Foundation of Quantum Understanding"*     Physics

## Career Highlights

- Credited as co-founder of twentieth-century physics
- Awarded Nobel Prize for Physics, 1918
- Had Germany's academy of science renamed for him (the Max Planck Institute), 1948
- Had Germany's highest scientific award named for him (the Max Planck Medal)

## Important Contributions

Max Planck was among the most pivotal scientists in history and ranks with Albert Einstein as one of the two founders of twentieth-century physics: He discovered the equation that founded quantum physics. Einstein, Bohr, Born, Heisenberg, Compton, and a host of other ground-breaking, Nobel Prize-winning physicists all based their work in part on the discoveries of Max Planck.

Planck discovered the quantum nature of energy at the atomic level and developed a formula for relating the energy content of a quantum to the frequency of the corresponding electromagnetic wave. The crucial role played in the development of quantum mechanics by Planck's Constant (a number relating the energy emitted by a body to the frequency of the radiation) led to the realization that it is one of the most important and fundamental of all physical constants. His work was the foundation upon which modern physics was built.

## Career Path

The black-body radiation problem should have been a simple mathematics exercise based on well-known physics and thermodynamics. It should have been, but it didn't work.

By the late nineteenth century, it was known that the radiation emitted by an atom was produced by vibration within the atom and that the magnitude of that radiation varried in a complex way as a function of its wavelength. To simplify the equations, scientists made these calculations for the heat absorption and radiation by a black, perfectly absorbing body. It should have been possible to use thermodynamics to produce an accurate expression for this black-body radiation.

But it didn't work.

Max Planck needed to find an equation that would allow him to correctly describe black-body radiation and solve this thermodynamic conundrum that had plagued him for a decade. He did not envision any grand discovery. He was a methodical, quiet teacher and applied mathematician, a pragmatic man. He only wanted to satisfy a very practical need and would have gladly used someone else's equation if only there had been one to use. While his struggle led to fame and triumph, Planck would have eagerly foregone both to avoid the nagging doubts and tragedy that plagued his later life.

Early in his life Max Planck developed a love of music and was leaning toward a career as a musician. However, teachers and parents praised his math skills while shunning his musical talents. So Max leaned toward a career in mathematics. Then a beloved teacher, Herman Muller, explained the principle of conservation of energy to him. The concept made such a strong impression on the young man that he decided on a career in physics. However, Professor Philipp von Jolly at the University of Munich told him that, "There was nothing new left to discover in physics." Max returned to mathematics and music.

When Max asked a music professor for advice on choosing a career he was told, "If you have to ask, don't choose music." Upon entering the university of Munich in late 1874, he still had not decided on his field. He initially signed up for math classes. However, he found that his interest drew him toward physics lectures. Max finally realized that he had a deep curiosity about the nature of the universe, which meant he should pursue a career in physics, in which he could use his math talent.

With his undergraduate degree from the University of Berlin, Max Planck conducted independent studies in thermodynamics for a year before transferring back to Munich for his doctoral studies. For his analytical work on the second law of thermodynamics, he was awarded a Ph.D. in 1879. Throughout the 1880s and early 1890s he taught and continued to struggle to reconcile experimental observations with the differing calculated results using thermodynamic principles. By his own admission, he had little success.

By the late 1890s the problems of calculating the heat radiation and absorption rates for different types of atoms tormented Planck. It should have been a simple thermodynamics calculation. But it didn't work. No one could make it work.

Planck hit upon the idea of correlating the entropy (a major thermodynamic concept) of vibrating atoms with their energy. As he followed his intuition for how to proceed with these calculations, he found himself treading new ground. No one had tried this approach to solving the perplexing black-body radiation problem.

Within a few weeks, Planck was able to derive a new radiation equation that was in close agreement with actual measurements under all conditions.It was not the formula, itself, that shattered old concepts and reordered the way all science viewed energy absorption and radiation by electrons. It was a concept in Planck's basic equation. He found that he had to introduce a constant of proportionality to make the equation fit with measured values and that this parameter could only take on discrete values found by multiplying an integer by several other terms.

The radiation absorbed by or emitted by a single electron could not be continuous, but could only happen at multiples of a set energy level, or quanta. Because measurements were made for a very large number of atoms all at the same time, it *seemed* that the energy readings were continuous. But at the level of a single electron, Planck discovered that they were not. Energy came in discrete bursts of fixed frequency and magnitude.

The energy bursts were soon called *quanta*, and quantum physics and quantum mechanics were born. The constant value that Planck deduced, $h$, which is one of the factors in determining the magnitude of an electron's quantum of energy, was named Planck's Constant and has been described as one of the most fundamental and basic physical relationships in our universe. This discovery earned him the Nobel Prize, and he had its value, $6.62 \times 10^{-27}$ erg.sec, engraved on his tombstone.

In the latter part of his career, Planck was wracked by nagging doubts. He believed in a deterministic world. Yet quantum theory, based on his work, pointed toward a universe of subatomic uncertainty. Could his initial calculations be wrong? Was there a way to reconcile his findings with his beliefs? Further, he couldn't make his equations compatible with Maxfield's field equations. Finally, he feared that his constant, $h$, and the entire constant of proportionality he had derived, were only mathematical conveniences and did not necessarily correspond exactly with the real world.

Planck's worries were never alleviated, but were instead replaced by personal tragedy, by World War II, and finally by his own failing health. His beloved wife died in 1909. One son had been killed during World War I, then his two daughters both died in childbirth, three years apart. A second son died of disease as a young and promising adult. His last living child, Erwin, was arrested for conspiring to assassinate Hitler. Nazi officials offered to release Erwin if Planck would sign a loyalty oath to Hitler (something he had steadfastly refused to do over the years). Proud to the end, Planck refused again. Erwin was executed in 1944. Planck said, "My sorrow cannot be expressed in words." To complete the tragedy, all his books, manuscripts, and notes were destroyed by an allied bomb during an air raid in May 1944.

Despite his personal setbacks, Max Planck will always be recognized and honored as the one who led the world past a terrible stumbling block and opened the door to understanding the atom. Few individuals in history have had a more profound impact on the development of science. None is more deserving of our praise than the quiet, practical man who set out to solve an equation and instead changed the world.

## Key Dates

| | |
|---|---|
| 1858 | Born in Kiel, Germany, on April 23 |
| 1879 | Received Ph.D. in physics from University of Munich |
| 1880 | Appointed to teaching post at University of Kiel |
| 1885 | Married Marie Merck; they had five children; she died in 1909; all five children died during Planck's life |
| 1889 | Appointed to teaching post in theoretical physics at University of Berlin |
| 1892 | Granted full professorship |
| 1918 | Awarded Nobel Prize for Physics |
| 1928 | Retired |
| 1947 | Died on October 4 |

# Advice

*Max Planck's primary advice to anyone planning a physics career is to master mathematics. Math is the language of science. If math is not your servant and ally, it will always be your enemy. During undergraduate studies gain a basic understanding of all fields of physics and related fields such as thermodynamics. Specialize in graduate school and commit yourself to staying with that field. It may take decades of struggle to arrive at a point where you can know what questions to ask, recognize the answers once you find them, or begin to understand the answers. Understanding math and being persistent now will produce understanding and advancement later.*

# References

Clive, Barbara. *The Questioners: Physicists and the Quantum Theory.* New York: Thomas Crowell, 1975. (Good review of Planck and the field.)

Heilbron, J. L. *The Dilemmas of an Upright Man: Max Planck as Spokesman for German Science.* Berkeley: University of California Press, 1987.

Planck, Max. *Introduction to Theoretical Physics.* Princeton, N.J.: Princeton University Press, 1949.

Planck, Max, and D. H. Williams. *A Survey of Physical Theory.* New York: Dover, 1994.

Risken, H. *The Fokker-Planck Equation: Methods of Solution and Application.* New York: Springer-Verlag, 1992. (Good technical piece on Planck's physics.)

Wasson, Tyler, ed. *Nobel Prize Winners.* New York, H. W. Wilson, 1987. (Summary review of Planck's important work.)

# Wilhelm Reich

*"Father of the Sexual Revolution"*                    Psychoanalysis

## Career Highlights

- Introduced brilliant new innovations in psychoanalysis and therapy
- Believed that neurosis represented excessive undischarged energy rooted in sexual repression
- Claimed that orgiastic impotence was primary cause of cancer, all neuroses, cardiovascular hypertension, and anemia
- Invented the "Orgone Energy Accumulator," designed to attract energy and help heal the body

## Important Contributions

Brilliant, radical, some say insane—Wilhelm Reich led a difficult life and, even though he died in 1957, his ideas are still analyzed, discussed, used, believed, misinterpreted, and misrepresented. Reich, sometimes called the "father of the sexual revolution," was a trained clinical psychoanalyst and served as an assistant to Sigmund Freud for almost 20 years. His greatest contribution to the field of psychoanalysis was his theory of the function of sexual release in determining both the physical and mental health of human beings.

## Career Path

The prison cell door slammed shut hard and brutal like the crack of a whip, and echoed with an ominous finality down the worn cement and metal corridor. The hands of unseen bodies extended through many of the cell bars in this federal prison at Lewisburg, Pennsylvania, as 59-year-old Wilhelm Reich slumped down on the narrow cot that would be his home until he died.

Two unfathomable questions revolved in his numbed mind: How did this happen to me? and What am *I* doing in prison?

There had been a time when the world considered Reich the rising star of psychotherapy and the heir apparent to Freud as the new leading psychotherapist in the world. So what was he doing in prison?

When Wilhelm Reich was around 12 years old, he witnessed his mother having an affair with his tutor. Wilhelm later hinted at the affair to his father, who used the young boy to force a confession from the mother, who then committed suicide. Later in life, these themes would appear in Reich's work: sexual repression and irrational condemnation of extramarital sexuality, the authoritarian father, the persecution of those who break society's sexual laws.

At age 14, Wilhelm left home for boarding school at Czernowitz, Austria. Three years later, his father died, also probably a suicide. (His father had taken out a large insurance policy, then deliberately stood in a pond for hours in cold weather, contracting pneumonia, which later turned into tuberculosis. His father died from the illness, but Wilhelm never saw any money from the insurance agency, a fact that led him to distrust insurance companies for the rest of his life.)

In 1916 Wilhelm joined the Austrian Army and fought on the Italian front in World War I. After the war, he enrolled in the law program at the University of Vienna. Soon, however, he switched to medicine, receiving his M.D. in 1922. He studied under Freud and was deeply influenced by Freud's theory that sexual repression was at the root of all neurosis. After graduate studies in neurology and psychiatry, Reich became the first clinical assistant at Freud's Psychoanalytic Polyclinic in 1922. In 1928 he advanced to become the clinic's vice-director.

In 1927, Reich published the first version of his most famous book, *The Function of Orgasm.* He had developed the belief that neurosis happened because of a person's inability to achieve a satisfactory sexual release. For him, this release was not just essential to the survival of the species in terms of reproduction; it was essential to the mental and physical health of humankind. Today, his view of the damming up of libido as the fundamental cause of neurosis has become commonplace among psychoanalysts.

Reich joined the Austrian Socialist Party in 1924 and, as a member, he wanted to establish socialist sex-hygiene clinics, which would offer psychoanalytic advice to the public as well as create an awareness of the sexual reforms that must accompany revolution. The clinics were closed down in 1930 by Party leaders who feared that the clinics were giving the Party a bad name.

Moved to Berlin, Reich joined the Communist Party, and once again began setting up his clinics. However, the Party closed his doors in 1933 and expelled him because of his advocacy of sexual politics. The next year, the

International Psychoanalytic Association excluded him because of his Communist associations.

During the 1930s, Reich's reputation nose-dived. Up until then, his writings had been taken as seriously as Freud's, and he contributed greatly to the theory and application of psychotherapy. His theories were considered a logical and reasonable extension of Freud's basic concepts. By the mid-1930s, however, Reich was viewed as a crank, and perhaps as a little mad. By 1939, Reich had been denounced by the Nazi Party and fled Germany for the United States.

Reich's research into microscopic plant and animal life revealed that not just sexuality but life itself operated in the pattern of release: tension and discharge, expansion and contraction. From this observation, he hypothesized that there must be a particular type of energy unique to sexuality. He believed he had discovered this ultimate life force, which he called Orgone energy. He devoted the rest of his life to studying Orgone energy and attempting to harness its healing powers.

It was Reich's contention that Orgone energy was a non-electromagnetic force that permeated all of nature, and that it could be demonstrated by means of Geiger counters. It could also be stored in accumulators, or "Orgone boxes," and used to cure mental and physical illnesses.

The claim that Orgone energy could cure cancer led the U.S. Food and Drug Administration to classify Reich's devices as drugs and therefore under their jurisdiction. In 1954, that agency obtained an injunction against the use of the Orgone energy devices. Reich called the claim ridiculous and refused to comply. In May 1956, he was found in contempt of court, convicted, and sentenced to two years in prison in Lewisburg, Pennsylvania. On June 5, 1956, two FDA agents and a federal marshal arrived to destroy the accumulators. On August 23 of that year, American authorities burned his books and notebooks at the Gansevoort Incinerator in New York. The American Civil Liberties Union protested the burning and issued a press release criticizing the burning of Reich's books; no major U.S. publisher ever printed the release. On November 3, 1957, the broken man died of a heart attack in the Federal Penitentiary in Lewisburg.

In retrospect, Reich's concept of Orgone energy is very similar to Yoga teachings on Kundalini energy. His innovations in therapy and clinical techniques are still popular with psychoanalysts today and are regarded as brilliant and insightful. His theories and lectures sparked the sexual revolution that spread from Scandinavia in the late 1940s and early 1950s through western Europe in the 1950s and to the United States in the 1960s. Whether Wilhelm Reich was just a clever crank, or a scientist of uncanny insight, only time will tell.

\* \* \*

## Key Dates

| | |
|---|---|
| 1897 | Born in Dobrzcynica, Galicia (now in Austria), on March 24 |
| 1915 | Passed his abiturium and joined the army, becoming an officer in 1916 and serving on the Italian front |
| 1920 | Graduated at the Faculty of Law, University of Vienna |
| 1922 | Received M.D. from the University of Vienna; became first clinical assistant at Freud's Psychoanalytic Polyclinic |
| 1924 | Joined Austrian Socialist Party |
| 1924–1930 | Became vice-director of Freud's Psychoanalytic Polyclinic |
| 1928 | Joined the Communist Party |
| 1930 | Moved to Berlin and established sex education for young people |
| 1933 | Expelled from the Communist Party |
| 1934 | Expelled from the International Psychoanalytic Association |
| 1939 | Left Germany to escape Nazis and moved to New York City |
| 1939–1941 | Was lecturer at New School for Social Research |
| 1942 | Published *The Function of Orgasm* |
| 1945 | Left New York City for Rangeley, Maine |
| 1954 | Defied Federal Food and Drug Administration injunction against use of Orgone energy devices to force a test case |
| 1956 | Held in contempt of court, convicted, and jailed for two-year term |
| 1957 | Died of a heart attack November 3 in federal penitentiary |

## Advice

*Wilhelm Reich would advise anyone considering a career in any branch of psychoanalysis to study and learn objective reasoning and observation. Observe nature and compare what you see with scientific coursework in that field. Study atomic physics and astronomy, courses in which conclusion is based on observation and inference. Theories as well as diagnosis must be based on objective, accurate observation. Finally, in addition to the standard courseload of medical school, add courses that expand creativity and your ability to see beyond conventional wisdom.*

## References

Erdelyi, M. *Psychoanalysis: Freud's Cognitive Psychology.* New York: W. H. Freeman, 1985.

Reich, Wilhelm. *Beyond Psychology: Letters and Journals 1934-1939.* Edited by Mary Boyd Higgins. Translated by Derek Jordan. New York: Farrar Straus & Giroux, 1995. (A collection of Reich's letters and journals, revealing the development of his revolutionary ideas regarding libido and human energy.)

———. *The Function of Orgasm; Sex-Economic Problems of Biological Energy.* New York: Noonday Press, 1986.

———. *Passion of Youth: An Autobiography, 1897-1922.* Saint Paul, Minn.: Paragon House, 1990.

Robinson, Paul. *The Freudian Left: Wilhelm Reich, Geza Roheim, Herbert Marcuse.* Ithaca, N.Y.: Cornell University Press, 1990. (Reissue.)

Sharaf, Myron R. *Fury on Earth: A Biography of Wilhelm Reich.* New York: Da Capo Press, 1994. (Reprint.)

# Charles Richter

*"Measuring the Beast"*                    Seismology

## Career Highlights

- Developed the Richter scale for measuring earthquakes
- Awarded the honorary medal of the Seismological Society of America, 1977
- Elected to Royal Astronomical Society, 1968
- Elected to the American Geophysical Union, 1965

## Important Contributions

Charles Richter was one of the earliest pioneers in developing the *science* of seismology. For centuries, the study of earthquakes had been treated more as a qualitative art. As part of scientific development, Richter created the open-ended, logarithmic Richter scale for measuring the magnitude of earthquakes. He was also the first to relate earth motion during a quake to the energy of the event. His books, written in the 1940s and 1950s, are still standard reference texts in the field.

## Career Path

It begins with a sound—like a truck just rumbling past—but it quickly builds to the sound of a pounding freight train roaring down on you. An earthquake rumbles through the Los Angeles suburbs. The ground groans. Trees violently sway. Plates rattle and crash from cupboard shelves. Chandeliers sway. Walls creak. Windows vibrate and explode. Shattered glass litters floors and lawns. People scream and run. Streets crack and buckle. A gas line breaks and explodes in a ball of fire, sending flames and smoke into the night.

Just as fast as it arrived, the earthquake passes and everyone rushes to radios, spinning the dial until they find a station that will tell them how big it was. Was it a 4.6, a 5.5, or a 6.2? Everyone knows the name and the scale: the Richter scale. But few know what the numbers measure or how much they have meant to scientists' ability to learn about these powerful earth waves. Charles Richter is the man who made these measurements possible.

When Charles Richter was nine years old, the family moved from rural Ohio to Los Angeles so that his father could take advantage of carpentry opportunities in the rapidly growing sprawl of southern California. Charles never felt at ease in this environment. His one high school activity was as member, and then as president, of the school's natural history club. The club took long, rambling hikes through the Arroyo Seco Canyon (now a freeway) and up into the rugged hills of the Los Angeles National Forest. Sometimes the hikes would last for days. Even teachers seemed not to mind that club members missed school when on a club expedition.

During these hikes, Charles saw the jagged scars across the landscape where earthquakes had shifted the earth. He even felt an occasional small quake. But no one in southern California seemed to mind. Small tremors were a natural part of life.

Charles always knew he would be some kind of scientist. Sciences were his passion. During his senior year of high school, he finally settled on astronomy, thinking it would be the best field to work in. After graduating at age 17, he enrolled in the University of Southern California to study astronomy.

After two years, Charles transferred to Stanford University because his interest had shifted toward physics, and Stanford had a better physics program. There he was exposed to the wondrous world inside an atom, and again shifted majors from physics to atomic physics.

Richter was offered a scholarship for graduate studies at the California Institute of Technology and began his studies toward a doctorate in theoretical physics. During his six years of study and research there, he served as lab and research assistant on a number of projects and gained a reputation as an excellent worker and clear thinker.

In 1927, Robert Millikan (Nobel laureate and president of Caltech) offered the young man a physicist research position at the campus Seismology Lab. Although his assigned job did not require it, Richter decided to immerse himself in the field of seismology. He studied geology and geography during his free time.

What Richter found was that, while researchers talked about earth movement and seismic forces, very little had been recorded about earthquakes. He recalled during a 1971 interview, "I wasn't supposed to do routine work on earthquakes. But someone had to find out where they originated and how big they were, so I just decided to do it."

Richter teamed with fellow research assistant Beno Gutenberg, a German-born geologist, to map all recorded southern California earthquakes. It took them over a year to compile a reasonably complete record of quakes over a 30-year period (1898–1928). They shocked local governments and the populace in general by showing that the region experienced more than 200 earthquakes every year. Admittedly almost all of them were small, but the number still seemed staggering.

The next problem was to determine the size of each quake. The only scale in existence to describe earthquakes had been developed by Italian geologist Giuseppe Mercalli, who had created an arbitrary 1 to 12 scale for evaluating earthquakes as a function of the damage and deaths they created. A "1" wasn't felt. A "12" caused extensive damage and loss of life. But a large earthquake got a "1" rating in an unpopulated area and an "8" or "9" if it occurred near a city. The same size earthquakes would receive different ratings depending on the quality of local construction and population density.

The Mercalli scale was useless for Richter's scientific purposes. The same earthquake that had rated as a "3" in 1880 might rate as a "5" in 1920 only because the southern California population had increased. He set out to devise a new scale, one that was quantitative and absolute. Richter realized he could use the physical size of the maximum wave amplitude of the earthquake as a handy indicator of the magnitude of the quake's energy.

To avoid creating a panic in the local population when an earthquake was recorded, Richter decided to make his scale seem "somewhat arbitrary with just small, simple numbers." After trying several different numerical schemes, he hit upon the idea of using the base 10 logarithm of the maximum amplitude of the seismic wave. On a logarithmic scale, a magnitude 7 earthquake wouldn't seem frighteningly larger than a magnitude 4 earthquake. In reality, of course, a "7" on that scale is 1,000 times larger than a "4."

Richter's scale was an instant hit. Within months of its first publication in 1935, it was being used worldwide and lauded as a significant new tool for seismic studies.

However, Richter never thought of the scale as anything more than a preliminary step toward what he really wanted to study: the amount of energy generated by an earthquake. Richter and Gutenberg spent a dozen years analyzing the scanty available data and retooling seismographs to collect more specific information. Their greatest frustration was that collection of data required them to stoically wait for an earthquake to happen along a fault line they were monitoring.

By 1950 Richter had mapped thousands of earthquakes from all over the world and was able to show that there was a direct correlation between seismic wave amplitude (Richter scale number) and quake energy. An increase of one number on the scale represented a ten-fold increase in amplitude, but a thirty-fold increase in released energy.

Richter continued to study seismic phenomena and to consult with city and county officials on earthquake safety for the rest of his life. He also maintained a full teaching load at Caltech and helped use the growing body of seismic data to work toward earthquake prediction. (To him, the word prediction "has more than four letters, but it's still a dirty word.") But he will always be remembered for the simple numeric scale he created. In the scale of things, it was a very valuable development for science.

## Key Dates

| | |
|---|---|
| 1900 | Born in Hamilton, Ohio, on April 26 |
| 1917–1918 | Studied at the University of Southern California |
| 1918–1921 | Received A.B. from Stanford University |
| 1927–1937 | Was assistant seismologist at the Seismological Laboratory in Pasadena, California |
| 1928 | Received Ph.D. in theoretical physics from California Institute of Technology (Caltech) |
| 1935 | Introduced the Richter scale |
| 1937 | Appointed assistant professor of seismology at Caltech |
| 1952–1970 | Appointed professor of seismology at Caltech |
| 1959–1960 | Worked as visiting professor at University of Tokyo |
| 1970–1985 | Appointed professor emeritus at Caltech |
| 1985 | Died on September 30 |

# Advice

*Charles Richter found great value in taking a roundabout path to reach seismology and would advise others to do the same. First master the basics of math and physics (including theoretical physics). The analytical tools developed in those courses apply to all other fields. Then follow your interest into the study of seismology and arts-related courses that help to free your creative thinking. Creative, original thinking is an invaluable tool to bring into the study of sciences. Finally, learn the theory and practice of the field and what others are doing and discovering in your field. You can't advance in your field until you understand its current state. That means becoming familiar with what everyone else has done and is doing, which requires long years of dedicated study.*

# References

Davidson, Charles. *The Founders of Seismology.* North Stratford, Conn.: Ayer, 1988. (Good historical review of the field.)

Devine, Elizabeth, ed. *The Annual Obituary, 1985.* Chicago: St. James Press, 1986. (Good summary of Richter's life and work.)

Howell, Benjamin. *An Introduction to Seismological Research: History and Development.* New York: Cambridge University Press, 1990. (Good overview of the field.)

Moritz, Charles, ed. *Current Biography Yearbook, 1990.* New York: H. W. Wilson, 1991. (Good review of Richter's work.)

Richter, Charles, and Beno Gutenberg. *Seismicity of the Earth.* New York: John Wiley, 1964. (Excellent primer on seismology and on Richter's views.)

# Sally Ride

## "The Most Fun I'll Ever Have"

## Astronautics and Astrophysics

### Career Highlights

National Aeronautics and Space Administration

- Was first American woman in space, 1983

## Important Contributions

Not too long ago, women were banned from the U.S. astronaut corps. An American woman simply could not become an astronaut. NASA lifted the ban only when it became increasingly difficult to find qualified scientists who were willing to work for salaries considerably lower than those of scientists employed by the private sector. Suddenly, women were allowed into the program, thereby widening the pool of qualified candidates and changing the face of American astronautics.

Twenty-two years after the United States sent up its first manned space capsule, Dr. Sally Ride, a 32-year-old astrophysicist and mission specialist, became the first American woman in space. While it was not her intention to become a symbol of progress for women, her achievements have made her one of the most famous women in the country.

## Career Path

The sun sat just above the blue Atlantic when, like a second sun, fire erupted from the rocket's engines. The ground shook and the thunderous roar was deafening even two miles away in the packed bleachers. A record number of members of the press—over 1,600—and several hundred thousand spectators shielded their eyes from the rocket's fireball glare and cheered. Over 200 press video cameras whirred. Lined shoulder to shoulder like Civil War riflemen, press photographers with monstrous telephoto lenses and camera motor drives clicked through miles of film.

Celebrities dotted the overflowing crowd, including Jane Fonda and Gloria Steinem. Many of the audience wore T-shirts emblazoned with "Ride, Sally Ride." Sally Ride hadn't planned to be a symbol, to change anything, or even to be an astronaut. She had seen the advertisement and thought space travel would be a kick. But as the *Challenger* shuttle lifted off into a clear Florida morning sky on June 18, 1983, Sally Ride made history.

Sally Ride was a born athlete, discovering tennis by age 10 at a club near her Encino, California, home. Under the instruction of four-time U.S. Open women's singles champion Alice Marble, Sally progressed to be a regular on the junior tennis circuit, ranking 17th nationally. Her tennis skills won her a partial scholarship to a private prep school in Los Angeles, Westlake School for Girls. It was there that the young athlete first discovered science through her favorite teacher, Dr. Elizabeth Mommaerts, whom she called "logic personified." Until that moment, Sally's sole focus had been tennis.

Science challenged and interested Sally in ways that other school subjects had never done before. Science made her want to learn and study. In 1968, Sally entered Swarthmore College in Pennsylvania to study physics. After three semesters, the lure of the growing crowds, exposure, and bigger purses on the women's tennis circuit led her to drop out of school to become a professional tennis player.

After a year on tour, however, Sally decided she would never become a top-ranked player. The call of science began to tug at her again. She returned to college at Stanford University in 1970, where she studied English and physics, earning her degree with a double major. Her graduate work at Stanford was all in physics and included X-ray astronomy and free-electron lasers. For her doctoral dissertation, she analyzed the theoretical behavior of free electrons in a magnetic field.

In 1977, Ride saw an advertisement in the campus newspaper that the National Aeronautics and Space Administration (NASA) was seeking young, athletic scientists to work as "mission specialists" on space flights. The qualifications exactly described her. She had never considered being an astronaut, had not planned for it or worked toward it. But the idea of space travel intrigued her and she applied, along with 8,000 others, including 1,000 other women. To Ride's amazement, she became one of 208 finalists. In October 1977, NASA flew her to Texas for a series of personal interviews, physical fitness tests, and psychiatric evaluations. She was one of 35 people chosen, including five other women.

Sally Ride then began the intensive training required of mission specialists at the Johnson Space Center. The year-long program included training in parachute jumping, water survival (in case the shuttle landed in the ocean), acclimatization to increased gravitational pull felt during acceleration, weightlessness, radio communications, navigation, astrophysics, and avionics. She logged hundreds of hours "flying" in the simulator and also learned to fly a jet, which she enjoyed so much that she took up flying as a hobby and qualified for a pilot's license.

After graduation from the NASA training program, Ride joined the core of astronauts working in ground-based assignments. She helped design the shuttle's remote mechanical manipulator arm for deploying and retrieving satellites. She also served as the capsule communicator, the astronaut who relays instructions from the flight director to the spacecraft crew, during the second and third flights of the space shuttle *Columbia*.

In April 1982, Navy Captain Robert L. Crippen, who had been selected to command the seventh space shuttle flight, chose Ride to be one of the four other crew members. She was to be mission specialist and flight engineer. The announcement of her selection drew immediate, widespread publicity. Both Ride and Crippen tried to downplay the significance of a woman chosen to fly in space and both fielded sexist questions about her emotional stability and suitability. Crippen adamantly defended her selection as the best person for the job: "There is no man I would rather have in her place."

The five crew members then began intensive training, rehearsing the flight over and over in the simulator. They tried to anticipate problems and design defects, sometimes spending 56 hours straight in the simulator.

Finally, on June 18, 1983, the space shuttle *Challenger* lifted off from Cape Canaveral, Florida. Ride was on board, becoming the first American woman in space. (Two Soviet female cosmonauts, Valentina Tereshkova and Svetlana Savitskaya, had preceded her, in 1963 and 1982, respectively.)

The flight was a stunning success, accomplishing 96 percent of the mission's objectives. The crew successfully launched two communications satellites, performed various scientific experiments in zero gravity, and successfully deployed and recaptured a German satellite with a 50-foot mechanical arm. The shuttle mission ended on June 24, 1983, when the *Challenger* touched down at Edwards Air Force Base in California (bad weather kept it from landing at Cape Canaveral, as planned). Commenting on the flight, Ride said, "I'm sure it was the most fun I'll ever have in my life."

Three weeks later, Dr. Ride took another assignment at NASA, that of liaison officer between NASA and private companies doing work on the space program. In October 1984, she flew on another *Challenger* mission, and then retired from NASA in 1987 to become a research fellow at Stanford University.

While Sally Ride has repeatedly insisted that she did not enter the space program to "become a symbol of progress for women," she has become that nonetheless. Her self-confidence and composure made her a world-famous role model and hero.

## Key Dates

| | |
|---|---|
| 1951 | Born in Encino, California, on May 26, 1951 |
| 1968 | Entered Swarthmore College in Pennsylvania to study physics, then dropped out |
| 1970 | Returned to college at Stanford University |
| 1973 | Received B.A. in English and B.S. in physics from Stanford |
| 1977 | Applied to NASA as a mission specialist |
| 1978 | Was chosen along with five other women, out of 8,000 applicants, for NASA shuttle program |
| 1978 | Received Ph.D. from Stanford University |
| 1981–1982 | Served as capsule communicator for the second and third flights of the space shuttle *Columbia* |
| 1982 | Selected by Commander Robert Crippen to be part of his crew for the seventh space shuttle flight |
| 1983 | Took off on June 18 in the seventh space shuttle flight from Cape Canaveral, Florida |
| 1984 | Flew on another space shuttle mission on board the *Challenger* on October 5 |
| 1987 | Instrumental in issuing the "Ride Report" |

1987–1989   Retired from NASA to become a research fellow at Stanford University

1989–present   Director of California Space Institute, UCSD

## Advice

*If you are interested in a career in the space shuttle program, Sally Ride would advise you to obtain, study, and adhere to the NASA qualifications statement for mission specialists. Find a sport and stay physically fit. Become involved in group, club, or team efforts. Gain a solid foundation in the general sciences and then specialize in one of the physical or life sciences. If you can afford it, learn to fly and get a pilot's license (a commercial pilot's license is even better). Being an astronaut is a lot of work, but Sally Ride believes it was definitely worthwhile. After her first mission, Ride announced that "I'd like to do it as many times as NASA will let me."*

## References

Blacknall, Carolyn. *Sally Ride: America's First Woman in Space.* Parsippany, N.J.: Silver Burdett Press, 1985.

Fox, Mary Virginia. *Women Astronauts Aboard the Space Shuttle.* Parsippany, N.J.: Silver Burdett Press, 1987.

Hurwitz, Jane, and Sue Hurwitz. *Sally Ride: Shooting for the Stars.* New York: Fawcett Columbine, 1989.

Kerrod, Robin. *Space Shuttle.* New York: Gallery Books, W. H. Smith, 1984.

O'Connor, Karen. *Sally Ride and the New Astronauts: Scientists in Space.* Danbury, Conn.: Franklin Watts, 1983.

Ride, Sally. *To Space and Back.* New York: Lothrop, Lee & Shephard, 1986.

———. *The Third Planet.* New York: Crown, 1994.

Wilson, Andrew. *The Shuttle Story.* New York: Hamlyn, 1986.

# Albert Sabin

*"A Better Vaccine"*                    Microbiology

## Career Highlights

- Developed the first oral live-virus vaccine against polio
- Isolated and developed a vaccine for dengue fever viruses
- Received the Bruce Memorial Award of the American College of Physicians, 1961
- Won the Lasker Clinical Science Award, 1965

## Important Contributions

Albert Sabin was not the first to create a polio vaccine. Jonas E. Salk had earlier created a dead-virus vaccine against polio, which was widely used. But Sabin believed that a dead-virus (or inactive) vaccine could be nothing more than a temporary safeguard, requiring the patient to be re-vaccinated at frequent intervals. He believed that only a living-virus vaccine could produce the necessary antibodies over a long period. Plus, a living virus could be taken orally because it would invade the body and multiply on its own, not needing to be injected like the Salk vaccine.

And so, in the late 1950s, Albert Sabin succeeded in developing an orally administered live-virus vaccine against poliomyelitis (polio). By the early 1960s, Sabin's vaccine had completely replaced Jonas Salk's dead-virus vaccine. His vaccine gave a stronger and longer-lasting immunity than Salk's vaccine and protected against both paralysis and infection.

While Sabin is best known for his development of the live polio vaccine, his long and distinguished career included research into and vaccines against many other serious diseases as well.

# Career Path

A line of volunteers shifted nervously in the waiting room of the University of Cincinnati medical clinic. Albert Sabin had persuaded his family to stand first in line. His children were far from eager to be guinea pigs in this experiment. "Do I *have* to, mom?" "Is he going to make me get a shot?" "I don't want to get polio. Why is dad going to give me polio?" In 1955, "polio," the cause of an unchecked epidemic of childhood paralysis in the first half of the twentieth century, was a word that struck terror into every heart. The rest of the line was made up of neighbors, colleges, and volunteer prisoners. All of them had to be coerced to show up for Sabin's first trial of a live polio vaccine.

Sabin, himself, went first and confidently smiled as he lifted a sugar cube saturated with his live polio vaccine. But his mind roared with burning questions. Was the virus so strong it would cause the disease? Was it so weak it wouldn't create a good immune response? Was the dose too large? Too small? Would the immunity last? The people in line saw none of these fears and concerns, just a beaming smile as Sabin popped the first live polio virus into his mouth. Only time would tell if he had just given himself polio or made the world safer from this dread disease.

Albert Sabin's family immigrated to the United States from Russia when he was 15 years old. As part of a struggling immigrant family, Albert worked at odd jobs, first while he learned English throughout high school, and then to put himself through college and medical school. He attended New York University and graduated with his M.D. in 1931. He interned at Bellevue Hospital in New York City, where he first became interested in virology. Paul de Kruif's *Microbe Hunters* was especially influential. "Melodramatic as it may sound," he says, "the book gave me a picture of what science meant to man."

In 1931, Sabin first began to study the polio virus at New York University, shifting to the Rockefeller Institute in 1936, where he continued his study of polio. He and a colleague, Peter Olitsky, were able to obtain live polio virus from monkeys (a natural carrier) and to grow the virus in tissue cultures from the brain cells of a human embryo that had miscarried.

The scientists' goal was to create a vaccine, but vaccines, in the early days of their development, were a risky venture. Appropriate dose size had to be determined by trial and error. Some people might get too large a dose and get sick. Some might not get enough and not become immune even though they thought they were. The public was skeptical and fearful of the concept of live vaccines.

Most people were afraid of voluntarily injecting even a small dose of a dreaded disease into their bodies and so preferred dead-virus vaccines. But dead-virus vaccines had to be administered through a shot and had to be repeated regularly because they didn't induce the body to produce strong antibodies. Live-virus vaccines, on the other hand, ran the risk of inducing the very disease doctors were trying to prevent.

Many researchers, like Jonas Salk, preferred dead-virus vaccines because they were safer. Sabin preferred live-virus vaccines because they were more effective. That preference brought with it a long series of problems and worries that dead-virus researchers didn't have to face. He first had to figure out how to weaken the virus so that each recipient's immune system could easily destroy it and the virus couldn't refortify itself. Then he had to find out how to keep the weakened virus alive long enough to be administered. Finally, he had to make sure he didn't weaken the virus too much or the body would not bother to produce a strong and lasting immune response.

Scientists believed that the polio virus entered the body through the nose. Sabin's experiments with monkeys demonstrated that, in fact, the virus was primarily an alimentary tract virus, so it had to enter the body orally.

Sabin's work was interrupted by service in the U.S. Army Medical Corps during World War II, after which he returned to the University of Cincinnati, where he resumed his polio virus studies with new growing techniques. He cultivated all three types of monkey polio virus in kidney tissues. Each virus strain produced its own variety of antibody, which was too feeble to produce the disease itself. Sabin weakened the virus by allowing it to infect a series of research animals, then he recultivated the resultant strains.

The resulting live (but weakened) vaccine worked by inducing a harmless infection of the intestinal tract, thereby simulating a natural infection without actually causing the disease. The tissues multiplied, giving rise to a mild and "invisible" infection, and the body subsequently formed antibodies against and, thus, immunity to the disease. The vaccine conferred immunity rapidly, which is particularly important during an epidemic. In addition, the vaccine rendered the alimentary tract of those vaccinated resistant to re-infection by the polio virus.

After years of patient research, Sabin tried the vaccine on himself, his family, and local volunteers, including prisoner-volunteers. By 1957, he was convinced of its safety and effectiveness and wanted to offer it for field trials. But the U.S. government refused to let him begin mass inoculations here. The Soviet Union and Mexico, however, welcomed Sabin's experiments, and during 1957 and 1958, millions of children in Russia and 200,000 children in Mexico were vaccinated.

In June 1959, Sabin announced the results of his inoculation studies at the meeting of the International Scientific Congress on Live Virus Vaccines. His vaccine was safe and effective. It gave a stronger, longer-lasting immunity than the Salk vaccine. It was also easier to give to children, being in the form of a sugar cube rather than an injection. In August 1961, the vaccine was approved for use in the United States, but it would take another year before it was manufactured in the United States and licensed for general distribution.

Over the course of his career, Albert Sabin also made many advances in our understanding of tropical diseases, encephalitis, and the B virus. His research helped save millions of lives and helped nearly eradicate poliomyelitis from the United States.

## Key Dates

| | |
|---|---|
| 1906 | Born in Bialystok, Russia (now in Poland), on August 26 |
| 1921 | Immigrated with his family to America |
| 1931 | Received M.D. from New York University |
| 1932–1933 | Trained in pathology, surgery, and internal medicine at Bellevue Hospital, New York |
| 1934 | Performed research at the Lister Institute of Preventive Medicine, London |
| 1935–1939 | Joined the staff of the Rockefeller Institute |
| 1939–1946 | Appointed associate professor of pediatrics at the University of Cincinnati |
| 1946–1960 | Appointed professor of research pediatrics at the University of Cincinnati |
| 1960–1970 | Named Distinguished Service Professor of Research Pediatrics |
| 1962 | Saw his polio vaccine used in Great Britain instead of the Salk vaccine; other countries soon followed |
| 1970–1972 | Became president of the Weizmann Institute in Israel |
| 1973 | Professor of biomedicine at the Medical University of Southern Carolina |
| 1973–1974 | Served as expert consultant to the National Cancer Institute |
| 1993 | Died on October 18 |

# Advice

*Albert Sabin found that microbiology focuses on laboratory experiments. Seek summer jobs working in a lab or volunteer as a lab assistant to both learn proper lab technique and find out if you enjoy long hours of lab work. Sabin believed you could successfully enter the field of microbiology either through medical school or through biological life sciences programs. Take chemistry (organic and inorganic) as well as biology and microbiology courses. During your undergraduate years, mix liberal arts and general sciences classes. Specialize in graduate school.*

# References

Barrett, James T. *Microbiology & Immunology Concepts.* Austin, Tex.: Pro-Ed Press, 1998.

Braude, Abraham I. *Microbiology: Basic Science & Medical Applications.* Philadelphia, Pa.: W. B. Saunders, 1982.

Daintith, John, et al., eds. "Albert Sabin," in *Biographical Encyclopedia of Scientists.* 2d ed. Philadelphia, Pa.: Institute of Physics Publishing, 1994.

Emmerson, A. M. *The Microbiology & Treatment of Life-Threatening Infections.* Ann Arbor, Mich.: Books on Demand, 1995.

Greene, Jay E., ed. "Albert Sabin," in *McGraw-Hill Modern Men of Science:* New York: McGraw-Hill, 1968: 411–412.

Hyde, Richard M. *Microbiology & Immunology.* New York: Springer-Verlag, 1995.

Rose, Noel R., and Almen L. Barron, eds. *Microbiology: Basic Principles & Clinical Applications.* Englewood Cliffs, N.J.: Prentice-Hall, 1983.

# Florence Rena Sabin

*"The Little Doctor"*

Anatomy and
Immunology

## Career Highlights

Archives of the National Academy of Sciences

- Was first woman faculty member at Johns Hopkins Medical School, 1902
- Was president of the American Association of Anatomists, 1924
- Elected to the National Academy of Sciences, 1925
- Made member of the Rockefeller Institute, 1925

## Important Contributions

Florence Sabin was a woman of many "firsts": the first woman professor at Johns Hopkins, the first woman elected to the National Academy of Science, and the first woman president of the American Association of Anatomists.

In addition, Sabin had not just one but three impressive careers. She was first a researcher and teacher at Johns Hopkins Medical School, where she specialized in the investigation of the lymphatic system, blood vessels, and the origin of red blood cells. Her discoveries about the lymphatic system, at first highly controversial, were eventually proved correct; her publications altered medical thinking and brought her many honors and awards.

**416**

Her second career was as a researcher of tuberculosis at the Rockefeller Institute. Her third and final career began after she retired at age 73, when she led an impressive (and successful) crusade to overhaul the public health system of her native state, Colorado.

## Career Path

Central City, Colorado, was a rough and tumble gold rush town in the 1870s. Company mine shafts were sunk fast and deep into rich veins of gold-bearing rock. Fortunes could be made overnight. Florence Sabin was born and raised in that "Wild West" environment because her father gave up the study of medicine to work as an engineer in the Colorado mines, hoping to get rich. Florence grew up with few children for playmates, no school, and more saloons than any other kind of business on the town's main street.

During her childhood Florence saw two of her younger brothers die in infancy and her mother die in childbirth, because their rugged Colorado high-mountain town was too far from medical help. Her feeling of helplessness in response to those deaths was a strong influence leading her toward the study of medicine.

Unable to cope with raising his two remaining daughters alone, Florence's father shipped her and her older sister to a boarding school in Denver. A few years later, her uncle, Albert Sabin, took the girls to live with him and his family for four years in Chicago. Florence later remembered those four years as happy and intellectually stimulating ones, contrasted with an otherwise bleak childhood. When she was 12 years old, Florence was shipped off again, this time to live with her grandparents on their farm in Vermont.

In 1889, Sabin was reunited with her sister at Smith College. There she became aware of the struggle for women's rights, an issue that she would quietly fight for all her life. But that interest did not sway her from her lifelong passion for medicine. By her sophomore year, she had settled on the biological sciences for her undergraduate studies, and after receiving her B.S. in 1893, began the search for a medical school that would accept women.

That same year, Johns Hopkins Medical School opened with the financial help of a group of Baltimore women who stipulated that women must be admitted on the same basis as men. Sabin applied to study there, but first needed to earn enough money to pay her tuition and expenses. For two years, she taught mathematics in Denver and for a year she taught zoology at Smith College. She finally enrolled as part of the fourth class admitted to Johns Hopkins, the best medical school in the country.

Sabin was an excellent student, winning one of four highly coveted internships in internal medicine upon graduation. Franklin Mall, professor of anatomy, proved to be the strongest influence upon her. He stimulated his students to learn on their own so that they might know the joys of discovery. While she was a student of Mall's, Sabin undertook a project to construct a three-dimensional model of the mid and lower brain. After studying over 100 brains obtained from the Baltimore morgue instead of studying existing textbooks, she published her findings in 1901 as *An Atlas of the Medulla and Midbrain*, which quickly became a popular text.

Because of her exceptional and original work, Sabin became an assistant in the anatomy department in 1902, the first woman faculty member at Johns Hopkins. She rose to the rank of professor in 1917, also the first woman to have joined the professorial rank at Johns Hopkins. Despite having obtained these prestigious positions, she experienced belittling discrimination. Her male colleagues called her "Miss" rather than "Dr." Sabin. When Mall died in 1917, Dr. Sabin, the assistant department chair, was not only *not* promoted to chair of the department, she was not even considered. Instead, one of her former students, Lewis Weed, succeeded to the chairmanship. She swallowed her pride and bitter disappointment and continued working at Johns Hopkins for another eight years, mostly because it was still better than any other teaching position a woman science and medical professor could hope to find.

In 1925 Sabin was the first woman elected to the National Academy of Sciences, and also the first woman to receive a full membership at the Rockefeller Institute in New York. She left Johns Hopkins that year and spent the next 13 years at the Rockefeller Institute, where she set up the Department of Cellular Studies. There she established a laboratory devoted to the cellular aspects of the immune response. She undertook the study of tuberculosis, which was a major health problem at the time, heading a team that examined how the body's disease-fighting immune system reacts to the bacterium that causes TB.

In 1938, after a 45-year career, Sabin retired to Denver, Colorado, to live with her sister. In 1944, however, she once again became active. Colorado Governor John Vivian asked her to serve on his Post-War Planning Committee to assist in assessing the state's health needs. Colorado had long seen itself as a health oasis; thus it came as a shock when Sabin and the subcommittee on public health published a report describing an inefficient, politically controlled board of health poorly funded, poorly trained, and with inadequate laws.

Florence Sabin became known as the "little doctor," as a dynamo and a powerful political force. She crusaded for basic public health reforms in Colorado, using her experience and skills to gather the necessary supporting facts and case studies. She traveled, spoke, and wrote extensively, persuading legislators and state officials to revamp the public health program. The series of health laws she fought for (called the Sabin program) was passed in 1947. She served as chair of the Interim Board of Health and Hospitals of Denver until 1951. In 1953, she died of a heart attack in Denver, Colorado.

## Key Dates

| | |
|---|---|
| 1871 | Born in Central City, Colorado, on November 9 |
| 1884–1889 | Attended the Vermont Academy in Saxtons River, Vermont |
| 1893 | Received B.S. at Smith College; Johns Hopkins Medical School opened |
| 1893–1895 | Taught mathematics privately in Denver |
| 1895–1896 | Taught zoology at Smith College |
| 1900 | Received M.D. at Johns Hopkins |
| 1901 | Published *An Atlas of the Medulla and Midbrain*; appointed to a fellowship in anatomy at Johns Hopkins |
| 1902 | Worked as assistant in anatomy department, the first woman faculty member at Johns Hopkins |
| 1917 | Worked as professor of histology, the first woman professor at Johns Hopkins |
| 1925 | Left Johns Hopkins to establish a laboratory at the Rockefeller Institute |
| 1938 | Retired to Denver, becoming emeritus from the Rockefeller Institute |
| 1944 | Made head of subcommittee on health for Colorado's Post-War Planning Committee |
| 1947–1951 | Was chair of the Interim Board of Health and Hospitals of Denver |
| 1953 | Died October 3 in Denver, Colorado |

## Advice

*Florence Sabin would offer the following advice to anyone considering a career in the fields of immunology and anatomy: First, become accustomed to finding answers by conducting your own experiments rather than by reading textbooks. Experience the joys of firsthand discovery. Certainly, read and study. But then, question, experiment, and analyze. Sabin believed that "it is more important for the student to be able to find out something for himself than to memorize what someone else has said."*

*Second, delay the commitment to rigid pre-med and medical school curriculum. First develop a broad-based undergraduate background in the general biological sciences and in philosophy and other arts that foster creativity. Also use this time to develop experimental skills and practice.*

## References

Bluemel, Elinor. *Florence Sabin, Colorado Woman of the Century.* Boulder: University of Colorado Press, 1959. (The most comprehensive book about Sabin.)

Campbell, Robin. *Florence Sabin: Scientist.* Junior World Biographies. New York: Chelsea House, 1996.

Phelan, Mary K. *Probing the Unknown: The Story of Dr. Florence Sabin.* New York: Thomas Crowell, 1969. (Biography for younger readers.)

Sabin, Florence. *An Atlas of the Medulla and Midbrain.* Baltimore, Md.: Friedenwald, 1901.

Stille, Darlene R. *Extraordinary Women Scientists.* Chicago: Children's Press, 1995.

# Carl Sagan

*"The Cosmic Explainer"*

Astronomy and
Astrophysics

## Career Highlights

- Authored more than 600 published scientific papers and popular articles
- Won the Pulitzer Prize for Literature, 1978
- Received the Apollo Achievement Award from the National Aeronautics and Space Administration (NASA), 1970
- Named Humanist of the Year, 1981
- Won three Emmy awards for the *Cosmos* series, 1981

## Important Contributions

Almost single-handedly, Carl Sagan brought astronomy and the space program to the American people. He was a vocal and untiring advocate of both the romantic and the popular sides of science. Although his primary interests were planetary surfaces and atmospheres, he also conducted pioneering studies in the possibilities of extraterrestrial life.

Sagan made significant contributions to the *Viking* mission to Mars, and he studied extensively the damaging effects of nuclear war on Earth's climate. He played an important role in developing the *Cosmos* series, one of the most successful series of any kind to be broadcast on PBS television. He authored many popular books, including *The Dragons of Eden,* which won a Pulitzer Prize. It is for this "popularizing" of science that he will be most remembered.

## Career Path

"What's a star?" It was an ordinary enough question for an eight-year-old boy to ask. But the ordinary adult response, "It's a light in the sky, kid," was not at all satisfactory to Carl Sagan, a very un-ordinary boy. So Carl hiked to a New York City branch library near his house to learn about the stars. Misunderstanding what he wanted, the librarian handed him a book on movie stars.

Carl took the book to a table and politely scanned it for five minutes before returning to the desk. "This isn't the kind of stars I want." The librarian returned with a book on stage and vocal stars. In five minutes an embarrassed Carl was back. "I want stars in the sky."

Finally comprehending, the librarian handed him a thick picture volume on "wonders of the galaxy." The young boy was stunned by what he saw and read in that book—the idea that stars were suns, just like our own sun, but so far away that they were only a twinkle of light, astonished him. He was hooked. Soon he learned about planets. Once he had discovered that there were suns out there and probably planets too, Carl felt certain there must be life out there too. By age nine, he was an amateur astronomer, convinced of the existence of life on other planets.

By age 10, Carl was captivated by the Mars novels of Edgar Rice Burroughs. With malignant enemies and rousing swordsmanship, the novels kept him entertained while they enthralled him with the possibilities of space. He began subscribing to a science fiction magazine called *Astounding Science Fiction*. There he reveled in Verne and Wells, finding the stories as thought-provoking as they were entertaining.

As Carl analyzed the novels and the magazines, however, he found they were all disappointing in one respect: "They ranked high in asking interesting questions but low in answering them." He wanted more hard science, more "meat" in the science.

When he was 12, Carl's grandfather asked him what he wanted to be when he grew up. "An astronomer," Carl answered confidently. "Fine," said his grandfather. "But how will you make a living?"

The question shocked the young boy, who had not thought about income in his plans for his life's work. He figured that his grandfather meant that astronomers were never paid and that he would have to hold some run-of-the-mill, unsuitable salesperson job during the day, then study his beloved astronomy at night and on the weekends. It was a glorious day in his sophomore year of high school when his biology teacher mentioned that Harvard paid astronomer Harlow Shapley a salary.

With the help of a series of scholarships, Carl Sagan obtained his B.A. from the University of Chicago in 1954 and a B.S. in physics a year later.

During his undergraduate years, he was an excellent basketball player, captaining a championship intramural basketball team. He also served as president of the Astronomical Society, which he founded.

Sagan stayed at the University of Chicago for his M.S. and his Ph.D. in astronomy, which he received in 1960. From 1962 to 1968, he served as a lecturer and assistant professor of astronomy at Harvard. But his flamboyant style, when coupled with the speculative nature of some of his research, was difficult for the old-line astronomy professors at Harvard to accept.

When he was denied tenure in 1968, Sagan moved to Cornell University. There he studied the bright and dark patterns on Mars and, with one of his graduate students, James Pollack, concluded that they were due to winds swift enough to whirl up dust storms in the thin atmosphere, sculpting huge variations in surface elevations. *Mariner 9* confirmed this theory three years later. Sagan was also the first to theorize that greenhouse gases were responsible for the very high temperature at the surface of Venus. The *Pioneer Venus* spacecraft later confirmed this theory.

Sagan was also interested in the origins of life on our planet. But the only way to study these origins was to recreate them in a laboratory. Over several years of experiments simulating the primitive atmosphere of Earth, he showed how organic molecules (such as amino acids and ATP) can be produced from commonly available inorganic compounds. The energy sources used for these syntheses included ultraviolet radiation (plentiful in the Earth's early atmosphere), heat, and high-pressure shock waves.

The experiment involved filling a flask with methane, ammonia, water, and hydrogen—things one would expect to find in the primitive atmosphere of a young planet—and passing an electrical discharge, like lightning, through the mix.

After each experiment Sagan was able to detect the presence of amino acids, the first step toward life. He also frequently detected ATP, a prime energy-storage compound. With the correct subsequent environmental conditions, these simple acids could develop into nucleic acids (proteins), the true building blocks of life.

In 1984, Sagan co-authored a paper called "Nuclear Winter: Global Consequences of Multiple Nuclear Explosions." The paper argued that even a relatively small nuclear exchange would create enough atmospheric smoke and dust to drop the Earth's temperature by 10 to 20 degrees Celsius, a condition that would last for months. This prolonged "nuclear winter" would destroy much of the world's industry and agriculture. The effect of this paper on politicians and the public was dramatic, even though it was widely criticized by other scientists, including Richard Feynman.

Sagan's work focused on virtually all aspects of the solar system. He researched the physics and chemistry of planetary atmospheres and surfaces, especially of Mars. In his later years, he focused on the long-term effects of nuclear war. Even though his work has brought great advancements to astronomy, Carl Sagan will be most remembered for popularizing science, bringing it to average Americans in a way that everyone can understand, appreciate, and enjoy through his many books, articles, and his television series, *Cosmos*.

## Key Dates

| | |
|---|---|
| 1934 | Born in New York City on November 9 |
| 1954 | Received B.A. with honors from University of Chicago |
| 1955 | Received B.S. from University of Chicago |
| 1956 | Received M.S. from University of Chicago |
| 1956–1957 | Worked as lecturer at University of Chicago |
| 1958–1959 | Worked as physicist at Armour Research Foundation |
| 1960 | Received Ph.D. in astronomy and astrophysics from University of Chicago |
| 1960–1962 | Appointed Miller Research Fellow in astronomy at University of California at Berkeley |
| 1962–1968 | Worked as lecturer and assistant professor of astronomy at Harvard University |
| 1962–1968 | Worked as astrophysicist at Smithsonian Institution Astrophysical Observatory |
| 1968–1970 | Worked as associate professor of astronomy and director of the Laboratory for Planetary Studies, Cornell University |
| 1970–1972 | Worked as professor of astronomy and space sciences at Cornell University |
| 1972–1981 | Served as associate director of Center for Radiophysics and Space Research |
| 1976 | Appointed David Duncan Professor of Astronomy and Space Sciences |
| 1981 | Became president of Carl Sagan Productions, Inc. |
| 1985 | Published first novel, *Contact* |
| 1996 | Died on December 20 |

# Advice

*Carl Sagan studied for a liberal arts degree before starting his science career. This intentional digression was designed to incorporate philosophy and the humanities into his later scientific work. He found that liberal studies fostered senses of wonder, curiosity, and creativity. Sagan once said that, for him, one of the most important factors in choosing his line of work was his sense of wonder, that he had developed himself into a questioner, one who always asked "why," and "what if."*

*Before settling into either astronomy or astrophysics study, Sagan would also suggest getting a good grounding in math and physics. Those courses will be the foundation for later astronomical explorations.*

# References

Cohen, Daniel. *Carl Sagan: Superstar Scientist.* New York: Putnam, 1987.

Englebert, Phillis, ed. *Astronomy & Space: From the Big Bang to the Big Crunch.* Detroit: Gale Research, 1996.

North, John. *Astronomy & Cosmology.* New York: W. W. Norton, 1994.

Sagan, Carl. *The Dragons of Eden.* New York: Ballantine Books, 1993.

Sagan, Carl (with P. R. Ehrlich and others). *The Cold and the Dark: The World After Nuclear War.* New York: W. W. Norton , 1984.

Terzian, Yervant, and Elizabeth Bilson, eds. *Carl Sagan's Universe.* New York: Cambridge University Press, 1997.

Von Baravalle, Herman. *Astronomy: An Introduction.* Fair Oaks, Calif.: Rudolf Steiner College Publications, 1991.

# Jonas E. Salk

## *"The Total Conquest of Polio"*

## Microbiology and Immunology

Photo by Jim Cox

### Career Highlights

- Developed the first successful vaccine against polio
- Founded, and was fellow and director of, the Salk Institute for Biological Studies
- Received the Bruce Memorial Award of the American College of Physicians, 1958
- Awarded the Lasker Award of the American Public Health Association, 1956

### Important Contributions

When the world learned, in 1955, that Jonas Salk had developed a vaccine that could prevent paralytic poliomyelitis, a wave of gratitude, love, and joy swept the world. People observed moments of silence, drank toasts, honked horns, waved flags, cried, laughed, hugged, and forgave each other.

In a seemingly unchecked epidemic, polio had claimed too many lives and crippled too many children's legs; the world was eager for a means of prevention—and eager to embrace the scientist who had created it. As headlines promised "the total conquest of polio," Salk became a hero, a hero who saved the lives and legs of thousands of people.

# Career Path

It was an odd recurring dream for a boy to have. Maybe it related to his mother, a driven perfectionist, who relentlessly demanded, drove, and directed him in every facet of his life to achieve similar perfection. The dream regularly returned: "Someday I shall grow up and do something important in my own way, without anyone telling me how." The dream resonated in Jonas Salk's being. As he turned from boy to young man, the dream took form: He would conduct important, original medical research in his own way and without outside direction. Jonas Salk became the image of his mother, a driven perfectionist bent on achieving his dream.

Raised in the Bronx, Jonas proved himself to be an excellent student, reading everything he could lay his hands on. He earned high grades in school and graduated from a secondary school for exceptional students. His mother saw to it that he excelled. As soon as her son had measured up to her standards, she raised them.

Jonas enrolled at the College of the City of New York for his undergraduate and pre-med courses. His work in virology and immunology began as a senior medical student at New York University. After receiving his M.D. in 1939, he worked for several months with Thomas Francis, who was studying methods of killing influenza virus without destroying the virus's ability to stimulate antibody production in the human body. Then he began a two-year internship at the Mount Sinai Hospital in New York.

Even as a student, Jonas Salk's perfectionism demanded that he exceed all normal standards of medical performance. No one carried out medical experiments with more care or determination than he did. Later, when he was developing the polio vaccine, he would work seven days a week, sometimes for 24 hours at a time.

Salk was considered an eccentric because of his perfectionism and unyielding determination. His peers did not see in him the creative spark they thought necessary for successful medical research. But Salk refused to consider any alternatives to his obsessive dream.

In 1942 Salk joined the research staff at the University of Michigan, where he again collaborated with virologist Thomas Francis. They developed a vaccine against influenza that was tested on 20,000 people and appeared to offer protection against influenza for about two years. This work brought Salk acknowledgment as an expert on the immunology of influenza.

During World War II, Salk worked as a consultant to control epidemic diseases in the armed forces. After another term at Michigan, he was invited by the University of Pittsburgh to join a special research unit to study the causes and treatment of virus diseases. It was there that he began working with the polio virus and the final pieces of his dream took shape.

By the time Salk began working with the polio virus, scientists had discovered that viruses could be grown in live chick embryos (mashed embryonic tissue, supplied with nutrients, with penicillin added to keep down bacteria growth). This ability to obtain sufficient amounts of viruses was essential to creating vaccines.

Salk studied the reaction of the polio virus to various chemicals and discovered that there were actually three types of polio virus. He concluded that a vaccine must immunize against all of them to be effective. He set about finding a way to treat the virus so that it could not cause the disease but could still produce an antibody reaction in the body. The public still vividly remembered the vaccine tragedy of 1935, when scientists had tested several dead- and attenuated-virus polio vaccines on over 10,000 children with disastrous results, including some cases of paralysis and death.

Salk collected spinal cord samples from polio victims and grew the virus in the new live-cell culture medium. He then suspended the virus in mineral oil and exposed it to formaldehyde for up to 13 days. (The formaldehyde ensured that the virus was killed—no live virus could be detected after three days of exposure.) He then tested the killed-virus vaccine on monkeys and found that it did indeed induce antibody formation. By 1952, he was ready to test the vaccine on people.

Injections were first given to children who had already had polio and were immune from the disease; results were good. The children's antibody levels increased. Next Salk tried the vaccine on his family and on children who had not had polio. Again antibodies were formed and none became ill. Salk felt the vaccine was ready to test in a large-scale clinical trial.

The United States had suffered a polio epidemic in 1952, striking more than 50,000 people and killing 3,300. Americans were demanding a vaccine. On April 26, 1954, vaccinations began in a field trial conducted and evaluated by Thomas Francis. During the course of this trial, 422,743 children between the ages of six and nine received three separate, spaced doses of the vaccine. Another large group was given placebo inoculations, and another large group was given nothing and simply observed. The results of the trial indicated that the vaccinations were 80–90 percent effective. On April 12, 1955, the vaccine was officially announced to be safe, effective, and potent.

Salk became a national hero. As hope surged for "the total conquest of polio" and plans were made to vaccinate 9 million more children, disaster struck. Two hundred children in California developed polio shortly after being vaccinated—11 children died as a result of the clinical trial.

The Surgeon General halted all polio vaccinations. After a brief investigation, it became clear that the children who were hurt all received vaccine produced by one particular laboratory. Technical improvements were made in the production process and inoculations resumed. By 1958, 200 million injections had been administered without causing a single case of vaccine-induced paralysis.

Shortly thereafter, Albert Sabin developed a live-virus polio vaccine, which replaced Salk's vaccine within a few years. However, Salk's vaccine made the first giant leap forward in the goal of eradicating polio and saved thousands of people from the crippling and often fatal effects of the disease.

## Key Dates

| | |
|---|---|
| 1914 | Born in New York City on October 28 |
| 1934 | Received B.S. from College of the City of New York |
| 1939 | Received M.D. from New York University |
| 1940–1942 | Interned at Mount Sinai Hospital in New York |
| 1942–1944 | Received a National Research Council fellowship |
| 1944–1946 | Served as consultant to the armed forces regarding epidemics |
| 1946 | Worked as assistant professor in epidemiology at the University of Michigan |
| 1947 | Worked as associate professor of bacteriology at the University of Pittsburgh |
| 1949–1954 | Worked as research professor of bacteriology at Pittsburgh |
| 1954 | On April 26, national field trials of his killed-virus polio vaccine began |
| 1955 | On April 12, vaccine was officially determined safe for general use; on May 7, polio vaccination was temporarily halted |
| 1954–1957 | Worked as professor of preventive medicine at Pittsburgh |
| 1957 | Named Commonwealth professor of experimental medicine |
| 1963 | Opened the Salk Institute for Biological Studies in San Diego |
| 1970 | Was adjunct professor of health sciences at the University of California at San Diego |
| 1995 | Died June 22 |

## Advice

*Jonas Salk attributed his success as a microbiologist and medical researcher to his drive for perfection in each experiment and procedure. He believed that there is no room in the field for imprecision or inattention to detail. Gain a solid foundation in chemistry, math, physics, and biological sciences before entering either medical school or microbiology post-graduate specialization. Medical school is not essential, but very valuable to advancement in the field. Above all, remember that any success in science requires prolonged and dedicated effort.*

## References

Carter, Richard. *Breakthrough: The Saga of Jonas Salk.* New York: Trident Press, 1966.

Gallo, Robert C. *Virus Hunting.* New York: Basic Books, 1991.

McCormick, Joseph. *The Virus Hunters: A Dual Memoir from the Frontiers of the Disease.* Atlanta, Ga.: Turner, 1996.

Powell, Michael F., and Mark J. Newman, eds. *Vaccine Design: The Subunit & Adjuvant Approach.* New York: Plenum Press, 1995. (Salk wrote the introduction.)

Silverstein, Arthur M. *A History of Immunology.* New York: Academic Press, 1989.

# Albert Schweitzer

*"Reverence for Life"*

Medicine,
Theology, and
Philosophy

## Career Highlights

- Won Nobel Peace Prize, 1952
- Awarded the Goethe Prize by the City of Frankfurt, 1928
- Received the Peace Award of the West German Association of Book Publishers and Sellers, 1951

## Important Contributions

Some people believe that we reach our fullest potential as human beings when we live our lives in service to others. Albert Schweitzer was one of those people.

At age 30, Albert Schweitzer was already renowned as a scholar, theologian, philosopher, and musician. He was a professor and principal at the Theological College of St. Thomas and could have easily settled into a life of comfort and luxury. Instead, he decided to "put into practice" the gospel of love. He quit his university position, went back to school to study medicine, and, in 1913, left his homeland to dedicate his life to working as a missionary doctor in French Equatorial Africa.

## Career Highlights

It's hard to convey convincingly the feelings of being unfulfilled and of needing to do something more when the world considers you have already excelled in every way. Holding two doctorates and the honored post of principal of a theological college, Albert Schweitzer was recognized as a leading expert in the fields of philosophy and theology. As a gifted musician, he was a foremost expert on Bach and on the pipe organ and had written popular books on both subjects. So it was difficult for him to solicit understanding for his gnawing need to throw it all away and find something more meaningful.

Albert Schweitzer had been raised in the Alsace region along the border between France and Germany and grew up speaking fluent French and German. His grandfather, a talented organist, encouraged Albert's musicianship, and by age eight, Albert had learned to play the organ. By age nine, he could substitute for the church organist at services. But music never felt like "enough."

Albert graduated from secondary school in 1893 and enrolled in the theological college of St. Thomas at the University of Strasbourg, where he majored in theology and philosophy. He passed his theological examination in 1897, and by spending the next summer studying philosophy at Strasbourg, he was able to win the Goll Scholarship, which allowed him to study philosophy at the Sorbonne in Paris. In 1899, he earned his Ph.D. in philosophy from Strasbourg; two years later, he received his Ph.D. in theology.

In 1902, Schweitzer accepted a position as professor of the Theological College of St. Thomas and later became its principal. During this time, he played Bach at organ concerts and became known as the foremost authority on Bach and an outstanding performer of his organ music. He even wrote a biography of Bach, as well as a book on the construction and playing of the organ.

Despite his contributions in theology and musicianship, Schweitzer felt unsatisfied and unfulfilled and wanted to give more to the world. He felt he had enjoyed many advantages in life and vowed at age 30 to devote himself "to the direct service of humanity." Undecided as to how to accomplish this mission, his interest was piqued by a magazine article written in 1905 by the Paris Missionary Society, describing the desperate need for doctors in Africa.

Although he was not a doctor, Schweitzer couldn't get the article out of his mind. Within a month, he had resigned his university position and enrolled in medical school. He gave organ recitals to defray his expenses and in six years passed the state medical examination. He qualified for a year's internship specializing in tropical medicine.

In 1913, Schweitzer and his wife sailed to Africa with copious good wishes and precious little funding to establish a hospital at a mission in Lambaréné (now Gabon). The need for the hospital was severe in this isolated area where, under primitive conditions, the Africans suffered from malaria, yellow fever, dysentery, leprosy, and sleeping sickness. The couple treated 2,000 patients in the first nine months alone.

Then came World War I, and because the Schweitzers were Germans living in a French colony, they were interned as enemy aliens in France for the duration of the war. After their release, they spent seven years in various countries in Europe, trying to pay off the debts they had incurred setting up the hospital in Lambaréné.

Also during this time in Europe, Schweitzer created a system of ethical principles called "reverence for life," which he published in two books in 1923. He explained his definition of ethics as follows: "It is good to maintain and further life; it is bad to damage and destroy life. And this ethic, profound, universal, has the significance of a religion. It *is* religion. . . . [Reverence for life] demands from all that they should sacrifice a portion of their own lives for others."

In 1924, Schweitzer returned to Lambaréné, only to find his hospital in ruins, reclaimed by the jungle. He selected a new site and rebuilt, this time in the model of a typical African village instead of in a European design. The hospital had no electricity (except for the operating rooms), animals roamed freely about, family members were allowed to stay and help patients during recovery. Schweitzer's goal was to win the trust of the Africans by practicing medicine in the familiar context of their own culture.

The remaining 40 years of Schweitzer's life were dedicated to that hospital. By the 1960s, the hospital could accommodate more than 500 patients.

Schweitzer won the Nobel Peace Prize in 1952 but would not leave his duties at the hospital to receive his award, so the prize was accepted for him by the French Ambassador to Norway. The doctor used the money to create a leper colony near the hospital at Lambaréné. In 1954, he delivered his Nobel lecture, "The Problem of Peace," in which he insisted that humanity must reject war because it makes us guilty of the crime of inhumanity.

In 1957, Schweitzer issued a "Declaration of Conscience," broadcast on radio, in which he urged people to demand that their governments ban the testing of atomic weapons. Not long after, 2,000 American scientists signed a petition to end atomic weapons testing. Arms control talks began in 1958, and the superpowers agreed to a test-ban treaty five years later.

Over the course of his life, Albert Schweitzer was both criticized and idealized. While some people said that his practicing medicine in the jungle was squandering his talent or simply escapism, most saw him as something of a saint. At the presentation speech for his Nobel Prize, one committee member noted that Schweitzer "has shown us that a man's life and his dream can become one. His work has made the concept of brotherhood a living one, and his words have reached and taken root in the minds of countless men."

Albert Schweitzer's humility and depth of service to those less fortunate touched the hearts of people worldwide. He was a model for the conscious use of science to serve the public interest, and he will be remembered for finding greatness in serving others.

## Key Dates

| | |
|---|---|
| 1875 | Born in Kaysersburg, Alsace, on January 14 |
| 1897 | Passed his first theological examination |
| 1899 | Accepted a post as a preacher at the Church of St. Nicholas |
| 1900 | Passed the licentiate (a degree higher than the doctorate in German universities) |
| 1901 | Received Ph.D in theology |
| 1902 | Received the post of *Privatdozent* in theology at the university |
| 1903 | Appointed principal of the theological college |
| 1905 | Published his French biography of Johann Sebastian Bach |
| 1905– 1911 | Studied medical science |
| 1911– 1912 | Interned at a Strasbourg hospital |
| 1913 | Arrived in Lambaréné, Africa |
| 1917 | Was interned in France during World War I |
| 1924 | Returned to Africa |
| 1952 | Awarded Nobel Peace Prize |
| 1957 | Issued "Declaration of Conscience" |
| 1965 | Died September 4 in Lambaréné |

## Advice

*Albert Schweitzer believed that academic effort, knowledge, and talent were the servants of dedicated service. Schweitzer earned three doctorates (an unprecedented achievement) but believed that they only had value when applied in the service of others. Schweitzer would advise anyone considering a career in the sciences to first determine how you want to use your career to serve humankind. Then build backwards from the work you want to accomplish to the necessary specialties, degrees, training, experience, and schooling. Save room in your coursework for philosophy classes to reconnect your studies with the human conditions you intend to serve.*

## References

Berman, Edgar. *In Africa with Schweitzer.* Far Hills, Calif.: New Horizon Press, 1986.

Gollomb, Joseph. *Albert Schweitzer: Genius in the Jungle.* New York: Vanguard Press, 1949. (For grades 7–8.)

Marshall, George, and David Poling. *Albert Schweitzer: A Biography.* Boston: Albert Schweitzer Fellowship, 1991.

Schweitzer, Albert. *Letters 1905-1965.* New York: Macmillan, 1992.

———. *Out of My Life and Thoughts.* New York: Henry Holt, 1933. (Reprinted 1990.)

# Glenn Seaborg

*"Father of the Transuranic Elements"*　　　Nuclear Chemistry

## Career Highlights

Lawrence Berkeley National Laboratory

- Discovered nine new elements and over 100 new isotopes, more than any other scientist in history
- Awarded Nobel Prize for Chemistry, 1951
- Awarded the Franklin Medal of the Franklin Institute, 1963
- Awarded the Priestley Medal of the American Chemical Society, 1979

## Important Contributions

Glenn Seaborg did more than any other scientist to explore, discover, and create the transuranic radioactive elements (those manmade elements heavier than uranium, element number 92). With his research team he discovered nine radioactive transuranic elements, including plutonium. He created, discovered, and studied over 100 isotopes of elements spread all over the Periodic Chart, including fissionable $U^{235}$. Both bomb-quality atomic fuels, plutonium ($Pu^{239}$) and the isotope $U^{235}$, were discovered by Glenn Seaborg.

Seaborg also created a structure for the transuranic elements within the framework of the Periodic Chart of Elements and was the first to catalog the characteristics of those elements. Singlehandedly, he opened the door to the transuranic elements and led the way into research on elements 93 through 106. Glenn Seaborg can truly be called the "father of the transuranic elements."

## Career Path

High school sophomore Glenn Seaborg thought it was magic, the first real magic he had ever seen. Day after day, in second period chemistry class, Glenn watched a theatrical chemistry teacher perform dazzling experiments to mystify and delight his students. Flashes of light in thin air, colors changing in test tubes before their eyes, smoke billowing in the air, metals whining, gases emerging from nowhere. It was the first time a school class had fascinated and mesmerized the young man. It was the first time he thought seriously about science. The mystical magic of chemistry opened a new sense of wonder and excitement that would burn in Glenn Seaborg for the rest of his life. He had found his field of study.

Glenn graduated from high school in 1929 as the class valedictorian. Still, he received no scholarship offers and so worked as a stevedore, an apricot picker, a farm laborer, an apprentice linotype operator, and a lab assistant for a rubber company, to scrape together enough money to cover tuition and expenses at college. He enrolled at the University of California at Los Angeles (UCLA) and graduated with a bachelor's degree in chemistry in 1934.

Seaborg then transferred to UC Berkeley to study nuclear chemistry under the noted chemist Gilbert Lewis. His study of the interactions of fast neutrons on lead, using the new cyclotron invented by Ernest Lawrence in 1931, earned him a Ph.D in chemistry in 1939. Lewis appointed him to a research associate position. In two years, at the age of 30, Seaborg moved up to the position of instructor of chemistry.

Glenn Seaborg was the first to take full advantage of the chemical research power of Ernest Lawrence's cyclotron, the first machine in the world capable of accelerating charged particles to near-light speed and massive energy levels and then accurately aiming those particles at a small target metal sample. The cyclotron gave researchers a level of control over their studies that had not existed before and allowed research to proceed hundreds of times faster than was previously possible.

In 1939, Ed McMillan, an assistant of Ernest Lawrence, used the cyclotron to bombard uranium with neutrons, attempting to study uranium fission. He found that not all the uranium particles underwent fission decay. Some absorbed a neutron and then underwent beta decay, thus increasing the atomic number from 92 to 93. With that unexpected finding, McMillan successfully created a new element, element number 93, the first element heavier than uranium ever discovered or created (called a transuranic element). McMillan named the new element neptunium because Neptune was the first planet beyond Uranus, the planet for which uranium was named.

In 1940 Seaborg decided to experiment with the unstable neptunium to see if he could create still heavier elements. Using the newest model of the cyclotron, he accelerated deuterons to 16 million electronvolts and slammed them into uranium oxide. As expected, he produced molecules of neptunium in the iron ore.

Seaborg then chemically isolated a tiny milligram of neptunium and tried to force additional beta decay. His team detected beta emissions from the unstable neptunium and were then able to measure the presence of molecules with an atomic number of 94 (94 protons in the nucleus) and an atomic mass of 238. Both elements 93 and 94 were studied and characterized. Seaborg gave the new element 94 the name plutonium, for the one planet beyond Neptune.

Further research showed that plutonium 238 ($Pu^{238}$) could absorb slow neutrons to become $Pu^{239}$. $Pu^{239}$ proved to be easily fissionable and released tremendous amounts of energy. It was the perfect fuel for atomic bombs. In early 1941 Seaborg managed to create a new isotope of uranium, $U^{235}$. Enrico Fermi confirmed Seaborg's findings that $U^{235}$ was far more fissionable than $U^{238}$. It, too, was ideally suited for atomic explosions.

Because of these two great chemical discoveries, Seaborg was asked to join the Manhattan Project, the U.S. secret effort to create an atomic bomb during World War II. He worked first with Enrico Fermi at the University of Chicago and then on his own to develop ways of isolating the tiny amounts of $Pu^{239}$ available in bombarded samples. He pioneered new experimental methods of working with and analyzing microscopic amounts of radioactive material. Once he had cataloged the characteristics of plutonium, trace amounts of naturally occurring plutonium were found in samples of pitch-blende and other mineral-rich ores.

After the war, Seaborg returned to his study of transuranic elements. He discovered that their characteristics followed a pattern similar to that of the lighter rare earth metals. With this insight, he was able to create spaces on the Periodic Chart for each of the known transuranic elements and to predict the characteristics and nature of two yet undiscovered elements. Within two years Seaborg and his team had created both elements and confirmed their characteristics.

By 1952, Seaborg had also created elements 97 through 102 and 106 and had earned a Nobel Prize for his transuranic discoveries. However, the work was becoming increasingly difficult because the higher number elements were increasingly unstable. While many isotopes of uranium have half-lives of thousands of years, unnilhexium, element 106, has a half-life of less than one second. Tiny samples decayed almost before Seaborg could create them. He had to pioneer new sampling, collecting, and analysis methods just to detect, let alone study, the new elements.

In 1954 Seaborg turned away from research to perform administrative duties, first for the Lawrence Radiation Laboratory, then for the University of California at Berkeley, and finally as head of the Atomic Energy Commission. Seaborg then finished his career as a graduate school chemistry teacher, letting others carry on the torch of exploration into the uncharted worlds of new elements and isotopes.

Glenn Seaborg left the world a legacy of over 100 new isotopes and nine new elements. Some have been used for peaceful purposes, some for war. But all have been critically important to advancing our scientific understanding of subatomic interactions and of the nature of elemental and nuclear chemistry.

**\* \* \***

## Key Dates

| | |
|---|---|
| 1912 | Born in Ishpenimg, Michigan, on April 12 |
| 1922 | Moved with family to Los Angeles, California |
| 1934 | Received B.S. in chemistry from UCLA |
| 1937 | Received Ph.D. in nuclear chemistry from UC Berkeley; appointed research associate there |
| 1940 | Discovered plutonium |
| 1941 | Discovered fissionable $U^{235}$ |
| 1942 | Joined the Manhattan Project |
| 1946 | Appointed full professor of chemistry at UC Berkeley |
| 1951 | Awarded Nobel Prize for Chemistry |
| 1954–1958 | Appointed assistant director of Lawrence Radiation Laboratory |
| 1958–1961 | Was chancellor of UC Berkeley |
| 1961–1971 | Appointed head of the Atomic Energy Commission |

1971–
1988    Worked as chemistry professor at UC Berkeley

1988–
present    Retired

## Advice

*Glenn Seaborg believed that success in chemistry or nuclear chemistry requires hard work, dedication, and long hours. Therefore, the specific field of science you choose must excite you to the point where you want to spend your free time pondering, studying, reading, musing, and theorizing about your science. Begin undergraduate studies by mastering math and by gaining a broad, general knowledge of physics and chemistry. Slowly focus on an aspect of chemistry that excites you and design graduate studies around that excitement.*

## References

Moritz, Charles. *Current Biography Yearbook, 1988.* New York: H. W. Wilson, 1989. (Excellent biographical review.)

Seaborg, Glenn. *The Chemistry of the Actinide Elements.* San Francisco: Routledge, Chapman & Hall, 1986. (Best description of nuclear chemistry.)

———. *The Elements Beyond Uranium.* New York: John Wiley, 1990. (Good description of the transuranic elements and of nuclear chemistry.)

———. *Modern Alchemy: Selected Papers by Glenn Seaborg.* New York: World Scientific Publications, 1993. (Review of nuclear chemistry.)

Tanor, Joseph, ed. *McGraw-Hill Modern Men of Science.* New York: McGraw-Hill, 1986. (Strong summary of Seaborg's work.)

Wasson, Tyler, ed. *Nobel Prize Winners.* New York: H. W. Wilson, 1987. (Summary of Seaborg's important work.)

# Roger Sperry

*"A Brain for the Brain"*　　　　Psychobiology

## Career Highlights

- Developed the current theories on left brain/right brain division
- Awarded the Nobel Prize for Physiology and Medicine, 1981
- Awarded the Ralph Gerard Prize for outstanding contribution to neuroscience, 1979
- Awarded the Albert Lasker Basic Medical Research Award, 1979
- Honored as California scientist of the year, 1972

## Important Contributions

Roger Sperry has been one of the major forces behind contemporary research into the mysteries of the human brain. His work formed the foundation of current theories on left brain/right brain division and activity. It was Sperry who discovered that the left brain was dominant in most people and controlled verbal and analytical skills. The right brain, he determined, controlled spatial skills and music.

But Sperry made significant discoveries before completing this Nobel Prize-winning research. He developed the still-dominant theory of chemo-affinity, which postulates that nerve fibers detect minute differences in chemical composition between individual cells to correctly attach themselves. Much of our current understanding of brain activity and function stems from the laboratory experiments of Roger Sperry.

## Career Path

It was dramatic. It was attention grabbing. But disproving two of the most popular prevailing psychological theories while still a student and post-doctoral intern—one developed by Sperry's graduate advisor and the other by the man who first hired him—was not a smart, safe way to begin a career. It was not a good way to please his bosses. But then, Roger Sperry never played it safe.

Roger Sperry was an excellent high school athlete and earned an athletic scholarship to Oberlin College in Ohio. There he starred on the varsity football, baseball, and track teams and captained the basketball team. In addition to sports, he scraped together enough study time to earn a B.A. in English in 1935, never having been drawn to any particular academic field.

Sperry was, however, intrigued by his introduction to psychology and stayed at Oberlin following graduation to pursue that subject instead of continuing his study of the humanities. Through his graduate advisor, R. H. Stetson, Sperry developed an emphasis on the biological aspects of psychology, which he maintained for his entire career.

By the time he received his M.A. in 1937, Sperry's interests had focused on the formation of the neural circuitry and its relation to higher functions of the brain such as memory, learning, and perception. He transferred to the University of Chicago to study under the renowned biologist Paul Weis, whose theories were reshaping scientists' views of the organization of the central nervous system.

After learning basic animal physiology and surgical technique, Sperry began a series of experiments designed to substantiate one of Weis's central theories on nerve functioning. He surgically crossed the nerves controlling the back legs of a rat. Weis claimed that the nerves would be slowly reeducated to correctly control their newly assigned muscles.

Sperry, however, found no proof of reeducation. When the left hind foot was stimulated, the right hind foot responded. His experiments shattered Weis's theory of central nervous system function, vaulting him into national prominence and earning him a Ph.D. in 1941 over Weis's grumblings and resentment.

Because of a strong feeling that he needed to continue his research, Sperry accepted a research fellowship at Harvard. His doctoral work had disproved a prevailing theory, but he had not proposed a replacement theory of his own. Using amphibians whose nerve cells were capable of regrowing, Sperry wanted to find out how nerves knew where to connect, that is, which cell they are supposed to stimulate. He cut nerve cells on hundreds of frogs and created physical obstacles to make it harder for the nerve to rejoin with the same muscle or optic cell.

Repeatedly Sperry found that the nerve cells groped their way to the correct attachment point. He theorized that nerve cells develop an acute chemical sensitivity to the exact concentrations of different chemicals in a target cell and will not attach to any other spot. He named this phenomenon "chemoaffinity." It is still a central tenet of psychobiology almost 60 years later.

Sperry shifted his research from nerve fibers to the brain itself, to try to chemically uncover how the brain functioned. He went to work at the Yerkes Laboratories of Primate Biology in Florida in 1942. Karl Lashley, who had hired him, had recently published the hypothesis that the two brain hemispheres had equipotential. The theory was hailed as a major advancement in psychobiology. Sperry was excited to work with Lashley and eager to extend the work of this famous researcher.

Using delicate surgical techniques, Sperry performed crosshatching of the cerebral cortex of cats and monkeys and implanted dielectric and conductor elements to measure brain electrical activity. His results totally disproved Lashley's theory.

Over the span of three years, Sperry had disproved prominent, popular theories of both his graduate advisor and his postdoctoral advisor, while each man was at the apex of his prominence. He is the only psychobiologist ever to perform this astounding feat. It vaulted him to the position of an acknowledged leader in the field.

Leaving the Yerkes Labs in 1946 because of the rift that had developed between him and Lashley, Sperry accepted an appointment as assistant professor of anatomy at the University of Chicago. Here he expanded on his research into the function of the two hemispheres of the brain. His principle technique in this work was to surgically sever the nerves connecting the left and right hemispheres of the brain and study the animal's behavior following surgery.

From these studies, Sperry observed that "each disconnected hemisphere behaved as if it were not conscious of the events and existence of the partner hemisphere." This finding was contrary to popular belief. Extending his surgical technique, he was able to isolate specific neural activity and to determine the relative influence of each hemisphere for different types of activity and thought.

When Sperry moved to Caltech at the request of Nobel laureate George Beadle in 1954, he was able to accelerate his research schedule. His focus remained on the function of the two hemispheres, using animal subjects, even though animal activist groups were loudly protesting Sperry's type of lab research and university officials requested that he minimize surgical experimentation. He remained undaunted and compared his results to clinical observations of human patients who had suffered severe injury to different parts of the brain (the only way to study and isolate brain function in humans).

Over time, Sperry was able to build a composite view of the functioning of the two brain hemispheres and of the communication between them through the *corpus callosum*, a thick bundle of 200 million nerve fibers connecting the two sides. In particular, his research discovered the amount of higher brain function information that is shared through the *corpus callosum* and the process by which sensory observations are converted into memory.

Roger Sperry's comprehensive studies of animal brains and functional behavior led to many of the advances in neural understanding of the twentieth century, including basic left brain/right brain division. His lifetime of research represents a fundamental contribution to understanding the human brain and affects the intertwined fields of psychology, neurology, and biology; for this work he earned a Nobel Prize. He stands alone as a leader in the field of psychobiology and in deciphering the most complex and wondrous machine of all, the human brain.

## Key Dates

1913    Born in Hartford, Connecticut, on August 20

1935    Received B.A. in English from Oberlin College, Ohio

1937    Received M.A in psychology from Oberlin College, Ohio

1941    Received Ph.D. in zoology from the University of Chicago

1941–   Appointed National Research Council postdoctoral fellow at
1942       Harvard University

1942–   Appointed research fellow at the Yerkes Laboratories of
1946       Primate Biology, Orange Park, Florida

1946    Appointed assistant professor of anatomy at University of
        Chicago

1952    Appointed associate professor of psychology at University
        of Chicago

1954    Given appointment as Hixon Professor of Psychobiology at
        California Institute of Technology

1981    Awarded Nobel Prize for Physiology and Medicine

1985    Retired

1994    Died on April 17

## Advice

*Roger Sperry would give three pieces of advice to anyone considering a career in psychobiology. First, use your undergraduate years to develop a broad base of liberal arts and general science knowledge with an emphasis on animal physiology. Second, develop excellent experimental skills. Work or volunteer as a lab assistant until you feel completely comfortable with experimental procedures and techniques. Third, when you have identified your desired specialty, study with the giants in your specific field. Study in the best laboratories under the best theoreticians you can find. But don't be in awe of them or of popular theories. Trust only what you can experimentally reproduce for yourself.*

## References

Erdmann, Erika, and David Stover. *Beyond a World Divided: Human Values in the Brain-Mind Science of Roger Sperry*. New York: Random House, 1991.

Kalat, James. *Biological Psychobiology*. Pacific Grove, Calif.: Cole Publications, 1987. (Good review of the field.)

Moritz, Charles, ed. *Current Biography Yearbook, 1985*. New York, H. W. Wilson: 1986. (Good review of Sperry's work.)

Tanor, Joseph, ed. *McGraw-Hill Modern Men of Science*. New York: McGraw-Hill, 1986. (Strong summary of Sperry's work.)

Trevarthen, Colwyn, ed. *Brain Circuits and Functions of the Mind: Essays in Honor of Roger W. Sperry*. Cambridge: Cambridge University Press, 1990. (Essays from students and colleagues reviewing 50 years of Sperry's experimentation.)

Wasson, Tyler, ed. *Nobel Prize Winners*. New York: H. W. Wilson, 1987. (Good summary of Sperry's work.)

# James Starrs

*"Leading the Science Orchestra"*

Forensic Science

The George Washington University

## Career Highlights

- Was consulting forensic scientist for investigations into the death of Lewis Merriweather, John Wilkes Booth, Jessie James, and other famous figures
- Awarded the Distinguished Fellow Medallion by the American Academy of Forensic Sciences, 1996
- Awarded the Jurisprudence Section Award by the American Academy of Forensic Sciences, 1988

## Important Contributions

Forensic scientist James Starrs has significantly elevated to a new level of precision and detail the science of the process of exhuming and analyzing long-dead remains. He has developed techniques and procedures to orchestrate and incorporate the expertise of over a dozen scientific fields and disciplines into his investigations to determine not only the long-ago cause of death (pathogenesis, a medical question), but more important, the manner of death (a legal question). Starrs is now an internationally recognized expert in the art and science of exhumation and the subsequent investigations. Forensics has become an important science for legal cases in recent years, and Starrs and others like him have helped promote this area of study.

# Career Path

Shovelful by shovelful the layers of dirt are removed from the grave in the misty morning light. Geologists and soil chemists scurry into the growing hole, examining each layer of exposed dirt, collecting and tagging samples for later analysis. A historian scribbles notes to compare with ancient records. Pharmacological, toxicological, radiological, and biological experts in gleaming laboratories stand ready at a nearby hospital where a scanning electron microscope has been borrowed and installed. Each of these technical experts periodically seeks direction over a walkie-talkie net from James Starrs, the leader of the investigation, who stands at the head of the grave. Another exhumation has begun.

Two events in James Starrs's childhood directly shaped his choice of forensic science as a career. Both happened when he was seven years old.

First, James's appendix ruptured. He was gravely ill and exposed to the limited technology available to medical science in the 1930s. Second, he was bitten by a rabid dog. Back to bed he went to undergo the painful, prolonged, and dangerous treatment for rabies while he slowly recovered.

These two experiences had a profound impact on James. First, his intimate exposure to medical technology made him feel closer to, and fascinated by, biological sciences and medicine. Second, he read the entire Sherlock Holmes series by Arthur Conan Doyle while recuperating. This reading planted in him "a permanent bug to resolve mysteries."

James graduated from high school in 1948 having won a competitive four-year college scholarship. He decided to attend Niagara University because his older brothers were there. James planned to study biology, but quickly floundered. By the end of his first year he had shifted his major to accounting. During his second year, he struggled through each accounting course (the struggle was made worse because he had little interest in the subject). He shifted again, this time to English.

In 1950, after two difficult years at Niagara, Starrs dropped his scholarship, abandoned school, and joined the U.S. Army to fight in the Korean War. By 1953 he had risen to the rank of staff sergeant. He spent his time writing commendations and reports for officers and decided that if he was going to do the work of an officer, he might as well get the privileges and benefits of being an officer.

Starrs resigned from the Army at the end of his three-year enlistment, got married, and got a job to support his family. But he was also determined to finish college in some professional school that would guarantee that he could reenter the Army as an officer should he be called up for another war. He wanted to enter medical school, but no med school offered night classes, a must for a working man who couldn't afford to leave his job.

The second choice was law. Luckily, St. Johns Law School offered night classes. Starrs crammed in as many classes as the law program would allow. He "felt behind" after wasting two years at Niagara and three in the Army. He was in a hurry to get through school and start a career, so he stuffed in additional classes to complete an undergraduate degree in biology. (Today it would be called molecular biology.)

By the time Starrs had completed his doctorate in law from New York University in 1959, he had also obtained an M.S. in biology. He was offered a teaching position in the law school of Rutgers University, which he accepted. On the side, he started a private law practice. Neither position worked out. He shifted to DuPaul University to teach family law. He lasted for four years there but knew that that wasn't what he wanted either.

In 1964 Starrs accepted a position in the law school at George Washington University in Washington, D.C. After he had spent several years on the faculty, representatives of the FBI visited the school looking for someone willing to put together a forensic sciences program. Starrs jumped at the opportunity, realizing that this was finally a way to incorporate his life-long interests in medicine and science into his profession of law.

Starrs's particular expertise as a forensic scientist is in the investigation of long-dead remains. There are parts of the total investigation that he performs himself, but he feels more like an orchestra leader conducting a whole team of scientists, determining the needs of each and ensuring that they do their jobs in harmony and on time.

Investigations always begin with extensive library studies to review life history and lifestyle information of the person to be exhumed. Charts of scars, fractures, wounds, cavities, and deformities are compiled. Handwriting samples are analyzed. Nutritional habits are recorded. Archaeologists search for probable burial sites.

While the body is being exhumed, chemists collect soil samples to search for any chemical abnormalities and to assess soil pH.

The exact analyses to be conducted vary depending on the specific questions to be answered. Standard elements include DNA analysis for positive identification and an analysis of teeth and bones to confirm the history of fractures, surgeries, and dental work. Results are also used to assess lifestyle limitations (limps, weak limbs, etc.). Bone and hair samples are chemically analyzed to indicate nutritional deficiencies. Pharmacological and toxicological investigations search for drugs and poisons. Radiological studies search for bone opacities and abnormalities.

Mountains of data are amassed from a dozen different disciplines. Starrs's job is to correlate all of these separate pieces and to ensure that the manner of their collection will withstand critical scrutiny in a court of law. The results of each scientific study are then pieced together to indicate the manner of death and, to the extent possible, how this person lived during the latter part of his or her life.

Forensic investigation is a painstaking and time-consuming, but fascinating, process, a chance to use modern technology and knowledge to solve centuries-old mysteries. Over the past 20 years, James Starrs has become one of the world's top experts in the practice of such investigations.

James Starrs searched until he was 38 to find the right field, position, and career for him, one that involved all of his passions and interests. Now he is one of the best-known and most-sought-after forensic scientists in the country and an internationally recognized expert on exhumations. His career is a strong testament to the power of persistence.

## Key Dates

| | |
|---|---|
| 1930 | Born in New York City on July 30 |
| 1948–1950 | Attended Niagara University |
| 1950–1953 | Served in Armed Forces during the Korean War |
| 1955 | Received B.S. in science and LL.B from St. Johns University |
| 1959 | Received LL.M and M.S. in biology from New York University |
| 1959–1960 | Pursued private law practice and worked as teaching fellow at Rutgers Law School |
| 1960–1964 | Worked as associate professor of family law at DuPaul University |
| 1964–1967 | Worked as associate professor of law, the National Law Center at George Washington University |
| 1967–present | Is professor of law at George Washington University |
| 1980–present | Is professor of forensic sciences at the Columbia School of Arts and Sciences, George Washington University |

## Advice

*James Starrs had so many interests (medicine, science, law, and mystery investigation) that he found it hard to pick one field. In fact, he found that his diversity of interests was a crucial asset for his forensic sciences degree. While there are many possible combinations of interests and skills that can build toward a forensic sciences degree, law and medicine are a must at the graduate level. Starrs would advise you to focus on biology and chemistry at the undergraduate level. Physics will be important, but not as crucial as those other two. A working mastery of math is a must.*

*You should also feel a strong attraction for solving mysteries and piecing together a hidden maze of clues and evidence. Study animal and human anatomy. Watch how animals move, how their parts function. Above all, challenge yourself constantly in every way you can. Growth and improvement come through challenge.*

## References

Jackson, Donna. *The Bone Detectives: How Forensic Anthropologists Solve Crimes and Uncover Mysteries of the Dead.* Boston: Little, Brown, 1996.

Jones, Charlotte. *Fingerprints and Talking Bones: How Real-life Crimes Are Solved.* New York: Delacorte Press, 1997.

Lewis, Alfred. *The Evidence Never Lies: The Casebook of a Modern Sherlock Holmes.* New York: Holt, Rinehart & Winston, 1984.

Otfinoski, Steven. *Whodunit?: Science Solves the Crime.* New York: Scientific American Books, 1995.

Silverstein, Herma. *Threads of Evidence: Using Forensic Science to Solve Crimes.* New York: Twenty-First Century Books, 1996.

# Howard Temin

*"Information Transfer"*        Virology

## Career Highlights

- Discovered the functioning of the deadly group of retroviruses
- Awarded the Nobel Prize for Physiology and Medicine, 1975
- Expanded our understanding of basic information transfer in living tissue by discovering that RNA could transfer information to DNA
- Awarded the Albert Lasker Basic Medical Research Award, 1974

## Important Contributions

Howard Temin was a research virologist. While studying the theoretically impossible behavior of one specific cancerous tumor-causing virus, he discovered how a whole group of deadly viruses, collectively called retroviruses, function. Temin extended the basic rules of information transfer in living systems. He discovered that RNA viruses could alter the DNA of living cells. That is, he discovered that information could travel from RNA to DNA. Previously it had been believed that information could only be transmitted from DNA to RNA to proteins. Finally, Temin discovered the enzyme that makes this information transfer possible and thereby provided the keys to understanding the deadly functioning of the group of retroviruses that cause many cancers, hepatitis, and AIDS.

## Career Path

Howard Temin graduated from Swathmore College in 1955 with a B.S. in biology and entered the California Institute of Technology (Caltech) for graduate work in experimental embryology. After one and a half years of study, he grew dissatisfied and switched fields to animal virology, where he worked in the laboratory of Dr. Renato Dulbecco.

As a newcomer to the field, Temin was given the lowest level research projects in the department, those assignments none of the other, more senior, students wanted. His first assignment was to conduct a background search of the literature for any information about the Rous sarcoma virus, a minor filterable virus discovered 30 years earlier in Plymouth Rock hens.

Temin grumbled at the insignificance of the project and the virus, but, knowing his lowly status as a transfer student, accepted the task and looked forward to better days. He didn't know it at the time, but he would spend the next 30 years studying that one virus and would gain fame and recognition far beyond that of any of the other students or professors in his department.

As a child, Howard had been recognized as a gifted student and showed a strong interest in biology. In high school, his parents arranged for him to spend his summers participating in a research program for gifted students at the Jackson Biological Laboratory in picturesque Bar Harbor, Maine. There he worked as a lab assistant and studied marine biology. These summer programs deepened his interest in biological research and gave him an invaluable foundation in proper laboratory experimental technique.

Howard entered Swathmore College in 1951, where he studied biology in the honors program. Between his sophomore and junior years, he spent the summer studying at the Institute for Cancer Research in Philadelphia. His studies there focused his interest on tumor growths, an interest that would stay with him for the rest of his career.

Temin entered the embryology department of Caltech for graduate studies. After a year and a half, he shifted to animal virology, where he began a study of the Rous sarcoma virus and, later, reticuloendotheliosis virus, a close cousin. He was not drawn to that particular virus, but rather to determining how viruses successfully attack the body. Just as field biologists typically have to specialize in one species to conduct in-depth studies, so, too, virologists typically specialize in one virus. Usually the result of such career-long studies is an understanding of that one organism. On rare occasions, these single-organism results lead to important generalizations. There is no way to anticipate such an occurrence. It's really a matter of luck. Howard Temin was lucky.

Having received his Ph.D. in 1959, Temin stayed at Caltech for an additional year while he completed preliminary studies of the Rous sarcoma virus. During this three-year research period, he made two significant findings. First, he and postdoctoral student Harry Rubin developed the first quantitative method for measuring the growth rate of viruses. Second, Temin's work with Rous sarcoma led him to hypothesize that certain viruses, Rous sarcoma among them, attack a living cell by altering the genetic information encoded in the cell's genes. This finding, while potentially important, was still very preliminary. He did not know how a simple virus could manage such a stunning, cunning, and deadly maneuver, nor could he trace the step-by-step process of the alteration. Further, he could not say why some viruses seemed capable of inducing genetic alterations while others were not.

Still, the finding was significant and earned Temin an offer from the University of Wisconsin to take a position as assistant professor of oncology (the study of tumors). His preliminary findings were puzzling because they seemed to violate accepted theory in two ways. First, Rous sarcoma had an RNA genome in it. All other known RNA viruses killed infected cells (rather than altering them). Temin's results indicated that Rous sarcoma did not do this. Second, it was a well-accepted tenet that information could only be transmitted from DNA to RNA to proteins. Temin's hypothesis implied that Rous sarcoma, an RNA virus, was transferring information from its RNA code to a cell's DNA.

Temin was, in part, thrilled by the job offer from the University of Wisconsin because his initial results had been met with general disdain and hostility by the virology research community. He had feared he might be snubbed and not find relevant work at all. The University of Wisconsin wanted him to continue his research and clear up the apparent discrepancies.

Knowing that he needed solid proof before either he or his thesis would be accepted by the general research community, throughout the early- and mid-1960s Temin conducted numerous lab experiments to conclusively demonstrate that Rous sarcoma RNA was transferred to, and encoded on, cell DNA in the cells it infected. The final proof, however, lay in finding the enzyme that must exist as the carrier to transfer the information. The race was on, with researchers around the country searching for this final link in the chain.

Temin dove into the search with boundless energy. He felt that this was *his* theory, and he didn't want someone else to beat him to the final discovery. In 1970 Temin isolated the missing enzyme at almost the exact same time that David Baltimore, working independently at MIT, reported its finding. Temin and Baltimore jointly agreed to call the enzyme "reverse transcriptase."

Temin later used the existence of active reverse transcriptase in an RNA provirus to identify a whole group of viruses he called retroviruses. This group of deadly viruses included many cancer-causing viruses as well as the hepatitis and AIDS viruses. His work revealed the basic mechanism by which retroviruses attack living cells. For that set of discoveries, Temin was awarded the 1975 Nobel Prize for Physiology and Medicine.

Howard Temin also conducted lab research that revealed valuable information on the role of serum proteins in the multiplication of healthy cells and the role of these proteins in stimulating excessive growth in cancerous cells.

Temin authored over 170 articles on his work and contributed to four books on virology and cell multiplication.

It took Temin 20 years of study and lab experimentation to fully understand the ways in which one simple virus, Rous sarcoma, functioned when in contact with a healthy living cell. Yet that long-term dedication has significantly advanced our basic knowledge of cell multiplication and information transfer, has made possible much of the subsequent advances in cancer treatment and AIDS research, and has saved millions of lives.

## Key Dates

| | |
|---|---|
| 1934 | Born in Philadelphia, Pennsylvania, on December 10 |
| 1950–1951 | Studied during the summers at the Jackson Biological Laboratory, Bar Harbor, Maine |
| 1951 | Entered Swathmore College |
| 1953 | Worked during the summer at the Institute of Cancer Research in Philadelphia |
| 1955 | Received B.S. in biology from Swathmore College |
| 1955–1959 | Studied at California Institute of Technology (Caltech); received Ph.D. in virology |
| 1959–1960 | Was postdoctoral fellow at Caltech |
| 1960–1964 | Was assistant professor of oncology at University of Wisconsin |
| 1964–1969 | Was associate professor of oncology at University of Wisconsin |
| 1969–1971 | Was professor of oncology at University of Wisconsin |
| 1971–1974 | Was professor of cancer research at University of Wisconsin |
| 1974–present | Is professor of viral oncology and cell biology at University of Wisconsin |
| 1975 | Awarded Nobel Prize for Physiology and Medicine |

# Advice

*Howard Temin shifted majors three times within the general field of biology. He found it valuable to study in different departments and would advise anyone considering a career in virology to take all the extra classes and studies you can early on. Get ahead in your studies. Find a field and subject that interests you and study it intensely. Don't be afraid to shift fields as your knowledge base grows and you refine your interests. Discoveries require long years of dedicated effort. You must be fascinated by your field to maintain energy and enthusiasm over such a long haul.*

# References

Abbot, David. *Biologists*. New York: Peter Bedrick, 1996. (Good review of the field and Temin's work.)

Tanor, Joseph, ed. *McGraw-Hill Modern Men of Science*. New York: McGraw-Hill, 1986. (Strong summary of Temin's work.)

Temin, Howard. "RNA-Directed DNA Synthesis," *Scientific American* (January 1972): 187–189. (Excellent review of Temin's central work.)

Wasson, Tyler, ed. *Nobel Prize Winners*. New York: H. W. Wilson, 1987. (Good summary of Temin's work.)

Weinberg, Robert. *Racing to the Beginning of the Road: The Search for the Origin of Cancer*. New York, Harmony Books, 1996. (Good historical review of the field.)

# Nikola Tesla

*"Lightning in His Hands"*  Electrical Inventor

## Career Highlights

- Invented practical AC electrical transmission and transformer systems on which all modern electrical systems are based
- Elected into American Institute of Electrical Engineers, 1903
- Offered 1912 Nobel Prize for Physics, but refused because it was to be shared with Edison

## Important Contributions

Nikola Tesla invented the alternating current (AC) system of electrical generation and transmission that is used worldwide today. More correctly, he invented the generators, high-voltage and low-voltage transformers, and motors that made AC transmission practical and feasible. He also invented the rotating magnetic field that made AC induction motors possible. The entire way in which we create, transmit, and use electricity can be traced to the inventions and vision of Tesla. Had it not been for the reclusive genius of Nikola Tesla, we might still be stuck with the inferior DC system that famed inventor Thomas Alva Edison was promoting.

# Career Path

October winds swirled crisp and cold off the Rockies as the city of Colorado Springs prepared for winter in 1904. Thunder rumbled across town from a clear, sapphire sky. Anxious citizens glanced up in fright and scurried for cover. Again thunder cracked like a whip, rattling windows and jarring nerves. The God-fearing dropped to their trembling knees believing the end had arrived.

But those on the east side of town also saw the flashes of lightning, bright as a second sun. The lightning came not from the cloudless heavens, but from the great coil Dr. Tesla had built in his laboratory. (Some said *mad* Dr. Tesla; some said he was a wizard or the devil who was trying to outperform God.)

Again lightning crackled from the Tesla Coil and leapt over 150 feet before blasting into the parched earth of Colorado Street. A jittery crowd began to grow at a safe distance from Tesla's lab, awaiting the retaliation of a wrathful God. But the lightning and thunder were not the act of a mad scientist or of some supernatural power. They were the natural outcome of the 5 million volts generated by Tesla's giant, super-efficient, high-energy, high-frequency oscillator. Unheard of and unprecedented in the annals of humankind, the Tesla Coil was mere child's play for Nikola Tesla, the master of electricity.

Nikola Tesla was born in a poor Serbian mountain village. By the age of seven he had developed a flair for math and science. He was especially drawn to the new force of electricity, which his mother, a skillful inventor of farm and home implements, feared as a force of evil and shunned in her inventions.

In 1881 Tesla graduated from college and took a job with the new telephone company in Budapest. During his year there he made his first important invention. This invention came not through long hours of careful work and experimentation or through systematic investigation, but rather, by Tesla's own account, it flashed into his head like a lightning bolt from nowhere.

Tesla was strolling through a Budapest park with a friend while reciting a passage from Goethe's *Faust* when, "the idea came in a single flash. In an instant I saw it all, and accurately drew the diagrams in the sand with a stick."

What Tesla envisioned that summer day was a rotating magnetic field to drive a multi-phase induction motor. This was not an improved design but an entirely new kind of electric motor. Such a thing had not existed in the world until that day. Yet it is the very electric motor design we still use in thousands of electric appliances and equipment.

In 1884, Tesla emigrated to the United States to work with famed American electrical inventor, Thomas Edison. Within a year the two split in a stormy fight when Edison refused to pay for an invention Tesla delivered, an improved DC dynamo motor design. It was the beginning of a bitter 20-year feud. In truth, the two seemed destined to fight. Edison was crusty, pig-headed, and curt. Tesla was borderline neurotic, easily offended, and had terrible interpersonal skills.

For a year Tesla worked for George Westinghouse, producing three commercial inventions that helped launch Westinghouse's new company. The most important of these was the industrial arc lamp, which is still used today, just as he created it.

But Nikola Tesla was neither a company man nor a team player. He parted from Westinghouse to form his own company and develop alternating current (AC) technology. While working with Edison, who deeply believed in the superiority of direct current (DC), Tesla had seen firsthand the two great limitations of DC systems. First, DC electrical energy couldn't be transmitted over long distances. After traveling only 30 miles through power cables, most of the energy, or voltage, was gone. Second, DC motors used a spinning disk, or drum, called a commutator, which sparked badly while spinning against wire brushes and was thus highly inefficient. Tesla eliminated both flaws as he created the generators, transformers, and motors to complete an AC system.

Tesla was able to convince his old friend—and now a wealthy business-man—George Westinghouse that there was profit to be made from AC current systems. Backed by Westinghouse money, he demonstrated his transmission system, sending AC current 186 miles with only a 22 percent loss of power. It was unimaginable efficiency for the time. In 1893 he built an AC power plant at Niagara Falls, New York, which lighted the Chicago World Exposition over 500 miles away.

The war was on for control of the growing American electrical system. Edison, the entire electrical industry, and DC power lined up on one side; Tesla, Westinghouse, and AC on the other. After a long, successful career of always being right, Edison refused to back down and used a long series of dirty tricks to undercut Tesla.

Edison talked the New York State Penitentiary into using AC current for their new electric chair and then ran ads calling AC a dangerous killer. He bribed state officials to reverse, or at least delay, decisions favoring AC systems. He wrote articles falsely discrediting Tesla and his work. But by 1906 it was clear that AC was superior, and every state and utility in the nation swung over to AC. So did industry and manufacturing.

Tesla had won. But in typical fashion, he seemed not to care. He had moved on to "high-frequency wireless transmission." The electrons flowing in an AC system changed direction (alternated) 50 or 60 times a second. Tesla found that if he increased the frequency from 50 to 10,000 cycles per second, electrical energy would fly off a wire and through the air to a distant receiving station. He moved his lab to Colorado Springs, Colorado, and set to work on wireless energy transmission and high frequency oscillators.

While AC systems are certainly his greatest contribution, Tesla created his best-known invention at Colorado Springs. Here he created the Tesla Coil.

As part of his high-frequency experiments, Tesla predicted voice radio over two years before Marconi (the inventor of radio) began his experiments. He actually transmitted a radio signal long before Marconi did. But he didn't pursue his transmitter for communication. He was consumed with the idea of transmitting electric power for household use.

In 1905 financier J. P. Morgan backed Tesla for a power transmission tower and system on Long Island. The 200-foot tower was built. The generating plant was begun. Then Morgan died and support was withdrawn. The tower was mysteriously dynamited. The project fizzled. Embittered, Tesla grew into a total recluse, refusing most human contact, and raised pigeons in a New York apartment until he died in 1943.

Nikola Tesla was often called a lunatic, a crazy man. Even his supporters called him a wild dreamer. He claimed to have received radio signals from other planets and to have created an electric death beam powerful enough to destroy 10,000 airplanes at a distance of 250 miles and to annihilate an army of 1,000,000 soldiers instantaneously—but refused to offer any proof.

Tesla was also an imaginative genius. He singlehandedly built over 700 significant electrical inventions, working with desperately little funding, and created the energy distribution system we still use. Tesla, more than any other individual (Benjamin Franklin and Thomas Edison included), shaped the way we create and use electricity, our most fundamental energy source.

## Key Dates

| | |
|---|---|
| 1856 | Born in Serbian mountain village of Smiljan on July 9 |
| 1875 | Attended Graz Polytechnic College in Austria |
| 1879 | Enrolled in University of Prague |
| 1881 | Left the university to support his mother when his father died |
| 1881 | Invented his first electrical device: multi-phase induction motor |
| 1882 | Hired by Paris-based Continental Edison Company |
| 1884 | Arrived in United States to work with Edison |
| 1885 | Quit Edison to work for George Westinghouse |

| 1887 | Left Westinghouse to form the Tesla Electric Company and become an independent inventor |
|------|---|
| 1888 | Electrical AC versus DC wars begin (won by Tesla and AC in 1906) |
| 1900 | Moved lab to Colorado Springs, Colorado |
| 1906 | Moved back to New York, increasingly became a recluse |
| 1943 | Died January 7 |

## Advice

*Nikola Tesla was an intensively private scientist. He preferred to live and work in seclusion and refused to teach or advise others. He was more of a visionary who made great inductive leaps than a careful scientist who tested each step along the way. Still, several of the principles by which he worked serve as valuable guides for students considering a career in research science. Immerse yourself in a subject or project. Allow nothing to distract you from your tightly focused work until you have produced results. If you study under someone at all, always work with the best, even if it requires great personal sacrifice. Finally, never accept physical limitations. History is filled with limits everyone accepted and acknowledged until one brave person broke them.*

## References

Anderson, Leland, ed. *Nikola Tesla, 1856-1943: Lectures, Patents, Articles.* Belgrade, Yugoslavia: Nikola Tesla Museum, 1991. (Good collection of Tesla's work.)

Hunt, Inez, and Wanetta Draper. *Lightning in His Hands: The Life Story of Nikola Tesla.* Denver, Colo.: EPIR Publications, 1964. (Excellent review of Tesla's life and work.)

Muir, Hazel, ed. *Larousse Dictionary of Scientists.* New York: Larousse, 1994. (Good sketch of Tesla's work and its significance.)

Seifer, Marc J. *Wizard: The Life and Times of Nikola Tesla, Biography of a Genius.* Indianapolis: Birch Lane Press, 1996. (Meticulously researched biography.)

Swezey, Kenneth. "Nikola Tesla, Pathfinder of the Electrical Age," *Electrical Engineering* 785 (1956): 786–794. (Good review of Tesla's work and times.)

# James Van Allen

*"Mapping Belts in the Sky"*                    Physics

## Career Highlights

- Discovered the Van Allen radiation belts
- Awarded the Louis W. Hill Space Transportation Award of the Institute of Aerospace Sciences, 1959
- Awarded the Gold Medal by the American Rocket Society, 1957
- Elected to National Academy of Sciences, 1959
- Elected chair of the Rocket and Research Panel, 1947

## Important Contributions

James Van Allen shaped and developed the direction of the early American rocketry program, and he designed and built the scientific instrument packages for on-board atmospheric testing. Van Allen was the first to seriously map the upper atmosphere, Earth's upper magnetic fields, and the radiation belts that bear his name. His work redefined our understanding of Earth's interaction with outer space and was an essential part of beginning human exploration beyond the atmosphere.

## Career Path

It should have been the crowning success of a lifetime and justified the government's expenditure of hundreds of millions of dollars on his program. But as data began to stream back from the *Explorer I* satellite in January 1958, James Van Allen's rich blush of triumph darkened to the bitter acid of fear.

Van Allen had fought for an orbiting satellite, claiming that the on-board instrumentation was the necessary key to proving his theories and filling the last gaps in his model of the upper atmosphere. As an expectant scientific community and suspicious government agents peered over his shoulder, he watched, bewildered, as the initial *Explorer I* data were spit out by a linked printer. The readings were as wrong as they could be. Where cosmic radiation levels were supposed to be high, *Explorer I* found they had dropped off to zero. *Explorer I* shattered the theories Van Allen had painstakingly developed over the years and, instead of confirming everyone's faith in him, left James Van Allen only able to say that suddenly he knew nothing.

James Van Allen had entered college in 1931 with no specific career plans or strong motivation. He had excelled in science in high school and so figured he should major in some aspect of either physics or chemistry.

Dr. Thomas Poulter, under whom Van Allen studied, was the one who unwittingly provided a focus for his career. Poulter was going to be a member of the Byrd Antarctic Expedition and used Van Allen to help him fabricate and test the cosmic ray instruments for that extended expedition.

As a freshman, Van Allen made his first measurements of cosmic ray intensity while testing and calibrating the equipment Poulter would use in Antarctica. He spent that summer trying to miniaturize the instrumentation package so that it could be more efficiently and easily carried through the cold.

Van Allen graduated in 1935 with a B.S. in physics and transferred to the University of Iowa for graduate school in nuclear physics. His dissertation centered on cosmic ray bombardment and on measurements of their intensity and characteristics. By the time he left the University of Iowa, his career specialization was fixed: the study of cosmic rays in Earth's upper atmosphere.

Van Allen took a post-doctoral position at the Carnegie Institute in Washington for three years. As a junior staff member, he spent most of his time assisting other people's projects and got little time and few resources to improve on his cosmic ray measurements.

Returning to civilian life after three years' service during World War II, Van Allen got the career break every researcher hopes for: his personal dream position. He was offered a position in charge of all high-altitude research at the Applied Physics Laboratory at Johns Hopkins University.

Van Allen laid plans on paper to launch instruments into the upper atmosphere to accelerate his cosmic ray studies. Two problems blocked him: funding and technology. At that time no manmade satellite had yet orbited the Earth, no manmade rocket had risen higher than 30 miles into the air. What rocketry there was, far exceeded Hopkins's budget.

Both problems, which could easily have been insurmountable, were solved by a grand coup. The entire stockpile of German V-2 rockets was turned over to the U.S. Army after the war. Most of them, with proper funding to support their use and research on their design, were given to Van Allen. He was as giddy as a child given free rein at a candy store.

Van Allen conducted tests of the V-2's stability, control, and thrust systems for almost a year. During this time he designed a smaller, simplified version of the V-2, named the Aerobee, which was tailor-made for upper atmosphere testing. In late 1946 he launched a V-2 to a height of 114 miles, a new world record. A year later a modified V-2, carrying sensitive magnetometers and photographic equipment, reached an altitude of over 250 miles before falling back into the Earth's lower atmosphere.

From the data recorded on these test launches, Van Allen began to build a mosaic of the cosmic radiation patterns in the upper atmosphere as well as their magnetic, electrical, and physical characteristics. But progress was slow. Funding existed for only a few launches a year. Many worthy projects competed for test equipment space in the tiny payload compartments. Van Allen was able to collect only a fraction of the data he needed and felt he was seeing only a shadow of the full picture of cosmic radiation.

In 1951 Van Allen transferred back to the University of Iowa but retained his control over Aerobee launches and data collection. As so often happens, new data provided not answers, but new questions. It became clear that an orbiting satellite probe was essential if he was to successfully map the upper atmosphere.

Van Allen spent several years pleading and arm twisting before convincing the U.S. government to launch its first satellite, *Explorer I*, called "baby moon," in January 1958. On board was an instrument package referred to as the "Van Allen package." But data from *Explorer I* were baffling. Cosmic radiation counts dropped off to zero at altitudes where he expected them to be high.

A year later, *Explorer II* carried a revised package of radiation and magnetic counters. Results were the same. Zero radiation beginning at an altitude of 250 miles.

At first Van Allen was depressed and baffled. Then he refused to believe the satellites' results. Instead, he proposed that a strong and unanticipated *increase* of radiation must have overpowered the counters and blanked out their recorders. He hypothesized that intense radiation belts were trapped by the Earth's magnetic field at high altitudes. Few believed him. Most thought it was a feeble attempt by a desperate researcher to cover a series of blunders.

Van Allen was allowed to redesign the instrument package for *Explorer IV*. He shielded all counters and made the probes less sensitive. The results confirmed his theory. Still, many researchers refused to believe that bands of intense radiation circled high above the earth.

To conclusively prove his theory, Van Allen received permission to perform a controversial experiment, Project Argus, a plan to explode a small nuclear bomb at an altitude of 200 miles above the Earth's surface and track the radiation to see if it gathered in the radiation belts he had detected.

Project Argus was exploded in August 1958. The distribution of charged particles from this explosion proved conclusively that Van Allen was correct and that the magnetic field of the Earth created a "magnetosphere" of radiation in the upper reaches of the atmosphere.

These radiation belts were later named the Van Allen belts in honor of their discoverer, the first scientist to conscientiously define the upper reaches of Earth's atmosphere. His work constituted the first comprehensive and serious mapping of the upper atmosphere and substantially revised the scientific community's view of space and of the interaction of Earth's magnetic field with open space.

## Key Dates

| | |
|---|---|
| 1914 | Born in Mt. Pleasant, Iowa, on September 7 |
| 1935 | Received B.S. in physics from Iowa Wesleyan College |
| 1939 | Received Ph.D. in nuclear physics from Iowa State University |
| 1939–1942 | Was research fellow with the Carnegie Institute in Washington, D.C. |
| 1942–1945 | Worked for U.S. Navy Ordnance Research Center |
| 1946 | Appointed head of high-altitude research at the Johns Hopkins University Applied Physics Laboratory |
| 1951 | Appointed head of physics department at University of Iowa |
| 1985 | Appointed Regent Distinguished Professor of Physics at University of Iowa |
| 1991–present | Retired |

# Advice

*James Van Allen's career was characterized by a number of false starts and was given shape by mentors. If you are considering a career in astronomy, Van Allen would advise you also to look for mentors. Every scientist must study and struggle on his or her own. But begin a career by learning from and apprenticing with a master who can act as guide and mentor to accelerate your career in a constructive and productive direction. Also master math and physics before concentrating on an astronomic specialty.*

# References

Asimov, Isaac. *Asimov's Biographical Encyclopedia of Science and Technology*. New York: Doubleday, 1974. (Strong review of Van Allen's life and work.)

Lemaire, J. *Radiation Belts: Models and Standards*. Washington, D.C.: American Geophysical Union, 1996. (Best technical review of the field.)

Moritz, Charles. *Current Biography Yearbook, 1976*. New York: H. W. Wilson, 1977. (Excellent biographical review.)

Tanor, Joseph, ed. *McGraw-Hill Modern Men of Science*. New York: McGraw-Hill, 1986. (Strong summary of Van Allen's work.)

Walt, Martin. *Introduction to Geomagnetically Trapped Radiation*. New York: Cambridge University Press, 1995. (Good technical review of the field.)

# Wernher von Braun

## *"The Father of NASA"*   Rocket Engineering

## Career Highlights

- Designed first successful supersonic ballistic missile
- Designed America's *Jupiter-C, Juno, Redstone,* and the *Saturn I, IB,* and *V* rockets
- Was a driving force behind the creation of NASA

National Aeronautics and Space Administration

## Important Contributions

Wernher von Braun was a rocket man. He seemed to dream of and work toward nothing other than space travel and the rockets to propel humans into outer space. He didn't care for whom he designed and built his rockets, so long as he was allowed to do it.

In the heyday of Germany's rocket development program in the 1930s, von Braun designed the A-1, A-2, and A-4 rockets, the first supersonic rocket and the first intercontinental ballistic rocket, for the German military. He also drew detailed plans for a German space station and shuttle system 40 years before any other country considered such a concept.

Following World War II, von Braun shifted his work to the United States and designed the *Jupiter-C, Juno, Redstone* and *Saturn I, IB,* and *V* rockets. Von Braun also lobbied the administration and Congress relentlessly for the creation of a U.S. space agency. Because of his tireless efforts, many call Wernher von Braun the "father of NASA" and believe that, without his efforts, America would never have achieved its prominence in space exploration.

## Career Path

Like a stiletto knife slicing through heaven and clouds, the thin, silver rocket rumbled into the sky, thick plumes of gray smoke dragging behind. Only 80 people were present to witness this historic launch in 1942 or to watch the rocket disappear into the distance far down range. Only a few German generals outside these 80 scientists even knew of the program.

Wernher von Braun, director of the German military rocket program, watched this launch of his first V-2 rocket with an odd mix of triumph, pride, and sadness. Triumph and pride because science had just advanced to a new plateau and he was the one who had ramrodded the project through from start to finish. Sadness because humankind had also just found a new and improved way to destroy itself.

Von Braun had always been fascinated by rockets and space travel. He collected toy rockets as a child and built his own small observatory. When he moved to Berlin to study at the Federal Institute in 1930, he joined the German VfR (*Verein für Raumschiffahrt* or Society for Space Travel). The thousand members of the VfR took the notion of space travel very seriously. Many well-known engineers were members and led the VfR in studying the problems of manned space flights.

In 1926 Robert Goddard launched the world's first liquid-fueled rocket. VfR member Hermann Oberth took on the task of studying Goddard's work and designs. Oberth later developed theoretical models for a two-stage liquid-fueled rocket capable of escaping Earth's gravitational field. Wernher von Braun became Oberth's assistant when he joined the VfR. By the time von Braun graduated in 1932, he and Oberth had test-fired several small liquid-fueled rockets and the former had taken over the lead in test analysis and design revisions.

The German Ordnance Department recruited von Braun upon his graduation. He agreed to join their effort on the provision that he could study first for a doctorate.

Von Braun's graduate studies were funded by the German military. His doctoral thesis was a detailed theoretical investigation, backed by experimental results, of the inner workings of a new generation of liquid-fueled rockets. For security reasons, the military retitled the paper, "About Combustion Tests" so it would not be noticed and read outside Germany.

By 1937, von Braun's group had grown to 80 scientists and engineers, mostly members of the old VfR. They successfully launched a rocket with a 100-pound payload and watched it climb 15 miles into the sky. They had also tested their liquid-fueled rocket engines as auxiliary engines on propeller-driven fighter planes. These tests were the first step toward the world's first jet aircraft.

In 1937 the Peenemuende Rocket Center was created by the German Army and Air Force. Von Braun was appointed civilian director of the Army portion of the center and moved his entire research group to Peenemuende. He was not overly interested in aircraft applications of his rocket engines. His sole interest and focus was on the development of rockets capable of supporting space travel.

In 1942, von Braun successfully demonstrated his improved A-4 rocket, the first supersonic ballistic rocket. It accurately delivered a missile to a target over 120 miles away. This rocket represented not only a giant boost in rocket design and improved power, but a giant step forward in on-board guidance and control technology. It was this rocket that the German Army renamed the "Vengeance Weapon 2," or V-2, and used in the 1944 and 1945 bombardments of England.

By early 1945 von Braun had also designed and tested a supersonic anti-aircraft missile and had detailed plans for A-9, A-10, and A-11 rockets. The A-11 would be capable of launching a payload of 30 tons into orbit and "maintaining a regular shuttle service to permit the building of a permanent space station circling the earth." It would be almost 40 years before the United States and Russia would reach a comparable point in their space planning and development.

When Germany collapsed at the end of World War II, von Braun delivered his entire team of engineers and scientists to the advancing U.S. Army. Still only 33 years old, he negotiated a deal by which the United States got all of his technical data and the existing stock of V-2 rockets in exchange for allowing von Braun and his team to continue to work on rocket development in the United States. His entire program picked up and moved to Ft. Bliss, Texas.

After von Braun's team relocated to the Redstone Arsenal in Huntsville, Alabama (later renamed the Marshall Space Flight Center), he split his time between designing the new Saturn series of rockets and working to review and assist commercial contractors for the new U.S. space program. The *Saturn I, IB,* and *V* rockets were all von Braun designs. Always his designs and thoughts were two and three generations ahead of the current technology. Always he fought to accelerate toward the day when humans would begin to explore distant space.

Von Braun's *Jupiter-C* rocket launched the first U.S. satellite, *Explorer I*, into space in 1958. His *Juno* and *Redstone* rockets were used for over 30 years to deliver military and commercial payloads into Earth orbit. They also served as the backbone of the U.S. intercontinental ballistic missile system.

When it appeared that the American government had lost its deep commitment to space exploration in the mid-1970s, von Braun left government service to work for Fairchild Industries, one of the principal space-related contractors. He retired from Fairchild in late 1976 and died the next summer.

Wernher von Braun was driven to promote space travel and to design the propulsion systems to make space travel feasible. Most of the successful rocket designs of the 1930s through the 1960s were his. Von Braun also wrote four books on rocketry and space exploration, none of which sold particularly well. But he will always be remembered for the rockets he gave to the world and for his vision of space exploration and development.

## Key Dates

| | |
|---|---|
| 1912 | Born in Wirsitz, Poland, on March 23 |
| 1932 | Received B.S. in engineering from the Federal Institute of Technology in Berlin |
| 1934 | Received Ph.D. from the University of Berlin |
| 1934–1945 | Worked for the German Ordnance Department |
| 1935 | Successfully tested A-2 rocket to an altitude of 1.6 miles |
| 1937 | Appointed civilian head of the Peenemuende Rocket Center |
| 1942 | Successfully tested his supersonic ballistic A-4 rocket |
| 1945 | Delivered his entire rocket team to the U.S. Army; they relocated to the Ft. Bliss, Texas, Ordnance Development Center |
| 1950 | Moved to Redstone Arsenal at Huntsville, Alabama |
| 1970 | Assigned to NASA headquarters in Washington, D.C. |
| 1972 | Left government service to work for Fairchild Industries in Germantown, Maryland |
| 1977 | Died on June 16 |

## Advice

*Wernher von Braun was not an academician and was reluctant to offer personal advice. However, he always mixed academic study with practical experimentation and would advise anyone considering a career in aeronautics, astronautics, or rocket design to do the same. Rely on universities for coursework, but depend on yourself for the design and conduct the experiments you need to gain a working understanding of theory. Join or form clubs to help relieve the labor and expense of experiments. Seek jobs in labs and schools emphasizing experimentation.*

## References

Arms, Thomas. *Encyclopedia of the Cold War.* New York: Facts on File, 1987. (Brief summary of von Braun's work.)

Daintith, John, et al., eds. *Biographical Encyclopedia of Scientists.* 2d ed. Vol. 1. Philadelphia, Pa.: Institute of Physics Publishing, 1994. (Summary entry on von Braun's work.)

Stuhlinger, Ernst. *Wernher von Braun: Crusader for Space.* Melborne, Australia: Krieger Publications, 1996. (Good biography.)

Tanor, Joseph, ed. *McGraw-Hill Modern Men of Science.* New York: McGraw-Hill, 1986. (Strong summary of von Braun's work.)

von Braun, Wernher. *Conquest of the Moon.* New York: Pennick Press, 1953. (Good review of von Braun's work on rocketry.)

Young, Hugo, and Peter Dunn. *Journey to Tranquillity: The Long Competitive Struggle to Reach the Moon.* Garden City, N.Y.: Doubleday, 1970. (Good review of the history of American rocketry.)

# An Wang

*"Technology Visionary"*

Electronics/
Computers

## Career Highlights

- Invented world's first electronic calculator and first word processor and holds over 40 patents for his electronic inventions
- Voted into U.S. Inventors Hall of Fame, 1987
- Awarded U.S. Medal of Liberty, 1986
- Awarded Medal of Achievement by the American Electronics Association, 1984

## Important Contributions

A successful inventor, technician, scientist, and entrepreneur, An Wang has been described as a "technology visionary," always able to anticipate future trends, demands, and developments. He holds over 40 patents for computers and word processors and invented the world's first electronic calculator, the LOCI. He is best known for inventing the world's first word processor with a display screen, simply called by users "The Wang."

But far more important, An Wang invented core computer memory. That invention was one of the key steps in moving computers from slow, unwieldy, overpriced toys into practical, high-powered pieces of necessary equipment.

## Career Path

When An Wang was born in Shanghai, China, in 1920, his parents gave him a name that means, "Peaceful King." But he grew up during a period of bloody civil strife and war known as China's "Age of Confusion," during which opposing forces fought for control of China. There was no peace and

An felt more like a powerless, drifting pawn dodging armies and bullets than a mighty king.

Civil war tensions eased as the boy turned 16 and entered Shanghai's Chiao Tung University, "the MIT of China." That same year, 1936, Japanese attacks on China began. During the bombing of Shanghai, An's mother was killed. In 1937 the Japanese seized Peking. War was on.

Wang immersed himself in the study of electrical engineering and communications as the world exploded in bombs and blood around him. He graduated in 1940 and joined an Army communications team building transmitters and radios for government troops. By 1945 he had lost both parents and two sisters to the war and had been evacuated to Chunking, where the feeble Nationalist Government hung on.

Because of his excellent knowledge of English (Wang's father taught English in a private school outside of Shanghai), he was one of 200 engineers selected to be sent to the United States for two years to observe U.S. construction and industrial methods. An decided that a graduate degree would be more useful than two years of watching others work and, instead of observing in a Virginia naval shipyard as he was assigned to do, he applied to, and was accepted by, Harvard University. During An's time at Harvard, Mao Tse-tung led Communist forces in a revolt against the Nationalist Government. He no longer dared to return to China because it appeared likely that the Communist forces would win. He applied for an extension at Harvard and stayed a third year to receive his doctorate in nonlinear mechanics.

In 1948 computers were in their infancy. An Wang had taken only one computer course. He had been interested in the course only for some of the mechanics it involved. He hadn't planned to work for a computer company and only applied to the Harvard Computational Laboratory because he desperately needed a job, it was easy walking distance across campus, and he confidently assumed he could do the work—whatever it might be.

Wang interviewed with Howard Aiken, the domineering Navy Commander who ran the lab. In 1944 Aiken had built the world's first computer, an electro-mechanical monster over fifty feet long and eight feet high called the Mark I. By 1948 they were up to the Mark III model. It ran at the astounding speed of 20 computations a second and filled an entire room. The lab's job was to operate, test, and improve on the Mark III.

During the interviews, Wang smiled and nodded confidently as if he had majored in electro-mechanical computer design. After two rounds of interviews (during which time Hughes Aircraft, Wang's first choice, turned him down for an engineering job), he was offered a research fellowship at the lab by Aiken.

Wang reported for work on May 18, 1948. On May 19, Aiken gruffly dumped Wang's first challenge in his lap. In truth, Aiken did not expect him to solve the problem. The existing staff had been working on this seemingly impossible task for several years without success.

But Wang didn't know that. All he knew was that Aiken had told him to find a way to read and record magnetic information without requiring mechanical motion.

To process information, the computer had to first read that information from punched cards, magnetic disks, or magnetic tape (like a tape recorder). For the computer to read, the tape had to rewind and play. The cards had to be fed through a scanner. The disks had to spin and readers had to scan to the right spot on the disk. The necessary mechanical motion made the process too slow. But no one knew how to speed it up.

From his mechanical engineering work Wang knew that information was stored in binary form, as either "1's" or "0's." He also knew that magnets could be used to orient the magnetic field, or "flux," of a small doughnut-shaped area of metal (called a core) in either a positive (up) or negative (down) direction. The direction of the flux could later be read electronically by passing a current through it. Information would be stored and read with no mechanical motion.

There was only one catch. The act of electrically reading the data would destroy the data. Wang was stumped. It seemed he had a solution to Aiken's problem, but his solution created an even bigger problem. It erased all the data it read.

Feeling all the pressure of a new employee whose boss was breathing down his neck, Wang struggled with the problem for two weeks before a solution leapt into his head one day while he walked across campus. It was all right to erase the data. Having read a byte of data and destroyed it, the computer could record it right back on the same core.

Data could now be electronically stored in and retrieved from banks of tiny memory cores. This was the first true internal memory for a computer. It is now common for computers to have a thousand-million bytes of data storage. Before An Wang's invention, the Mark I only had several hundred bytes.

Wang's invention became the standard system for computer information storage and instantly increased the speed of computers a thousandfold. At the time, no one recognized the immense importance of his discovery. He thought he was just doing his job and didn't realize for several years that he had revolutionized information storage technology.

In 1951, An Wang quit the lab and founded his own company, Wang Laboratories. In the mid-1960s he developed the first desk calculator, the LOCI (logarithmic calculating instrument), which was the first effective substitute for a slide rule. A decade later he invented the world's first word processing machine, the Wang Computing System. It made Wang the second largest computer manufacturer in the world.

An Wang began his business in 1951 with a walk-up rented room above an electrical fixtures store. Thirty years later he employed 15,000 people and had factories throughout the world. But the discovery that touched us all most had come earlier, when he threw off the computer's mechanical yoke and made information storage truly electronic.

## Key Dates

| | |
|---|---|
| 1920 | Born in Shanghai, China, on February 7 |
| 1944 | Received B.S. from Chiao-Tung University, China |
| 1945 | Left China for the United States; entered Harvard Graduate School |
| 1948 | Received Ph.D. in physics from Harvard |
| 1948 | Hired by the Computational Lab in Cambridge, Massachusetts |
| 1948 | Invented computer memory |
| 1951 | Formed Wang Laboratories |
| 1955 | Became naturalized U.S. citizen |
| 1963 | Invented digital logarithmic converter (first calculator) |
| 1975 | Developed world's first word processor |
| 1990 | Died March 24 of cancer |

## Advice

*An Wang would advise under-graduates to look far into the future when picking classes and specialty areas to study within the general fields of electronics and computer sciences. Piece together clues to see ahead 10 years to what future trends will be. Design your study program to position you to be a part of those future trends. Exercise discipline in your studies and in your work. These are the keys to finding success.*

*Wang also advised youth to grab the opportunities that present themselves and then persevere. "The longer you are able to survive and succeed, the better you are able to further survive and succeed." Perseverance creates confidence. Confidence builds success.*

## References

Gareffa, Peter, ed. *Contemporary Newsmakers, 1986, Issue #1*. Detroit: Gale Research, 1986. (Biographical review.)

Ingham, John, and Lynne Feldman. *Contemporary American Business Leaders*. New York: Greenwood, 1990. (Biographical review.)

Moritz, Charles, ed. *Current Biography Yearbook, 1987*. New York: H. W. Wilson, 1987. (Biographical review.)

Wang, An. *Lessons: An Autobiography*. Reading, Mass.: Addison-Wesley, 1986. (Autobiography.)

# Annie Wauneka

*"Badge Woman"*                    Community Health

## Career Highlights

Navajo Tribal Museum

- Awarded the Presidential Medal of Freedom, 1963, the first Native American ever to win this medal
- Awarded the Arizona State Public Health Association's Outstanding Worker in Public Health Award, 1959
- First woman ever elected to the Navajo tribal council

## Important Contributions

Annie Dodge Wauneka was one of the most influential and inspiring American community health activists of the twentieth century. She successfully bridged traditional Navajo medicine and beliefs with modern (Western) medicine and singlehandedly led the fight to conquer a long-standing tuberculosis epidemic on the Navajo reservation.

Wauneka fought for improved sanitary conditions and isolation of the sick and to make the best possible health care practices an accepted and expected way of life for her people. Her efforts are credited with literally saving her people.

# Career Path

Winter snows swirled around the Ft. Defiance, Arizona, school as an eight-year-old, serious, broad-faced Navajo girl finished filling and cleaning the lanterns for use in the makeshift school infirmary that night. The school had given up trying to hold classes with hundreds of students lying pale and weak with deadly influenza in the rows of beds in what had been the gymnasium.

Everyone knew of the influenza epidemic that swept through the Navajo reservation in that winter of 1918, killing thousands. But it hadn't seemed important to eight-year-old Annie Dodge until the disease struck her school and she had to watch helplessly as the light of life faded from friend after friend. Four and five a day were carried away in a wagon to be buried.

Annie had a mild case of influenza and so volunteered to help the one school nurse tend to sick children. Each morning she cleaned and filled a hundred kerosene lanterns used to light the clinic at night. She fed soup to sick children. She washed their faces with cool cloths, she read them stories, and she watched some of them die. She would never forget the look of those poor, dying faces.

Annie Dodge was born in her mother's hogan on the sprawling Navajo Indian reservation near Sawmill, Arizona. A hogan is a traditional Navajo dwelling: a round, one-story building, with no windows, thick stick and mud walls, and a central hole in the ceiling for smoke. Her father, Henry Chee Dodge, was a wealthy Navajo rancher who lived in a large, Western-style house. After living with her mother for one year, Annie moved to her father's house and into a life of relative privilege.

Besides living in a Western-style house, Henry Dodge spoke English (rare among the Navajos of the time) and he believed in education for all, even for women (unheard of in the tribe at that time). There were no schools on the vast reservation, and education meant traveling to an expensive boarding school.

When Annie was eight she was sent to Ft. Defiance, Arizona, to school. During her first winter at school the terrible influenza reduced the school population by half. Less than a year later a second epidemic struck the region. This time it was an eye condition that led to blindness. Native Americans were especially susceptible to it. Annie and other Navajo students were moved to an Albuquerque school to avoid being infected. Thousands on the reservation were blinded before the terror passed.

These two epidemics made a powerful impression on the young girl. She wondered why the Navajos were in such poor health that they were especially susceptible to disease. Annie made up her mind to become a nurse and learn more about her people's health problems.

While Annie was in Albuquerque, her father was elected chairman of the entire Navajo tribe. He spoke for improved education and for adoption of Western schooling systems. He met with much resistance from a people steeped in the value of tradition.

After eleventh grade, 18-year-old Annie Dodge abandoned her education to tour the reservation and assist her father. She saw a side of reservation life she had never known. Elsewhere on the reservation she saw great poverty and much illness. She came to appreciate her father's belief that improved education was the way to solve the Navajos' problems. But Annie saw poor health and sanitation as even more pressing problems.

Although Annie married George Wauneka and produced eight children, she still remained deeply involved in her community's health. Consistently, she saw three interrelated factors that drove her people into continual poor health: poverty, lack of cleanliness, and inadequate (or non-existent) medical care for the sick.

Wauneka began to speak out against traditional dirt floors in hogans and for improved cleanliness in the home. More often than not she made people angry. They thought she was attacking Navajo traditions. She argued for separating the sick into clinics or government hospitals to protect the healthy, but was shunned because the Navajos didn't trust American medicine, government clinics were poorly staffed and supplied, and hospitals were often hundreds of miles away.

Annie Wauneka lobbied the government for more and better clinics and was turned down because of a lack of available funding. Still she persisted, even as a tuberculosis (TB) epidemic took a steadily firmer grip on the reservation.

In 1951 Wauneka was elected to the tribal council, the first woman ever so elected. Now she thought she would have the power to create change. She decided to concentrate her fight on TB. She went to the reservation's government doctors and asked to be taught. She spent weeks in hospitals and laboratories run by the Public Health Service studying and learning about TB. She visited Navajos inflicted with the dread illness and told them in language they could understand what TB was and what the doctors were doing to cure them.

Still Wauneka faced much resistance. Part of that resistance was a lack of communication between the Navajo people and government doctors. Wauneka had to invent new Navajo words to describe much of Western medicine. She wrote a book that listed Navajo medical terms defined in English, and American medical terms described in Navajo.

Much of the resistance she faced, however, came from a belief that she was trying to undermine the prestige and lofty position of medicine men within the Navajo society. Over a period of several years, Wauneka slowly convinced the medicine men that TB was an "outside" disease and that it was appropriate for them to use "outside" medicine to fight it.

Wauneka successfully linked medicine men and government doctors to work in concert on all Navajo health issues. She also convinced the tribal council to appropriate almost half a million dollars for flooring and windows in the hogans of poverty stricken families. Because of her work, the TB epidemic was halted.

Beyond that specific victory, Wauneka successfully integrated Western medicine into the lives and community rhythm of the Navajo people and substantially upgraded the medical care that was available to the Navajo. In recognition of her efforts, President Kennedy awarded her the Presidential Medal of Freedom, the first Native American to be so honored. Out of respect for this award, always pinned to her blouse, the tribe began to proudly speak of her as "Badge Woman."

Annie Wauneka will always be remembered as a warrior who saw the enemy both in a specific disease and in the conditions in which her people lived. Like other legendary warriors, she took up the battle even though it seemed an impossible fight.

## Key Dates

| | |
|---|---|
| 1910 | Born in the Navajo Nation near Sawmill, Arizona, on April 18 |
| 1928 | Completed eleventh grade and returned home to assist her father |
| 1932 | Married George Wauneka; they had eight children |
| 1951 | Won a seat on the Navajo tribal council, the first woman ever to do so |
| 1952 | Appointed chair of the Navajo health committee |
| 1956 | Received B.S. in public health from the University of Arizona |
| 1959–1969 | Broadcast a weekly health radio program to the Navajo people |
| 1963 | Was first Native American ever to win the Presidential Medal of Freedom |
| 1978 | Retired from the tribal council |
| 1997 | Died on November 11 |

## Advice

*If you are considering a career in community health, Annie Wauneka would offer this advice: To successfully work in a community you must work with the community. Carefully blend the best of what exists with new ideas that others have to offer. Respect both local community values and traditions and new outside ideas. Fight fears and prejudices in all forms.*

*Education is the one and only key to success both for an individual health worker and for a society as a whole. Education does not guarantee success in bringing about change, but a lack of education almost guarantees failure. Study history, sociology, and psychology as well as physiology, virology, and health.*

## References

Bataille, Gretchen, ed. *Native American Women*. New York: Garland, 1993. (Summary entry of Wauneka's work.)

Nelson, Mary. *Annie Wauneka*. Minneapolis, Minn.: Dillon, 1972. (Excellent biography of Annie Wauneka.)

Gridley, Marion. *American Indian Women*. New York: Hawthorn, 1974. (Good biographical review of Wauneka and her work.)

Kunitz, Stephen J. *Disease Change and the Role of Medicine: The Navajo Experience*. Comparative Studies of Health Systems and Medical Care, 6. Edited by Charles M. Leslie. Berkeley: University of California Press, 1989.

Steiner, Stan. *The New Indians*. New York: Harper & Row, 1968. (Good summary entry of Wauneka's work.)

Trennert, Robert A. *White Man's Medicine: Government Doctors and the Navajo, 1863–1955*. Albuquerque: University of New Mexico Press, 1998.

Witt, Shirley. "An Interview with Dr. Annie Wauneka," *Frontiers* 6 (Fall 1981): 64–67. (Good look at Wauneka and her beliefs.)

# Cyril Wecht

## *"Modern Murder Mysteries"*

## Forensic Pathology

## Career Highlights

Allegheny County Department of Pathology

- Awarded Career Achievements Award by New York Society of Forensic Sciences, 1996
- Awarded Gold Medal Award by the American College of Legal Medicine, 1996
- Elected into *The Best Lawyers in America: Directory of Experts,* 1990
- Awarded President's Certificate of Appreciation for Meritorious Service by the American College of Legal Medicine, 1979
- Elected president, American Academy of Forensic Sciences
- Elected president, American College of Legal Medicine

## Important Contributions

Dubbed the Sherlock Holmes of forensic medicine, Cyril Wecht is the most sought after medical expert witness in the country. He is a leading practioner of the science of creating and using hard medical evidence to accurately reconstruct the events of a crime.

Cyril Wecht is a forensic pathologist. Forensic means of or relating to the law. Pathology is the study of diseases and their cause. A forensic pathologist bridges medicine and law to conduct medical investigations into the causes and circumstances surrounding death or injury to assist in making legal decisions. Wecht has consulted on some of America's most famous courtroom cases and is, in many people's mind, the very definition of a forensic pathologist.

## Career Path

As the witness is sworn in and takes his seat, the packed courtroom quiets to a hushed murmur of anticipation. The defendant leans tensely forward, straining to catch every nuance of every word. The jurors shake themselves out of the lethargy created by a string of boring technical witnesses.

Everyone knows that the verdict hangs in a delicate balance and that this witness and the next few minutes of testimony may determine the outcome of the case. Nationally acclaimed forensic pathologist Cyril Wecht is about to begin his expert testimony. It had been a long road and a hard climb for Dr. Wecht to reach this point.

Cyril Wecht's parents were both first generation, struggling immigrants who wanted their only son to succeed. During an interview Dr. Wecht once said, "How did Jewish immigrant parents in the 1930s define success? A doctor. My father always *told* me I would be a doctor."

It wasn't that Cyril didn't want to be a doctor; he simply never stopped to consider other possible careers. Luckily, he was a gifted student. He got excellent grades and graduated from high school as valedictorian with highest honors. He never had to reassess the family's assumption that he would be a doctor.

In high school Cyril developed an early liking for politics. He ran for office in his junior and senior years and, in his senior year, was both class and student body president. After high school graduation, he enrolled in the University of Pittsburgh pre-med program.

In college, Wecht kept his connection with politics fresh while he studied medicine. He was elected president of his fraternity and president of the Student Congress. He served as president of the debate team and was active in journalism and drama. Everyone assumed that these activities meant Wecht was aiming for a law degree.

It wasn't until Cyril Wecht graduated cum laude from Pittsburgh's pre-med program and was a student at the University of Buffalo School of Medicine that he first considered combining the law he so enjoyed with the medicine he felt predestined to practice into one career. During his second year of medical school, the American Medical Association (AMA) put him in touch with Dr. Louis Regan, the nation's leading forensic pathologist. In the spring of that year (1954), the AMA and the American Bar Association

(ABA) held their first-ever joint conference. Regan invited Wecht to meet him there and discuss careers in forensic pathology.

After that conference, Wecht knew he had found his future: forensic pathology. This meant, however, that he had committed himself to master *both* of the most rigorous and difficult academic programs on Earth: medical school and law school.

Wecht completed his medical studies at the University of Buffalo in 1954 and spent two additional years completing his M.D. degree at the University of Pittsburgh. He then began his medical internship and also entered law school. He paused halfway through law school to complete a two-year residency in pathology. Then he completed his law degree at the University of Maryland and the University of Pittsburgh in 1962.

By the time he passed the Pennsylvania bar exam in 1962, Wecht had completed 14 years of intensive study and training. Now, finally, he could go to work in his chosen field. The two most common places for a forensic pathologist to work are as a coroner or in private practice. Typically, he chose to do both.

As a coroner, Wecht is responsible for the investigation of mysterious or suspicious deaths or injuries. He must search for medical and factual clues that allow him to rebuild the events of the case and determine what happened and how it happened. His duties include investigation of crime scenes, autopsies to determine both time and cause of death, wound analysis, slide analysis of tissue and blood samples, investigations of public institutions such as hospitals or the police department, court testimony, and public health investigations.

A typical autopsy takes between one and two hours. Wounds are measured and their exact cause determined. Major organs are examined. Fluid and tissue samples are collected for lab analysis. Following this examination of the body, additional hours or days are consumed with chemical analysis of body fluids and with microscopic examination of tissue samples. When all information has been compiled, 95 percent of the time Wecht is able to explicitly and definitively recreate the events that led to injury or death.

As a consulting forensic pathologist, Wecht is asked to review evidence collected by others and to both interpret that information and critique the collection, handling, and processing of key evidence. While he has consulted on many of the most famous murder cases of our times (John F. Kennedy, Robert Kennedy, Nicole Brown Simpson, Vincent Foster, JonBenet Ramsey, David Koresh, and others), Wecht says that the most intense and interesting cases are often product liability and medical malpractice cases.

Wecht believes he has conclusively shown that the "single bullet theory" of how President Kennedy was killed is a joke. It is impossible. The same, he says, is true for the Robert Kennedy assassination. "Sirhan Sirhan was convicted of firing a shot. But that shot did not and could not have killed Robert Kennedy."

"The police bungled the JonBenet Ramsey investigation from the very beginning," Wecht has said, "to the point where they may never get a conviction." He concludes that "there is no evidence of forced entry. I'm sure the parents did it." On reviewing the Nicole Brown Simpson murder, Wecht concluded, "There is some evidence to suggest that there was a second suspect present at the murder scene."

Famed lawyer F. Lee Bailey called Wecht "the best medical expert witness in the country." This reputation stems from his thorough, impartial, and consistently accurate investigation of events and examination of evidence. He is the embodiment of the best and highest application of the precepts and practice of science.

Wecht is also one of the busiest people in the country. Besides his full-time job as county coroner, he is the consulting pathologist to four regional hospitals, an adjunct professor and lecturer at five universities and colleges, an active member in 26 professional societies, and a member of six national advisory boards. He has performed over 13,000 autopsies and reviewed over 30,000 others. He is on the review board of 15 professional journals, speaks at dozens of conferences each year, and is the author of five books and over 350 articles.

## Key Dates

| | |
|---|---|
| 1931 | Born in Pittsburgh, Pennsylvania, on March 20 |
| 1952 | Received B.S. in pre-med from University of Pittsburgh |
| 1954 | Graduated from University of Buffalo School of Medicine |
| 1954–1956 | Received M.D. from University of Pittsburgh School of Medicine |
| 1956–1959 | Interned at St. Francis General Hospital, Pittsburgh, Pennsylvania; attended University of Pittsburgh Law School |
| 1959–1961 | Did residency in pathology at the Veterans Administration Hospital in Oakland |
| 1961–1962 | Attended University of Maryland School of Law |
| 1962 | Completed law degree at University of Pittsburgh |

| 1962–1964 | Worked as pathologist at Leech Farm Veterans Administration Hospital, Pittsburgh, Pennsylvania |
|---|---|
| 1964–1978 | Was director of Pittsburgh Pathology and Toxicology Laboratory |
| 1970 | Was first elected Allegheny County coroner |
| 1973–present | Is chair, Department of Pathology and chief pathologist, St. Francis Medical Center, Pittsburgh, Pennsylvania |

## Advice

*Cyril Wecht loves his work and would encourage you to pursue this field. "It will always be around. It's something society will always need." The academic programs for pre-med (undergraduate), med school, and law school are pretty fixed. You won't get electives until your third year of med school. To get some exposure to a coroner's duties, volunteer during the summers to work in a coroner's office. Finally, Dr. Wecht would remind you that the field of forensic pathology requires the curiosity to solve mysteries and the conduct of logical, consistent, and impartial investigations. Look for these qualities in yourself before you commit to this career.*

## References

Drusdale, Alan. "People Making News: Cyril Wecht," *Executive Report*. (September 1997): 10–15. (Good review of the duties and functions of a coroner.)

Gaensslen, R. *Sourcebook in Forensic Serology, Immunology, and Biochemistry*. Washingotn, D.C.: U.S. Department of Justice, 1996.

Wecht, Cyril. *Cause of Death*. New York: E. P. Dutton, 1993.

———. *Grave Secrets*. New York: E. P. Dutton, 1996.

———. *Who Killed JonBenet Ramsey?* New York: Penguin, 1998.

# Steve Wozniak

*"The Electronic Whiz Kid"*

Computer Technology

Photo by Carolyn Caddes, © 1995

## Career Highlights

- Invented the Apple II computer
- Co-founded Apple Computer Corporation
- Received the National Medal of Technology from President Ronald Reagan, 1985

## Important Contributions

When Steve Wozniak invented the Apple computer, it was not the first personal computer, but it was the first revolutionary one, and the best anyone had ever seen at the time. Steve Jobs the entrepreneur saw the potential of Wozniak's invention and devised a plan to market it. Together they founded Apple Computer in a garage in 1977, where they built their first computers. In only six years, Apple made the *Fortune* 500 list, the youngest firm ever to reach that list. The Apple computer revolutionized how computers were designed and used and made the founders phenomenally rich in the process.

## Career Path

Steven Wozniak was 11 years old when he got an idea for his first machine. It seemed like a simple, straightforward project to the young boy, whose father was an electrical engineer and had shelves of electrical manuals and spare parts. Steve began to build the machine in his room and soon his desk, his bed, and his floor were covered with mounds of resistors, capacitors, and transistors. Miles of colored wire, endless diagrams, and stacks of circuit boards and metal framing strips were heaped in tangled piles.

The project grew too big for Steve's room and sprawled onto the kitchen table and livingroom floor. As if the machine were alive and growing on its own, what he thought would be compact bits of circuits became sprawling mazes of wire, boards, and components. When he finally finished the machine, it weighed more than he did and was bigger than the stove. But when he turned it on, it worked! He had built a machine that could play tick-tack-toe! At 11 years old, Steve Wozniak had conceived, designed, and built his first computer.

While Steve Wozniak was an excellent student and a natural electronics tinkerer, he was not adept at making friends. He was shy and quiet and loved to "lose himself" in books. By the fourth grade, Steve had discovered that he loved math.

In the fifth grade, Steve read a book about a ham radio operator. Inspired, he enrolled in an adult-level neighborhood class to get a ham radio license. He learned Morse code and built his own ham radio transmitter and receiver from a kit. Yet because most ham operators were adults, he felt too shy to join in their conversations. He lost interest in the ham radio and turned his attention to other electronic projects.

After building his tick-tack-toe computer, Steve and a neighborhood friend constructed house-to-house intercoms. Using inexpensive parts they bought with their allowance money, they stretched a wire across yards and over fences. With microphones, speakers, buzzers, lights, a power converter, and relays, the boys were able to communicate with each other through the late-night hours.

At age 13, Steve won a blue ribbon at the Bay Area Science Fair for a 10-bit parallel digital computer that he built for his eighth-grade science class. The most impressive part of his project was that he himself had designed the integrated circuit the computer used. Integrated circuits had only been recently discovered (in 1958 by Jack Kilby), but Steve understood the technology so well that he was able to improve on the design, creating one that was simpler, faster, and "cleaner" than those developed by major electronics companies. His science teacher admitted that the boy was way beyond all of his teachers in "technological know-how."

In high school, Steve finally found a group with whom he could overcome his shyness, other electronics whiz kids. He was elected president of the Electronics Club, and he gave lectures and wrote papers for the club that explained electronics principles he learned on his own.

Steve's electronics teacher, John McCollum, knew that high school could not offer Steve the kind of rigorous challenge he needed. McCollum arranged for him and another excellent electronics student to spend afternoons of their senior year programming computers for Sylvania. Steve also received a grant from the National Science Foundation that allowed him to attend lectures at the University of Santa Clara and other colleges with a select group of high school students. When he took his S.A.T. exam, he earned an 800—a perfect score—on math.

Steve was not just a smart kid, however. He was also a prankster. For fun, he built a gadget that would set off the school fire alarm. He designed a television jamming device and amused himself by watching people try to "fix" their reception while Steve himself was jamming the signal. Another time he built an audio frequency oscillator that was supposed to make a sound like a dripping faucet, but his sounded more like a ticking clock. As a joke, he wrapped the contraption in foil and stuck some wires in it. Then he placed it in the locker next to his. A full-scale bomb scare followed. The principal was not amused. He called the police, had Steve arrested, then suspended him from school for a week.

After high school graduation, Steve attended the University of Colorado, but only for one year, because out-of-state tuition was very expensive and he did not prove to be a very dedicated student. The ski slopes lured him away from classes, and his pranks lured him from his homework (he began using his television jamming device in the dormitories).

For his second year of college, Wozniak went back to Sunnyvale and studied at DeAnza Community College. For his third year of college, he went to the University of California at Berkeley. Money problems forced him to put off his fourth year of college and get a job instead. He wound up working at Hewlett-Packard as an engineer. There he taught himself how to write programs incorporating graphics, something that had never been done before on a computer.

Wozniak's good friend Steve Jobs worked at Atari, and the two of them joined the newly formed Homebrew Computer Club, where members swapped ideas, showed off new designs, raffled off computer parts, and generally had fun. Wozniak built a new, improved circuit board for a computer. He connected it to a television (the monitor), a power supply, transformers, and a keyboard. The whole thing worked using programs he had written. When he demonstrated his newest invention at the club, Jobs immediately saw its potential. Never before had computers been so small, so affordable, and so easy to use! He knew others would want one—he knew there was a market for this creation.

Jobs convinced a reluctant Wozniak into forming a company to market the new computer. They picked the name "Apple" because they were looking for something fresh, a name that reflected a break with tradition (after all, whoever heard of a computer named after a fruit!). On April Fool's Day, 1976, they officially formed the Apple Computer Company. They sold Job's Volkswagen and Wozniak's programmable calculator to raise $1,350 to begin making computers.

One month later, they got their first order for 100 circuit boards, and Apple Computer Company was on its way. Within a few years, the Apple II computer would be the largest-selling computer in the world. In reflecting on his remarkable achievement of being the sole designer of a major computer system, Wozniak said, "Designing a computer is the hardest work you could ever do. You've got to concentrate on hundreds of little details and how they interplay. It's like solving the hardest puzzle that ever was." Steve Wozniak proved to be one of the world's best puzzle solvers. His computer, the first personal computer, revolutionized both the field of computer design and the fundamental human-computer interface.

## Key Dates

| | |
|---|---|
| 1950 | Born in San Jose, California, on August 11 |
| 1968–1969 | Attended the University of Colorado, Boulder |
| 1971 | Attended the University of California at Berkeley |
| 1972 | Worked for Electroglas in Menlo Park |
| 1973 | Worked as engineer for Hewlett-Packard |

1976    Officially formed Apple Computer Company with Steven Jobs on April 1

1981    Ceased active work for Apple

1982    Founded Unuson ("Unite Us in Song"); festivals lose money but Wozniak continues as president

1985    Worked for Apple Computer again but retired to escape the corporate bureaucracy

1986    Received B.S. from U.C. Berkeley

1986– 1990    Created Cloud Nine company to produce remote control devices; abandoned it in 1990

1990– 1997    Trained teachers on use of Macintosh computers

1997– present    Rehired as consultant to Apple Computer

## Advice

*If you are considering a career in computer technology, Steve Wozniak would advise you not to specialize too soon. Spread yourself over several disciplines. You must have a foundation in the basics—math, physics, materials science, electrical engineering—but don't be afraid to study anything else that interests you. Search for new ways to combine departments and disciplines to your advantage.*

*Wozniak adds, "And never think that it's all been done already. People probably thought that way in Rome thousands of years ago. There will always be new inventions simply because there's a need inside us to express our creativity and inventiveness."*

## References

Butcher, Lee. *Accidental Millionaire: The Rise and Fall of Steve Jobs at Apple Computer.* New York: Paragon House, 1988.

Herz, J. C. *Joystick Nation: How Videogames Ate Our Quarters, Won Our Hearts, and Rewired Our Minds.* Boston: Little, Brown, 1997.

Kendall, Martha E. *Steve Wozniak: Inventor of the Apple Computer.* New York: Walker , 1994.

Moritz, Michael. *The Little Kingdom: The Private Story of Apple Computer.* New York: William Morrow, 1984.

Sullivan, George. *Screen Play: The Story of Video Games.* New York: Frederick Warne, 1983.

# Chien-Shiung Wu

*"Courageous Hero"*                    Nuclear Physics

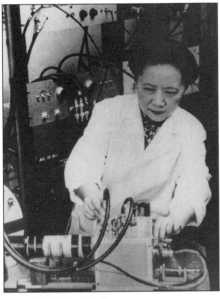

AIP Emilio Segrè Visual Archives

## Career Highlights

- Was one of the world's leading experimental physicists
- Experimentally confirmed Feynman's and Gell-Mann's theory of conservation of vector current in beta decay, 1963
- Awarded the Comstock Award of the National Academy of Sciences, 1964
- Elected to the National Academy of Sciences, 1958

## Important Contributions

In 1957, Chien-Shiung Wu announced the results of an experiment, which instantly changed the way scientists viewed the structure of the world. Although the experiment was highly technical in its nature and results, her findings on the nature of beta radiation decay proved that existing theories of atomic structure and interaction had to be incorrect.

As a result of Wu's efforts, science arrived at a more accurate understanding of the nature of elementary particle interactions, which are at the core of much of the progress in atomic and subatomic studies of the last 50 years.

## Career Path

It was not going to be a normal summer for a girl who had just graduated top of her class from high school. Instead of parties and congratulations, Chien-Shiung Wu would be desperately studying. Based on her grades, Chien-Shiung had been selected to attend China's elite National Central University in Nanjing. She loved, and wanted to study, physics, but had had little math and science in high school and so dared not apply for that program.

Chien-Shiumg's father disagreed. He said there was plenty of time—two months—to prepare herself for any program she cared about. He brought her advanced textbooks on math, chemistry and physics and would not listen to her protests that there was too little time, or that she couldn't learn years' worth of material in one short summer. As a renowned physicist, Wu later said that without her father's insistent encouragement, she would probably be "teaching grade school somewhere in China now."

Born in 1912 in Liuhe, near Shanghai, Chien-Shiung Wu had a father who fervently believed in equal rights and equal education for women. He decided that his daughter should attend the best school possible, no matter how far away it was. So at age 10, Chien-Shiung Wu was shipped off to the Soochow Girls School, about 50 miles from Shanghai. The school offered a Western curriculum, and professors from American universities frequently lectured there. For seven years Chien-Shiung lived at the boarding school, only coming home for winter and summer vacations.

The Soochow Girls School was divided into two parts: a teacher training school and an academic school. Because the teacher training school was free and the graduates were offered positions, Wu enrolled there. Soon, however, she realized that her friends in the academic school were learning much more about science and foreign languages than she was. So she devised a solution: In the evenings, after her friends had finished with their schoolbooks, they turned them over to her, and she worked late into the night teaching herself mathematics, physics, and chemistry. She soon realized that she preferred physics to everything else.

Despite her initial fears about her readiness to study college-level physics, Wu excelled in the physics program at the National Central University and graduated in 1934. She spent two more years there, teaching and researching, but because China had no graduate programs in physics, she would have to travel abroad to further her studies. In 1936, her uncle helped finance her move to the United States for graduate studies. She intended to get her degree as quickly as possible and then return to her family in China, but that would not happen. She would never see her family again.

It had been arranged that Wu would get her Ph.D. at the University of Michigan. But at Michigan women were not allowed to use the student union building. In addition, Michigan already had over 600 Chinese students, and Wu wanted to meet Americans. Besides, U.C. Berkeley was where all of the great physicists were working, like Robert Oppenheimer and Ernest Lawrence. The deciding factor was that a young man whom she liked immediately and would later marry, Luke Yuan, enrolled at Berkeley. Without telling her family, Wu chose Berkeley instead.

In 1937, Japan invaded China, and Wu was cut off from home. She would have no contact with her family for eight years. She immersed herself in work to forget about the war, working late into the night at the university lab, often until three or four o'clock in the morning. When university officials worried about her safety walking home alone after her evening study sessions in the department lab, they arranged to have another graduate student pick her up and drive her home each night.

By the time Wu received her Ph.D., she had logged enough study and experiment hours to become well enough known as a fission expert to make a six-month lecture tour across the United States. Despite her prominence, however, Berkeley would not hire her. None of the other leading universities had women physics professors. Also, because she was Asian, she was looked on as suspect, as were all Asians during World War II, even though the Chinese had been fighting Japan longer than any other nation.

Wu settled for a teaching position at a women's school, Smith College. While she enjoyed the teaching, it left her little time for research. When the United States joined World War II a year later and physicists were in great demand, she received offers from eight universities. She chose Princeton, and, at age 31, became Princeton's first female professor.

In 1945, after Japan's surrender, Wu finally heard from her family. They were well and had survived the war, but she could not go home to visit because China was now in the midst of a civil war between Chiang Kai-shek and the Chinese Communists, and the United States would probably not let her return once she left. When the Chinese Communists won in 1949, all relations were severed between the United States and China. (It would not be possible for Wu to visit China again until 1973. By then, her brothers and her parents were all dead.)

Wu plowed her energy into her work, this time studying beta disintegration (a form of radioactive decay). In 1956, she proved that parity was violated in weak interactions; this nonconservation of parity observed in beta decay suddenly changed the way scientists viewed the structure of the world. A few years later, she reported confirmation of another new fundamental theory in nuclear physics, the theory of conservation of vector current in nuclear beta decay.

Chien-Shiung Wu also demonstrated that electromagnetic radiation from the annihilation of positrons and electrons is polarized, which supported

Dirac's theory and proved that the electron and positron have opposite parity. In more recent years, she has studied biological problems, focusing on the structure of hemoglobin.

It must have taken a great deal of courage for Wu to leave her family in China and move, alone, to the United States for her education. It was braver still for her to singlehandedly challenge the theories of the leading physicists of our time. It is appropriate, then, that in Chinese her name means, "Courageous Hero." Taking those courageous steps helped bring about many of the recent advances in atomic and subatomic physics.

## Key Dates

| | |
|---|---|
| 1912 | Born in Shanghai, China, on May 31 |
| 1922–1930 | Attended the Soochow Girls School |
| 1934 | Received B.S. from the National Central University in China |
| 1936 | Moved to the United States |
| 1940 | Received Ph.D. from U. C. Berkeley |
| 1942 | Taught at Smith College, Northampton, Massachusetts |
| 1943 | Became Princeton University's first woman instructor |
| 1944 | Joined the scientific staff of the Division of War Research at Columbia University |
| 1946 | Became a staff member at Columbia University |
| 1954 | Became a naturalized U.S. citizen |
| 1957 | Was professor of physics at Columbia |
| 1997 | Died February 16 |

# Advice

*Chien-Shiung Wu offered two pieces of advice to new nuclear physics students. First, "You must work very hard in the beginning. It is hard to push the door open and to get inside such a complex subject. But once you understand it, it is very interesting." Second, gain a general, liberal arts education in your early years. Then devour every math, physics, and nuclear physics class you can find. You can never spend too much time learning and studying in the field.*

*On reviewing her life, Wu emphasized how much her father encouraged and supported her. She once recalled his advice her to: "Ignore the obstacles. Just put your head down and keep walking forward." Wu would offer similar encouragement to students today.*

# References

McGrayne, Sharon Bertsch. *Nobel Prize Women in Science: Their Lives, Struggles, and Momentous Discoveries.* New York: Carol Publishing, A Birch Lane Press Book, 1993.

Marton, L. L., and Claire Marton. *Methods of Experimental Physics: Nuclear Methods in Solid State Physics.* Vol. 2. New York: Academic Press, 1983.

Shriprakas, Patel B. *Nuclear Physics: An Introduction.* New York: Halsted Press, 1991.

Wu, Chien-Shiung, and Luke C. Yuan, eds. *Elementary Particles: Science, Technology & Society.* Berkeley: University of California Press, 1981.

# Rosalyn Sussman Yalow

*"The Fighter"*             Medical Physics

## Career Highlights

- Was first American-born woman to win a Nobel Prize for Science
- Developed the radioimmunoassay procedure, which virtually started the new science of neuroendocrinology
- Received the National Medal of Science, the nation's highest science award, 1988
- Was first woman to win the prestigious Albert Lasker Basic Medical Research Award, 1976
- Received 47 honorary degrees from universities and colleges

## Important Contributions

Rosalyn Yalow (with Solomon Berson) developed the radioimmunoassay (RIA) procedure, which revolutionized endocrinology. For the first time in history, doctors could diagnose conditions caused by minute changes in hormones. Many routine procedures such as screening blood banks for deadly diseases, testing athletes for drug abuse, checking fetuses for serious deformities like spina bifida, and even treating hormonal disorders like diabetes would not be possible without Yalow's RIA.

For this discovery Yalow won the Nobel Prize, but not first without years of struggle to make the scientific community understand the value and the potential of her work.

# Career Path

On Rosalyn Yalow's desk sits a worn and faded photograph of tiny, five-year-old Rosalyn wearing boxing gloves and standing over her ten-year-old brother, who lay sprawled at her feet. "That's the attitude that made it possible for me to go into physics," she quipped. Indeed it was. Yalow was a fighter; she had to be. She fought her way into the scientific world, she fought to make her mark, then she fought to make her work understood when the rest of the world refused to believe her.

By age eight, Rosalyn Sussman had decided that she wanted to be a "big-deal scientist." She liked knowing things; she liked logic. At age ten she enrolled in an all-girl junior high school and narrowed her science goals to medical research. She completed three grades in two years and so impressed one teacher that he called her "a genius."

Rosalyn graduated from high school when only 15, but her parents could not afford tuition to send her to college. Fortunately, her excellent grades won her admittance to Hunter College, a highly competitive women's college that didn't charge tuition. She desperately wanted to go on to medical school after Hunter, but discrimination based on sex and religion were rampant in graduate schools at that time. Rosalyn was female, Jewish, and had no money. No medical school in the country would accept her.

Unwilling to accept defeat, Sussman took a part-time secretarial job in Columbia University's medical school during her senior year at Hunter, with the understanding that, in return for learning stenography and working as a secretary, she could take science courses at Columbia. Thus, odd as it sounds, in January 1941, she graduated from Hunter College with high honors in physics and chemistry—and entered secretarial school.

When the United States entered World War II, the draft quickly depleted graduate programs of their male students. For a few short years, graduate programs opened their doors to women. The University of Illinois, the most prestigious school Sussman had applied to, offered her a teaching assistant-ship in physics. She was the first woman admitted to the engineering school (which included physics) at the University of Illinois since World War I.

At Illinois Rosalyn Sussman met Aaron Yalow, an aspiring nuclear physicist, and they were married in 1943. In 1945, she received her Ph.D. in nuclear physics and moved back to New York City as the first woman engineer at the Federal Telecommunications Laboratory, a research lab. The research group folded a year later, and she retreated to Hunter College to teach while she sought another research position.

Radioisotopes were just coming into use in medicine, and in 1947, Yalow went to work for the Veterans Affairs Medical Center in the Bronx, where she turned a janitor's closet into one of the first radioisotope labs in the United

States. At the VA Center Yalow met Solomon A. Berson, a young resident physician in internal medicine. They formed a research partnership that would last 22 years.

Berson knew physiology, anatomy, and clinical medicine; Yalow knew physics, mathematics, chemistry, and engineering. They taught each other their fields. They both loved their work and were willing to work 80-hour weeks.

Yalow and Berson focused on insulin research, injecting patients with radioactively tagged insulin and taking frequent blood samples to measure how fast the insulin disappeared from the patient's system. Surprisingly, the tagged insulin took *longer* to disappear from diabetics than from nondiabetics who had never had insulin.

After repeated studies, Yalow reasoned that the human immune system must be producing antibodies to fight the foreign insulin. But the conventional wisdom of the day said that an insulin molecule was too small to produce antibodies. They wrote their findings into an article, but no one believed them. *Science* refused to publish their work. *The Journal of Clinical Investigation* would not publish it until the words "insulin antibody" were removed from the title.

Then Yalow and Berson realized something startling: Their technique measured the antibodies to a hormone; the inverse of this procedure would measure the hormone itself! They called this method radioimmunoassay (RIA) because it used radioactive substances to measure antibodies produced by the immune system.

This test worked by taking a patient's blood sample (which included the hormone they wished to measure) into a test tube. They added the hormone's antibody and mixed in a small amount of the radioactive form of the hormone. Then they waited. It could take a few hours to a few days, but eventually the natural hormone and the radioactive hormone would fight to combine with the antibody molecule. By measuring how much of the radioactive hormone actually bonded with the antibody, they could calculate how much of the natural hormone had been present in the patient's body.

This technique had several excellent attributes. First, it was astoundingly sensitive. It could detect a spoonful of sugar in a body of water 62 miles long, 62 miles wide, and 30 feet deep. Second, it was a test-tube operation, so no radiation entered a patient's body. Third, the test only required tiny amounts of plasma for each test—a tenth of a cubic centiliter was all that was required from the patient. Fourth, it worked for nearly every hormone, and different substances could be tested simultaneously. It was a major breakthrough!

Berson and Yalow published their findings in 1956, but most scientists thought the concept too complicated, too unbelievable. The two researchers didn't give up. Instead they began training scientists how to use RIA. After

10 years, the scientific community finally realized the value of what Yalow and Berson had done.

In 1972, Berson died of a heart attack. Because Nobel prizes are not given posthumously and had never been given to a surviving partner of a research team, it was generally believed that Yalow would never win a Nobel even though RIA was unquestionably worth the prize. In addition, sexism was still a problem. She was a woman, and some people said her career was over without Berson.

Yalow set out to prove herself all over again. For the next four years, she worked 100-hour weeks. She took over Berson's editing and speaking engagements. She published 60 articles and won a dozen awards. Finally, on October 13, 1977, Rosalyn Yalow became the first American-born woman to win a science Nobel Prize—and the first survivor of a partnership to win.

## Key Dates

| | |
|---|---|
| 1921 | Born in the Bronx, New York, on July 19 |
| 1931 | Enrolled in an all-girls junior high school |
| 1941 | Graduated from Hunter College |
| 1941 | Worked as teaching assistant in physics at the University of Illinois |
| 1945 | Received Ph.D.; became an electrical engineer at a telecommunications laboratory |
| 1946–1950 | Worked as teacher at Hunter College |
| 1947 | Was consultant to the Bronx Veterans Administration Hospital |
| 1956 | Published idea for radioimmunoassay |
| 1992–present | Retired from the VA; became senior medical investigator |

## Advice

*Rosalyn Yalow believed that medical physics research is almost too broad a field for any one researcher to fully grasp. In school, combine as many fields as possible into your curriculum. The broader your base, the easier it will be to advance. Physics, nuclear physics, chemistry, and math are essential starting points. Virology, physiology, and other biologically related courses form the next layer of your knowledge base. Beyond those basics, let your chosen area of research define additional necessary studies.*

*Yalow would also add that you should make sure you choose a research field that you love enough to at work 80 to 100 hours per week. Progress is slow and painstaking, but the personal and professional rewards of carefully executed research are great.*

## References

Hutchings. *Medical Physics.* Cincinnati, Ohio: South-Western Publishing, 1990.

McGrayne, Sharon Bertsch. *Nobel Prize Women in Science: Their Lives, Struggles, and Momentous Discoveries.* New York: Carol Publishing, A Birch Lane Press Book, 1993.

Stille, Darlene R. *Extraordinary Women Scientists.* Chicago: Children's Press, 1995.

# Appendix A

## Internet References

The World Wide Web is bulging with excellent sources of information on every conceivable field of science. It is also overflowing with inaccurate, unreliable, and downright wrong information. While Web sites come and go faster than fashion fads, the sites listed below are stable and dependable for the science information they contain. Most of these sites also serve as valuable links to a vast number of other reliable science Web sites.

Any of the major search engines (for example, Yahoo, Netscape, Web Crawler, Go To) list enough valuable science sites to more than fill up any available time for additional reading and research. While we previously have used many of the sites listed here for research purposes, all of them were checked and verified during October 1998. While this is by no means an exhaustive list, it includes solid sites through which you can reach information on any of the major science disciplines.

**NOTE**: The necessary prefix http:// has been omitted from this listing for any sites beginning with www.

| Web Site | Host and Content |
| --- | --- |
| www.discover.com | Over 100 top picks of science sites by the senior staff at *Discover* magazine, a top science periodical. Updates monthly. |
| http://imagine.gsfc.nasa.gov/ docs/teachers/lifecycle/LC_ main_p1.html | NASA info on the life cycle of stars and links to related sites. |
| www.cdc.gov | Center for Disease Control links to over 20 related specialty sites on various fields of medical health. |
| http://medicine.wutl.edu | Detailed logs on comets and meteor showers and links to related sites. |
| www.civeng.carleton.ca | Information on all earthquakes worldwide and links to related sites. |
| http://gdbWWW.gdb.org | Mapping of the human genome project, related information, and links to related sites. |
| http://spacelink.msfc.nasa.gov | NASA's prime space information "hot line" site. |

| | |
|---|---|
| http://nyelabs.kcts.org | Site of "Bill Nye the Science Guy" with links to many valuable science sites. |
| www.si.edu | Main site for the Smithsonian Institution. Includes a site index for all major collections and areas of research. |
| www.arc.nasa.gov | Main NASA-Ames science education site. Includes links to many valuable science sites. |
| www.outbreak.org | Comprehensive information on microbiological research and worldwide outbreaks. Many informative links. |
| http://robotics.jpl.nasa.gov | Main Jet Propulsion Laboratory site for robotics and artificial intelligence with links to other related sites. |
| www/reston.com | Information site for space discoveries with links to many related specialty sites. |
| www.nasa.gov | NASA home page. Information on their programs and an enormous number of linked sites on many fields of science. |
| www.seti.org | Home page for the SETI (Search for Extra-Terrestrial Intelligence) work. Wealth of information on space exploration. |
| http://hurlbut.jhuapl.edu/NEAR/ndisp.html | Fun site for information about future near-earth passes by comets and asteroids. Links to related sites. |
| http://mpfwww.jpl.nasa.gov | Information site for the Mars Missions with links to related JPL departments and other, related sites. |
| www.periodictable.com | Prime science education and information site with separate areas of chemistry, physics, geology, and other major fields. |
| www.elibrary.com | Major source for science-related articles and information from thousands of books, magazines, journals, and newspapers. |
| http://decaf.talkway.com | Networking site to link with countless others having and seeking information on any major science field. Links to hundreds of related sites. |

| | |
|---|---|
| http://geology.miningco.com | Good site for solid geology information (as well as chemistry, physics, and others). Includes many links to related sites. |
| http://walrus.wr.usgs.gov | Home page for the USGS western US coastal and marine geology research with links to other governmental and university sites. |
| www.geol.umd.edu | Good university site (University of Maryland) with loads of information and valuable links to other institutions. |
| http://edgesci.com | Good site for technical geological information (about, for example, rocks, minerals, crystals) and links to related sites. |
| www.toptenlinks.com | Networking site that lists their ten top links for any given field of science. |
| http://stormy.geology.yale.edu | One of Yale's better sites. Good source of geology information and of links to other activities at Yale and other geology-related institutions. |
| www.earth.ruu.nl | Good general information site on geology with links to other disciplines. |
| www.geology.indiana.edu | Strong site for its breadth and depth of geological information. Good links to other departments and related institutions. |
| www.seismo.berkeley.edu | One of UC Berkeley's better Web sites. Solid information on the field and courses and links to other, geology-related activities. |
| http://chemengineer.miningco.com | Technologies, trends, databases related to chemical engineering and links to other related sites. |
| www.search-beat.com | Directory site for searching top-rated science sites in various disciplines. |
| http://chemistry.miningco.com | Main chemistry-related home page for this technology information and science information site. |
| http://hackberry.chem.niu.edu | Listing of the best chemistry Web links for 1995, 1996, and 1997. |

| | |
|---|---|
| www.chem.vt.edu | Home page for the chemistry hypermedia project. Good links to other related institutions. |
| http://webbook.nist.gov | Extensive listing of chemistry information, calculations, and other links. |
| http://ijc.chem.niu.edu | Internet listing of major chemistry-related journals and information. |
| www.shef.ac.uk | Key site for world-wide information on the elements and related research. |
| http://ci.mond.org | Networking connection site for chemistry-related research, information, and academia. |
| www.chem.icla.edu | Good university site. Loaded with current information and links to other important departments and institutions. |
| www.ecrc.cr.usgs.gov | Major USGS site for information and links related to environmental contaminants. |
| www.cchem.berkeley.edu | Home page for major university chemistry information and links to other departments and institutions. |
| http://pubs.acs.org | American Chemical Society site, stuffed with information, current research, and links to other significant sites. |
| http://chemsw.com | Good technical information site for general, organic, inorganic, and advanced chemistry information. |
| www.chemweb.com | Site features searchable chemistry journals, databases, jobs, and software with links to other related sites. |
| http://astronomy.miningco.com | Good technical information on astronomy, space research, journals, and software, with links to other sites. |
| http://observe.ivv.nasa.gov | Strong public access site for Earth and space data. |
| http://planetary.org | Planetary search information and links to other institutions. |
| www2.astronomy.com | Online astronomy magazine with news, reviews, and appropriate links. |

| | |
|---|---|
| www.cv.nrao.edu | Site with links to astronomy/astrophysics sites and information on the Web. |
| www.seds.org | Site of an independent, student-based organization promoting exploration and development of space. Good information and links. |
| www.astro.washington.edu | Strong university site with current research and links to other institutions. |
| http://donald.phast.umass.edu | Excellent site of a major university department with reviews, course information, current research, databases, and links to other major institutions. |
| www.pparc.ac.uk | Particle Physics and Astronomy Research Center site with extensive particle physics and astrophysics information and research. |
| www.whoi.edu | Main site for Woods Hole Oceanographic Institute, the largest independent oceanographic research institute in the world. Vast information, research databases, and links to related institutions. |
| www-ocean.tamu.edu | Good university-based oceanographic science site with links to other universities and departments. |
| www.skio.peachnet.edu | Site for Skidaway Oceanographic Institute with links to many other related sites. |
| http://scilib.ucsd.edu | Scripps Institution of Oceanography main Web information site. |
| www.benthos.com | Ocean industry links to major development, research, and information. |
| http://www6.etl.noaa.gov | Home page for meteorology and oceanography divisions of National Oceanic and Atmospheric Administration. |
| www.tos.org | Home page for the Oceanography Society. Information, education opportunities, current research, and links. |

| | |
|---|---|
| http://aslo.org | Home page for the American Society of Limnology and Oceanography. |
| http://bigisland.miningco.com | Good site for technical ocean development and research information and links to other disciplines and institutions. |
| www.ibwpan.gda.pl | Directories of useful links to the World Wide Web virtual oceanographic and scientific library. |
| http://physics.org | Home page of the Institute of Physics. Information, reviews, journals, current research, and links to other sites. |
| www.physicsnet.com | Alternate site for the Institute of Physics. |
| www.aip.org | Extensive main site of the American Institute of Physics. Thousands of pages of free articles and information. |
| www.cern.ch | Home page of CERN, the central European physics research center. Extensive information and links. |
| www.slac.stanford.edu | Information page for the Department of Energy lab at Stanford. Great store of current research and physics information with an emphasis on nuclear and particle physics. |
| http://nssdc.gsfc.nasa.gov | Home page for the National Space Science Data Center. Thousands of pages of information, data, research, and links. |
| www.physics.wisc.edu | Good university physics site. Course and educational information, current research, and links to other departments and institutions. |
| http://tagg.colorado.edu | Extensive university physics site. 1,000 site references for physics information and links to NASA activity and other ongoing research. |
| www.search-beat.com | A one-stop Web site for science web listings. |
| http://golgi.harvard.edu | Bioscience links from Harvard; includes extensive on-campus activity, opportunities, and research. |

| | |
|---|---|
| http://expasy.proteome.org.au | Information page of the Swiss Institute of Bioinformatics. Major worldwide molecular biology server. |
| www.journals.asm.org | American Society of Microbiology journal site. Articles, reviews, information, and links to other sites. |
| www.radonc.stanford.edu | Site of the Division of Radiation Biology. Technical information, program information, and links to other departments and institutions. |
| http://conbio.rice.edu | Central clearinghouse for conservation biology information, resources, university programs, and related links. |
| www.mcb.arizona.edu | Information page for a training and research program in biology and microbiology; contains extensive information and links. |
| www.iob.org | Site of the Institute of Biology, with extensive information on related professions and job opportunities as well as research and general information. |
| www.ummp.lsa.umich.edu | University of Michigan Museum of Paleontology site. Information, databases, journals, educational opportunities, links to other sites. |
| www.global-expos.com | Site surveys, rates, and lists all the paleontology Web sites this staff can find. Great index of Web information. |
| www.geo-science.com | Good, university-based site for general information about geology and paleontology. |
| www.dinosaur.org | Ultimate dinosaur Web site. Extensive information, reviews, and educational information as well as multiple links to other paleontological sites. |
| www.cincmuseum.org | Site by the Cincinnati Museum Center; features links to hundreds of other sites of related universities, professional organizations, government agencies, and institutions. |

| | |
|---|---|
| www.balogh.com | Good listing of geology and other earth science books and journals with appropriate links. |
| http://128.173.184.74 | Online laboratories of Paleontology Department of University of Virginia. Also information about ongoing research and links to other departments and institutions. |
| www.dinosauria.com | Extensive dinosaur information site with links to other academic pages. |
| http://merchant.calweb.com | Good index to electronically available paleontology resources. |
| http://world.std.com | Museum and journal collaborative site containing extensive listing of rocks, minerals, and related information. |
| http://ecology.miningco.com | Good general review of ecological systems, habitats, and environmental sciences with links to other Mining Company sites and those of other related institutions. |
| http://sevilleta.unm.edu | Site by the University of New Mexico Long-Term Environmental Research Program. Good data and conceptual source. |
| www.ramas.com | Site sharing applied biomathematics software, research, results, and related data. Specializing in biology, wildlife, and human health risk analysis. |
| http://wlm13.umenfa.maine.edu | Site of the Department of Wildlife Ecology at the University of Maine, one of the oldest and most highly regarded wildlife programs. Educational opportunities, field databases, research listings, and links to other departments and institutions. |
| www.cossa.csiro.au | CSIRO Office of Space and Applications site features remote sensing and earth observation data and program information as well as current research and valuable links. |
| www.evergreen.edu | Networking site for information about ecological programs and related funding opportunities across Canada and the northern United States. |

| | |
|---|---|
| maine.edunhsbig.inhs.uiuc.edu | Clearinghouse site for wildlife ecology-related software, habitat analysis, diversity indexes, population dynamics, and general simulations. |
| www.silvafor.org | Site created to locate and distribute information about ecologically responsible forest use. Provides direct access to publications, manuals, maps, journals, and related graphics. |
| www.eeb.princeton.edu | Site of Princeton's Department of Ecology and Evolutionary Biology. Provides information about the field, educational opportunities, and links to related departments and other institutions. |
| http://microibiology.utmp.edu | University of Texas Medical Branch Web site offers information about the field, educational programs, ongoing research, and links to other institutions. |
| www.mikrob.slu.se | Resource site offering integrated evaluation of physical, chemical, and biological properties of soil with links to other sites. |
| www.bugs.uah.ualberta.ca | Designed as a public health and microbiology information site; gathers data from all over North America. |
| www.tmb.lth.se | Extensive information related to university courses in microbiology and related disciplines. |
| www.isleuth.com | Internet Sleuth is a collection of searchable databases related to microbiology. |
| www.lsumc.edu | Combined site of LSU's Microbiology, Immunology, and Parasitology Departments with data, general information, numerous links, and educational information. |
| www-micro.msb.le.ac.uk | News and information gathering site for all fields related to microbiology. |
| http://microbes.micro.iastate.edu | Valuable university departmental site featuring filed information, ongoing research activity, educational opportunities, databases, and links to other institutions. |

| | |
|---|---|
| http://osu.orst.edu | Ohio State University's botany site, featuring a library of information on the field, current research, educational opportunities, and ongoing university activities. |
| www.sysbot.uu.se | Uppsala University's Systematic Botany page. Good reference for general information and links to related activities. |
| www.ou.edu | Site collects and disseminates information on careers in botany and on working with plants. |
| www.botany.org | Home page of the Botanical Society of America. Features extensive links to other institutions, searchable databases, and general information. |
| www.botany.hawaii.edu | University of Hawaii's botany page lists extensive research and related results and data as well as links to other Pacific institutions and career and educational references. |
| http://141.211.110.91 | Extensive searchable database on plant taxonomies and related species information, characteristics, and distribution. |
| www.ucl.ac.uk | Extensive European database on anthropology maintained by the University College London Anthropology Department. |
| www.ameranthassn.org | Home page of the American Anthropological Society. Listing of journals, articles, research, issues, data, and related institutions. |
| www.lib.ua.edu | Site of resources designed to facilitate the Internet search for material related to the field of anthropology or to related courses. |
| www.sharonburton.com | Site designed to act as focal link to anthropology technical writing, reviews, software analysis, books, programs, and research. |

| | |
|---|---|
| www.umma.lsa.umich.edu | Home page of the University of Michigan's Museum of Anthropology, one of the major archaeological research and teaching facilities in the country. |
| http://library.jmu.edu | Site designed to facilitate a search of Internet resources related to anthropology. |
| http://anthap.oakland.edu | Central site housing information on graduate-level programs and research efforts related to anthropology and archaeology at over 100 major American universities. |
| http://landau.phys.clemson.edu | Site linked to many other university-level research departments on atmospheric sciences. Excellent database and general information. |
| www.atmos.albany.edu | Merged site for the Departments of Earth Sciences and Atmospheric Sciences at the State University of New York. Good information on a full range of specific research fields as well as general information, educational programs, and links to other universities. |
| http://java.science.yorku.ca | Site covers data, research, and general information for the departments of pure and applied sciences at York University. Includes links to major research and activity on atmospheric sciences across Europe. |
| www.unavco.ucar.edu | Working group site focusing on research related to atmospheric applications of Global Positioning Satellite, including both ground and space-based meteorological sensing. |
| www.webdirectory.com | Web directory of organizations engaged in environmental, atmospheric, and natural sciences. Includes data, organization information, research descriptions, and links. |

| | |
|---|---|
| www-eps.harvard.edu | Site of the Earth and Planetary Sciences at Harvard; features information on geology, geochemistry, paleontology, solid-earth geophysics, atmospheric sciences, ocean chemistry, and other disciplines. Information includes educational opportunities, general information, databases, research efforts, and links to other active institutions. |
| http://maps.fls.noaa. gov | National Oceanic and Atmospheric Administration site for information about atmospheric sciences and related activity across the country. |
| http://toaste.ag.rl.ac.uk | Transport of Ozone and Stratosphere-Troposphere Exchange is a European commission tasked to study and monitor ozone transport and stratospheric-tropospheric exchanges. Site includes much data and research information as well as links to related organizations worldwide. |

# Appendix B

## Scientists by Field of Specialization

The 100 scientists chosen for this book represent all of the major fields, and most of the sub-fields, of science. Here they are listed by their disciplines of specialty within the three general groupings of science: physical sciences, earth sciences, and life sciences. The work of many of these scientists spreads across more than one discipline. These scientists are listed under the field that we felt contained their most important contribution.

### PHYSICAL SCIENCES

*Astronomy*

Burnell, Joycelyn Bell
Hale, George
Harris, Wesley
Hubble, Edwin
Penrose, Roger
Sagan, Carl
Van Allen, James

*Chemistry*

Asimov, Isaac
Carothers, Wallace
Curie, Marie
Henry, Warren
Land, Edwin
Lucid, Shannon
Pauling, Linus
Seaborg, Glenn

*Electronics*

Bardeen, John
Bushnell, Nolan
Farnsworth, Philo T.

Gates, William
Hoff, Ted
Kilby, Jack
Wang, An
Wozniak, Steve

*Physics*

Alvarez, Luis
Bohr, Niels
Born, Max
Dirac, Paul
Einstein, Albert
Fermi, Enrico
Feynman, Richard P.
Gabor, Dennis
Geiger, Hans
Goddard, Robert Hutchings
Gould, Gordon
Hawking, Stephen
Heisenberg, Werner
Hofstadter, Robert
Jackson, Shirley
Lawrence, Ernest
Mayer, Maria Goeppert
Meitner, Lise
Michelson, Albert

Oppenheimer, Julius Robert
Pauli, Wolfgang
Planck, Max
Ride, Sally
Tesla, Nikolai
Von Braun, Wernher
Wu, Chien-Shiung

## EARTH SCIENCES

### Atmospheric Science

Bjerkness, Jacob
Lorenz, Edward

### Environmental Science

Brower, David
Carson, Rachel
Muir, John

### General Earth Sciences

Eiseley, Loren
Nye, Bill

### Geology

Chouet, Bernard
Henson, Mathew
Hess, Harry
Holmes, Arthur
Richter, Charles

### Oceanography

Ballard, Robert
Clark, Eugenie
Cousteau, Jacques

### Paleontology

Bakker, Robert
Chin, Karen
Gould, Stephen Jay

## LIFE SCIENCES

### Anthropology

Leakey, Louis
Mead, Margaret

### Biology

Burbank, Luther
Carver, George Washington
Claude, Albert
Cobb, Jewel Plummer
Cohen, Stanley
Commoner, Barry
Cori, Gerty Radnitz
Crick, Francis
Duggar, Benjamin
Ehrlich, Paul
Elion, Gertrude
Fossey, Dian
Goodall, Jane
Moss, Cynthia

### Genetics

Beadle, George
McClintock, Barbara

### Medical Science

Brody, Jane
Dausset, Jean
Franklin, Rosalind
Hamilton, Alice
Reich, Wilhelm
Sabin, Florence Rena
Sabin, Albert
Salk, Jonas E.
Schweitzer, Albert
Sperry, Roger
Starrs, James
Temin, Howard
Wauneka, Annie
Wecht, Cyril
Yalow, Rosalyn Sussman

# Index